Marketing Interfaces

Exploring the Marketing and Business Relationship

Marketing Interfaces

Exploring the Marketing and Business Relationship

Edited by Ian Wilson

PITMAN
PUBLISHING

PITMAN PUBLISHING
128 Long Acre, London WC2E 9AN

A Division of Longman Group UK Limited

First published in 1994

© Longman Group UK Limited 1994
© Chapter 10 The Design Management Institute, Boston 1994

British Library Cataloguing-in-Publication Data
A CIP catalogue record for this book can be obtained from the British Library.

ISBN 0 273 60286 1

Typeset by 🡒 Tek-Art, Croydon, Surrey
Printed and bound in Great Britain by Bell and Bain

The Publisher's policy is to use paper manufactured from sustainable forests.

CONTENTS

CONTRIBUTORS

Ian Wilson is Senior Lecturer at Staffordshire University Business School.

Dr Michael Carter is Principal Lecturer at Staffordshire University Business School.

Dr Rachel Davies Cooper is Research Fellow at Centre for Design, Manufacture and Technology, University College Salford.

Gavin Dick is Senior Lecturer at Staffordshire University Business School.

Richard France is Senior Lecturer in Finance at Staffordshire University Business School.

Karen Freeze is Director of Research, Design Management Institute, Boston.

Ann Hollings is Senior Lecturer at Staffordshire University Business School.

Keith Moreton is Senior Lecturer at Staffordshire University Business School.

Leslie Nicol is Principal Lecturer at Staffordshire University Business School.

Dr Gordon Pearson is Lecturer at Keele University and Director of Keele Management Development Centre.

David Williamson is Principal Lecturer at Staffordshire University Business School.

PREFACE

It has been said that if all the economists in the world were placed next to one another head to toe they still could not reach a conclusion. Marketers have experienced similar difficulties in explaining exactly what marketing is. Definitions of marketing are legion, and nearly twenty years ago Crosier (1975) assembled a list of some fifty attempts. Despite this preoccupation, misunderstandings among the general public and among industrialists are commonplace. Marketing is still commonly seen as either 'selling', or 'advertising' or 'research'. Rarely are all its functional components identified, let alone the perspective of marketing as a business or as a crucial component in business strategy. To some extent, academics – and practitioners – do not help: the former are continually revising their views as to how marketing should be presented and what emphasis should be accorded to relevant dimensions; the latter tend to interpret marketing within their own environment, often failing to recognise that, while the fundamentals remain constant, key requirements and practices can differ significantly between different situations.

Many explanations of marketing include references to its relationship with other parts of the firm. There seem to be two main points which are made in this context. First, marketing is seen as a co-ordinating activity. Cannon (1986), for example, writes: 'Co-ordination with other departments within the firm – finance, personnel, production – is as important as managing the specific aspects of the marketing mix under their control.' Second, it appears that an organisation cannot be marketing-orientated unless all its members embrace the marketing concept. Cowell (1984) writes: 'The centrality of the customer to the enterprise will permeate all departments of organisations which are truly marketing-oriented.'

Although these two fundamentals are almost universally accepted in the marketing literature, there is little in the texts on marketing which provides any conceptual or practical help on the implications of these fundamentals. This book attempts to address that need. It examines the tasks and philosophies of the main functional areas with which marketing has to interface. It examines these from the perspective of the function concerned, rather than of the marketer. From a marketing point of view this has great merit since it implies trying to understand the needs, attitudes and values of the customer (in this case the customer being finance, production and other functional areas, and internal marketing being the particular variant of the marketing concept used).

The book thus aims to provide marketers with a necessary understanding of the operations and capabilities of the other main business areas, and their impact upon marketing strategy and implementation. It also aims to give non-marketers a new perspective of marketing and of their own role in contributing towards the development of marketing orientation and strategy.

BIBLIOGRAPHY

Cannon, T. (1986), *Basic Marketing: Principles and Practice,* London: Cassell Educational.
Cowell, D. (1984) *The Marketing of Services*, London: Heinemann.
Crosier, K. (1975) 'What Exactly is Marketing?', *Quarterly Review of Marketing,* Vol. 1, No. 2.

CHAPTER 1

Marketing Faces and Interfaces

Ian Wilson

INTRODUCTION

In the opening section of the chapter we consider some different perspectives of marketing itself, focusing particularly on several of the functional activities within marketing, especially those whose boundaries with other functional areas are often disputed. Later sections look at marketing orientation and marketing strategy – both of which are seen as crucial to a full appreciation of marketing and as of great importance to all members of an organisation.

MARKETING MIX FUNCTIONS AND BEYOND

Borden (1964) was responsible for first concocting the notion of the marketing mix during the 1950s. His original list of twelve mix elements was subsequently reduced and popularised by McCarthy (1960) as the '4 Ps', i.e. product, price, promotion and place (distribution channels). More recently, writers have expanded the number of 'Ps' and for organisations in service industries it is now normal to refer to the '7 Ps'. The three extra Ps represent a recognition of the importance to service marketing of the 'people' element, the 'process' of providing the service and the 'physical evidence' of the environment within which the service is provided.

The following brief survey of the mix identifies the main activities within it and discusses the interfaces with other functional areas on which these activities depend. The particular scheme used incorporates six mix elements, of which the first five are also used to 'position' the organisation and its offerings within the marketplace. The topic of positioning is explained in depth under Business Unit Marketing Strategy, at p. 50. The mix elements involve:

- the management of brands and products
- customer service
- marketing channels
- marketing communications (promotion)
- pricing
- marketing research.

Product and brand management

Product and brand management is particularly concerned with the development and maintenance of a balanced range of strongly branded products. It also, of course, requires a suitable product deletion policy. Marketers must be conscious of the life cycle of products and services and aware of the need to adjust mix elements at different stages. They need to be able to recognise when products (or brands) should be phased out and when it is more appropriate to regenerate them by means of, for example, upgrades, line extensions, new versions for different market segments – or simply through more effective promotion. Some writers talk about 'old product development' as a process which focuses on sustaining the strength of existing products by the use of progressive quality improvements, continual cost-reduction exercises and communications activities which treat promotional expenditure as an investment. Old product development, or range updating, requires marketers to indicate the direction of change but its implementation requires the participation of manufacturing, engineering, R&D, design and other functional areas.

'New product development', while often seen as the proving ground for marketers, in fact – especially in high-technology industries – not only requires the participation of other functional areas but may even need to be led by them. The role of technologists and marketers in this context is considered under Marketing orientation and organisational success at p. 47.

The process of branding is – in the popular mind – associated predominantly with communication activities, particularly advertising and the use of symbolic devices. Certainly these can be key ingredients in building a successful brand but are probably secondary to the qualities of the product and service itself.

One of the main reasons many brand leaders of fifty years ago are still brand leaders today has been the way that careful management of brand mix elements has ensured that brand values and personality remain both intact and yet relevant to the current period. Changes to both product and promotion have been made, but made gradually and judiciously. The value of high-profile brands began particularly to occupy minds in the 1980s when large corporations were looking to impress shareholders both by associating corporate identity with top product brands and also by boosting balance sheet strength by valuing their brands in the accounts – often for the first time. In November 1988 Ranks Hovis McDougall added £678 million to its assets as a reflection of the value of such brands as Hovis, Bisto, Saxa and Mr Kipling. The criteria developed by Interbrand consultants, against which the valuations were made, included position in the marketplace, age and stability, the industry the brand competes in, degree of international repute, consistency and amount of promotional spending, the market trend, the extent to which the trade mark is protected, and earnings power. The accountancy profession has not issued its own guidelines on how and if such valuations should be undertaken.

Marketers may well find themselves in conflict with corporate planners over this relationship between corporate identity and product brands. In some cases, of course, a product brand may enhance corporate identity and may in turn benefit from corporate ownership endorsement. This applies to the strong association between ICI and Dulux where ICI's perceived values of competence and reliability are linked with the warm, homely image of Dulux (*Marketing Week*, 1993). In other situations, however, the indiscriminate linking of a corporate logo to a product may damage a brand's image. The danger is most likely to occur where the organisation has a number of brands in widely varying product fields. One example was the use of the Allied-Lyons logo (*ibid.*) in adverts for Castlemaine XXXX, which could jeopardise the brand's expensively developed image. In managing brands, therefore, marketers have to pay attention to the relationship of corporate and product image, of umbrella brands to individual brands and to the new product and market areas into which existing brand names can be extended.

Another important brand-related issue which faces marketers in a wide variety of industries is whether or not to supply own-label (known alternatively as distributor, retailer or house brands) in addition to – or instead of – their own proprietary (manufacturer) brands. Many factors affect and are affected by the decision, not least those which involve the way that the manufacturing function is organised and indeed the whole organisational culture. Some of these issues emerge in the Snacks and Nibbles case study in chapter 9.

From a marketing perspective, some of the factors influencing the own-label decision are:

- the costs of supplying own-label
- the costs of manufacturer branding
- amount and flexibility of production capacity
- relative prices achievable from manufacturer brands and own-label
- impact on power relationships between manufacturer and distributor/retailer
- degree of differentiation of existing manufacturer brands
- manufacturer ability to invest in new brand development
- effect on manufacturer brand sales of also agreeing to supply own-label.

Customer service

Customer service is rarely picked out as a separate component of the marketing/positioning mix. In the sense that most buyers of tangibles expect an element of service to be provided with the products, it could be included within the product package or could perhaps be seen as a lubricant which can enhance the performance of each element in the marketing mix and therefore the experience of customers. However, because the issue receives scant attention in some organisations, while in others it has become *the* main basis of differentiation from competition, it appears justifiable to draw individual attention to it.

One way of thinking about customer service is to visualise it as being two components – services additional to the basic product and the quality levels with which products and services are supplied – each of which needs planning at three basic stages: pre-sale, during the sale and after the sale. Examples are shown in Fig. 1.1.

	Pre-sale	*During sale*	*Post-sale*
Additional services	Technical advice Feasibility study	Test facilities	Installation Guarantees Maintenance
Service level	Prompt quotations One-stop contact point	Order status information Delivery precision Delivery time	Availability of spares Call-out time

Fig 1.1 The components and planning stages of customer service

Particular attention has been paid in recent years to the notion of customer care, an aspect of customer service which focuses on the 'moments of truth' when an organisation and its employees interact with customers. Customer care programmes can be aimed at improving reliability of staff (competence, accuracy, keeping promises), their responsiveness to customer needs (willingness to help and deal with complaints, prompt provision of information and services) and their personal approach (honesty, friendliness, courtesy). While many of the staff who deal with customers are in marketing functions, many – for example, telephonists, delivery drivers, credit controllers – are not. The provision of customer care and customer service thus depends crucially on the behaviour of so-called part-time marketers. Their behaviour (and that of all members of the organisation) has to be sustained by the overall organisational culture. This is discussed in chapter 8.

Marketing channels

Marketing channels relate to the route through which three key activities are conducted: the physical distribution of goods, the provision of customer services (discussed above), and the selling process itself. In many situations the same channel is used for all three purposes. In other cases two or three different channels may be used. The selection or design of a selling (or trade) channel is a central aspect of marketing strategy. Options may range from direct marketing (within which there is a range of possibilities for developing a direct relationship between supplier and user) to channel systems with a number of vertical and horizontal levels. An example of the latter type is shown in Fig 1.2.

Marketers use a variety of criteria to choose an appropriate channel structure, some of which are listed in Table 1.1.

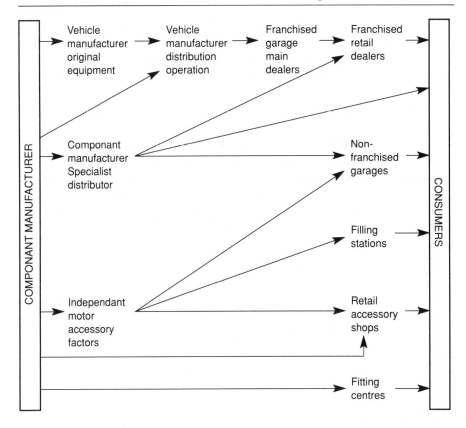

Fig 1.2 Distribution channels for automotive spare parts

Table 1.1 Channel selection criteria

Channel establishment costs
Channel operating costs
Price levels achievable
Sales volumes achievable
Impact on positioning strategy
End user market coverage
Degree of control over way product/service is marketed
Risk
Adaptability to changing market circumstances
User needs and preferences
Degree of competitive advantage through using innovative channels
Capacity of channel intermediaries to be motivated
Capacity of channel intermediaries to offer loyalty
Channel credibility

At an operational level, the management of such channels – and particularly the recruitment, motivation and control of independent intermediaries – is a key responsibility of marketing and sales personnel.

In providing physical distribution and customer services there are significant interfaces with other functional areas, and this aspect is discussed next.

Marketing and logistics

Among the many chestnuts in the folklore of marketing is the saying that 'distribution is the first law of marketing'. If the product or service is not available, you can't sell it. Of course, this view – applied literally – holds good in only a limited number of circumstances. Many customers are prepared to wait but what they generally want is delivery precision, i.e. a firm, acceptable delivery period which is adhered to. Indeed in many markets, either ex-stock delivery or delivery precision may be the key order-winning criterion. Partly in recognition of this importance to making a sale the 'physical distribution' function is sometimes organised as an activity within the marketing department. Marketers are made responsible for the level of finished stocks and for the distribution of the stocks to depots or to customers' warehouses and for associated order-processing activities and information flows.

In addition to its key role in 'delivery' of customer satisfaction, there is another argument for locating physical distribution within marketing. For those organisations which need to use a channel through which to market their products, the selection, development and management of that channel are tasks of overriding importance. Sometimes the uses of a channel for selling purposes and for physical distribution purposes are inextricably linked. Contract furniture manufacturers sell to office equipment dealers because they are needed to display and deliver furniture as well as to sell it. On other occasions a particular channel may be used only for selling purposes or only for delivery purposes. Thus the furniture manufacturer might sell through interior designers but actually deliver direct (or use a carrier) for any orders passed on by the designer. Particularly in the former case, it is the responsibility of marketers to develop channels based not only on their ability to provide delivery and display services but on their capabilities in other areas of marketing such as selling, provision of market information, and the like. Because of this need to integrate physical and other channel activities, there is an argument for all aspects to be under the control of one functional area.

This close relationship between marketing and physical distribution is perhaps captured by the concept of the 7 Rs which echo the 4 Ps of marketing. The 7 Rs consist of the right product, in the right quantity and the right condition, at the right place, at the right time, for the right customer, at the right cost. Increasingly, however, there has been a tendency to integrate physical distribution activities, which are generally defined as relating to finished goods, with activities related to raw materials and work in progress. These material-flow or material-management tasks, combined with physical distribution tasks, are now frequently referred to as logistics. Fig. 1.3 illustrates this development.

Such an integrated approach to logistics can often be justified in terms of

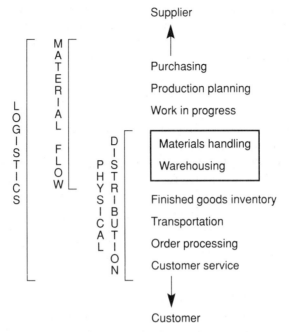

Fig. 1.3 Logistics

extra efficiency gained by reducing throughput time and/or minimising total costs. The gains which can be achieved clearly depend on the nature of the industrial processes involved and the complexity of market needs. Thus some industries (e.g. aerospace) source from thousands of suppliers but market to a very limited number of customers whose needs have been clearly established years in advance. At the other extreme (e.g. chemicals) some industries use a limited number of raw materials which may then be processed into a huge variety of products with a huge array of needs in terms of storage, packaging and transport. In between, there are industries where the complexity between inbound and outbound activities is much more even.

The key point from a marketing perspective is not the locus of control but that the output of the logistics or physical distribution system meets the needs of consumers. It is clearly vital that distribution costs, which typically account for a fifth of all costs in a company, are kept to a minimum. However, it is also vital that significant marketplace advantages can be achieved by consistently providing the right level of customer service. It is the responsibility of the marketing function to specify service levels required by different customers and the extent to which those customers are prepared to trade price for service. Of course, achieving customer service satisfaction *is* more difficult if responsibility for packing and storing, for example, is placed with the manufacturing manager and responsibility for carriage with the transport manager, and each of these functional heads has his or her own set of targets – none of which may be related to customer service. Either some sort of matrix organisational structure is required or great emphasis must be placed on the internal role of marketers to persuade colleagues that the targets specified in the marketing plan must override narrow departmental perspectives. Some of these issues are developed in chapter 3.

The question of establishing service levels is closely related to the issue of segmentation, which is discussed in the next section. Suffice to say here that not all customers require the same 'level' of service, expressed in terms of product availability, packaging, delivery method and distribution or any of the other elements of an after-sales-service package. Indeed, it may be possible to segment customers specifically in terms of their different service-level needs. In this way, scarce resources such as finance and space for finished goods or rapid transport, might be reallocated in such a way as to improve service where it is needed and *reduce* service levels where they may currently exceed needs. Such readjustments may be reflected by differential prices and may also increase the profit contribution of distribution activities.

Marketing communications

Marketing communications embrace a wide variety of methods for the transmission of messages to and from customers and other target publics. The marketer's task is to select an appropriate combination of methods in relation to a relevant set of criteria. Table 1.2 notes the main communications options together with a typical set of criteria.

Table 1.2 Marketing communications

Promotion method	Criteria
Selling – personal	Communication objective (e.g. awareness/
– telephone	comprehension/conviction/purchase)
Direct mail	Strength and immediacy of persuasion
Media advertising	Credibility of source of persuasion
Sales promotion (trade and/or consumer)	
– money off	Contact cost
– free product	Speed at which message can reach target
– samples	Selectivity with which message reaches target
– competitions	Ability to control timing, content and context of message
Exhibitions/seminars	Longevity of impact
Sponsorship	Possibility of obtaining feedback
Point of sale display	Impact on positioning and branding
Packaging	Available budget
Public relations	

The nature of the interface between 'sales' and 'marketing' and PR and 'marketing' is discussed in some depth below. There is also a significant interface between marketing and manufacturing in respect of packaging. For firms which market products like tea or coffee, packaging represents the largest part of the 'manufacturing' operation and yet it is also of crucial concern to marketers. This shared interest stems from the multiple roles of packaging, which can be summarised as:

- *protection* against deterioration, damage, pilferage, contamination
- *convenience* in handling, storage, usage
- *promotion* through identification, display, presentation.

In some industries, new forms of packaging are the principal means of competitive advantage and the principal direction for new and old product development. Increasingly, issues in respect of labelling and disposal of packaging are becoming more important as a response to both legislation and consumer demand.

Marketing and selling

Selling is obviously a part of marketing when viewed in functional terms. Or is it? It is still probably true that in a majority of organisations which have marketing and sales departments they are seen as dissociate activities, generally reporting to different functional heads. Further than this, a recent text on sales management (Lynch, 1990) stated:

> Marketing is *not* an activity carried on in an ivory tower by specialists; it is an integral part of the sales effort, its aim should be to create the environment that most effectively and most quickly helps the sales force to do their job and it shall be headed by *salespeople* who know best what the sales force needs and what customers buy.

Putting aside for the moment the final comment, the extract clearly demonstrates a relationship between marketing and sales, but one in which the academic interpretation of this relationship is inverted. The author goes on to define the job of the marketing department as being to establish a corporate style for publications, letterheads, give-aways; arrange product launches; ensure that the company and its products are presented in a positive light; provide the sales force with promotional material; arrange seminars and conferences.

With this type of thinking on the one hand, and Drucker's (1980) famous claim that 'the aim of marketing is to make selling unnecessary' on the other, it is worthwhile reviewing how marketing and sales can and should relate.

There are some very powerful reasons for proposing that the job of selling is but one of the functions within the range of tasks which can be logically grouped within a marketing department. One reason is that in many, if not most, organisations the sales team is often large and powerful itself. Unbridled, it might lead to a company orientation usually described as the 'selling orientation'.

While a competent and motivated sales force can sometimes legitimately be the key to success, using sales pressure to persuade customers to make purchases which may not be right for them is ultimately doomed to failure. The sales force must be responsible for implementing marketing strategy and its behaviour must be consistent with the marketing concept, not at variance to it. In a real sense, what the salespeople do at an individual customer level must reflect marketing strategy at a segment level.

A second reason is that the ultimate task of salespeople is persuasive communications. They are not always, however, the only channel through which such communication can take place. Some firms choose not to use field salespeople at all and carry out all communications using direct response or direct mail advertising. Within the financial services industry some organisations have recently introduced salespeople ('advisers') where none existed before, while others have replaced field salespeople with brokers or with non-personal forms of communication.

Even where such direct substitution is not possible, the amount of expenditure on personal selling activities or other forms of marketing communications can be varied. For example, would the short- or long-term sales response be greater if we hired an additional salesperson or allocated an equivalent annual amount to the media advertising budget? Furthermore, additions to advertising expenditure might even increase sales force productivity through a variety of mechanisms – such as generating a large number of enquiries, 'warming up' prospects before a sales visit, moving product faster through trade channels, and others. Allocating communications/promotions expenditure between different areas is a complex task – one made more difficult if the potential recipients of those funds have different functional directors. Rivalry makes it hard to achieve the optimum balance between personal and non-personal marketing communications expenditure.

A third reason is that it is crucial that the sales force carries out the role specified for it within the marketing plan – a role which has to be consistent with marketing strategy because it is a key element in the implementation of that strategy.

There are a number of sales forces which exhibit two particularly damaging features. First, individual field salespeople are not clear about their key tasks. Is their main objective to make short-term sales or to develop relationships over time? To win new customers or to retain existing customers through concentration on after-sales service? To disseminate information and advice or to chase up debts? Is it to compete with or to support distributors? The second – and related – feature is that salespeople are often not certain which customers to call on. This is not only a question of existing and potential customers, 'hot' or 'cooler' prospects but also a fundamental aspect of the market segmentation strategy. Should salespeople concentrate on large or small customers; on price-sensitive or service-centred customers; on those in the electronic components industry or the automotive industry? Sales management may be happy with any type of sale made to any type of customer. The marketing strategy may call for a much tighter definition of the salesperson's task and the target customer.

Of course, having the same functional head is not the only solution to these differing orientations. The real solution lies in a mutual appreciation of the roles and problems of marketing strategists and salespeople. Such understanding depends on factors like good communications, training and job rotation – but it all becomes that much easier to achieve when organised within one functional area.

Marketing and public relations

Public relations (PR) activity is popularly viewed as being concerned primarily with manipulating the media. The PR business has itself become more public in recent years, partly as a result of its increasing role in politics and in finance, particularly in take-over activity. Regrettably, much of the public face of PR has been shown in an unpleasant light, for example the battle between BA and Virgin, which has featured allegations of feeding misinformation to the press about competitors' financial health.

PR can, however, be interpreted much more widely than press relations. The Institute of Public Relations defines PR as 'the deliberate, planned and sustained effort to establish and maintain mutual understanding between an organisation and its public'. Public, here, means all the 'publics' which might have an influence on organisational success and thus includes, in addition to the media itself, end users, trade customers, consumer lobbies, environmentalists, government, the local community, investors, employees, unions and even suppliers and competitors – and finally 'Joe Public'. Developing an understanding, of course, involves more than just persuading; it entails listening to what the relevant 'public' is saying and taking account of it in strategy development. In this way, PR is very much a two-way process. It is also an ongoing activity that proceeds in accordance with planned objectives and strategies. Interestingly, one of the growth areas in PR has been crisis management, but even here some form of contingency planning is appropriate. It could be argued, for example, that had Perrier formulated an effective response to the discovery of traces of benzene in its bottled water – 'just in case . . .' – it could have limited the short-term sales damage. Since Perrier water contained benzene naturally, such a disclosure might reasonably have been anticipated. In the absence of an effective and speedy response, speculation increased as to whether Perrier's process quality control was at fault or whether the product itself was polluted – a possibility completely at variance with its image of natural purity. Indeed, it could be argued that PR is no less than the task of creating and projecting the personality of an organisation. Haywood (1984) believes that 'Public Relations should begin before the policy making stage – when attitudes towards the issues are being developed by management and policies being formulated.'

Thus, for example, PR activity might involve dissemination of organisational policies and culture throughout the organisation. This aspect of PR is very close to the concept of 'internal marketing' in that it relates to the recipient employees as if they were customers. Their needs are recognised, as is their value as the ultimate determining factor in whether marketing plans are implemented and (external) customer satisfaction is achieved. Another example might be the use of PR in terms of establishing policy in relation to new product development. Car manufacturers are adopting highly visible stances in terms of features and benefits incorporated into new products. Ford is concentrating on its contribution to safety through ABS braking; Fiat on environmental protection through the use of catalytic converters and recyclable components. Some 10 per cent of Fiat's R&D budget is now devoted to environmental issues.

In short, PR should be more than skin deep. Just as the nature of PR can be viewed in a variety of ways, so can its relationship with marketing. On the one hand, marketing could be seen as part of PR. The justification for this perspective would be that organisational success depends on favourable dispositions and responses from many publics (the province of PR) while marketing activity is aimed primarily at customers, just one of those publics. At the other extreme is the view that PR is a subset of marketing. The justification here is that marketing activity embraces a variety of approaches for communicating with customers, of which one might include PR activity.

Some writers speak in terms of 'corporate public relations' and 'marketing public relations', where the former would be concerned primarily with issues management, public affairs, lobbying and corporate advertising, all aimed at a variety of publics, while the latter would concentrate largely on media relations and press agency in support of promotion of products to customers. The distinction is not without ambiguity, and indeed promotional vehicles such as media advertising, sponsorship, exhibitions and seminars, films and videos, and house journals can be used for either corporate or marketing purposes. Of course the two are not mutually exclusive but should be mutually interactive (Kitchen and Proctor, 1991). A favourable corporate image makes an organisation more attractive to do business with.

What is clear is that in many industries and companies the proportion of the market communications budget being allocated to traditional PR activities in support of marketing, as opposed to spending on conventional product/brand advertising or personal selling, is increasing. The cost and credibility advantages of press editorial (often perceived as unbiased even when it clearly originates from a supplier) over advertising have become more widely recognised. PR activities can be used to support as well as supplement other activities. Often it is necessary to educate a market as to what a new product is, and can do, before consumer acceptance and take-up can be achieved. The BT share issue is an unusual but interesting example. Six times larger than any previous UK share issue, success required that people who had never considered investing in financial assets became shareholders in large numbers. This needed not only conventional promotional activities aimed at generating awareness and providing inducements to buy, but also an education programme which explained what shareholding entailed. Booklets were issued on how to buy and sell shares and a share information office was established.

The relationship between marketing and PR is thus complex, with overlapping targets and parallel techniques. In organisations where different departments are responsible for PR and for marketing activities, there is ample scope for conflict and inconsistency. Such dangers need to be avoided by early discussion of philosophies and objectives during corporate and marketing planning processes. Readers are referred to Kotler and Mindak (1978), who have proposed a framework for planning PR and marketing activities in tandem.

Pricing

The price has often been referred to as the 'signal of quality'. It is also the only variable within the marketing mix which feeds immediately into the 'bottom line'. Although widely recognised as one of the 4 Ps, most evidence suggests that in a majority of organisations cost-plus methods of determining price are still the norm. Whilst there are some valid arguments in support of cost-plus techniques, price has a crucial role to play in positioning a product, in giving value to the customer and in bringing about a balance between demand and supply. Too low a price, for example, may either result in excess demand leading to supply shortages and consumer disappointment, or may not attract the target consumer who perceives the product as unlikely to meet either quality standards or need for status recognition.

Thus prices have to be set with regard to a number of influences, requiring interfaces with a variety of external and internal interests. The final responsibility for determining price levels must rest with general management. Marketers' main tasks should be to advise on price levels which:

- are consistent with positioning strategy and the other elements in the marketing mix;
- are likely to suggest the desired competitive stance (e.g. do we want to be the price leader, to be aggressive or to be a price follower and maintain the status quo?);
- bring a balance between supply and demand at all stages in product life cycle;
- where appropriate, assist in the pursuit of marketing objectives which may demand either the rapid growing of a new product/market and discouragement of competitors (penetration price) or, alternatively, the creaming of high unit profits at the expense of sales volume and market growth (skimming price);
- where distributors are employed, allow for attractive margins;

- are seen to be reasonable in the eyes of customers and government;
- provide the required level of profit (*see* below).

It will be the task of the finance department to ensure that the organisation's cost levels are accurately entered into the equation and that the critical relationships between costs, volumes and prices and profits are clearly recognised and understood. The relative impacts of altering costs or prices should be modelled over a variety of sales and output levels, and marketers should be asked to comment on the real-world feasibility and effects of the alternative scenarios.

Marketing and profit

Kotler (1980) has said that 'In some companies there is a trade-off between sales growth and profit growth; but marketing is an alternative that proves that you can have your cake and eat it.'

Indeed, many strategists believe that higher sales, particularly if they are synonymous with higher market share, result in higher profitability. Whatever the arguments for and against this particular proposition, yet other commentators have questioned whether, in fact, profit generation should be a responsibility of marketing. The Chartered Institute of Marketing's definition ('the management process responsible for identifying, anticipating and satisfying customers' requirements profitably') makes it clear where mainstream marketers stand on this issue. However, in another context, when discussing the boundaries imposed on marketing by the strategic planners, even Kotler (1980) suggests: 'It may be that in future, marketers will have to see themselves as demand managers rather than simply demand stimulators, or perhaps as engineers controlling the level, timing and size of demand.'

Piercy (1982a) argues that 'marketing determines the potential for profit by managing demand and achieving sales volume targets'. Piercy's proposition is that the great danger in cost and profit analysis in marketing is that it overemphasises the apparent need to make short-term profits, which may well dampen entrepreneurial dynamism and also result in the reduction of long-term profitability.

This more limited role for marketing has its advantages. It is easily understood. It avoids the problem of determining exactly which measure of profit marketing should be responsible for, e.g., net profit, gross profit or other. It perhaps focuses marketing skills on better execution of operational marketing. On the other hand, most of Piercy's case for marketing not being responsible for profits hangs on the assumption that it causes a preoccupation with short-term profit and the associated emphasis on techniques of distribution cost analysis used to assess the profit contributions of markets, segments, distribution channels, customers, sales personnel, advertising, etc. However, this short-term orientation surely stems from the general culture within which British (and

American) business functions. If shareholders and banks, and thus managers, accepted a longer-term view of product and market profitability, it would actually increase the scope for more effective marketing and permit a more rational approach to marketing mix decisions. This issue is discussed in chapter 5 on the financial interface with marketing.

The discussion above of functional marketing's responsibility for profit assumes that profit generation is an organisational objective. It should be noted that this is not always the case and there has, in recent years, been an explosion in the demand for marketers in 'not for profit' organisations.

The marketing mix in services

When the 4 Ps are extended to encompass the additional 3 Ps (process, physical evidence, people) thought to be appropriate to marketing mixes in service industries, the interface between marketing issues and other functional tasks is equally clear. Cowell (1984) writes: 'In service systems the marketing implications of operational performance are so important that the two functions have to co-operate. In services, marketing must be just as involved with the operational aspects of performance as operations managers; that is with the "how" and the "process" of service delivery.' A good example is provided by McDonald's, whose first joint venture in Moscow serves 45,000 customers each day – on average, within one minute once inside the restaurant (Vikhanski and Puffer, 1993). To achieve customer satisfaction (and benchmarks established by McDonald's elsewhere) with the food and service has required a huge investment in catering facilities and equipment, in seating and cash registers and particularly in developmental activities for employees in all functions. The process is virtually inseparable from the product and the customer benefit.

Physical evidence such as buildings, layout, furnishings and so on may also require close attention from marketers. An interesting example is provided by Ladbrokes, which undertook a complete redesign and refurbishment of betting shops in order to dispel their seedy image and reposition betting as a rather more wholesome activity.

Finally, the role of people has been repeatedly referred to either in the context of internal marketing or as part-time marketers. This latter role is particularly important in service marketing where the people providing the service may be virtually inseparable from the service itself. Retail shop assistants, airline stewards and the famous Kwik-Fit fitters are obvious examples of where human resource development is a key ingredient in marketing success. In the more competitive environment faced by the professions, some dentists are explaining to patients what options there are and what the experience will be like for the patient. How long will it be before the marketing-orientated doctor requires more than just the current half-day session on bereavement counselling in the five-year training period?

Marketing research

Marketing research encompasses a wide variety of activities. Its scope is indicated in Table 1.3.

Table 1.3 Scope of marketing research

Buyer behaviour
Basic needs and motivations – purchase decision criteria and processes
– awareness and perception of brand, organisation and product class

Market size and structure
Trends – segmentation – marketing channels

Competitor research
Share – strategy – strengths and weaknesses

Product and price research
Concepts – test marketing – portfolio analysis – packaging research
– buy response curve – bid analysis

Communications research
Media research – pre- and post-testing – tracking studies – evaluation of sales
force, PR, sales promotion

Distribution research
Measurement of outlet penetration, service quality – evaluation of distributors

Environmental research
Economic, social, technological and demand forecasting

The task of the marketer is to recognise which decisions will benefit from the use of research, what information is needed, which combination of research techniques is appropriate and whether the research should be conducted in-house or be subcontracted to a research agency.

There are two main areas where marketing research activities interface with other functional areas. First, there are a number of situations where there is a need for other functional areas to become involved in research. The task of forecasting, for example, requires input from finance and manufacturing, and a model for organising this is proposed in chapter 6. A second example recognises the limitations faced by 'conventional' researchers in seeking and evaluating new opportunities in hi-tech markets. This issue is discussed under Marketing orientation and the marketing concept at p. 36, where the need for the involvement of R&D technologists is advocated. A third example arises in many organisations including those where the sales operation is integrated into the marketing function. Field sales staff tend to accumulate a wealth of information about customers, competitors, ideas for new products and feedback about the organisation. Unfortunately, very little of this information tends to be used because of the difficulty of recording and retaining it, and because – in some organisations – it is not seen as part of the salesperson's job. Valuable market-ing information can be collected by staff from a variety of functional areas and attempts need to be made to capture it and capitalise on it.

This brings us to the second main area where marketing research interfaces with other functional areas. Increasingly, organisations are thinking not just in terms of the collection of *ad hoc* research but the design of integrated systems for collecting, sorting, retrieving and disseminating data on a systematic basis. Such marketing information systems (MKISs) are planned to draw upon data for marketing which emanates not only from marketing research studies but also from environmental scanning systems and internal accounting systems. Such systems are generally in an embryonic state but are ultimately intended to incorporate full-blown modelling and decision-support systems.

In turn this has led Piercy (1987) to maintain that:

> if the marketing department (or, it should be noted, some other subunit) does not convert the uncertainty of the marketing environment into the sales forecast, there is no basis for planning production, manpower or the financing of operations. In this sense, the management of information is at the very centre of the status of marketing management and the implementation of the marketing concept in the company.

Christopher, McDonald and Wills (1980) go even further, when they write that 'marketing management becomes first and foremost an information processing activity'.

Chapter 7 (on information management) discusses the nature of the relation-ship between marketing management and those responsible in an organisation for the development of information systems. The interface is even more impor-tant than that suggested by the crucial need to obtain, evaluate and use envi-ronmental and internal information in decision-making. The reason is that, in today's world, information and information technology can be a major com-petitive weapon.

From marketing mix to marketing orientation

Interestingly, the concept of the mix is beginning to attract criticisms as being an unrealistic model of modern marketing, particularly in areas other than repeat-purchase consumer items. The idea of manipulating the Ps to achieve sales and customer satisfaction belies the importance in so many markets of promoting and fostering relationships between seller and buyer whose pur-pose is to maintain stable and co-operative transactions to the benefit of both parties. This point is developed further under Relationships, pp. 41–2. It also ignores the fact that in some markets it is increasingly the *buyers* who initiate transactions by searching for suppliers who can meet their needs. It is then the task of the potential supplier to see if they can offer a package which is appro-priate. Nevertheless, the concept of the mix is useful as a means of readily referring to the main functional areas within marketing.

We have briefly seen some of the main marketing functional activities. These functions are *inputs* into a marketing (or positioning) mix. The main *outputs* with which functional marketers are concerned are indicated on the matrix in Table 1.4.

Table 1.4 Marketing functional activities

Output	Input					
	Product/ brand planning	Customer service	Marketing channels	Marketing communi-cations	Pricing	Marketing research
Information						•
Image	•	•	•	•	•	
Relationships		•	•	•		
Satisfaction	•	•	•	•	•	
Volume/profit	•	•	•	•	•	

Marketing mix functional activities are the most visible face of marketing and it is easy for organisations to mistake the undertaking of some of these functions for marketing itself. It is often possible to recognise within organisations typical patterns that reflect the degree to which marketing functions have been adopted and to which the organisation has moved in the direction of marketing orientation. These patterns, or stages of development, are necessarily stereotypes but they can be illuminating.

Stage 1 has been described as peripheral marketing. Typically, one or more of a number of 'marketing services' may be provided. Such services might include publicity or market research.

Stage 2 might involve the expansion of the range of services and their organisation within a marketing department. At this stage, departmental functions might include advertising, exhibitions, sales promotions and other forms of marketing communication. They might include marketing research, involving a wider brief than most market research. However, 'marketing' would still probably be less important than the sales or finance department.

Stage 3 might see the transfer of pricing to the marketing department, the transfer of sales and the transfer of responsibility for physical distribution and after-sales service. In an engineering company the application engineers who previously reported to the technical director might be transferred to a newly appointed marketing director. In a consumer products firm, even R&D staff might be transferred to marketing. At this stage, marketing is perhaps pre-eminent among departments. It should be noted that this is a description of an evolutionary pattern and does not suggest that the marketing department has any valid claim to pre-eminence.

Stage 4 might see the marketing department taking on an integrative role within the organisation as a whole. The department might be charged with this task for a number of reasons. There is a 'time relationship' which normally exists during the planning process (Foster, 1974). Thus market research and sales forecasting precede, for example, manufacturing and finance plans. However, as we note elsewhere in this chapter, these activities should not be performed by marketing staff in isolation. For example, forecasting should be a joint activity, as should design of new products. These issues are discussed in the chapters on forecasting and design. In general, however, other functional plans are based on marketing plans which themselves subsume sales forecasts and sales budgets. This time relationship also ends with activities often associated with aspects of the marketing function. It is, for example, the responsibility of marketing to ascertain whether customer needs have been met and whether customers are satisfied with the relationship they have with their supplier. This monitoring activity may be carried out by sales personnel and also by market researchers.

Whilst the origin of the sustainable competitive advantage of an organisation may lie with manufacturing, design or finance expertise, or with skills and resources possessed by any functional area, it is the task of marketing management to harness these for the benefit of selected market segments. This task is the formulation of marketing strategy and is pivotal to organisational survival and success. It is also the role of the marketing function to make customers aware of these advantages (marketing communications), to secure customers' commitment to them (sales) and to ensure they are delivered.

The third reason is not related to marketing's functional activities at all. One of the manifestations of marketing is that it is a company-wide philosophy: it does not 'belong' to a particular functional area. Marketing orientation is the province and the responsibility of all departments. To quote Drucker (1973): 'Marketing is so basic that it cannot be considered a separate function on a par with others such as manufacturing or personnel. It is first a central dimension of the entire business.'

For a company to be good at 'marketing' it has to be marketing-orientated, good at all the functional areas within a firm (from R&D to manufacturing and finance) and good at co-ordinating all those areas so that the natural tendency to conflict is minimised and everyone pulls in the same direction. One vehicle through which co-ordination and integration should take place is the marketing plan. While this is only one of several functional plans developed by organisations and which sum to form the corporate plan, it is a key plan at both the strategic and operational levels. Strategically, it specifies customer segments to be targeted and the basis on which they will be competed for. At the operational level, detailed sales budgets and forecasts are the basis of manufacturing and finance activities. To perform this co-ordinating role, marketers need to be able to integrate marketplace possibilities with company capabilities, all within the directions specified in the corporate plan. This issue is covered in more depth in the section on Marketing Strategy.

Stage 5 of the process really takes us into the next section: marketing orientation and the marketing concept. At this stage, marketing assumes a cultural orientation in addition to a set of functional and integrative tasks. Traditional departmental boundaries are broken down and replaced by company-wide ownership of and commitment to marketing orientation.

MARKETING ORIENTATION AND THE MARKETING CONCEPT
Customers, segments and markets

It is over thirty years since Levitt's (1960) influential marketing myopia 'manifesto' appeared. In it Levitt uses a variety of examples to illustrate the crucial importance for an organisation of defining the business it is in. Because, he claimed, basic questions about customer needs and wants were seldom asked, organisations risked collapse as more satisfying ways of meeting these (generic) needs were made available by (new) competitors.

The reason that this happened was that management was conditioned to concentrate on product and technical aspects of an organisation, giving to marketing only 'stepchild' status. The railways thought they were in the railway business. A marketing-orientated approach would have shown that the customer's need was for transport, and that need could be satisfied in an increasing variety of ways. Management needed to reorientate its thinking. As Levitt said, 'the organisation must learn to think of itself not as producing goods and services but as *buying customers*, as doing the things that will make people *want* to do business with it'.

Some interesting conceptual and practical issues follow from the above considerations. For example:

- How broad or how narrow should the definition of the generic need be?
- To what extent does the marketing concept allow for the creation of needs or wants rather than just their identification?
- What criteria or starting points are used in determining those customers whose needs are to be served?

To take the last point first, is there a suggestion that a truly marketing-orientated organisation actively seeks a (changing) group of customers who are likely to offer a (profitable) market for something, the nature of the something being immaterial? The answer for almost all *existing* organisations is no. It is flying in the face of reality to ignore the practical limitations placed on an organisation seeking to chase opportunities wherever they may lie. Spillard (1980/81) has proposed a useful framework which marketing strategists can use to help guide business directions. The framework consists of a set of 'logics' which any organisation will possess to a greater or lesser extent and whose nature and strength need to be appreciated when considering any major change in direction. (Changes which offend against basic and powerful logics will require skilful internal marketing if they are to become marketplace realities.) Spillard's logics are shown in Table 1.5.

Table 1.5 Spillard's logics

1 *Raw Material Logic*
   Possession and exploitation of one or two key raw materials drives the organisation's strategy.

2 *Process Logic*
   This could take many forms: for example, retailing, refining, assembling.

3 *Technical Logic*
   A multitude of products and services could be linked as a result of a common technological base. Obvious examples today would include the harnessing of microprocessor technology to applications as disparate as word processors and telecommunications. Indeed, the fusion of microprocessor and telecommunication technology has stimulated the growth of a host of new markets.

4 *Product Logic*
   Often described as the product concept and much maligned as such by Levitt. Organisations see their business in terms of the provision of a specified range of products or services like bicycles, cranes or insurance.

5 *Market Logic*
   This involves specifying customers, markets or market segments and can be done in a wide number of ways. Market segments are discussed in detail in the next section.

6 *Product/Market Logic*
   A combination of the two above.

7 *Personality Logic*
   Behaviour responds to and affects the personal preferences of the dominant individual or power groups. This logic often occurs in family organisations built up over time but may also occur elsewhere.

8 *Philosophical Logic*
   A rather nebulous logic stemming from strongly held values such as willingness to innovate or take risks, beliefs about growth rates and rates of return, desire to be cosmopolitan, etc.

While for some organisations, the dominant logic might be the market logic, it should not necessarily always be so. Even if it *does* dominate, there will also be degrees to which some or all of the other logics are present and may constitute forces which will make strategic moves in a particular direction more difficult.

Amstrad provides an interesting example of how logics can be chosen. It has defined its customers in terms both of age (seventeen to thirty-five) and of socio-economic groups (B, C1, C2, D), the price levels they are prepared to pay and in terms of the volume of sales that can be achieved. If the potential product is, or could be made, a mass consumer market product (defined as sales in excess of 200,000 units a year for a minimum of two years), has an electronics base and satisfies the needs of the target consumers, then it is a candidate for Amstrad.

Once a decision has been reached as to the general strategic direction of the organisation, we then need to consider how broadly or narrowly to define the concept of needs. The point made by Levitt was that in any product/market situation it is crucial to identify the generic need being met and to recognise that competition includes any organisation which can meet that need irrespective of the format in which it is supplied. Thus the manufacturer of expensive fountain pens may compete with the manufacturer of carriage clocks and document cases as alternative means of meeting the need for prestigious gifts. Equally, failure to appreciate generic need may lead to failure to exploit lucrative markets. For example, a scaffolding manufacturer may see itself as just that and restrict its market to builders. Seen as a supplier of temporary staging, however, customer groups could include pop show promoters and garden festivals.

There is a danger, however, in viewing generic need too broadly. Clearly there are products and services which serve the same generic need but which cannot be viewed realistically as competitors. Generic need and competition need to be defined at a level which is sufficiently operational for the organisation. Thus, personal computers, word processors, manual typewriters, pens and pencils can all be used to meet the need for written communication but they cannot all be included within the same competitive set. Some of them meet other generic needs as well. On the other hand, some personal computers will suffer a greater threat from word processors than from other personal computers.

One of the hindrances to both the study and practice of marketing is the existence of too much jargon – and too many different interpretations of the same piece of jargon. Given this, it is rather disappointing that marketers have generally failed to provide adequate definitions of such basic constructs as 'market', 'industry', 'business' and 'strategic business unit (SBU)'. As Curran and Goodfellow (1989) write, markets are frequently described in product terms (the market for men's fragrances), need terms (esteem/social/hygiene/security) or demographic (ABC, a youth market or ethnic market) or geographical terms (the UK market). Depending on the purpose at hand any of or any combination of these might be appropriate. This in itself is difficult enough to translate into a workable/operational definition. On top of that is the problem of finding a definition that is appropriate at different levels of the organisation. Thus, at the strategic level of management, Abell (1980) suggests that a market is defined by the provision of particular functions to particular customer groups, irrespective of the technology used to perform those functions. For most purposes, however, a somewhat tighter definition might be more useful.

In product terms, for example, markets can be broken down into:

- product class, e.g. electric hoists
- product form, e.g. electric chain hoists, electric wire rope hoists, compressed air hoists
- product variants, e.g. low headroom
- product features, e.g. number of speeds, safety devices.

These classifications are, of course, arbitrary. For example, a low headroom hoist could be viewed as being a particular product form rather than a product variant, while some would view the mode of power or the choice of chain or wire as being more variants. Electric hoists themselves are part of the wider materials handling market and in some cases could be substituted, on the one hand, by hand operated hoists and, on the other, by lifts or robots.

Two things are important. First, that the firm views its products – and choice processes and criteria for them – in the same way as customers. Second, that the firm adopts a classification which permits necessary analyses to be made. Such analyses might include market share and market leakage analysis. Thus, to take our hoist example, if our firm produces only electric chain hoists it will wish to monitor market share development compared to all other electric chain hoist manufacturers. In auditing its absolute share of this market, it will also want to know the extent of 'leakage' resulting from the following factors:

- product variant/feature not offered
- product size/style/colour not offered
- customer segment deliberately not competed for (e.g. low price/no distribution)
- customer deliberately not competed for (policy decisions relating to, for example, size of customer, nature of relationship).

Reverting to the rather more strategic level, the firm will want to monitor general trends in the material handling market which may affect customer behaviour and operations concerning the relationships between different forms of electric hoists and between electric hoists and other means of moving goods from one point to another.

As well as viewing markets broadly, marketers – in most instances – will also need to break down markets into constituent components, or segments. Such is the importance of the concept of segmentation to marketing orientation and particularly to marketing strategy that it will be discussed next in some depth.

Most product markets can be split into groups within which consumers have similar needs and responses, but which differ significantly from those of other groups. Some of these segments exist naturally, others are created by marketers. There are also, in general, many different ways in which markets can be segmented, and segments will often overlap. The examples which follow show some of the different segmentation bases which could be used:

Segmentation in industrial markets

Industry group

The traditional approach categorises customers on the basis of standard industrial classification. One large engineering components company developed seven major segments on this basis (including, for example, an automotive segment, a heavy industry segment, an electrical segment) and these were further subdivided into some forty-two sub-segments. Marketing planning activities, albeit at different levels of detail, were implemented for each of these sub-segments. The rationale for this approach is that similar industries are likely to require similar marketing packages; others are likely to need a different approach. The simple, generalised example in Table 1.6 will serve to illustrate some differences in respect of what could be the same basic product line.

Table 1.6 Different needs of marketing packages

Automotive customer	Heavy engineering customer
Standard product	Custom features
Bulk packaging	Individually wrapped
Price level below full cost	Average profit margin
Price determined by annual contract	Price negotiated individually
Delivery 'just in time'	Delivery two months from order
Communications: continuous, linked via computer systems	Frequent, ad hoc communications
Promotional media: sponsorship	Promotional media: exhibitions, direct mail

There would be, of course, similarities between the two segments in terms of some of the marketing mix variables, for example:

- distribution channels – direct
- after-sales service – both need a high level of technical and commercial after-sales support
- personal selling – intensive relationship-building, combined with technical expertise.

The key point, however, is that to serve effectively each of the two segments requires different strategies, operational activities, organisational support and different people dedicated to their respective needs and objectives.

An engineering component may be sold to a customer who is the final consumer (end user), or it may be sold to a manufacturer of some other product (original equipment manufacturer (OEM)) for incorporation into that product, and it may be sold to some form of dealer/distributor who then resells it to the final consumer. Clearly, each of these three types of customer has different needs, and can be grouped into segments on the basis of what each does with the product.

The third variant also recognises that the use of the product may vary – but this time in a technical sense. In some applications, usage may be continuous and heavy and the reliance on the component may be extreme. In others, use may be sporadic and the component not have such a key role to play. Again, differing needs will call for differing marketing mix packages if supplying firms are to be successful.

Customer size

Our firm could choose to segment potential customers by the amount of business they are able to place (often, but not always related to the size of their organisation). Customers could, for example, be classified as A, B or C. The As might be the 20 per cent of customers who, after Pareto, typically account for 70–80 per cent of existing and potential business. They can be singled out for particular emphasis, perhaps with a customer marketing plan formulated for each of them. C customers perhaps represent very small levels of existing and potential business and distribution cost analysis (DCA) techniques might well show they produce net losses. Such customers could perhaps be passed on to a distributor and no longer be serviced directly by our firm. B customers might well be retained but would receive a reduced level of service compared with A customers. They may, for example, be visited by a salesperson only monthly compared with weekly for A customers.

Organisational buying processes and characteristics

The ways in which organisations buy can differ in a number of ways and will call for different marketing mixes. A few of these will suffice to illustrate:

- single sourcing or multiple supplier philosophy
- sophisticated vendor screening procedures or simple tenders
- size and composition and relative influence on the members of the decision-making unit (DMU)
- decision-making styles and personalities of DMU members
- degree of loyalty of customers – Garda (1988) refers to 'entrenched' customers, who may presently be loyal to either you or one of your competitors, and 'open' customers, who have not committed themselves to any degree and may be ready to switch suppliers on each procurement occasion.

Geography

It is clearly possible to segment customers according to their geographical location. In some industries suppliers traditionally limit themselves to marketing on a regional basis, often because they believe their products would be uncompetitive further afield. Sometimes this premise is not justified and profitable opportunities may exist further afield, particularly in rich markets which have been segmented using other bases.

In terms of international marketing, exporters are frequently exhorted (ITI Research, 1979) to limit their activities to a smaller number of countries. This is generally known as market concentration. On the other hand, there are occasions when this type of geographical segmentation is inappropriate. For a passive exporter, who receives rather than seeks orders from overseas, it may be more profitable to deal in a superficial way with a large number of geographical markets. This would be known as market spreading. The relative advantage of concentration and spreading are discussed by Piercy (1982b). Equally, for a firm producing a product with a very specialised application, it might be necessary and easy to identify all those applications and seek business, wherever they are located. Segmentation should be by product/application rather than by geography in that particular area.

Product

Although not perhaps a *true* form of segmentation, many firms are faced with the decision whether to compete in all product forms or variants. In bearing manufacturers, for example, Timken makes only tapered roller bearings and INA only needle roller bearings. Other manufacturers make ball bearings, cylindrical bearings, spherical bearings, etc., as well as tapered roller and needle roller bearings. Whatever their decision as to 'width' of product range, firms also have to decide on 'depth' of range, e.g. how many sizes, how many different materials or tolerances, etc.

Customer benefit

In so far as there should be one preferred segmentation basis (see below), it is surely segmentation on the basis of customer benefit, or buying criteria. As with the markets for most products or services, there is a segment which buys predominantly on price, i.e. the main benefit the customers are seeking is lower procurement cost. Other segments are less concerned with price than with performance – however this may be defined. Unfortunately, rarely do customers make purchases having regard to only one or two criteria. They usually consider a number of criteria, but their relative importance is likely to differ between different groups of customers.

A survey of customers for food manufacturing machinery revealed the following eight purchase criteria in overall order of importance:

(1) ability to cope with variable (often high) production volumes;
(2) flexibility easily to accommodate new food product styles;
(3) quality of end food product (e.g. no marking by machinery);
(4) cleanability of equipment;
(5) reliability;
(6) after-sales support package (commissioning, maintenance and spares);
(7) price (initial purchase);
(8) degree of technical innovation.

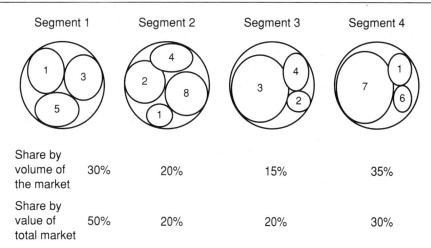

	Segment 1	Segment 2	Segment 3	Segment 4
Share by volume of the market	30%	20%	15%	35%
Share by value of total market	50%	20%	20%	30%

Fig. 1.4 Different segmentation of purchase criteria

However, within this overall picture it was possible to identify and build segments of customers attaching different priorities to these criteria. Four possible segments are shown in Fig. 1.4. The numbered circles indicate the main purchase benefits.

In consumer and service markets it is a popular practice to attach labels to segments and we might refer to segments 1, 2, 3 and 4 in Fig. 1.4 as, respectively, the 'volume', 'experimenters', 'quality' and 'price conscious' segments. Again, prospective suppliers who have perceived the market segments in this way can choose to market to one, some, or all of them, either with an undifferentiated offering or with a distinct marketing mix for each segment.

As mentioned previously, and as seen in Fig. 1.4, segments may overlap. Another supplier might decide that the needs of segments 2 and 3 could be treated as sufficiently similar to merit being treated as one, thus providing it with a bigger target at which to aim. Obviously, for firms to want to base strategies on segments, those segments need to be large enough, to exist over a reasonable period of time, to be identifiable by measurable characteristics (e.g. market size and competitor share, price levels, etc.), and to be uniquely reachable in terms of marketing communications and channels of distribution.

However, marketing embraces a number of activities, and sometimes it is appropriate to segment customers in different ways for different purposes. Using simple computer databases and spreadsheets, it is easy to code customers in respect of the various characteristics, including their response to manipulation of marketing variables. Each customer could be assessed, for example, for its degree of price consciousness. At the time of price increases, changes can then be made on a differential basis according to the predicted customer response. In a similar way customers can be classified according to size of business, the share of that business held by different suppliers, degree of support needed and a whole host of the variables as well as basic data relating to location and industry sector. Customers can then be easily sorted into different segments for different purposes.

An important point is the search for segmentation bases which are appropriate to the firm and to customers, manageable in practice, innovative and may provide the basis for a sustained competitive advantage. For example, research into the diffusion of innovations through industrial markets (Hayward, 1977) has shown that some organisations are more receptive to the purchase of new technology/processes than are others. Suppliers of such hi-tech equipment could well segment the market in terms of attitude to new technology and plan to target such different segments at different points in time and by stressing different benefits.

There are great dangers for those firms which fail to recognise the (changing) pattern of segments in a market. They can find themselves easily outmanoeuvred by smarter competitors who have better understood given groups of customer needs. Equally, the fruits of segmentation are often difficult to achieve if firms have chosen an inappropriate basis for segmentation or have generated too many segments which fail to be sufficiently distinctive in terms of real customer needs. These difficulties are also readily apparent in markets for consumer goods and services, which will now be reviewed briefly.

Segmentation in consumer markets

Traditionally, the main approaches to segmentation in the consumer goods industries were based on classification by consumer characteristics. Geography and demographics (age, sex, social class, etc.) were emphasised in the early days and are still used as classification variables in the majority of consumer market research studies. Later extensions of basic demographics resulted in such classifications as life cycle, which helps to explain purchase behaviour in terms of stages of life: bachelor, newly married, with children (full nest), where children have left home (empty nest), through to solitary survivor. Classification systems such as Sagacity and Acorn interlace a number of dimensions such as life cycle, income, occupation, household facilities and others in attempts to improve the ability of the segments they describe to discriminate efficiently between different types of behaviour.

Another approach to consumer classification, and one that has increased in use in recent years, is alternatively referred to as psycho-sociological, psychographic or, more popularly, lifestyle segmentation. A good example, developed by advertising agency Young and Rubicam, is known as '4 Cs'. A great advantage of lifestyle approaches is that they paint a picture of the target consumer, which can be very helpful for marketers and advertisers in planning campaign themes and slogans. Well-known adverts which appeal to four of Young and Rubicam's groups are:

- Halifax cash card – appeals to *Aspirers*
- British Airways Club Class – *Succeeders*
- *Guardian* – gives you the whole picture – *Reformers*
- Legal and General umbrella – *Mainstreamers.*

Yet, like all consumer classification techniques, 4 Cs is a stereotype, a surrogate for real behaviour which may not be applicable in specific product situations. Segmentation in terms of consumers' behaviour towards benefits sought from specific products and specific brands is a better method for many marketing purposes.

Consumer behaviour not only relates to benefits sought but also allows segmentation in terms of other behavioural variables. For example, we could segment by:

- usage status: light users of the product, heavy users
- potential users, lapsed users, first time buyers, etc.
- loyalty status: hard core loyals, switchers
- occasion.

As for industrial markets, two of the criteria for successful segmentation are that it should be imaginative and yet meaningful. Techniques for uncovering and/or creating segments will generally involve qualitative market research (such as group discussions) to uncover consumer attitudes towards product fields and brands and towards more general aspects of values and lifestyle. Such information can then be subjected to quantitative research which will measure and link it to other data on demographics and consumer purchasing behaviour. Cluster analysis may then be used to uncover segments composed of multi-dimensional variables. For a more detailed account of such procedures, readers are referred to Lunn (1986).

A final point about segmentation: if firms decide to market to only one or a few of the segments they uncover or create, they need a set of criteria against which the attractiveness of different segments can be measured. A number of such criteria are:

- durability (life cycle of segments/needed products)
- price levels
- strength of existing competition (size, ability, resources, entrenchment)
- ease of customer identification and reachability
- customisation costs (entry investment, share building and maintenance)
- ease of entry for new direct competitors and substitute products
- degree of consistency with overall marketing objectives, strategies and positioning
- degree of interdependency with other segments.

The task of the marketers in respect of market selection is thus a complex one. At one extreme they will be deciding in which segments of a market to compete and how to tune finely the marketing mix offering. At the other extreme, they need to be conscious of the dramatic and discontinuous shifts in whole industries which may render the entire existing market and competitor environment obsolete. Abell (1978) refers to these discontinuous changes as 'closing strategic windows for incumbent competitors and an opening window for new entrants'. He identifies four major ways in which change can take place:

(1) *New primary demand.*
(2) *New competing technologies*   Technological innovation in one industry may result in its owners seeking to apply it in other industries, thereby leapfrogging over the traditional barriers to entry. Examples abound in the replacement of metal components with plastics, mechanical parts by solid-state electronics and with optical fibres. Such is the importance of this that Abell was prompted to say: 'The nature of technological innovation and diffusion is such that most major innovations will originate outside a particular industry and not within it.'
(3) *Market redefinition*   This may occur in different ways, but particularly as a result of a general trend towards marketing a package of equipment which constitutes a system solution to a need rather than individual pieces of hardware. Thus, in automotive engineering, a complete wheel hub is replacing the individual components – hitherto supplied by different manufacturers. In this way, new or existing entrants to the industry can redefine the market.
(4) *Channel changes*   As distribution channels develop for products, perhaps because they broaden to cater for additional uses and users, the possibilities for existing users of those channels to enter the market for the product increase. It becomes a case of product development and the use of existing marketing skills to make use of synergy between the new and existing products.

Thus marketers need to be receptive to the possibilities that strategic windows may either open or close. Chapter 2 examines whether this role is simply the strategic application of marketing or whether it should more properly be within the province of corporate planning staff. Certainly, significantly different skills are required to evaluate strategic windows than for the tactical and operational planning and implementation of marketing activities.

Customers, competitors and capability

Marketing orientation places customers and their needs at the focal point. Some authors have, however, made a distinction between marketing orientation and customer orientation. They see the latter as characterised by too little attention paid to either the competition (Porter, 1985) or the needs of the organisation (Middleton, 1989). In a recent paper, Kotler (1991) appears to have come full circle in concluding that the 'best attack on a competitor is probably to be knowing where the market is going, and being aligned with the customers and their needs for new benefits and services'. Davidson's (1987) concept of offensive marketing reconciles organisational and customer needs in the following definition: 'Marketing is the process of balancing the company needs for profit against the benefits required by consumers, so as to maximise long term earnings per share.' He claims that long-term success requires an organisation to pursue both 'market led marketing' (searching for unsatisfied consumer wants to fill) *and* 'asset led' marketing (directing existing skills and resources to an appropriate marketplace).

The foregoing illustrates the way in which marketers are continually reappraising both the emphasis on the various elements within the marketing concept model and the operationalisation of the model. In order to confirm the view that customer focus is not exclusively a concern of the marketing department, some authors prefer the labels 'market orientation' or 'market-led organisation' to 'marketing orientation'. In a way these are also unfortunate in that they emphasise the market and not organisational capability. We shall use the terms 'market-led' organisation and 'marketing orientation' interchangeably but stressing the proviso that they both reflect an organisation-wide ownership of the concept and they both imply a recognition of the need to take account of organisation capability and competitors as well as customers.

Among the hallmarks of a market-led organisation we can list the following (helped by a simple alphabetical mnemonic). A market-led organisation:

- Anticipates
- Balances
- Creates
- Delivers
- Exploits
- Fosters
- Galvanises
- Harmonises
- Integrates.

Anticipates

A market-led organisation anticipates effects of shifts in customers, competitors, technologies and other environmental factors. An ability to read the times – or, rather, to predict future times – seems to be a product partly of an effective environmental scanning system, partly of closeness to the customer, partly of inspiration and partly of the way in which effective organisations ensure that representatives of the different functional activities have freedom to hone and apply their particular skills in the outside world. More is said about this last point later in this section.

At the other extreme is the identification of new applications and new customers for existing products. Perhaps less of a hallmark of a true market-led organisation, it is no less valid an activity. The steel balls designed for use in rolling bearings have found additional uses in weapons and as a grinding medium. The ubiquitous Post-it notes resulted from the imaginative use of an existing adhesive formulation.

Common to these examples of anticipation and identification is the principle of interpretation of future and current customer needs and wants.

Balances

Matching the competing needs and attentions imposed by customers, competitors and company capabilities and departmental perspectives has already been identified as the crux of the marketing concept. In many organisations there is an imbalance among these factors.

An example of an imbalance among different departmental interests and orientations was provided by a manufacturer of domestic tableware, selling a large proportion of its products through mail order houses. Believing that the critical success (or survival?) factor was low-cost production, the company invested heavily – and continuously – in plant and equipment which, run at full capacity, would shave fractions of a penny from the cost of producing tea or dinner sets. There was felt to be a marketing justification for this, in that it was believed that consumers shopped within price points and that the mail order houses would source only at manufacturer prices that allowed them to advertise at these retail 'psychological' price points. In fact this was a case of production orientation rather than marketing orientation. The company skills base was heavily orientated towards production management and cost reduction was pursued without reference to alternative strategies. The marketing budget was virtually non-existent. There was no marketing research other than the information collected informally by the sales director and the two salespeople; no promotional activity other than major account selling. Expenditure on design was limited to a few hundred pounds a year. In Porter's terms, this could resemble a low-cost strategy aimed at a focused market. But it was a strategy which resulted from an imbalance of skills and orientation rather than from a thorough evaluation of alternative positioning, and it was likely to result in customer offerings inferior to those of the competition. A reallocation of only a small proportion of the plant and equipment budget to allow some investment in design and image building would have paid handsome dividends in a number of ways. It could have permitted a move into a higher, more profitable price point. It could have afforded access to more design-conscious channels of distribution. It could have increased business security, since in a price-sensitive market with a limited customer base the company was highly vulnerable to imported competition which might increase dramatically with only small exchange rate movements.

It is also possible for organisations to direct too much attention towards beating a specific competitor, perhaps at the expense of focusing on customer needs. It can be argued that the best way to beat the competition is by providing the best long-run satisfaction to the customer. Certainly there may be dangers in trying to beat the competition through strategies that overemphasise a frontal attack (head-on collision) on a principal competitor at the expense of attention paid to customer need and satisfaction. The battle between lawnmower giants Flymo and Qualcast is perhaps a good example. In 1980 Qualcast's attempts to resist the growth of Flymo centred on negative advertising. The campaign slogan 'It's a lot less bovver than a hover' began an expensive 'knocking copy' war. Flymo retaliated with 'Why slowmo when you can Flymo?' The ability of Qualcast cylinder mowers to collect cuttings was not an advantage that was sustainable in the longer term and in 1989 the attack shifted to stress a benefit which hovers could never replicate: stripes. The new slogan – 'The difference shows where a Qualcast mows' – stressed quality. Flymo countered with its own quality-based campaign: 'A great finish starts with a Flymo'. Both companies now have full product ranges and both are basing their competitive advantage on quality. Both are investing in excess of £3 million per annum in advertising. It would not be surprising if all this resulted in both customer confusion and dyadic myopia. While Flymo claims 39 per cent of UK unit sales of lawnmowers, Qualcast claims its share of 36 per cent is higher than Flymo's. But Black and Decker also claims 28 per cent and with 103 per cent so far there has been no mention yet of Honda, Yamaha, Mountfield, Ibea and several others. While the big guns are trained on one another, opportunities arise for other competitors who may be better at listening to the customers.

Creates

A market-led organisation does more than predict and interpret environmental change. One school of thought proposes that such organisations actually create the future. Hiroshi Yamauchi, president of Nintendo, has said of the $6 billion hi-tech video games business: 'This is a market that Nintendo created through its own course and strategies. Because this was created by Nintendo worldwide, I would say that only Nintendo can anticipate or forecast what will become of this market' (*Sunday Times Magazine*, 1992). This somewhat complacent statement nevertheless illustrates the principle. But creating the future does not have to mean originating completely innovative products or services. Some organisations have created new market segments merely by innovative thinking and have thus captured a unique position in the marketplace. Market segmentation strategy is discussed in a later section, but a good example of creating new segments is shown by the footwear industry. Sports shoes have been developed for a variety of sports, for serious athletes and amateurs, for the fashion conscious and for everyday wear, for those who are looking for comfort, for style or for street credibility!

Creating – and safeguarding – the future can also be achieved by leading the development of industry technical standards, which leaves other competitors with the options of following, quitting or competing with a large disadvantage – perhaps only in niche markets.

Delivers

Perhaps the ultimate yardstick of a market-led organisation is that it delivers satisfaction to its customers. It provides value for money products and it offers excellent customer service. One organisation which is synonymous with this positioning is Marks and Spencer and while other retailers have suffered dramatically in times of recession, M&S has so far been able to depend on customer loyalty to maintain (and even increase) profits. It is no accident that M&S is also renowned for the quality of relationships within the company as well as between company and customers. One other point worth noting here in the context of ability to deliver satisfaction, is that 80 per cent of M&S's suppliers are based in the UK. This permits M&S to exercise more control and more flexibility over supplies, and offers a measure of protection against the effects of the devaluation of sterling. It illustrates again the importance of harnessing the contribution of all areas within the organisation to providing competitive advantage and customer satisfaction.

Exploits

Not every market-led organisation will have growth among its key objectives. Some will quite deliberately wish to remain small scale in order to maintain exclusivity, or acceptability in a niche market (Morgan Cars) while others may feel that expansion would be risky, perhaps financially and culturally. Others, however, will want to grow and will need to exploit their competitive advantages effectively.

Virtually first in the world with a mini-car at a time when car ownership was about to explode, BMC failed to exploit its position. Seen on a global scale, leadership was rapidly surrendered.

Advantages must be aggressively exploited for the time that they remain differential advantages. Care must be taken, however, not to over-exploit. The fashion industry makes its money from licensing, which subsidises the business of creating new designer clothes. With several hundred products being marketed under licence, however, the credibility of some fashion brands is being stretched with the real risk of killing the goose which laid the golden egg.

Fosters

While advantages must be exploited they must also be carefully fostered and nurtured, lest they be dissipated by the ravages of time and competition. One of the most valuable of the so-called 'marketing assets' that an organisation might possess is the power of its brands. Well-managed brand names bring recognition, clearly signal positioning and breed consumer loyalty. Such loyalty is reflected not only in market share but also frequently in premium prices and thus larger than normal profits. Fostering brands requires the type of old product development activity referred to on p. 2 under Product and Brand Management.

Galvanises

In a market-led organisation, leadership, culture and communication and a clear marketing strategy galvanise all members towards the achievement of corporate goals. Internal marketing is practised and those who have roles as full-time and part-time marketers are fully aware of their contribution towards customer satisfaction.

These issues are discussed in chapter 8. They are not new. In 1970 the Machine Tools Economic Development Committee claimed that, for successful firms: 'Every executive in these companies – from top management down through the entire management structure – was personally oriented towards the customer.' We would argue that it is not only executives who should be customer-orientated. In more recent times, organisations which are generally considered to have goal- and customer-orientated and enterprising cultures are those such as Apple Computers and Microsoft. Hierarchical structures are out – everybody is involved.

Of course, it is not sufficient simply to have the 'right' sort of culture and communication. There has to be a coherent direction, and the marketing plan is a key mechanism to co-ordinating the relevant activities in the same direction.

Harmonises

Strategic management has the task of developing a harmonious fit between the needs of customers and the capabilities of the organisation. At the corporate level this fit requires a matching of company skills and resources to the triad of customer groups, functional needs and alternative technological solutions. At the business unit level, the matching is more likely to be between the needs of particular product market segments and a particular set of marketing mix elements.

Not all organisations recognise the need for this corporate level fit. For example, the diversified engineering company Tomkins bid to take over food giant Ranks Hovis McDougall. Tomkins believes that it does not matter what sector a company is in – any company makes a suitable acquisition if it is underperforming, undervalued and can be revitalised through more effective management. However, in general, in recent years there has been a tendency to divest 'non-core' businesses and to concentrate managerial effort on those areas where the organisation has a clear competitive advantage.

As mentioned at the start of the chapter, a company's competitive advantage may arise from particular expertise or skill in any of its functional areas, or indeed in the combination of those areas. Companies like Guinness, Mars or Heinz benefit from a long history of building successful brands. Their success is based on the quality of their product and advertising management. The success of De Beers has been based on its (to date) ability to regulate the supply of a large proportion of the world's diamonds. This has maintained both the image of exclusivity of diamonds and their premium price.

In many cases, it is possible to reduce weaknesses (and to build strengths) so as to develop competitive advantage further. In some cases it is even possible to alter this structure of strengths and weaknesses fundamentally so as to allow a company to reposition. This, however, is difficult and for most companies it is far easier and cheaper to try to match existing company capabilities with product-market and segmental needs. A key task within a marketing-orientated company is, therefore, the effective diagnosis of capability. Whilst in the case of firms like Mars, functional marketers might play the lead role in this activity, elsewhere this must be a shared activity led by top corporate management. In a major contribution to corporate strategy, Prahalad and Hamel (1990) discuss their concept of core competences: 'the collective learning in the organisation, especially how to co-ordinate diverse production skills and integrate multiple streams of technologies'. As an example, Honda's core competence is in engines and this gives it competitive advantage in such widely diverging end products as cars, motorcycles, generators and lawnmowers. Although in apparently unrelated product markets Honda has been able to build image and customer loyalty through its umbrella brand name.

According to Prahalad and Hamel core competences need to meet three qualifying criteria: provide potential access to a wide variety of markets, make a significant contribution to provide customer benefit of the end product and be difficult to eradicate. Thus, while core competences are likely to be technologically based, they become meaningful only in marketplaces. Top management has to provide the organisational structure and culture which promotes the vision to ally what technology makes possible with what customers want. Chapter 2 revisits the work of Prahalad and Hamel.

Yet again, the Japanese seem to provide the clearest examples of how these ideas might work in practice. In order to design the Lexus – Toyota's prestige car developed to compete with Mercedes and BMW – members of the design team lived the lifestyle of the target consumer. Based in California, they behaved as the intended customer so as fully to understand their motives, perceptions and values. Japanese technology then provided this – speedily. The issue of harmonious fit between organisation and environment will be encountered again when discussing auditing the macro environment on p. 44.

Integrates

There are two main aspects to the issue of integration. First, the marketing-orientated organisation acts in an integrated way in relation to the marketing strategy. The subject of marketing strategy is dealt with later in the chapter but the point to be made here can be stated simply. If, in Porter's terms, a firm pursues a low-cost strategy, it must strive to drive down costs in every activity within the value chain and also between activities. (Sometimes overall costs may be minimised by accepting a higher cost in a particular activity.) Development costs will be driven down, as will manufacturing costs, likewise selling and other promotional costs. The organisation will then be behaving in a consistent, integrated fashion in the light of a clear strategy and a low-cost culture will develop.

The second aspect of integration relates to achieving a parallel consistency among the elements of the positioning mix. Again, this relates to marketing strategy and is developed further later. Consistency is needed to ensure that customers receive the appropriate messages and that mix elements combine synergistically. Two examples should serve to illustrate the point. Perfume manufacturers such as Chanel have been engaged in strenuous attempts to prevent their products from being sold by discounters like Superdrug. Among the reasons are, first, that lower prices are destroying the image of exclusivity, believed to be a key product benefit. Second, discount stores do not provide the appropriate physical ambience within which perfume should be purchased, nor do they offer a suitable level of customer service and advice.

The other example relates to the combination of elements within the marketing communications mix. Many organisations use different agencies to handle their media advertising and their sales promotions. This means that the consumer may receive two different and even conflicting messages. Whilst there is no need for words and pictures to be copied from one medium to the other, there is a need for a clear strategy reflected by core themes extending across both media.

MEASURING MARKETING ORIENTATION

Having considered some general characteristics of marketing orientation, let us turn now to specific criteria which can be used to evaluate the degree to which such orientation exists in an organisation. A number of alternative approaches will be reviewed and then synthesised. It is well known among marketers that grafting a marketing manager, or a whole marketing department, on to an organisation is – of itself – no indication of a movement towards marketing orientation. Equally, changing the sales director's title to sales and marketing director is unlikely to bring any concomitant change to organisational culture and processes. In practice, such changes often result in no more than a temporary increase in market research activity and various sales support activities. The leopard's spots remain the same.

Ames (1970) drew attention to this phenomenon and proposed a series of 'tests' to check for 'real' marketing orientation. Some of these questions are recast below and are as valid today as when Ames first coined them in 1970.

- Has the organisation evaluated more than three strategic focuses for each product/market business?
- Have specific steps been taken to block international and home competitors?
- Has the product/service package developed to meet changing segmental needs?
- Do top and functional management exchange ideas on development and execution of product/market strategies?
- Is there an organised communication channel to ensure that staff in contact with customers assist the identification of product needs and opportunities?

Ames's approach focuses on the presence of certain activities or behaviours, each of which is necessary to marketing orientation. A slightly different approach is to focus on the outcomes of successful marketing. Davidson (1987) has developed criteria for rating an organisation in terms of its prowess in 'offensive marketing'. Examples include:

- strong and differentiated customer proposition
- success in launching profitable new products/services
- new markets successfully entered
- clear long-term strategy refined where necessary, but strongly adhered to
- commitment to constant improvement in quality and value for money
- high level of investment compared with competitors (facilities, advertising, research and development, people development).

Narver and Slater (1990) have constructed a means of measuring market orientation, which they define as consisting of customer orientation, interfunctional co-ordination and competitor orientation together with a long-term focus and profit/revenue objective. The components of the three behavioural items include:

(1) Customer orientation
   - customer commitment
   - creation of customer value
   - understanding of customer needs
   - constant satisfaction objectives
   - after-sales service.
(2) Interfunctional co-ordination
   - joint customer calls
   - shared information
   - functional integration in strategy
   - all functions contribute to customer value
   - shared resources with other business units.

(3) Competitor orientation
- salespeople share competitor information
- rapid response to competitors' actions
- top managers discuss competitor strategy
- targeting of opportunities for competitive advantage.

The synthesis below addresses the key elements of marketing orientation and poses fundamental questions. It is neither a detailed audit of each element nor a marketing audit. For a detailed list of questions concerning some of the topics, and additional ones relevant to marketing operations, the reader is referred to Wilson (1993). Interestingly, in a seminal article on the marketing audit itself, Kotler, Gregor and Rogers (1977) make no specific reference to the need to check for the level of marketing orientation, though this is implicit in many of their questions.

Customers
- Do we understand the customer's underlying needs?
- Do we understand segmental buying criteria?
- Do we understand the buying process?
- Do we know how the customer perceives us?
- Do we know all this for end users and middlemen?

Relationships
- Is there an ongoing process of developing network relationships with our customers?
- Is there an organisation-wide commitment to customer satisfaction, service and care?
- Are there adequate feedback loops for customer communications and satisfaction measurement?

Our organisation
- Do we understand the source(s) of competitive advantage?
- Are corporate objectives clear, realistic, ambitious and adequately disseminated?
- Is top management committed to marketing orientation and culture?
- Do we have effective and creative marketing planning and control systems?
- Do manufacturing, R&D, purchasing, finance, logistics participate in the marketing planning process?
- Do organisational objectives *really* override departmental perspectives?
- Are organisational structures sufficiently flexible to encourage creativity and multi-disciplinary task orientation?

Competitors
- Do we know the main local and global competitors?
- Do we understand their strengths and weaknesses?
- Can we identify their objectives and strategies?
- Do we know how the customer perceives them?

- Have we selected strategies targeted at specific competitors?

Macro-environment
- Have we given adequate consideration to the impact of changing economic, social and cultural climates?
- How might changes in product and process technology upset the existing market structure and competitive balance?

It is now appropriate to explore some of the key issues listed above.

Customers

The importance of understanding end users' underlying needs was illustrated in the previous section. Many firms, however, fail to recognise that if they market through middlemen such as retailers and/or wholesalers/dealers, they need to understand *their* needs as well. To market effectively, manufacturers have to maximise the operating efficiency and effectiveness of the whole marketing channel. Instead of co-operation, many channel systems are characterised by conflict. There are many reasons for the emergence of conflict but a fundamental one is the failure of manufacturers and middlemen to appreciate that each has different objectives and different needs from the relationship and views it from different perspectives.

Marketing-oriented organisations – whether manufacturers or middlemen – understand the needs of the other party, understand the value of the contribution they make, and do not exercise apparently superior power at the expense of the other party.

Understanding customer needs, of course, includes understanding the buying process and the buying criteria that customers use. Interestingly, while many firms claim to know intuitively what motivates their customers to source business with them, their understanding is often shallow and rarely do they attempt to get 'under the skin' of customers. Buying practices vary dramatically between industries and between organisations within the same industry. Two examples serve to illustrate this point.

A well-known charity was in the market for a computer software system to handle its subscriber lists. It developed its own computer-based screening model to reduce the number of shortlisted suppliers to three. The screening model contained a wide variety of purchasing criteria, each weighted appropriately. In contrast to this was the manner in which a small firm was awarded a large contract to supply a pie production line. In-depth interviews with members of the client's decision-making unit revealed that the successful supplier was not even initially invited to quote but was an after-thought, included because of geographical proximity. This client also used a supplier rating system but the price/specification criteria which dominated it were largely outweighed by other factors. The client was very impressed by the quality of the relationship which developed between the chief executive, the sales manager and the design and production engineers from the supplying firm and the team formed by the client to be responsible for procurement. The client formed the view that 'these were people we felt we wanted to work with'.

Firms thus need a clear understanding of buyer criteria and processes. A number of successful firms use these varying processes as the basis of their market segmentation strategies. Further, many firms do not recognise how customers and potential customers perceive them. The market positions them differently from their imagined positioning. This leads to inappropriate strategic and operational marketing decisions. Often the market's perceptions are based on outdated information or false assumptions, but if the firm is unaware of this it does not respond appropriately. A firm in the food processing industry felt it was not obtaining as large a market share as it wanted because its products were seen as outdated. Research showed that the problem in fact lay in the perception that the firm was expensive and was geared only to meeting the needs of very large-scale food processors. Neither of these perceptions was true.

More is said about positioning and perception in Business unit marketing strategy, pp. 50–55.

One way of assessing the extent to which a firm understands its customers and then tries to build relationships with, and value for, them is to look at its success in moving customers through a hierarchy of loyalty, i.e. from suspect to prospect to customer to client to advocate. And so to the question of relationships.

Relationships

When marketing to organisations, firms need to realise that effective marketing is primarily a relationship-building activity which links supplier into buyers. Increasingly, traditionally adversarial relationships between buyer and supplier are being replaced by longer-term co-operative relationships which emphasise joint commitment as being a better route to mutual satisfaction. This is occurring increasingly in engineering, for example, and between manufacturers and retailers in the food industry. In major construction projects, this type of activity has been undertaken for a long time, with one of the key roles of the sales representative/account manager being to establish and develop the networks between key staff from all functions of both organisations.

There are some suggestions that UK firms have often been poor at this activity in comparison to some European competitors. They have failed to devote sufficient attention and time to identifying and building relationships and have also failed to involve sufficiently senior people from the UK side.

Where networks can be established, customer feedback should be assured as long as it is then channelled to appropriate decision-makers in the supplying firm. However, for organisations where customers are not large enough to justify a network of relationships, careful attention must be paid to designing mechanisms to capture customer feedback. Research shows that most customers are lost because of neglect. They are neglected not only in the sense that selling effort often tends to be concentrated on potential new rather than existing customers, but also as sources of feedback on the supplier's performance and of new product ideas and improvement.

In building relationships with customers it is important to reorganise the role of those who we have previously described as part-time marketers. They are not part of the conventionally organised marketing function but they may (and should?) have frequent customer contact. Typically such people are found in positions in the credit control or transport departments or on the switchboard. They might also include, on the one hand, members of quality circles in manufacturing departments whose remit includes direct links with customers and, on the other, customer visits by chief executives. The weekly visits to one of his stores by Tesco Chairman, Sir Ian Maclaurin, would be a good example.

Whilst the focus has been primarily on relationships with customers, it is important to recognise that other types of relationships may need development.

- Good working relationships between departments which can impact on either customer responsiveness or the implementation of marketing strategies.
- Good relationships with its suppliers can give a firm a significant competitive advantage, perhaps through improved quality, delivery or new product innovation.
- Good relationships with partners, such as joint venture partners, are often the difference between success and failure.
- Collaboration ventures of all kinds are becoming a key aspect of modern business, whether between major multinationals seeking to enter or defend major product-market areas or simply between firms indulging in joint sales promotions.

Our organisation

As shown earlier, marketing orientation requires a balance to be achieved between an organisation's assets and its market and competitor opportunities and threats. This means that its competitive advantage need not just be grounded in marketing mix variables but may 'arise anywhere in a firm's value chain' (Porter, 1985). SKF, the Swedish bearing multinational, provides some examples.

In the 1970s SKF was beginning to develop its marketing expertise. Marketing planning, market research and effective marketing through distributors were high on the agenda. But so, too, was a long-term manufacturing and logistics strategy whose motivating force was the need to remain competitive with the Japanese in manufacturing costs. The strategy was basically in two stages. First, through a programme known as GFSS (Global Forecasting and Supply System) the production of particular types of bearing were located in one manufacturing site and the whole group's requirements were provided from the one site. Compared with the previous practice where the same bearing might have been made in as many as eighty manufacturing sites worldwide, the benefit from economies of scale was enormous. (Of course, there was an increase in transportation costs but the net gain was still large.)

Stage 2 involved the 'robotisation' of each main manufacturing plant. What was originally batch production or mass production was to become flexible production, twenty-four hours a day *and* with a minimum of labour: 20,000 manufacturing jobs were to be shed over a period of ten years. This was not a re-emergence of the 'production concept' or the introduction of a Porter-like 'low-cost strategy'. It was a recognition that competitive prices are either a qualifying or an order-winning criterion in many industrial market segments. It is crucial to performance and survival that costs are driven down, and manufacturing and logistics have key roles to play in this respect.

SKF also provides a useful illustration of the contribution that information technology can make. The success of GFSS depended upon computerised forecasting procedures, instructions to factories and shipping instructions. SKF's expertise in information technology also gave it a huge competitive advantage in dealing with distributors. Installation of advanced computer-based enquiry and order-handling systems in distributors' premises allowed them – at the touch of a button – to access for information and ordering purposes stocks held in regional depots and main warehouses in the UK and in several other European countries. At one and the same time purchase was made very easy for distributors and their purchase transactions and stockholding costs were reduced. An enormous competitive advantage was achieved.

Marketers must be able to diagnose the sources of competitive advantage and ensure they are translated into customer benefit.

Most of the remaining questions within the heading 'Our organisation' relate primarily to the existence of effective planning and control systems and the incorporation of appropriate objectives. These are discussed later in the chapter. However, we shall also note here issues arising from the work of Peters and Waterman, which form a bridge between issues relating to organisation and those concerning relationships. Peters and Waterman (1982) have had great success in persuading management that 'excellent' firms can be distinguished by a set of eight organisational design attributes or principles:

(1) bias for action;
(2) closeness to the customer;
(3) autonomy and entrepreneurship;
(4) productivity through people not systems;
(5) strong values for employees to feel proud of;
(6) growth through internal development of core business;

(7) lean and simple staffing;

(8) achieving a balance between autonomy and control.

Although subsequent research (Capes et al., 1991) has cast doubt on their methodology, there is likely to be a relationship between the structure and culture of organisations and their performance. Whether organisation is the driver or facilitator of performance is not clear, but its importance in contributing to marketing orientation is discussed in chapter 8.

Competitors

In many markets firms are able to monitor market share changes accurately. Movements of a fraction of a percentage point can be the cause of celebration or sacking. Whilst it is important to monitor progress against competition (using market share or other benchmarks), it is perhaps more important to have a good understanding of competitor strengths and weaknesses, of the basis on which they compete in their target markets and of their strategic intentions.

Firms must also be able to assess the determination of potential competitors and the ability of apparently 'backward' competitors to catch up. In 1978 microwave ovens were being made in their millions in the US and Japan, while Samsung was taking its first faltering steps towards building a prototype in Korea. Within ten years Samsung was making 80,000 ovens a week (Magaziner and Patinkis, 1989). In the early 1970s in the UK, Honda cars were ridiculed. Today they hold their prices better than any other.

Macro-environment

Long-term economic trends and the superimposition on them of cycles in economic growth are fundamental determinants of the growth and health of businesses. Many of the business success stories of the 1980s resulted from the surge of opportunities which were allowed to flourish in a period of strong consumer and industrial demand. A significant number of those businesses were not appropriately positioned to cope with the harsh recessionary climate which prevailed from the end of 1988.

The key tasks of top corporate management are, first, to position an organisation in terms of the businesses in which it wishes to compete and, second, to determine the contribution that each of these businesses should make to the total organisation. Just as marketing-orientated functional management needs to assess individual business internal and competitor strengths and weaknesses in order to position within markets and segments, top corporate management needs to assess organisational strengths and competencies as well as environmental factors. Marketing-orientated top corporate management is sensitive to, and has a clear view of, the impact of environmental factors on markets and thence businesses.

Putting together a recession-resistant business is arguably becoming more difficult. Increasingly, overseas markets are experiencing the same stage of cycles at similar points in time. Within the domestic UK market, a feature of the recent recession is that it has left few sectors of the economy untouched. Within broad sectors, however, some market segments have fared better than others. While the market for new cars slumped, that for second-hand models – especially those auctioned – held up rather better. W. H. Smith's home-improvement division fared very poorly whilst its distribution activities remained solid.

The marketing-orientated firm not only seeks to position to minimise the impact of cycles and seasonality but also monitors economic growth and makes contingency plans to allow appropriate adjustments to enable significant deviations from planning assumptions to be better coped with. Such an organisation is crucially aware of the links between falling orders, inventory build, cash flow and borrowing issues. It has clear models of how environmental relationships impinge on it and how internal relationships interface with one another to minimise damage and maximise opportunity.

Marketing-orientated firms are also able to interpret other environmental trends such as those presented by social and cultural change. Although it is dangerous to stereotype periods of time, as it is people or groups, the 1980s have clear characteristics distinguishing them from other decades. 'Reading the times' has more significance for marketers of consumer goods and services, perhaps, than for those of industrial goods but even here marketers need to be sensitive to changes in customer needs. Safety and environmental impact are examples of purchase criteria that have grown in importance in response to changing times. In consumer markets changing lifestyles present both opportunities and threats to those who are alert to changes and act to capitalise on or moderate the impact they have. A well-known example would be the targeting of BMW cars at the 1980s 'yuppie' and their repositioning to appeal to the caring instincts of the family man which were presumed to emerge in the 1990s. Such repositioning was a recognition not only of demographic and income distribution changes, but also of forecasted changes in consumer priorities.

Alertness to changing technology is also a crucial part of marketing orientation. It does not mean product or technical orientation but the vision to recognise how technological change can redefine markets. It is fundamentally no different from the point Levitt was making when he described the railways' failure to recognise the impact of technology improvements in one industry on its ability to meet underlying customer needs more effectively in an apparently unconnected industry. The difference today, however, is in the much more rapid pace of change.

MARKETING ORIENTATION AND ORGANISATIONAL SUCCESS

One of the many stumbling blocks which has hindered the spread of true marketing orientation among organisations has been the marketing profession's failure to point to sufficient, enduring, incontrovertible evidence that it actually produces the desired results – and produces them across a spectrum of applications covering consumer and industrial products, consumer, industrial and professional services, profit and non-profit organisations. As with many of the operational areas within the marketing function, it is also difficult to establish numerical relationships between activities and attitudes and the concomitant results. The impact on production costs, quality and volumes as a result of investment in new plant can be readily calculated. The impact of many types of marketing expenditure and of improved attention to customers and competitors is less easy to prove. On top of this, marketing has its critics – from among customers, industrialists and other professions, and from academia. We shall review some of the criticisms and then examine some evidence in support of marketing orientation.

Criticisms of marketing fall into a number of categories. The first covers sharp practices such as pyramid selling, over-aggressive selling and misleading promotions. Unfortunately, many people still associate marketing principally with promotional practices aimed at persuading people to buy things they don't really need. Where such malpractice exists it deserves to be highlighted and castigated. But the criticisms are of unethical operational practices; they are not fair criticisms of the marketing concept.

Poor marketing practice, which can take myriad forms, e.g. badly targeted marketing communications, and the very high rate of new product failure also attract criticism. Star (1989) claims that the problem with marketing stems from 'functional limitations on the implementability of the marketing concept'. As an example he comments that marketers know that 'consumers who share a common set of attitudinal, perceptual, and sociological characteristics are more likely to share a particular set of needs than, say, consumers in the same age or income group'. Yet when it comes to implementing campaigns, consumer segments to be targeted are invariably specified in terms of age, income or social grade. Clancy and Krieg (1990) also criticise marketers for their failure to select appropriate marketing strategies when introducing new products. They say there is a 'tendency to evaluate *too few* options for every decision in the marketing mix and then to do this evaluation by focusing on whatever option produces the *biggest numbers*'. They claim that today's information technology should allow marketers to evaluate – in terms of effect on profitability, not merely numbers of customers or sales – the impact of selecting *thousands* of different market segments to target, different product concepts, different promotional messages.

Chaston (1990) suggests that management in industry frequently has negative perceptions of the marketing function and its contribution to corporate success. He attributes this to marketers placing too much emphasis on the importance of their own role and to poor marketing practice. According to him, marketers are guilty of, among other sins:

- resisting attempts to place controls on their performance
- lacking financial managerial skills
- indulging in creativity without analysis
- using market research to justify preconceptions
- starving other departments of resources
- having insufficient understanding of business.

These – and other – criticisms may well be true of many marketers but they are probably also true of many other functional practitioners. Poor marketing practice is a reason for better marketing, not less marketing. There is clearly a need for better education and training of marketers and there is also a need for a better understanding of marketing throughout an organisation. This is, to a large extent, the responsibility of marketers themselves (internal marketing) but it is also the responsibility of the chief executive to provide the climate within which marketing is understood and practised at all levels and by full- and part-time marketers.

More fundamental perhaps, is the allegation that the marketing concept itself is flawed: not only flawed but actually inimical to organisations. Several critics have argued that firms which find out (using conventional marketing research techniques) what consumers want, and then produce it, are unlikely to spot major new profitable growth opportunities. That is because these opportunities result from the creative application to new products of the explosion in technological advances. Consumers themselves can express only reactions to present products or new concepts which are small departures from present offerings. They are unable to articulate wants for radically new products or formats because they cannot conceive of their potential existence. Only insightful technologists have the imagination to do this.

Again, this seems to be of a criticism of marketing practice rather than of the marketing concept. There are many products which consumers will not buy if there is no value for them. Being innovative is not sufficient of itself. There has to be a need and there may well be better approaches to identifying latent needs than those generally used by marketers. In their article on expeditionary marketing, Hamel and Prahalad (1991) describe an approach to new product introductions which is based on (1) simultaneous – rather than sequential – effort on new product development by marketers, R&D technologists and production engineers, and on (2) understanding consumer needs and response to new products through a 'series of low-cost, fast-paced market incursions' rather than by traditional market research processes. Rapid 'real' learning allows unsuccessful new products to be replaced by others or reformulated, the emphasis being placed on the speed and low cost of such replacement/reformulation.

It is also important to note that many firms which successfully exploit new technology products employ cross-company (multi-disciplinary) project teams to achieve speed and creativity. Equally, the technologists spend time with the consumers so that their creative energies can be directed towards new products which fulfil real (if initially latent) needs and lifestyles. But, again, these new approaches are not indicative of any failure of the marketing concept. Rather, they are a recognition that there may be better ways of discovering consumer needs and disseminating them through the organisation. Remember that true marketing orientation does require *all* areas of an organisation to be in tune with the customer.

What then, of the evidence for a positive contribution from marketing to organisation success? A study carried out at Strathclyde (Baker and Hart, 1989) investigated policies and practices which discriminated between above and below average companies of varying sizes and across a range of industries. Average performance for each industry was measured by a composite of sales growth and profit margin. Factors examined were classified into three broad areas: the organisation and status of marketing within the companies, the degree of attention paid to strategic marketing planning, and the approach taken to a number of specific marketing tasks such as new product development, market research, customer service, sales and distribution channel management, promotion and pricing.

In all three areas researched, the study found support for the view that some differences in attention to marketing variables were often associated with some differences between above and below average companies. However, in summary, Baker and Hart found: 'Overall it is possible to say that relatively few of the factors studied actually accounted for differences in performance.' They suggested that all the firms in their sample could be considered successful 'given that they survived the recession of the early 1980s' and that they, therefore, 'tend to be similar in terms of their policies and practices'. They conclude by claiming that discriminating factors are 'much more subtle than earlier commentators would have us believe' and that the important message is not so much 'what you do' as 'how you do it!'. As suggested previously, there has been much criticism of current competence in marketing. The subject of how to measure excellence *in* marketing (rather than through it) is discussed by Hansen, Gronhaug and Warneryd (1990).

A different interpretation is that the classification of firms into above and below average (or excellent and non-excellent) is itself methodologically unsound. Doyle (1992) argues that uni-dimensional or other limited measurements of performance are misleading and dangerous. Creative accounting can disguise true financial strengths, for example. Short-term results can always be improved at the expense of long-term health. He claims that the 'conventional measures of excellence lack robustness' and this explains why a large proportion of those firms considered 'excellent' at one time or another have failed to demonstrate excellence over a longer period.

Another possible explanation, of course, is that variables other than those connected with 'marketing' play a larger part in differentiating between above and below average performers. In an American study of 140 business units within one corporation, but spread between a variety of commodity and non-commodity products, Narver and Slater (1990) attempted to research the effects of marketing orientation plus situational variables affecting profitability. Their research thus attempted to establish relationships between buyer power, supplier power, seller concentration, ease of entry, market growth, technological change, size relative to largest competitor, total operating costs in relation to largest competitor, and return on investment as well as the effects of market orientation. Market orientation was measured by a combination of customer orientation, competitor orientation and interfunctional co-ordination as described in the earlier discussion on marketing orientation.

Narver and Slater's results allowed them to claim: 'The findings do suggest that after controlling for important market-level and business-level influences, market orientation and performance are strongly related.' However, they warn that the study needs to be replicated over time and in diverse environments in order to give more confidence and generalisability to the findings.

It is thus difficult to establish unequivocal support for a relationship between organisational success and the existence of particular functional marketing activities. It is also difficult to establish a clear-cut relationship between marketing orientation and success. Many further elements including other functional skills, strategy planning and organisation culture play their part as well. It is our contention, however, that a market-led organisation has a culture where all members of the organisation subscribe to, and participate in, the development of marketing orientation and marketing strategy.

The nature of strategy in marketing planning is considered specifically in the next section while the nature of corporate planning is covered in chapter 2.

MARKETING STRATEGY

One of the difficulties associated with the term 'strategy' is that it has different connotations in different contexts. It embraces a number of different dimensions. On the one hand, a strategy is a means to an end; it states the broad-brush methods by which one intends to achieve predetermined objectives. On the other, the strategic (planning) process includes the very establishment of those objectives. At another level, strategy can be considered to relate to the organisation as a whole and yet the term can also be applied at a functional level, e.g. marketing strategy or finance strategy. Finally, strategy is often viewed as being of grand and comprehensive substance and long term in its impact. And yet a salesperson will probably have a 'strategy' for gaining access to the decision-maker during his or her next call. It is thus clear that strategy can legitimately mean different things under different circumstances.

The remainder of this chapter discusses marketing strategy at the corporate level, and then at the business unit level. (A third level relates to more detailed strategies for each element within the marketing mix.)

Corporate marketing strategy

At the corporate level, marketing strategy is concerned principally with influencing which businesses to compete in and assisting in setting objectives for those businesses. As an example, Goodwin plc is a medium-sized engineering firm engaged in a variety of product businesses. It has businesses which manufacture pumps, valves and dental casting equipment, and even operates foundries. The link between these apparently dissimilar businesses is historical and steeped in the possession of natural resources and production engineering. Goodwin's most recent move, however, has been into a business with quite different characteristics. Facing generally static demand in its existing businesses, Goodwin sought a growth business which would utilise existing skills and assets and in which it could establish a competitive advantage. It selected maritime and air surveillance equipment – a growth market in which the manufacture of precision radar needed its mechanical engineering design and production skills. Radio frequency design skills were acquired by the purchase of a small company at the forefront of radar design. The specific designs available to this company also provided a significant competitive advantage. This combination of growth markets plus existing capability plus competitive advantage is the hallmark of marketing orientation.

The decision to enter the new business was a corporate board-level decision, made following an extensive marketing research programme to identify a business with the appropriate characteristics. Clearly, the objectives set for the new business are based on a 'build' strategy, appropriate for a new entrant with a competitive advantage in a growth market.

Business unit marketing strategy

At the individual business (SBU) level, marketing strategy requires the resolution of five key questions:

(1) where to compete;
(2) on what basis to compete;
(3) with whom to compete;
(4) when to compete;
(5) how to enter new competitive areas.

Questions (1), (2) and (3) revolve around the issue of *positioning*, yet another ambiguous term within the vocabulary of marketing. It is, however, central to marketing strategy. Positioning first joined the list of marketing buzzwords in 1969, and was used by Ries and Trout (1982) to describe what was essentially a communications technique. It involved doing something to the 'mind of the prospect' by powerfully associating the product uniquely *with* a particular consumer benefit and also *against* the competition. Choice of brand name was crucial to this process as was the allocation of sufficient marketing expenditure to maintain the position.

Today, positioning is seen as a rather broader approach. Kotler describes it as the 'act of designing the company's offer so that it occupies a distinct and valued place in the target customers' minds'. This book regards 'positioning' as the task of combining competitive advantage strategy and segment strategy, resulting in a clear position *vis-à-vis* customers and competitors. The market needs to have a clear and accurate perception of who the firm is and what it is trying to do.

In approaching the task of positioning, firms need first to establish how customers presently position it. Perception surveys often reveal that consumers 'see' a firm in quite a different way from that imagined by the firm. It can then be decided whether to reinforce this existing positioning or whether some other positioning is preferred, in which case appropriate activities need to be undertaken in order to reposition the firm and/or its products. Positioning is triangulated by reference to customers (segments), competitors and competitive advantages. The perceptual map in Fig. 1.5 has been constructed from consumers' perceptions of competing brands of footwear against two key dimensions. Clearly, there may be other significant dimensions but these have been chosen as key purchase attributes in this instance. Each manufacturer needs to decide whether the existing positioning in respect of these attributes and its competitors is satisfactory or needs redefining.

In making this decision the firm would need to consider a number of factors.

- The importance to the customers they are seeking of these – and other – purchase attributes: for example, if Dunlop were aiming at status-conscious leisure footwear users, it would need to consider how it could reposition.

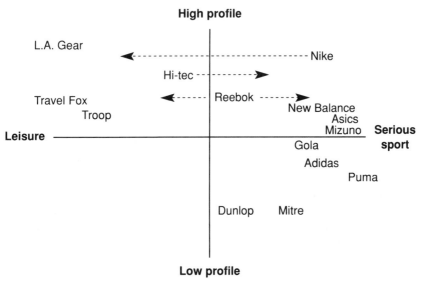

Fig. 1.5 Positioning in the trainers market

● The ability of the firm – in terms of skills and resources – to reposition: if repositioning required 'real' improvements in terms of particular attributes, it may not be possible. Even if possible, such 'real' changes might involve other functional departments such as manufacturing, logistics and R&D.

● The degree of competitor strength in purchase attributes and their ability to respond to the firm's improvements.

When reviewing its strategic options in terms of segments and SCAs (sustainable competitive advantages), the two basic questions which must be answered are 'How many?' and 'Which ones?' We shall address the segment issue first.

Segments (where to compete)

It has become fashionable for marketing strategists to make use of Porter's (1985) work to present the main options. According to this, firms can choose to compete within a narrow target or across a broad target. Chapter 2 delves more deeply into Porter's approach. Prior to Porter's popularity marketers tended to refer to three basic options:

(1) undifferentiated marketing, which ignored segmental differences and made available the same 'offering' to any consumer who wanted it;

(2) concentrated marketing, whereby the firm recognised a number of segments but chose to serve only one (or a small number) and tailored its offering specifically to meet segmental needs;

(3) differentiated marketing, where a firm chooses to market to a number of identifiable segments, altering its offering for each targeted segment.

Unless the strategy adopted is an undifferentiated one, typical selection criteria for selecting target segment(s) (such as those shown on p. 29) would be used to determine the best option(s).

SCAs (what to compete on)

Marketers differ as to whether it is better to stress one strong consistent positioning message or to stress multiple benefits. The former approach is reminiscent of the creative advertising strategy approach advocated by Rosser Reeves (White, 1988). It is also consistent with much sales training conventional wisdom which advises that the salesperson probes for the customer's 'hot button' and ignores the other benefits his firm may offer but which are not particularly relevant to the immediate individual customer prospect. On the other hand the multi-SCA approach allows appeals to several benefit segments and also recognises that many customers seek a particular combination of benefits. In organisational markets these may be embodied in a wider vendor rating scheme which includes both order-qualifying and order-winning criteria.

SCAs must have value or benefit for customers but there is a rich variety of types of advantage. Table 1.7 lists some.

Table 1.7 Examples of competitive advantages

Superior product benefits:
  Performance
  Reliability
  Safety
  Usage: ease of, comfort in
  Durability
  Maintenance: ease of/lack of
  Design: colour, shape, materials, ergonomics
  Cost: procurement, running, depreciation
Superior image benefits
Superior service/services
Superior relationships: with suppliers, partners, customers
Size advantages: muscle, economy, experience from large scale
Size advantages: flexibility, responsiveness from small scale
Legal advantages:
  Patent protection
  Exclusive rights
  Government preference
Better functional marketing skills and resources

Who to compete with

The changing emphasis of marketing orientation, from customer to competitor and perhaps back again, has already been mentioned. Wherever the emphasis should lie, the fact remains that organisations need to consider how the existence of particular competitors might influence their marketing strategy. Some firms make explicit decisions not to compete in certain segments because of the dominance of existing suppliers or they may decide to opt for a 'follower' strategy so as not to upset the relationship with market 'leaders'. Alternatively, they may decide to compete, but to develop differential advantages specifically designed to defeat or circumvent known competitors. Finally, they need to consider likely competitor reactions to any strategic moves they plan.

In most cases then, the nature and strength of competitors will influence the selection of product and market segments and the choice of competitive advantage. In some cases, however, competitor strategy will be the focal point of marketing strategy. For example, the battles between Coke and Pepsi or between Flymo and Qualcast suggest that the major aim of strategy has been to beat specified competitors. Similarly, in some firms – even where competitor battles are less conspicuous – targets will be set for the amount of market share to be taken from targeted opponents. For firms selling to large organisational customers such planned share changes will be detailed at individual customer level.

This analysis of planned share change has an important benefit for marketing planning. It forces firms to accept that share gains can be made only by taking business from someone else and that the someone else has to be identified and is unlikely to be a willing participant in the process; it will have its own plans and responses. This tends to induce an element of realism into planning for share gain. In fact the only situations where this may not apply are where growing markets obscure share changes so that firms believe they are gaining when in fact they are losing share, and, second, where firms have entrenched positions within customers/segments which themselves have an increasing or decreasing share of the market.

When to compete

The issue of when to compete is concerned with new product and new market entry decisions. It is also closely related to competitor strategy and aspects of competitive advantage. For example, it involves general decisions as to whether to lead or follow competitors in new product market areas and in this sense helps to position a firm. Barclays, for example, is generally considered to be an innovator in these terms and has focused in some recent advertising campaigns on the lead that it has taken in such initiatives. However, it also involves specific decisions as to the appropriate time to enter particular markets or to add or delete particular products. Schnaars (1981) has carried out an analysis of new product introductions which have resulted in lasting success for the pioneer in some cases, while in others, later entrants into the market have been able to wrest away market leadership from the pioneer.

How to enter new competitive areas

The first four elements of strategy relate to the way in which a firm or business unit is perceived by and competes in its existing chosen product-market areas. If the firm makes a strategic decision to enter new segments or markets or to introduce new product lines, it may need to review a range of strategic options for new market entry or new product development. (Of course, decisions may be made to withdraw from markets and products.) Increasingly, for example, firms are developing 'strategic alliances' or partnerships with other organisations. Sometimes these are defensive arrangements, established to ward off threatened attacks by large predators or aggressors. However, such alliances are often established in order to enter new markets or launch new products. The costs (and risks) of such ventures can be of such magnitude in certain product fields (e.g. aerospace, pharmaceuticals, automotives) or when approaching new markets on a regional or global scale, that they can only be undertaken jointly.

Strategic alliances may take many different forms and are only one out of a number of possible options. For a firm making a decision to enter a new overseas market, for example, the range of market entry options might include:

- selling direct from the domestic market to the final user customer overseas
- selling through an export house

- selling to a buying office
- appointing an export manager
- forming a co-operative/federated marketing group
- piggy-backing
- appointing an overseas agent
- selling through an importer
- appointing an overseas distributor
- appointing an overseas licensee
- establishing a franchise operation
- setting up an overseas branch office
- establishing an overseas marketing subsidiary
- establishing a joint venture
- setting up an overseas manufacturing and marketing operation.

All these options vary in terms of the degree of investment they require, risk they entail, and active commitment they imply to the new market. They are all strategic, however, in terms of how critical they are to organisational success and how long lasting they will be in their implications for the firm in the market.

Strategic deployment of the marketing mix

Implementation of business unit marketing strategy requires that all relevant elements of the marketing mix are integrated so as to be consistent with and support the chosen positioning. Thus, in the case of Swatch, the marketing strategy called for the watch to be repositioned from permanent timepiece to throw-away fashion accessory, from older to younger customers. Prices had to be set to allow this new behaviour and distribution channels had to be widened to encompass sports shops and boutiques as well as jewellers. Product design had to change from functional-aesthetic to a continuously changing range of themes and colours, whilst product quality needed to be consistent with 'Swiss manufacture'. Promotion had to be reorientated to include merchandising and sales promotional activities. There was virtually no need for distributors to provide after-sales facilities.

But the new marketing strategy also called for new approaches from manufacturing, without which the marketing strategy would not have been feasible. Thus new manufacturing technology was needed to drive down unit costs. The number of moving parts was cut by over half and watches were sealed by welding instead of screws. Swatch clearly illustrates the interface between manufacturing and marketing strategy and the fact that both 'sides' have to understand the needs – and limitations – of the other. Both contribute to the marketing strategy.

Strategy, implementation and planning

Just as marketing orientation is underpinned by organisational culture, market-

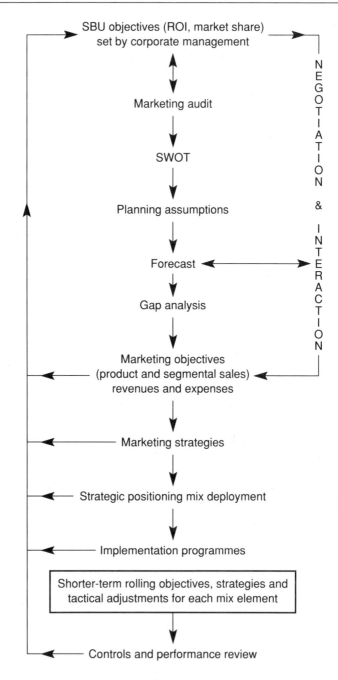

Fig. 1.6 Stages in developing a marketing plan

ing strategy is underpinned by a suitable marketing planning system (itself also dependent upon organisational culture). As McDonald (1992) says: 'The overall purpose of marketing planning, and its principal focus, is the identification and creation of sustainable competitive advantage.' At the heart of the process, therefore, is the generation of alternative strategies and the selection of marketing strategies. Fig. 1.6 shows a typical sequence of interactive and iterative stages in the development of a marketing plan. Despite the widespread awareness of such processes, all the evidence suggests that only a minority of organisations actually follow them with any degree of rigour or make use of the accompanying array of planning tools and techniques.

Many of the reasons for this are reviewed by McDonald (1992) in an excellent summary of the state of marketing planning. Among them is the ever present issue of organisational culture, and in particular the notion of a planning culture. Clearly, a marketing planning system – if it is to work – has to be supported by the chief executive and functional directors. Their role should not end with 'handing down' and negotiating SBU objectives and establishing planning guidelines but they should be seen to be ambassadors of this process and should ensure that the resulting plans are the basis for both future action and control.

The interface with senior corporate management can be problematic for some in that it raises the issue of the relationship between strategic marketing planning and corporate strategic planning. Certainly is difficult to separate the two activities in the sense that the processes and techniques used are largely the same (although not necessarily equally appropriate) and they are both aimed at meeting customer needs profitably. Some authors (including the author of the next chapter, Gordon Pearson) prefer to label longer-term planning involving strategic issues as business strategy planning, leaving to marketing planning responsibility for implementing these plans through the planning and control of the marketing mix elements. There is certainly an argument for this if it means that the adoption of a strategic planning approach is made easier by the terminology being more politically acceptable to other functional disciplines. On the other hand, as described earlier, the term marketing strategy is applicable at different levels in an organisation and may be the responsibility of corporate managers, SBU managers, or marketing department functional managers. It is not intended (here, at least) as an attempt at domination by marketing departments. Additionally, the term 'business strategy' encompasses all the functional areas of the organisation rather just those specifically related to markets.

One argument in favour of marketers being responsible for marketing planning at both the SBU strategic level and the functional level, is that there is so much (and needs to be so much) interdependency between position decision, implementation via marketing mix programmes and tactical adjustments to mix variables. Since one of the key characteristics of good strategy is that it is capable of implementation, perhaps those responsible for implementation should also contribute largely to strategy selection. Fig. 1.7(a) and (b) shows two examples of the extent to which marketing management take responsibility for strategic marketing planning. In (a), general management decide on marketing strategy, leaving only mix planning and implementation to marketing whereas in (b) marketing strategy becomes part of the marketing functional area.

The process shown in Fig. 1.6 is therefore treated here as strategic marketing planning, which implies a time frame of some three to five years. Within the framework of the strategic marketing planning process, annual marketing plans need to be developed. These will tend to follow a similar set of procedures, but with strategy options relating to different marketing mix permutations (rather than to basic positioning strategy) and to short- and medium-term action.

Interfaces among different functional areas are often tense at annual plan level as well as at the strategic marketing level. For example, different approaches to forecasting and budgeting used by marketing departments, finance and manufacturing can be a source of disagreement both at monthly (or weekly) review meetings and when inputting into next year's marketing plan. Chapter 6 proposes a method by which forecasting can become a force for integration rather than conflict. The terms 'forecasts', 'budgets' and 'targets' may even be interpreted differently by different functional areas. Attempts must be made to establish a planning framework and terminology which is understood and accepted throughout an organisation.

Another potential source of interface disharmony can occur in both strategic and annual marketing planning. In many organisations, the planning process is often driven by the finance department, with the emphasis on covering costs and making the numbers balance. Of course the numbers must balance (even marketers need to be numerate and realist) but this can render the process mechanical at the expense of creativity. Strategy search and selection, at whatever level, need to be wide-ranging and imaginative.

Whilst the value of an appropriate strategic planning process has already been stressed, perhaps the more important point is that members of the organisation *think* strategically. Schnaars (1981) charts the changing emphasis in strategy from budgeting in the 1950s through long-range planning in the 1960s, formula planning in the 1970s to strategic thinking in the 1980s. Strategic thinking is more flexible, more creative and is undertaken by operational managers, not ivory tower planners. According to Schnaars: 'Ideally every member of the organisation thinks strategically about consumers' needs, competitors, and competitive advantage.'

The need to be 'profitable' on a short-term basis may also be a source of conflict between marketers and accountants. In one organisation where I worked, progress towards strategic marketing plan objectives was constantly frustrated by the finance department requiring price increases to meet short-term cost and volume variances. Annual price plan development became inconsistent with the longer-term price development required by the strategic plan. Clearly, marketing planning – whether at the strategic or annual level – necessarily involves a high degree of interdisciplinary interfacing.

Marketers are increasingly beginning to realise that they have as big a task in 'selling' their plans internally as in the marketplace. Piercy (1992) has proposed that, during strategy development, marketers should also prepare strategies for persuading the rest of the organisation to commit to the plans. Without participation and commitment from manufacturing, design, R&D, logistics, finance, human resources, marketing plans won't work: they are unlikely even to be referred to.

Roles of individual functional areas may also vary according to the particular task involved. In recognising this, Hutt and Speh (1984) have proposed an approach to decision-making within the organisation which is analogous to the concept of the 'decision-making unit' typically found in the buying process

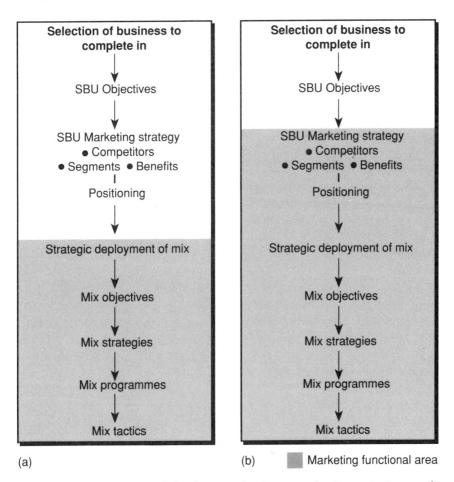

(a)   (b)   ▨ Marketing functional area

Fig. 1.7 Alternative views of the demarcation between business strategy and marketing planning

used by organisational customers. They suggest that some people/departments take the initiative in proposing courses of action (responsible), some make the decision (approve), some need to be consulted (consult) during the decision process, some carry out the decision (implement) and others need to be advised of the decision (inform). The correct identification of roles within tasks then makes it likely that interfacing problems will be minimised, and that commitment to strategic and operational decisions and implementation will be increased.

As an example, a marketing manager initiating a new product development proposal in order to compete in a new market segment might face the following scenario. The Business Unit Manager may be the individual responsible for taking the decision but would do so only after extensive consultation with, and approval from, his corporate level operating superiors, corporate planning staff, and Business Unit managers in Finance, Manufacturing and R&D. The SBU manager might futher consult with sales management and technical/engineering support functions. Implementation of the new strategy would depend on the co-operation of all the above and the commitment of operational staff in sales, manufacturing and technical areas. The marketing manager needs to take into account the inter-disciplinary nature of developing and implementing marketing strategy and to learn how to adapt his or her influence skills to each situation. They further need to understand which individuals exercise informal power aside from that arising from their formal position authority.

CASE STUDY

Michelin

This case study is intended to demonstrate the 'classical' role of marketing and some of the associated interfaces with other functional areas. It also reveals a shift towards increasing marketing orientation and a clear product market strategy. It relates principally to the development of the Michelin MXT tyre as a successor to the MXL, both tyres being aimed at the replacement market for mass market cars (T speed rated). It concludes with an update on Pilot – Michelin's latest tyre offering in the V and ZR high speed rated segment.

In line with Michelin's tradition for excellence in product quality and performance, the MXL had established a reputation for grip, handling, comfort and long life. However, a number of changes taking place in the environment and in the industry itself suggested a re-evaluation of what was required from a tyre. These changes involved, for example, more female motorists, more recreational motoring (including abroad), and more second cars. At the same time, vehicle manufacturers have been reducing the life cycle of car models, increasing the number of options within each model range, and producing cars capable of higher speeds and faster acceleration and requiring lighter steering and more responsive braking. Furthermore, government legislation has been forcing improvements in terms of safety standards, fuel efficiency and noise reduction. In developing new products, Michelin had traditionally relied upon the experience and feel of R&D staff. In the case of the MXT, however, a Europe-wide survey of 7,000 motorists was commissioned. Quantitative research was supplemented by in-depth interviews and group discussions.

Research commenced in 1986 with market analysis of future trends and forecast of volume potential, and qualitative research (phase A) into the main consumer demands of an S/T-rated tyre. The prime objectives were to:

- make recommendations to R&D for the design of a new tyre which matched these needs as far as possible
- provide the marketing department with information about the appropriate publicity/communications message and promotional requirements.

The qualitative phase involved target group motorists, tyre distributors and Michelin's own sales force. This progressed to a quantitative phase (phase B), whose objectives were to quantify:

- the relative importance of each problem or 'customer need', identified in phase A
- the performance attained by existing tyres as far as these needs are concerned, i.e. a satisfaction index of current products
- the importance of beliefs held by users as to which tyre characteristics are viewed as not compatible (e.g. 'handling performance in the wet' with 'treadlife').

The list of criteria (shown below) generated as a result of phase A was then tested for relative importance.

- to have a low noise level
- to have a high mileage
- no need for regular pressure maintenance
- to have an attractive lettering on the sidewall
- to be comfortable
- to be resistant to kerbing
- to have a built-in and practical method of checking the tyre pressure
- to have a tread pattern which wears evenly
- to be particularly resistant to hazards on the road (e.g. stones, glass)
- to be suitable for driving on different types of road surface
- to have shoulders which are broken up into segments/blocks
- to be wide
- to have a protective band on the sidewall to reduce impact of kerbing
- to be a tyre which helps reduce the fuel consumption of the car
- to be particularly resistant to punctures
- to have large channels going from side to side across the tread

Research indicated – in contrast to R&D traditional beliefs – that increased mileage was not motorists' main priority but that good grip, in a variety of weather conditions and throughout the tyre's life, was now paramount. (Motorists in the UK were particularly concerned with grip on wet roads immediately following a dry spell whilst German motorists were more concerned with aquaplaning!)

Another 'unexpected' research finding was that it was not sufficient to make a tyre which met the performance requirements, but that the tyre must *look* as if it did. The challenge to R&D staff was therefore to design a tyre with significantly better wet grip but without sacrificing mileage, comfort and noise criteria – and to make it convey the right visual messages. Research also indicated how motorists interpreted functional design features such as grooves, blocks, sizes, shoulder design and sidewall design as quality and performance cues.

The challenge for manufacturing is to be able to respond to such design changes and, in today's environment, to be able to manufacture economically but with more model variants and consequently shorter production runs.

Traditionally, manufacturing has been resistant to increases in model variants owing to cost and disruption factors. The need to respond to the demands of the marketplace has been recognised, however, and manufacturing has a key role to play in providing marketing with competitive advantage. The improvement in tyre build flexibility in the commercial vehicle market illustrates this: in the 1970s it took two days to change a mould for one truck tyre to another; today it takes twenty minutes.

The importance of design to the new tyre was recognised in the launch to Michelin staff and distributors. The slogan used was 'MXT – a work of art' and this theme was pursued throughout a series of presentations at stately homes, even down to the use of an 'art gallery' featuring well-known paintings incorporating tyres. Similar presentations were made to other Michelin employees including *all* members of the workforce in order to communicate the strategy and values behind the new product.

A feature of the more proactive approach to marketing in Michelin has been a more thorough understanding not only of the needs imposed by changes by car manufacturers and changing priorities of tyre consumers but also of the needs and motivations of the tyre distributors which themselves have undergone a marketing revolution in recent years. Spurred partly by competition from high street retailers like Halfords and Kwik-Fit, they have revamped their level of customer service and image. Specialist tyre distributors may be tempted to offer consumers a cheaper tyre, perhaps with a view to 'helping' the customer and also making the sale easier. The task of Michelin's sales force is to convince the distributor that, for those consumers that can afford Michelins, the extra benefits outweigh the price premium and provide better value for money in the long term. Michelin estimates that some 60 per cent of mass market replacement tyre customers are potentially receptive to such a message.

The introduction of the new product also provided a golden opportunity to add to distributor motivation through consumer promotions which help 'pull' sales through outlets. Michelin's consumer advertising launch was based on the slogan 'Miles More Grip', which married the new MXT grip benefit to the traditional Michelin image of high mileage. The extent of the investment in operational marketing activities is reflected in a European launch budget of some £20 million. The promotional campaign was also accompanied by extensive pre- and post-testing among motorists, including testing against advertising produced by Pirelli, Dunlop and Continental. Evaluation of consumer response to product performance, advertising concept and message as well as sales figures has confirmed the success of the MXT. The progression towards increasing marketing orientation (and also the scope of functional marketing) has continued at Michelin and is illustrated by the approach taken to launching its new entries in the replacement market for high-performance tyres.

Research among high-performance drivers (defined as drivers of sports, hot hatch, performance and luxury cars which need V and ZR speed-rated tyres) has revealed that they can be segmented according to driving style. These segments relate to a predisposition towards speed, comfort or high mileage, and a new range – branded Pilot – has product variants (suffixed SX, CX or HX respectively) tailored to the needs of each segment. The use of brand name plus consumer-friendly approach again signals a change of approach from a company which has been product-orientated to one where a clear positioning strategy is being implemented to cut through confusion in the marketplace. As in the case of the MXT launch, investment in communication activities was heavy, including national press and poster campaigns and rally car sponsorship. The trade launch also echoed that of the MXT, but this time the 'Pilot' theme required regional presentations in air museums.

Extra consumer choice (six different tyre configurations alone for a segment which accounts for less than 10 per cent of the market) places yet more reliance on the R&D, design and manufacturing functions to make the marketing strategy feasible. The importance of explaining the strategy throughout the organisation is crucial to securing understanding and commitment.

SUMMARY

This chapter – particularly the opening section – has discussed a number of interpretations, or faces, of marketing. However, it views the essence of marketing as consisting of three key faces (shown diagrammatically in Fig. 1.8): conceptual (otherwise referred to as marketing orientation, marketing philosophy or market-led), strategic and functional. It is perhaps fortuitous that the acronym which results (CSF) is also commonly used to refer to 'critical success factors' – those key customer factors which must be present in order to succeed in a given marketplace.

Fig. 1.8 Marketing faces

The marketing concept and marketing strategy are both themselves based on a triad: customer–competitor–company capability. Marketing orientation (concept) requires the organisation to know its customers, its competitors and itself (see Fig. 1.9). Marketing strategy requires that, in the light of this knowledge, the organisation follows a coherent and consistent path towards an agreed destination.

Both marketing orientation and marketing strategy are seen as being 'owned' by the organisation as a whole. It must understand the strategy, be committed to it and be culturally and technically capable of supporting it. As we have said earlier, while competitive advantage needs to be based on customer benefit it may well be founded in distinctive competence residing in any one or more functional areas within the organisation. Equally, limitations in such functional

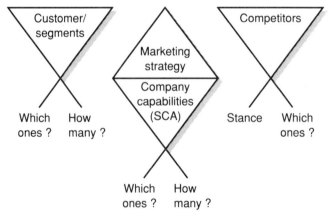

Fig. 1.9 From marketing orientation to marketing strategy

areas may make some marketing strategy alternatives untenable.

Finally, the key positioning elements have to be deployed strategically in order to guide the development of operational plans for marketing activities. Fig 1.10 illustrates this mechanism. The interfaces with other functional areas (and their strong contributory roles) in achieving the desired positioning and its successful implementation should be clearly recognised.

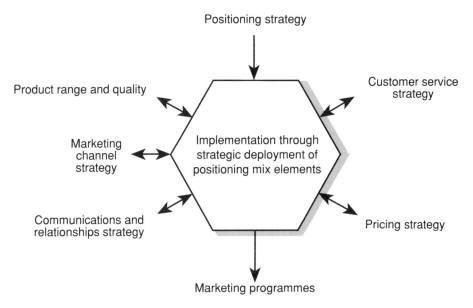

Fig. 1.10 From marketing strategy to implementation of marketing programmes

BIBLIOGRAPHY

Abell, D. F. (1978) 'Strategic Windows', *Journal of Marketing*, July.

Abell, D. F. (1980) *Defining the Business: The Starting Point of Strategic Planning*, Englewood Cliffs, NJ: Prentice-Hall.

Ames, B. C. (1970) 'Trappings vs Substance in Industrial Marketing', *Harvard Business Review*, July–August.

Baker, M. J. and Hart, S. J. (1989) *Marketing and Competitive Success*, Oxford: Philip Allan.

Borden, N. (1964) 'The Concept the Marketing Mix', *Journal of Advertising Research*, June.

Capes, N., Farley, J. V., Hulbert, J. M. and Lei, D. (1991) 'In Search of Excellence Ten Years Later: Strategy and Organisation Do Matter', *Management Decision*, Vol. 29, No. 4.

Chaston, I. (1990) *Managing for Marketing Excellence*, Maidenhead: McGraw-Hill.

Christopher, M., McDonald, M. and Wills, G. (1980) *Introductory Marketing*, London: Pan.

Clancy, K. and Krieg, P. (1990) 'From Myopic Maximisation to Panaromic Optimisation: New Directions in Financial Services Marketing and Marketing Research in the 1990s', *Marketing and Research Today*, August.

Cowell, D. (1984) *The Marketing of Services*, London: Heinemann.

Curran, J. G. M. and Goodfellow, J. (1989) 'Theoretical and Practical Issues in the Determination of Market Boundaries', *European Journal of Marketing*, Vol. 24, No. 1.

Davidson, H. (1987) *Offensive Marketing*, Harmondsworth: Penguin.

Doyle, P. (1992) 'What Are the Excellent Companies?', *Journal of Marketing Management*, Vol. 8, No. 2.

Drucker, P. F. (1973) *Management: Tasks, Responsibilities and Practices*, New York: Harper and Row.

Drucker, P. F. (1980), quoted in 'Sitting at the Feet of Marketing's Latest Game', *Marketing Week*, 7 March.

Foster, D. W. (1974) *Marketing Imperative*, London MacDonald.

'Game Wars' (1992) *The Sunday Times Magazine*, 1 November.

Garda, R. A. (1988) 'Strategic Segmentation: How to Carve Niches for Growth in Industrial Markets' in B. A. Weitz and R. Wensley (eds), *Readings in Strategic Marketing*, NY: Dryden.

Hamel, G. and Prahalad, C. K. (1991) 'Corporate Imagination and Expeditionary Marketing', *Harvard Business Review*, August.

Hansen, N., Gronhaug, K. and Warneryd, K. E. (1990) 'Excellent Marketing: The Concept, its Measurement and Implications', *Marketing and Research Today*, June.

Hayward, G. (1977) 'The Adoption of New Industrial Products', *Marketing*, November.

Haywood, R. (1984) *All About PR*, Maidenhead: McGraw-Hill.

Hutt, M. D. and Speh, T. W. (1984) 'The Marketing Strategy Centre: Diagnosing the Industrial Marketer's Interdisciplinary Role', *Journal of Marketing*, Vol. 48.

ITI Research Ltd (1979) *The Barclays Bank Report on Export Development in France, Germany and the United Kingdom* , London: Barclays Bank International.

Kitchen, P. J. and Proctor, T. (1991) 'The Increasing Importance of Public Relations in Fast Moving Consumer Goods Firms', *Journal of Marketing Management*, Vol. 7, No. 4.

Kotler, P. (1980) 'Sitting at the Feet of Marketing's Latest Guru', *Marketing Week*, 7 March.

Kotler, P. (1991) 'Kotler on . . . *Management Decision*, Vol. 29, No. 2.

Kotler, P. and Mindak, W. (1978) 'Marketing and Public Relations: Should they be Partners or Rivals?', *Journal of Marketing*, October.

Kotler, P., Gregor, W. and Rogers, W. (1977) 'The Marketing Audit Comes of Age', *Sloan Management Review*, Vol. 18, No. 2.

Levitt, T. (1990) 'Marketing Myopia', *Harvard Business Review*, July–August.

Lunn, T. (1986) 'Segmenting and Constructing Markets', in R. Worcester and J. Downham (eds), *Consumer Market Research Handbook*, Maidenhead: McGraw-Hill.

Lynch, J. (1990) *Managing the High-Tech Sales Force*, Sigma Press.

McCarthy, E. J. (1960) *Basic Marketing: A Managerial Approach*, Boston: Irwin.

McDonald, M. H. B. (1992) 'Strategic Marketing Planning: A State of the Art Review', *Marketing Intelligence and Planning*, Vol. 10, No. 4.

Machine Tools Economic Development Committee (1970) *A Handbook for Marketing Machinery*, London: HMSO.

Magaziner, I. C. and Patinkis, M. (1989) 'Fast Heat: How Korea Won the Microwave War', *Harvard Business Review*.

Marketing Week (1993) 'The Rise and Rise of Name Dropping', *Marketing Week*, 22 January.

Middleton, V. T. C. (1989) 'Marketing the Margin', *Quarterly Review of Marketing*, Winter.

Narver, J. C. and Slater, S. F. (1990) 'The Effect of a Market Orientation on Business Profitability', *Journal of Marketing*, October.

Peters, T. and Waterman, R. (1982) *In Search of Excellence. Lessons from America's Best Run Companies*, London: Harper and Row.

Piercy, N. (1982a) 'Cost and Profit Myopia in Marketing – Strengthen Your Marketing Department by Reducing Its Profit Responsibility', *QRM*, Summer.

Piercy, N. (1982b) *Export Strategy, Markets and Competition*, London: George Allen and Unwin.

Piercy, N. (1987) 'Developing Marketing Information Systems', in M. J. Baker (ed.), *The Marketing Book*, London: Heinemann.

Piercy, N. (1992) *Market-led Strategic Change. Making Marketing Happen in Your Organisation*, Oxford: Butterworth-Heinemann.

Porter, M. E. (1985) *Competitive Advantage. Creating and Sustaining Superior Performance*, NY: Free Press.

Prahalad, C. K. and Hamel, G. (1990) 'The Core Competence of the Corporation', *Harvard Business Review*, May–June.

Ries, A. and Trout, J. (1982) *Positioning: The Battle for Your Mind*, NY: Warner Books.

Schnaars, S. P. (1981) *Marketing Strategy: A Customer-Driver Approach*, NY: Free Press.

Simmonds, K. (ed.) (1982) *Strategy and Marketing: A Case Approach*, Oxford: Philip Allan.

Spillard, P. (1980/81), 'Ansoff Revisited: Logic, Commitment and Strategies for Change', *Quarterly Review of Marketing*, Vol. 6, No. 2.

Star, S. H. (1989) 'Marketing and Its Discontents', *Harvard Business Review*, December.

Vikhanski, O. and Puffer, S. (1993) 'Management Education and Employee Training at Moscow McDonald's', *European Management Journal*, Vol. 11, No. 1.

White, R. (1988) *Advertising: What It Is and How to Do It*, Maidenhead: McGraw-Hill.

Wilson, A. (1993) *Marketing Audit Checklists: Guide to Effective Marketing Resource Realization*, Maidenhead: McGraw-Hill.

CHAPTER 2

The Marketing/Strategy Interface

Gordon Pearson

INTRODUCTION

The interface between marketing and strategy is both obvious and confusing; at the same time clear and yet decidedly fuzzy. It all depends on what is meant by marketing and what is meant by strategy. The connection between the corporate strategy of a financial conglomerate, such as Hanson, and the marketing department of its main subsidiary is no doubt extremely tenuous. However, the connection between the business strategy of a firm such as Marks and Spencer and the marketing philosophy which drives the company is clearly close and direct.

The term 'marketing' can refer to a set of techniques, a function, a department of a business, or a philosophy. The interface with strategy is relatively simple if it is assumed to mean technique or function. In such a case marketing becomes simply a means to the end of implementing strategy. However, marketing as a philosophy is more complex. Marketing philosophy is what supposedly drives many of the most successful and progressive businesses and consequently it must, according to many writers, take the leading part in business strategy and indeed guide the whole process of strategy formulation.

The interface becomes even more problematic when terms such as marketing strategy and strategic marketing are loosely used and, more particularly, when the tools and techniques of marketing are misused by strategists and the tools and techniques of strategy are misused by marketers.

There is no clear consensus of view about where marketing ends and strategy begins, but it is hoped that the evidence in this chapter will provide some clarification.

STRATEGY

Strategy is perhaps an even more widely misused term than marketing, if this is possible. It clearly means many different things, depending on the situation. The position of icebergs was strategic to the *Titanic*, but not to the *Hindenberg*; the supply of horseshoe nails was of strategic importance at the battle of Flodden

Field, but not at Waterloo; advertising is strategic to Coca Cola, but not to the corner paper shop; one person's strategy is another person's tactics. So whose strategy are we concerned with?

One way out of answering this is to define strategy in terms of a hierarchy:

- *Corporate strategy* refers to issues concerning the company as a legal-financial entity and is measured in terms such as earnings per share growth, returns on equity and so on.
- *Business strategy* refers to issues concerning the business units (SBUs) of the company as competitive entities within product market and technological environments. Typically, though inadequately, such strategies are measured in terms of market share, sales volume growth and gross margins.
- *Functional strategies* refer to the orientation and long-term thrusts of the business functions such as marketing, production, R&D and finance and are measured in terms appropriate to the function.

In this view of strategy the position of marketing as a function is made quite explicit. Marketing strategy refers simply to the strategy of the marketing function, i.e. the strategic control of marketing variables such as price, product, promotion and distribution. Even using this very simple definition there are problems: in practice there are few businesses where key decisions on product or price are treated as the sole responsibility of the chief marketing executive. They are clearly profit decisions and profit is generally regarded as the responsibility of general management.

These difficulties arise even with a relatively pedestrian definition of marketing and strategy. If one goes further and uses a Kotleresque, 'Segmentation–Targeting–Positioning' definition of marketing strategy the difficulties are compounded. Quite clearly these issues overlap with the concerns of business strategy as identified above. Further still, using the marketing as philosophy definition, the interface becomes exceedingly problematic. For the time being, this confusion is simply noted while clarification will be sought from a more in-depth look at strategy.

The problem with strategy is its intrinsic complexity. In even the smallest single-product business, strategy has to take account of many different factors: customer needs, production capability, financial strength, market structure and growth, competitive activity and many more. In order to get to grips with these, managements have tended to make use of simplifying models.

Since the days when corporate strategy was synonymous with long-range planning, and in most cases amounted to little more than cranking the annual budget over an extra four years, there have been just two strategic models of real consequence: portfolios, first introduced by Boston Consulting Group, and Porter's model of competitive strategy. In addition, marketers have also advocated and practised an approach to business which overlaps, even operationalises, other less effective models. Finally, a new approach appears to be emerging which seems likely to dominate strategic thinking up to the millennium. In considering the strategy marketing interface, each of these models will be discussed in turn.

THE BOSTON MATRIX

The first model was Boston's business portfolio (Boston Consulting Group, 1968) and its derivatives. Business portfolios were based on the empirically tested idea that total costs fall as experience is gained in making and selling a product. Boston's own work centred on an analysis of twenty-four different commodities (e.g. germanium transistors, silicon diodes, crude oil, ethylene, polystyrene, titanium sponge, refined cane sugar, Japanese beer), and it has been replicated many times (e.g. Exhibit 2.1).

If costs fall with experience, simple logic suggests that the business which gains the most experience will enjoy the lowest costs. Thus, assuming a general market price (which is a perfectly valid thing to assume in the case of commodity products), such a business would also enjoy the highest profits. Therefore, increasing market share in order to achieve a rapid increase in experience would be highly profitable. In a young and rapidly growing market, experience will be quickly doubled, thus multiplying the cost reduction benefits. Thus in such markets it was extremely worthwhile to achieve a large market share. By comparison, on low-growth, mature markets the cost benefits accruing from experience were extremely low and the value of increasing market share, in order to gain cost advantages, minimal. Worse, in such businesses the result of maturity is not so much experience-generated cost reductions, but the progressive accrual of additional overhead in the form of managerial discretionary status, perks and other non-business expenses. The experience curve should not therefore depict continuous cost reductions as Boston suggested, but reductions during the growth phase, with cost increases during maturity.

Boston's portfolio had two dimensions: market growth rate and relative market share. From this the four Boston categories were derived: stars, cash cows, dogs and problem children, and the three strategic prescriptions: invest, ration investment, and withdraw, i.e. the decisions of an investment manager running a portfolio, not of a marketer managing a mix of products.

Boston originally emphasised that the cost-reducing effects of experience were of significance only in situations of high growth rates, and originally pre-

Exhibit 2.1 The fruits of experience

In 1957 Western Digital's plant in Allentown, Pennsylvania, used 4,000 workers to produce five transistors per worker per day at a unit cost of $2.50. By 1983 the same plant, using the same number of workers, was producing 5.3 million transistors per worker per day at a unit cost of thousandths of a penny.

sented their matrix with the cut-off point between high and low growth at the 10 per cent a year mark. Below this level it was acknowledged that the effects of experience were less material and, by implication therefore, the model itself would not be relevant. This suggested that the model would not be pertinent to the vast majority of American or European businesses, but may well be relevant to firms enjoying the growth rates then widely experienced in Japan.

Paradoxically, American and European (especially British) businesses adopted the Boston portfolio very widely in trying to achieve strategic control (if that term is not a contradiction in terms), while the Japanese resolutely refused to submit.

A firm's relative market share was measured as share relative to its largest competitor and the split between high and low share was usually drawn at between 1 and 1.5 (i.e. market share between equality with, and 1.5 times that of the largest competitor). Thus in any industry there could be only one business with a high relative market share. In industries experiencing low growth this could have been somewhat catastrophic because the Boston prescription for low-growth, low-share businesses was simply 'divest'.

On this basis, Boston suggested that the vast majority of British industry should be divested and, in fact, it seems this process has gone some way over the past two decades. Fortunately, many managers were too shrewd, or optimistic, to follow through the Boston prescription. They used the Boston model very widely, but apparently did not take its prescriptions too seriously if they did not accord with what they were going to do anyway!

The Boston prescriptions are clearly limited. So far as managing the business was concerned they were more or less silent, being restricted to versions of the

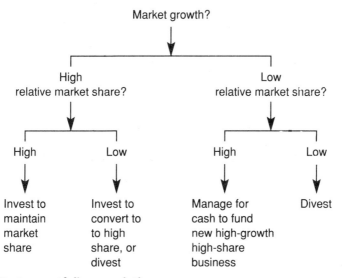

Fig. 2.1 Boston portfolio prescriptions

Exhibit 2.2 The Boston matrix in practice

During the 1970s many British and American firms adopted the Boston matrix to formulate their corporate strategies and as a strategic guideline for acquisitions and for major capital investments. Under this system it became extremely difficult for managers of a business which was designated a 'dog' to achieve head office support for major investments. The consequence was that the managements concerned became demoralised and inevitably the business ceased to be technologically competitive. Head office attention then was focused on cost reduction and divestment.

'buy', 'sell' or 'hold' type of decision as illustrated in Fig. 2.1. There is no qualitative substance in these statements and little to assist strategic management apart from investment/divestment. The Boston prescriptions are therefore restricted to those of the manager of an investment trust, or perhaps the corporate HQ staff of a conglomerate whose main activity is the buying and selling of businesses.

Nevertheless the model has been used far beyond this genuine portfolio application. Corporate strategists have used the Boston portfolio to guide their investment decisions between businesses (see Exhibit 2.2).

Marketers too have (mis)used the matrix very widely to maintain a balanced portfolio of products, and every standard marketing text contains an explanation of the Boston matrix and how it may be used. But for them the limitations of the model are even more profound. Its empirical foundations are entirely based on an analysis of commodity products selling at market prices, while the essence of marketing is concerned with differentiating products for customers prepared to pay higher than base prices.

The Boston model has, of course, been widely criticised by strategists and marketeers alike (e.g. Alberts, 1989). Strategists have objected to the fundamental proposition that the strategic success of a business could be determined by just two quantifiable factors. This seems too simplistic and could be true only if it was assumed that management itself could not make a difference. But management, for whom the Boston portfolio was created, exist only to make a difference - if they do not make a difference they may as well be replaced by robots. Marketers also level the same criticisms, but for them the validity of the model is even less appealing. The fact that the Boston matrix is still included in standard marketing texts, and is apparently still widely used, only serves to confuse the strategy:marketing interface.

OTHER MATRICES

The original Boston matrix is the only business portfolio model for which there is any documented empirical support. It was early recognised as simplistic and was variously enhanced, not least by Boston Consulting itself. However, the two best-known models were General Electric's Business Assessment Array (BAA) and Shell's Directional Policy Matrix (DPM) (Gluck, 1985). These enhancements related to both the inputs and outputs of the model.

On the input side, the two quantitative measures of share and growth were replaced by much more detailed analyses of both the market and the business. For example, instead of market growth, the BAA model sought to measure market attractiveness indicated by such factors as size and growth of the market, cyclicality of growth, product life cycle position, industry profitability, ease of entry, business environment (e.g. government regulation, industrial relations), degree of competition and concentration of competitors, investment intensity, availability of labour and materials, marketing intensity and customer concentration. Similarly, instead of relative market share the BAA sought to measure business strength indicated by such factors as market share and change in relative market share, profitability, technological competence, brand loyalty, managerial calibre, product differentiation, production economics (age/obsolescence of plant), plant capacity, company reputation and image.

The outputs of these enhanced models retained the simple buy, hold or sell prescriptions with only minor sophistications. The matrix was generally divided into nine cells rather than four, and the BAA prescriptions were 'invest/grow', 'improve/defend' and 'harvest/divest'.

Clearly these models were less simplistic than Boston and required far more detailed analysis, which itself would result in greater understanding of the business situation. Despite this, the prescriptions remain essentially limited to the options of an investment trust manager. If 'buy', 'sell' or 'hold' are the only strategic options, then business strategy is a relatively trivial pursuit, which it may not be.

Portfolios have been widely adopted and misused by marketeers to assist in the achievement of a balanced portfolio of products -i.e. a balance between today's breadwinners and tomorrow's (cash cows and stars), but this is really no advance on Drucker's analysis of over thirty years ago and only trivialises the basic Boston research. In addition such misuse also clearly adds to the confusion of where the strategy:marketing interface should be drawn.

PORTER'S COMPETITIVE STRATEGY MODEL

Porter's (1980) approach focused on essentially the same two dimensions. Though he did not overtly define a portfolio matrix, one is nevertheless implicit in his analysis, as indicated in Fig. 2.2.

Instead of relative market share or business strength Porter goes directly to the simple measure of business profitability, which he uses as a test of competitive advantage (discussed later in more detail). Instead of market growth or industry attractiveness, Porter simply uses the idea of industry profitability and then focuses on the factors which determine it. The factors he identifies are

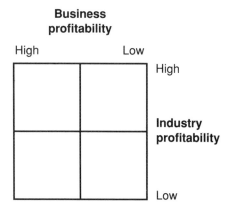

Fig. 2.2 Porter's implied matrix

a further development of the measures of industry attractiveness described above. He divides them into five categories which he describes as the 'forces driving industry competition'. These are used as a checklist and include most of the industry attractiveness factors, dividing them according to economics categories: competitors, substitutes, new entrants and the transactional power of suppliers and buyers.

Enumerating these five 'forces' is somewhat arbitrary, especially when a sixth force, government regulation, is often the most important factor in determining the profitability of an industry. Porter himself investigated the pharmaceuticals and airline industries and found that government regulation and deregulation was the key to profitability in both (Porter, 1988).

The detailed industry analysis commended by Porter leads, in one sense, to a dead-end. In the former models the purpose of assessing industry attractiveness was quite clear - to answer: 'Shall we buy into this industry, get out of it, or stay put?' But Porter is more concerned with what goes on inside a business and how it can be improved, rather than the simple 'buy', 'sell' or 'hold' decision set.

Industry analysis does not play a major role in the subsequent definition of competitive strategy. However, the assessment of business profitability, the other dimension of Porter's implied matrix, is developed much further. The analysis of profitability starts from the very basic assertion:

Profit = Revenue – Costs

This relationship is both a statement of the obvious and the starting point for the profit-maximising model of classical micro-economics, which requires only the assumptions of perfect competition for it to be amenable to solution by calculus. It may not look too promising as the foundation of a practically useful strategic model but that is how Porter used it.

The question is 'How can a business maximise its profitability, or at least

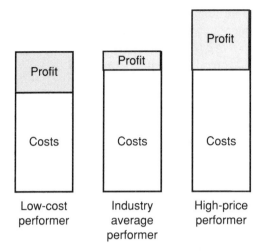

Fig. 2.3 Profitability of industry participants

become the most profitable performer in its industry?' Fig. 2.3 illustrates the two different approaches suggested by Porter, compared against the industry average performer. Maximum profitability can, in principle, be achieved in only one of two ways: by minimising costs or by maximising prices. Thus any effective business strategy must aim to pursue one or other of these aims: to be the lowest-cost producer or the highest-price seller. It would be convenient to refer to these two strategies as cost leadership and price leadership except that 'price leadership' is used by economists to mean something rather different.

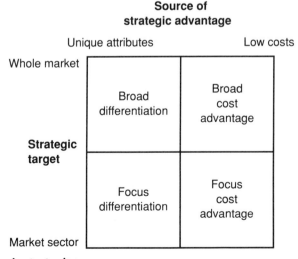

Fig. 2.4 Generic strategies

Consequently, the terms initially used by Porter were 'cost leadership' and 'differentiation', the latter referring to the means by which a premium price is earned. These two were referred to as 'generic' strategies because they are the only two ways, in this model, in which profitability can be maximised, i.e. the only two sources of competitive advantage (see Fig. 2.4).

Porter (1988) is emphatic that 'failure to make the choice [between cost leadership and differentiation] means that a company is "stuck in the middle", with no competitive advantage. The result is poor performance.' This is undoubtedly a great danger, as has long been emphasised by many other writers (e.g. Drucker's (1964) assertion that 'concentration is the key to real economic results'. Moreover, the basic concept of strategic direction seems to imply much the same thing. Many companies which have a clear direction and a distinct position are also demonstrably either cost leaders or differentiators, but not both. Names like Porsche, Bic, Yves St Laurent and KwikSave, for example, immediately classify themselves in one camp or the other.

However, there is nothing *intrinsic to the model* which suggests a firm cannot successfully combine aspects of both cost leadership and differentiation. The most profitable firm in an industry could well be both a cost leader and a differentiator. Cases have been reported of firms which appear successfully to combine low-cost strategies with differentiation (see Exhibit 2.3). Some researchers have even suggested that the most effective strategies for some situations comprise systematic oscillation between cost leadership and differentiation (Gilbert and Strebel, 1988). Thus, 'stuck in the middle' is not an intrinsic rule of the model, but a pragmatic enhancement to warn of the dangers; a rule of thumb which may knowingly be broken with advantage.

The original introduction of focus as a generic strategy obscured the simple basis of the whole model: that profits could be maximised by achieving either lowest costs or highest prices. Competition erodes profits by the various means indicated in Porter's analysis of industries (i.e. substitutes, new entrants, etc.) and perfect competition erodes profitability perfectly. A way of minimising this erosion would be to minimise competition. This can be done by focusing on areas of the market where there are the fewest competitors. Hence the focus strategy. But focus is not a strategy as such, more a question of degree – at the

Exhibit 2.3 Differentiation and cost leadership

Hall (1980) found that high-performing businesses all 'used careful strategic analysis to guide their investments'. The basis of differentiation did not seem to matter – it might be to do with any attribute or combination of attributes of the product or service. It might also be related to a combination of differentiation and cost leadership. Philip Morris, for example, was found to 'combine lowest cost fully automated cigarette manufacturing with high cost branding and promotion production to gain industry profit leadership without the benefit of either largest unit volume or segment market share'.

end of the day all strategies are focused to some extent. Even Ivory Soap (Porter, 1988), which has a very broad appeal, is carefully positioned as a multidimensional brand aimed at a fully researched customer profile. Focus, like stuck in the middle, is a pragmatic addition to the model. Its consideration may be important, but it is not itself a generic strategy.

Competitive strategy was the leading orthodoxy of the 1980s and, like the portfolio model, also enjoyed around a decade of dominance. But while Boston's model was explicitly market-, though definitely not marketing-, oriented in its key measures, Porter's is more intimately concerned with serving the customer in some distinctive and valued way. Porter emphasises that the point of differentiation has to be valued by the customer to the extent that the customer must pay for it, but he fails to indicate ways in which this can be measured or identified. For this we have to look to more orthodox marketing methods, of which Porter himself appears to be virginally innocent.

THE STRATEGIC MARKETING MODEL

Porter's model essentially lacks a way of identifying an appropriate generic strategy. This is provided by the strategic marketing approach. This is not simply strategy for the marketing function, but strategy for the whole business based on the marketing philosophy, i.e. a management orientation to determining the needs of target markets and to satisfying those needs more effectively and efficiently than competitors do. To do this the marketing philosophy must be all-pervasive. Everyone on the firm must be customer-oriented: one employee who doesn't give a damn about the customer can undo months, even years, of painstaking reputation building.

Peters and Waterman (1982) found that the excellent companies were invariably customer-orientated: they accorded a far higher priority to giving the customer value, quality and service, than they did to operating efficiently in cost terms, or being technological leaders. Customer orientation may be vital to 'excellence', but this is no different from what marketing textbooks have been saying for decades. The fact that customer orientation is not widely practised hardly makes the message more stimulating. The point about customer orientation is that it has to be focused and strategy-driven. IBM's customer orientation is focused on providing service, because that is the cornerstone of its strategy. Service is not the cornerstone of every business. Some thoroughly successful firms have prospered through the simple and valid strategy of 'pile it high and sell it cheap', or 'any colour so long as it's black'. Such cornerstones are intrinsically no less customer-oriented than 'service'. It all depends what customer need the product is satisfying.

Selznick (1957) suggested that every viable business has some 'distinctive competence', something at which it is peculiarly effective. It may not be unique and the firm may not be the best, but at least, in some aspect, it must be better than the common herd. If it were not so, the firm would go out of business. For the distinctive competence to be of any strategic value it must be embodied in the product the customer buys. For example, a firm may be peculiarly effective in R&D, but if the fruits of its research are not incorporated in the firm's product this competence will avail it nothing. Similarly the distinctive competence might relate to some aspect of cost, but if that strength is not embodied in the product in the form of reduced price, or increased quality, etc., it will have no strategic impact.

If the distinctive competence accords with the customer need and is embodied in the product, it creates a leadership position. The idea that 'economic results are only earned by leadership, not by mere competence' has been a central Drucker concept over the years (Drucker, 1964). While he is sometimes accused of making things seem too simple, his concept of leadership is in fact much more subtle than some of the later contributions, such as Boston's. Leadership, for Drucker, did not mean that a business had to have the dominant share of the market, or that it had to be first in every product line, or the most technologically advanced. Leadership had merely to relate to 'something of value to the customer'. It might be in service, or distribution, or some quite narrow aspect of the product, it might even relate to the firm's 'ability to convert ideas into saleable products'.

Potentially, then, a leadership position attaching to anything which the customer values provides the business with economic results. With no leadership position, even if the firm has the major share of the market, the business will at best be 'marginal'. The problem with this concept of leadership has been how to make it operational. Its generality makes it difficult to measure. If it cannot be measured, it can only remain a generality. Within the main strands of strategic management literature there is no definitive method for how a firm might identify a worthwhile leadership position, much less how it might achieve one. But the idea that it has to be of value to the customer, and therefore embodied in what the customer buys, leads to consideration of the product. This is the point where strategy has to draw directly on the mainstream of marketing.

An expensive bottle of wine is not usually purchased simply to satisfy a thirst. Similarly, an automobile is not bought solely as a means of transport. Products are loaded, both physically and psychologically, with many extras that may be important determinants of sales success. Marketing literature is replete with descriptions of the many and various components that comprise the modern conception of a product. One widely held view sees the product as having three layers: the core benefit or service, the formal product and the outer, augmented product layer which includes such things as warranty, service support and so on (Kotler, 1984). This onion-like model implies that the product can be unpeeled to reveal hidden depths. The analogy only partly stands up to scrutiny. The various attributes of a product are not necessarily related in any predictable fashion, onion-like or otherwise. All that can be said is that there are many and various attributes that could be categorised for convenience as physical, implied and psychological, as shown in Table 2.1.

Table 2.1 Product attributes

Physical attributes	Implied attributes	Psychological attributes
Price	Distribution	Corporate image
Quality	Delivery	Brand image
Performance	Reliability	Product image
Design	Warranty	Need image
Packaging	After-sales support	
	Advertising	
	Service	

What matters about this complex product is the customer's perceptions of its various attributes. Producing the best mousetrap is of no avail if it is not perceived as such by potential customers. The customers' perception of the product is an amalgam of their perception of the various product attributes, any of which may be critical. They may buy it because the price is right – it satisfies their economic needs; or its performance may be what attracts them; or its quality; or it might be some more deep-seated psychological need which is satisfied by the product's sexy design, or image.

The customer's perception of products is not necessarily compatible with a commonsense notion of reality. Too great a divide between perception and reality is likely to be only short-lived, but there will nevertheless be differences, and some of them may be important. Even an attribute as apparently unambiguous as price may be affected by this dichotomy between customer perception and reality. A product which is actually cheap relative to its competitors, may in fact be perceived as being relatively expensive. If customers regard price as the critical attribute, then their perception of the product's price will dictate the buying decision. If they perceive Brand A as cheaper than Brand B they will buy it, even if the reality is that Brand B has the lower price.

Customer and potential customer perceptions are a crucial ingredient of strategic marketing and their identification is a key step in defining an effective competitive strategy. A differentiation strategy can be avowed simply by managerial decision without any recourse to customer perceptions. Such differentiation may fail because it is quite irrelevant to the customer who is not particularly concerned with the attribute being differentiated. Effective differentiation must therefore be based on a sound knowledge of customer perceptions.

Such precise information is unlikely to be achieved simply by being 'close to the customer'. Obsessions with service and quality, effective nichemanship and listening to the customer are what Peters and Waterman identify as 'close to the customer', but understanding the real needs and perceptions implies a more systematic form of customer orientation which has to include a technically reliable form of enquiry. The process of identifying what need the customer satisfies when he or she buys the product can be approached quite systematically using tried and tested marketing research methods.

The strategic marketing approach is not infrequently used in conjunction with a Porter model of strategy and this no doubt contributes to much of the present confusion over where the interface between marketing and strategy should be drawn. Some of this confusion may be eradicated by the final strategic model to be considered. This is the approach identified by Hamel and Prahalad (1993), based on their study of global industries, which promises to become the leading strategic model of the 1990s.

CORE COMPETENCE AND STRATEGIC INTENT

More than thirty years ago Selznick (1957) used the term 'distinctive competence' to denote what a particular business is uniquely good at by comparison with its close competitors. Selznick suggested how distinctive competence and what he called 'organizational character' - what we would now call 'culture' - could be combined to fulfil an organisation's basic mission.

Selznick's idea of distinctive competence highlighted the competitive element which differentiates one business from another. Such differentiation is no longer enough because the current speed of technological development means that competitive advantage based on a singular competence is unlikely to be sustainable for long.

Drucker (1964) developed a parallel theme in his enunciation of business leadership: a business must be the leader in something – it mattered not what that something was, so long as the customer genuinely wanted it and was prepared to pay for it. Drucker's idea of leadership is not market leadership, most often measured simply in terms of market share: 'examples abound of companies that have the largest share of the market but are far behind in their profitability compared to competitors of much smaller apparent stature' (Drucker, 1964, p. 38).

The idea of core competences, promulgated by Prahalad and Hamel (1990), differs from both these antecedents. The idea resulted from studies of the way successful firms, mainly Japanese, appeared systematically to acquire and exploit combinations of fundamental technologies in order to develop generic or core products with which to dominate global markets. Core competence is not simply the possession of a particular technological or managerial capability. This would be unlikely to differentiate a firm from its competitor possessing a similar capability. Core competence is a combination of such capabilities which provide the firm with a leadership position in the development of certain generic or core products. This is what gives the business a sustainable competitive advantage.

The fact that Hamel and Prahalad's work has been based almost entirely on global businesses is not accidental. The ever increasing scale of investment required by advancing technology means that the exploitation of that technology must be rapid for it to be profitable. Speed of exploitation means that immediate access to a large market, ideally global, is essential. Thus changes in the global environment arise from global technology development (Miller, 1990). The assiduous pursuit of a global market results inevitably in convergence of consumer tastes (Ohmae, 1989). Just a few decades ago the cultural differences between, say, Japan and Britain meant that it would be difficult to envisage the same consumer product succeeding equally in both markets. Now, tastes for many technically advanced consumer durables clearly coincide and the same product can be marketed in London and in Tokyo with only superficial promotional differences.

The globalisation of technology makes it essential that all businesses, large and small, take a global view. Even a localised business like Carter's (see Exhibit 2.4) with no global pretensions themselves must take full account of global developments in markets and technologies potentially relevant to their business. This global awareness is essential to the maintenance of technological position (Clark, 1989).

Exhibit 2.4 Carter's Gold Medal soft drinks

Carter is a medium-sized UK producer of soft drinks, with sales largely confined to the Midlands region. The firm has no plans to achieve global leadership in its product markets. It does not seek to emulate Coca-Cola and would no doubt regard any comparable business which did have such aspirations as naive and unrealistic.

Nevertheless, Carter regards it as vital to make full use of the latest technology in the industry from wherever it comes, and through its use to deliver value to customers. The firm recently opened a new factory, described as the 'world's most advanced automated soft drink bottling plant', which permits it to respond flexibly to changes in demand. In the press release announcing the opening of this new facility, Chairman Tony Marchmont said:

In this industry, flexibility means tripling production because of a heat-wave. It means a special promotion for a single retail store wanting, say, pink bottles with a special label. It means producing ten lines of 1,000 bottles as cheaply and quickly as one line of 10,000 bottles.

Carter is not a global leader, but recognises the need to exploit global technology to achieve its strategic aims.

(Pearson, 1992, p. 12).

A firm's existing core competences can be identified by analysing its product or service. What are the fundamental skills and knowledge on which successful products are based? They may relate to straightforward world leadership in specific technologies or they may be more related to particular organisational or managerial skills. Examples include:

- Benetton: fast cycle times through computer-aided, just-in-time manufacturing, rapid customer response, distinctive product aesthetic design
- Toyota: fast cycle times
- Honda: engines, power trains
- Coca-Cola: brand strength, geographic spread
- Carter's Gold Medal soft drinks: flexibility of bottling facilities; responsiveness to customer requirements.

Companies that successfully build global leadership in more than one core competence are few and far between; those that have done so in several are extremely rare. Global leadership in two or more complementary fundamental competences provides the ability to create a stream of new products. Some of them (e.g. personal hi-fi, electronic personal organisers) may be unimaginable, with no known demand, and in this way go some way beyond the marketing side of the strategy:marketing interface.

Most of the firms Hamel and Prahalad give as examples are global players, but their cases are instructive for every business whether or not their intentions have a global dimension. Most of the global players began their quest for core competences as small and relatively obscure players and became global only through persistence over decades of following an explicit and well-understood strategic intent. Moreover, every business, whether in services or manufacturing, is affected by the new technologies which are themselves global. Even for those businesses which have no global ambitions whatsoever and appear not to be vulnerable to global competition, the concept of core competences, though writ small, is equally relevant. Every management needs to know what competences form the foundation of its most successful products, so that they can develop those competences and nurture the people on whom they depend.

For many businesses, the acquisition and development of core competences are somewhat haphazard. As Mintzberg (1987) noted, even the clearest strategic positions may emerge from a process of repeated trial and error, or even as a result of simple good luck. The extent to which strategic positions emerge, as opposed to being deliberately planned, can never be known – many emergent strategies are post-rationalised to give the impression of careful and sophisticated planning. For example, whilst Honda's development is apparently based on the overt exploitation of its position in engines and transmissions, its ultimately successful entry into the American motorcycle market was a saga of learning from trial and error. Honda simply had a product, the light-weight

Super-Cub bike, which it wanted to sell in Harley-Davidson-dominated America. In 1957 Soichiro Honda thought he had agreed to sell 7,500 motorcycles a month while his American agent had thought they were talking about an annual sale. 'Seventy-five hundred a month!' the agent exclaimed when he realised the misunderstanding. 'That's out of the question. Preposterous!' (Gilder, 1986, p. 187). A few years later Honda was selling around 20,000 a month in America.

The breakthrough idea, or product, is by definition 'preposterous'. If it were not so it would already have happened. Such breakthroughs can themselves lead to the development of new core competences which provide the basis of sustainable leadership positions. The idea that Canon should set out, as a leading camera manufacturer, to beat Xerox in the copier market was preposterous, but Canon did it. Such successes do not arise solely as a result of trial and error or good luck, but are based on a clearly articulated strategic intent which is painstakingly implemented over many years, as outlined in Exhibit 2.5.

Core competences are the basis of competitive advantage in achieving strategic intent. To acquire and nurture competences that are not core is simply a waste of resources and effort and serves only to dissipate concentration. It is much better to buy in non-core competences (Quinn, Doorley and Paquette,

Exhibit 2.5 Canon's attack on Xerox

Canon's attack on the photocopier market involved the following eight steps:
(1) Establish the strategic intent to 'beat Xerox'.
(2) Identify Canon's existing core competences.
(3) Understand the Xerox technology and patents in order to identify the necessary core competences.
(4) License the technology to gain market experience and begin to acquire the core competences not already owned.
(5) Invest in R&D to improve on the existing technology to acquire and start to exploit core competences, primarily to achieve cost reductions, e.g. by standardisation of components, improving ease of maintenance and replenishment, etc.
(6) License out own technology to fund further R&D and thus further consolidate the core competences required to beat Xerox.
(7) Open challenge, first by attacking markets where Xerox was weakest, e.g. Japan and then Europe.
(8) Finally, innovative, rather than imitative, attack on markets were Xerox was strongest, e.g. by selling rather than leasing, distributing through office equipment retailers rather than direct, and focusing promotion on end users rather than corporate functional heads.

Source: Hamel and Prahalad, 1989

1990) and focus all internal efforts on the acquisition and development of what really matters.

A firm's capacity for competitive innovation is based on its ability to acquire relevant core competences and to apply them effectively in the development of core products. Capability is infinite. It is not constrained by the competences you already have, or even the resources at your disposal, but can be extended by the careful definition of the competences required and the means of their acquisition and development. Missing competences can be painstakingly developed internally through focused investment in R&D or acquired externally through various forms of collaborative arrangements. Success by internal development may provide a sustainable leadership position where the acquisition of new technology is a continuous process with each advance laying the foundation for the next. Internal development is, however, extremely expensive and beyond the means of all but the largest organisations. Moreover, in an era when the diffusion of technology is rapid, the resultant competitive advantage may be short-lived. Also, a lot of new technology is not protectable and there is little commercial benefit in being the holder of patents the essence of which are immediately copied by competitors. As Ouchi and Bolton (1988) suggest, internal development is not the best way to progress in areas where the intellectual property may be 'leaky'.

So for a variety of reasons, the acquisition of core competences through collaboration has become an attractive proposition. It is a way of reducing costs and eliminating wasteful competition especially in R&D (Telser, 1987). It is also likely to be quicker to buy in technology, rather than develop it in house. And it also opens up the potential of a business to the establishment of core competences far beyond those it could develop with its own resources, as the example of Canon shows. Canon used primarily a combination of external licensing and internal R&D to build the competences to beat Xerox.

It is a way forward which accords very well with the business environment of the 1990s. Communications with suppliers, customers, competitors, shareholders, technological suppliers and independent sources of knowledge and expertise such as research associations, universities and commercial technology consultants, have never been more important to the success of a business. Diffusion of innovations has never been more rapid, so the need to know what is happening in new technology throughout Europe, America, Japan and elsewhere has never been greater. Consequently we are operating in an era of increasingly open communications.

Buyer – seller relationships have moved from the adversarial to collaborative (Spekman, 1990) so that transactions are not seen as one-off profit-maximising deals, but as part of longer-term mutual dependencies where close collaboration can work to the benefit of both parties.

It used to be thought that to compete globally you had to be big, but this is no longer true. The logic behind the trend to alliances and collaborations is based on the need to globalise when clearly it is beyond the scope of the businesses concerned if they operated alone. Collaboration, even between competitors, has thus become one of the key business issues, and examples of successful and disastrous collaborations abound. Businesses are having to adjust to this more open world of technology exchange, alliance and research (Ramo, 1989). The tremendous cost of maintaining, in isolation, a leading position in a globalised market or technology is beyond the capacity of all but the very largest corporations. Collaboration, rather than cut-throat competition, is becoming an imperative for smaller businesses if they are not to be left hopelessly behind.

However, collaboration can be disastrous for the unwary. Hamel (1987) highlights two different approaches to collaboration. Typically, the Japanese adopt the role of students or learners in their approach. They seek to learn and understand as much as they possibly can from the arrangement. Western countries, on the other hand, typically adopt the role of teacher. The result is that the Japanese firms learn and the Western companies give up their special expertise. The Japanese may learn a technology, but more often nowadays it is market understanding which they gain from collaborations. The Western participants may gain today's technology (or even yesterday's) relatively cheaply, but in so doing stand out of the technology race and miss the long-term development, making it very difficult for them to climb aboard at some later stage. Therefore 'collaborate with your competitors, but be careful' (Hamel, Doz and Prahalad, 1989). Know exactly what you are trying to achieve through collaboration.

The strength of a business is not seen in terms of a particular product, sector of the market or distribution channel, but in its underlying capability to generate a range of rapidly evolving products or markets. The traditional rationale for structuring an organisation as a collection of strategic business units, each with maximum autonomy, becomes questionable. Instead, the overriding requirement is for the development and acquisition of common strands of expertise which cut across products, markets and business units.

This may lead to some apparently strange combinations of business activities. For example, 3M's products include 'Post-It' notes, magnetic tape, photographic film, pressure-sensitive tapes and coated abrasives. These all have quite different production technologies, end consumers and channels of distribution. The rationale is based on the core competences in substrates, coatings and adhesives. Or again, what would be the justification for a product range including lawnmowers, generators, motorcycles and cars? These are all quite different markets with their own unconnected distribution channels. Honda's success with this diverse range – 200 per cent growth between 1980 and 1988 – is based on the deliberate exploitation of its core competences in engines and power trains.

Prahalad and Hamel (1990) quote several such examples of the use of core competences. The success of NEC (see Exhibit 2.6) resulted directly from this approach. In similar vein, between 1980 and 1988 Canon grew by 264 per cent to beat Xerox with a range of core products including image scanners, laser printers, copiers and cameras, based on core competences in precision mechanics, fine optics and microelectronics.

Honda's application of its core competences resulted in the introduction of four-wheel steering and multi-valve engines among others. These developments can be introduced to give the competence owner enhanced competitive advantage. For example, Canon manufactures around 80 per cent of desktop laser printer engines even though sales under its own name are relatively small. The Hewlett-Packard IIP laser printer, which led the personal laser market using a Canon engine, was quickly faced by a Canon product with the same engine but with the added feature, at no additional cost, of infinitely scalable fonts. Hewlett-Packard was forced to respond with a similar feature built into the IIIP model.

Core competences are not the sole preserve of manufacturing industry. The same concepts apply equally in services, though the competences may be related to technology imported from manufacturing. For example, fast cycle times are a critical factor in providing customer service in many industries. Sportswear producer and retailer Benetton owes its success and explosive growth almost entirely to fast cycle times made possible by the use of information technology (Bower and Hout, 1988). It starts in new product development with a CAD system which automatically explodes a new design into a full range of sizes and transmits the patterns to computerised cutting machines to await customer orders. Undyed fabric is stored at demand scheduled just-in-time (JIT) factories and cut and dyed strictly to order. Retail outlets are also

Exhibit 2.6 NEC's use of core competences

NEC adopted the core competences approach by systematically exploiting the convergence of core competences in computing and communications (C&C). A 'C&C' committee oversaw the development of these core competences and resulting core products. This was supported by other co-ordination groups and teams which cut across the traditional organisation structure and ensured that each member of the organisation knew and understood the strategic intent. NEC developed competences internally and also through more than 100 purposive collaborations and alliances with other organisations.

Between 1980 and 1988 NEC's sales grew from $3.8 billion to $21.9 billion and the company became the world number one in semiconductors and a leading player in telecommunications and computers. Over the same period, its American competitor GTE enjoyed sales growth from $10 billion to $16.5 billion and had to withdraw from several of its major business areas.

Source: Prahalad and Hamel, 1990, pp. 79–91

run on a minimum stock JIT basis. Cycle time, from placing the order at the retail store to receiving the specially made product, takes fifteen days, which both satisfies customers and avoids over- and under-production.

Most firms, whether in manufacturing or service sectors, are not competing on a global front and do not seek to be global leaders. Nevertheless, every firm is operating in a global context: the technologies used are available globally and every customer is conditioned by standards of quality and service which apply globally. Thus every firm must ensure it is aware of all the available technological capabilities and must decide which core competences are needed to implement its particular strategic intent. Strategic intent concerns a business's long-term direction and if identified simply and succinctly can have a profound effect on the firm's stakeholders, both internal and external. Employees know what they are trying to achieve and therefore how they should make their greatest efforts; customers know what the firm's products and services embody; suppliers understand what the key elements are when dealing with the firm.

Strategic intent needs to be defined with precision and to be supported by indications of how fast and far the firm proposes to travel. Thus milestones along the route need to be spelled out and progress at each stage monitored and the people involved rewarded according to progress.

'Become the leading world producer of photocopiers' is a statement of strategic direction which could be a powerful organising and motivating concept. The strategic intent of 'beat Xerox' is still more powerful, focusing as it does on the major competitor and thus identifying standards to be beaten, or mechanisms to be avoided, right across every aspect of the business.

The way Canon achieved its strategic intent is shown in Exhibit 2.5. In essence the process is one of spelling out the strategic intent in terms of a competitive challenge, identifying the existing and required competences and then setting about acquiring those competences that need to be added in order to achieve the challenge set. The following are examples of strategic intent expressed in simple, mainly unambiguous terms:

- Komatsu: encircle Caterpillar
- Canon: beat Xerox
- Coca-Cola: put a Coke within 'arm's reach' of every consumer in the world
- NEC: exploit competence in computing and communications
- US Space Programme: put a man on the moon by the end of the decade.

These are statements of mission or long-term objectives capable of initiating and galvanising action and being converted into competitive challenges which are staging posts along the way. The expression of strategic intent in terms of a competitive challenge identifies a gap between the actual competences possessed and those required in order to achieve the strategic intent.

This 1990s approach to strategy, through the definition of strategic intent and competitive challenges and the development and exploitation of core competences, is clearly on the strategy side of the strategy: marketing interface. It is much more clearly so than the previous models that have dominated strategy practice and which have been discussed in this chapter. This model is explicitly concerned with the technology of the business, the organisational structure of the business (organised as cross-cutting strands of technological competence rather than product-based business units), the actual and potential core products of the business (which may or may not be conceivable) and the strategic intent of the business, which clearly cannot be expressed in orthodox marketing language.

CONCLUSION

Marketing is both the foundation and the sharp end of business strategy. It provides some underlying analytical framework as well as the means for identifying an effective form of differentiation. As a philosophy, marketing has long been regarded as the foundation stone of effective business strategy. As a set of techniques, marketing plays a vital part in identifying customer perceptions and preferences as a basis of strategy. As a function, it plays an important role in implementing an agreed business strategy.

In all these ways marketing is crucial to effective business strategy. However, strategy itself is not the responsibility of marketers. The identification of a strategic intent which is capable of mobilising the business to an inconceivably greater future, the specification of the core competences necessary to the achievement of that strategic intent, and the acquisition and exploitation of those core competences are all strategic issues beyond the scope of marketing and marketers. In this new era of rapid global technological development, the place of marketing may not be quite so dominating as it has been in the past. The old arguments about technology push and demand pull may today have a different outcome. Certainly, the innovations produced by the subjects of Hamel and Prahalad's enquiry are not of the 'bigger fins and stripes in toothpaste' variety. The strategy:marketing interface may be emerging from a period of relative confusion.

The real strategic issues remain the responsibility of general managers, not marketing managers. Nevertheless, it is to be hoped, the new general managers will always be imbued with the marketing philosophy.

BIBLIOGRAPHY

Alberts, W. W. (1989) 'The Experience Curve Doctrine Revisited', *Journal of Marketing*, July.
Boston Consulting Group (1968) 'Perspectives on Experience', Boston Consulting Group, Boston.
Bower, J. L. and Hout, M. (1988) 'Fast Cycle Capability for Competitive Power', *Harvard Business Review*, November–December, pp. 110–18.
Clark, K. B. (1989) 'What Strategy Can Do For Technology', *Harvard Business Review*, November–December.

Drucker, P. F. (1964) *Managing for Results*, New York: Harper & Row.

Gilbert, X. and Strebel, P. (1988) 'Developing Competitive Advantage' in J. B. Quinn, H. Mintzberg and R. M. James, (eds), *The Strategic Process*, Englewood Cliffs, NJ: Prentice-Hall.

Gilder, G. (1986) *The Spirit of Enterprise*, Harmondsworth: Penguin.

Gluck, F. W. (1985), 'A Fresh Look at Strategic Management', *Journal of Business Strategy*, Fall.

Hall, W. K. (1980) 'Survival Strategies in a Hostile Environment', *Harvard Business Review*, September–October.

Hamel, G. (1987) 'Corporate Strategies and Technological Cooperation', paper given to UACES Conference on European Technological Co-operation, Brunel University, 14 May.

Hamel, G. and Prahalad, C. K. (1989) 'Strategic Intent', *Harvard Business Review*, May–June.

Hamel, G. and Prahalad, C. K. (1993) 'Strategy as Stretch and Leverage', *Harvard Business Review*, March–April.

Hamel, G., Doz, Y. L. and Prahalad, C. K. (1989) 'Collaborate with Your Competitors – and Win', *Harvard Business Review*, January–February.

Kotler, P. (1984) *Marketing Management*, Englewood Cliffs, NJ: Prentice-Hall.

Miller, W. F. (1990) 'Technology and Global Strategy', *Strategic Direction*, January.

Mintzberg, H. (1987) 'The Strategy Concept', *California Management Review*, Fall, pp. 11–32.

Ohmae, K. (1989) 'Managing in a Borderless World', *Harvard Business Review*, May–June.

Ouchi, W. G. and Bolton, M. (1988) 'The Logic of Joint Research and Development', *California Management Review*, Vol. XXX, No. 3.

Pearson, G. J. (1992) *The Competitive Organisation*, Maidenhead: McGraw-Hill.

Peters, T. and Waterman, R. H. (1982) *In Search of Excellence*, NY: Harper and Row.

Porter, M. E. (1980) *Competitive Strategy: Techniques for Analysing Industries and Competitors*, NY: Free Press.

Porter, M. E. (1988) *Michael Porter on Competitive Strategy*, video film and pamphlet, Harvard Business School Video Series.

Prahalad, C. K. and Hamel, G. (1990) 'The Core Competence of the Corporation', *Harvard Business Review*, May–June.

Quinn, J. B., Doorley, T. L. and Paquette, P. C. (1990) 'Beyond Products: Services-Based Strategy', *Harvard Business Review*, March–April, pp. 58–68.

Ramo, S. (1989) 'National Security and Our Technology Edge', *Harvard Business Review*, November–December.

Selznick, P. (1957) *Leadership and Administration*, NY: Harper & Row.

Spekman, R. E. (1990) 'Buyer Seller Relations', *Strategic Direction*, February.

Telser, L. G. (1987) *A Theory of Efficient Cooperation and Competition*, Cambridge University Press, Cambridge.

CHAPTER 3

The Interface with Manufacturing

Leslie Nicol

INTRODUCTION

This chapter presents, first, an overview of the relationship between manufacturing and other parts of the organisation and the way this relationship has changed over a number of years, supported by an analysis of the role and purpose of the managers of manufacturing functions as perceived by themselves and by their peers in other functions. Based on an exposition of the nature of operations, the chapter then attempts to identify the interfaces between manufacturing and its external contacts, principally the markets for provision and consumption of its materials.

Some well-known marketing models as perceived from the manufacturing function are analysed, which readers may find will complement their understanding of these models from their own disciplinary perspective. A more inward-looking approach follows by defining the place of manufacturing strategy and developing a number of specific subordinate strategies within the manufacturing domain.

The discussion is then set in context by a detailed description of the concept of the 1990s, which is presented by some as the potential saviour of manufacturing operations and certainly the principal way manufacturing can give an organisation a competitive edge. This has been labelled 'world class manufacturing' by its originator and its impact is seen as extending well beyond the perimeters of the manufacturing departments themselves.

Finally, although the wider issues of forecasting are addressed in chapter 6, we try to look into the future by some limited extrapolations from current social and economic developments to assess whether these trends might have a major impact on the further pressures on manufacturing and its interface with marketing.

OVERVIEW
The task and the organisation

'Manufacturing's task is to provide, better than the company's competitors, those criteria which enable the products involved to win orders in the market-place.' (Hill, 1985).

This statement presupposes a definition of the marketplace, a definition of the product, and identification of the strategic position of the product in that market. Of course, the strategic development of corporate marketing objectives cannot be completed without consideration of product development and feasibility of manufacture. This is clearly, in most cases, a cyclic and iterative procedure. Failure to complete the cycle and repeat the iteration leads to undue dominance of one function (product design, manufacturing feasibility or marketing strategy) over the other two. Most companies, if they examine their consciences, can find examples of instances where such dominance occurred. In UK national terms, such imbalances have, historically, arisen in many industries.

Thus, the 1960s was the decade of production leadership, encouraged by short memories of the post-war surplus of demand over supply. Following a period of domination by accountants, the latter part of the 1970s and the greater part of the 1980s were typified by marketing ascendancy. We look forward to the rest of the 1990s with some confidence that customer orientation of manufacturing and of service provision will bring new hope.

These imbalances are reflected in the power and influence structure of the organisation, shown in Figs 3.1 to 3.4 by the information and influence flows. They are typical of the situations that existed in the scenarios outlined above. Fig. 3.1 represents the key elements of the supply of manufactured goods. Fig. 3.2 models a production-led organisation. Technical capability and capacity define the product from which, after limited interaction with the design team, its order-winning criteria are specified. The appropriate marketing policies are then developed to react to this product specification. Fig. 3.3 models a market-

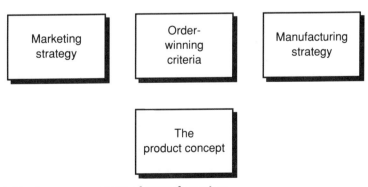

Fig. 3.1 The key components of manufacturing

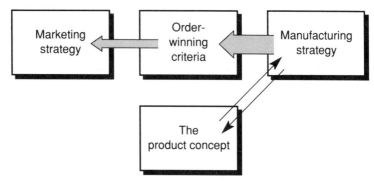

Fig. 3.2 Production-led

ing-led organisation. Definition from the marketplace of the product specification is imposed upon production, which is also required to respond to the order-winning criteria previously established. Fig. 3.4 models a product-led organisation. Sophisticated product development defines both the production organisation and the marketing policies. The common factor in all four models is the need for a clear definition of the order-winning criteria.

Perceptions of the role of manufacturing managers

From the descriptions above, the relative development of the major functions and the role of manufacturing in new product concepts, it can be seen that the status of the manufacturing manager is not always commensurate with that of the function. The decline in influence was not due solely to the increased competitiveness of world markets and the installation of additional capacity, or to the development of sophisticated financial and marketing analytical techniques.

Considerable research has been carried out to determine the dimensions of the present situation and its causes. The clearest analyses were carried out for the UK by Hill (1985) and internationally by Hayes and Wheelwright (1984).

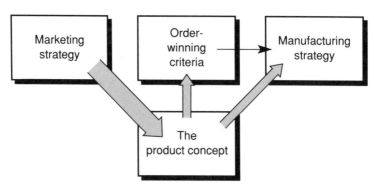

Fig. 3.3 Marketing-led

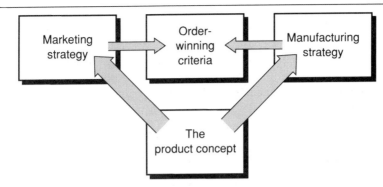

Fig. 3.4 Product-led

Manufacturing now occupies a reactive role in corporate strategy for some or all of the following reasons.

- *The manager's view of himself or herself*   The manager expects to respond to changes initiated elsewhere, rather than to create change. His or her recruitment and education (largely from engineering or problem-solving disciplines) reinforce this attitude.
- *The company's view of the manager*   He or she is expected to spend the majority of his or her time on short-term problems. This month's output generally has to take priority over next year's plans.
- *The manager is introduced too late into the debate*   Too many new product ideas are conceived by marketing and general management, with technical feasibility discussion with design, and are then submitted to manufacturing as (nearly) fully developed concepts. The opportunity for radical redevelopment may not exist.
- *The 'can't say no' syndrome*   Manufacturing takes a pride in being able to do anything and is expected to continue to do so. It is therefore expected not to say no to changes in volume variety, delivery or product.
- *Lack of language skills*   Perhaps by the nature of their tasks and the need to communicate with personnel of all levels of ability in direct and explicit terms, the opportunities to develop intellectual skills in articulation and debate (in particular on conceptual issues) are more limited than for sales, accounts, design or general management.
- *Functional goal definition*   Targets and goals may be expressed for the organisation in terms of financial value of sales revenue or profits, whereas the corresponding goals for production (of operator or machine performance, standard hour or machine hour content, etc.), are available only after a complex conversion process. The production manager uses different language and different units of measure from his peers.
- *Tenure*   In an age of increasingly short tenure of managerial positions, the period required to implement long-term strategy in manufacturing, which can exceed five years, may be seen as a career block or stagnation.

Although some of these reasons are less important now, their existence has been checked on a number of occasions and their consequences are widely recognised. Awareness of this decline in status has led to resentment by manufacturing of other higher-profile managers, much of it directed at marketing, so creating an immediate antagonism. This image of manufacturing has percolated into the City, where it was for many years a less than favourite sector, exaggerating the low availability of investment capital. In schools, the image has led to poor recruitment from the brighter school leavers (thus indirectly reinforcing one of the reasons given above for decline). The UK is not alone in this situation, but it contrasts unfavourably with other leading growth economies of recent years such as Germany and Japan.

THE INTERFACES

Manufacturing–marketing interdependence

In Skinner's (1983) traditional view of manufacturing problems, he identified the key issue as the trade-offs between one aspect of manufacturing's task and others. St John and Hall (1991) extended this to the trade-offs between manufacturing and marketing. The basic conflict is between customer response and cost consciousness, leading to the selection of either product-focused or differentiated strategies (customer responsive) or a cost leadership strategy (production responsive). Taking a more positive view, they have highlighted a number of areas of interdependence between what they regard as the two departments which most strongly influence the ultimate success or failure of the enterprise. These areas of interdependence are:

- Capacity planning and long-range sales forecasting: plant investment, which may take many months or even years to implement, depends on the success of marketing in translating uncertain market performance into realisable forecasts. Errors result in lost sales or overstocking and underutilised facilities.
- Production scheduling and short-term sales forecasting: rigid schedules prevent flexible customer responses. Frequent changes in sales requirements create increased costs, late deliveries and unstable inventory levels.
- Inventory and delivery speed: inventory is sought by manufacturing, to smooth variations in supply and demand, and by marketing, to provide flexible, fast customer service – but at a price.
- Quality assurance: manufacturing depends on marketing's ability to keep it up to date with additional or revised customer specifications and product features to ensure that both are working to a common purpose.
- Breadth of product range: the search for additional volume or markets may appear to be in direct conflict with manufacturing's desire to achieve focus in methods, facilities and skills.

- Cost control: especially when pricing is perceived to be an effective marketing tool, manufacturing will seek stable specifications, volumes and deliveries.
- Product development: a vital tool for continuing and extending the life cycle; may involve new plant, additional infrastructure problems and complex controls.

A general classification of operations

Manufacturing is only one aspect of the operations function, which can generally be divided into four major classes:

Class I   Manufacture, which is a change of *form*. In this the output is generally different from the input.

Class II   Transport, which is a change of *location*. The nature of input and output is generally identical.

Class III   Supply, which is a change of *possession*. The output is again generally identical to the input.

Class IV   Service, which is a change of *state*. In this there is a change or modification to the input.

All four types of operation can exist within both the manufacturing sector and the service sector. There are changes of form in the service sector as well as changes of state in the manufacturing sector, but manufacturing is principally associated with classes I and IV (change of form and of state) and the service sector more usually with classes II and III (changes of location and possession). Exhibit 3.1 gives examples.

Exhibit 3.1 Examples of the classification

Change of form
Machining and assembly of mechanical products
Making sandwiches

Change of location
Delivery of washing machines from factory to customer
Movement of commuters from suburb or further to city centre

Change of possession
Sale of copper futures in the commodity market
Issue of an invoice for manufactured goods

Change of state
Heat treatment, curing, testing or counting work in progress
Adding knowledge of holidays to enquirer at travel agency or reassurance to worried patient in doctor's surgery

Management of all these activities comes under the generic heading of operations management. An understanding of the existence of the four classes and their application in any particular company or industry is vital to the management of the interface between the operations function and all other management functions.

The emphasis of this chapter, however, is on the subset of operations that comprises manufacturing only. Especially in this area the term 'supply chain' is increasingly being used to describe the interfaces with external contacts. The four crucial interfaces are – in process order – the supplier, the pre-operations stock, the post-operations stock and the customer. There are two uncertainties: volumes and the products.

This chapter does not address the internal mechanisms and techniques by which manufacturing seeks to solve its problems, but the four interfaces and the two uncertainties are discussed in the sections that follow.

Interfaces and uncertainties
The first interface: the supplier and purchasing

The manufacturer/supplier relationship is, of course, the inverse of the seller/ customer relationship. The profit potential of an efficient purchasing department is, however, frequently underestimated. Consider the following product cost structure:

Materials	£40
Labour	£15
Overheads – fixed	£30
– variable	£15
Margin	£25
Selling price	£125

In order to increase total profit by 20 per cent (£5), it would be necessary to increase labour productivity by 33 per cent (generally unrealistic, unless present operations are inefficient); to increase sales volume by 20 per cent at constant prices or by 50 per cent with a 4 per cent promotional discount (perhaps possible in a growing market, but difficult elsewhere); to reduce overheads by 33 per cent (which would seriously destroy the infrastructure); or to save 12.5 per cent on the total raw materials bill by price reductions and substitutions.

The purchased material option is by far the most accessible way to increase company profit, and the response to this situation has been to adopt an aggressive purchasing policy. The key elements are an antagonistic approach to suppliers and strict adherence to the principles of dual sourcing.

The theory of dual sourcing is that it will keep suppliers insecure and therefore determined to improve service or reduce prices in order to retain the contract. Other benefits supposedly include additional cover in case of financial failure or industrial relations disputes with one supplier. But disadvantages are also significant. If industrial troubles hit one supplier, they are likely to be transferred to its competitors; if financial difficulties affect one firm, demand from its customers will tend to be transferred to the same limited range of competitors, creating supply shortages and price premiums. The lack of security frequently leads to demands for larger part tool costs or less enthusiastic commitment to product development and investment.

Antagonistic negotiation places emphasis on the personal skills of buyer and seller and reduces the rational-economic content of decision-making. It usually involves disseminating only the barest essential information. Manufacturing details are passed to suppliers only on a need to know basis (since they are also supplying the firm's competitors), to minimise opportunities for accidentally or intentionally revealing commercial secrets.

Manufacturing's view of supplier relationships has, however, undergone a major change in the last two decades. Although the change is not yet universally accepted, it is becoming increasingly prevalent and the effect on the marketing and sales functions will be dramatic when universally adopted.

The new view is that relationships with suppliers should be collaborative working partnerships. Since the profitability and survival of both organisations depend on the success of the same product, they have a common interest in the outcome. If a supplier has difficulties in meeting the requirements of the product a joint product development activity will result in improvements for both parties. It is becoming common for the larger of the two firms (or the more expert in key technologies) to use its skill and expertise to help to solve the other's internal problems. Use of common databases for scheduling and delivery of components is being introduced, especially in the automotive sector. Professional advice and consultancy on infrastructural systems may assist in the profitability and survival of the weaker. If one has debtor or cash-flow problems, the other may contribute its financial systems, credit references or debt-collection facilities. It is in the interests of neither for the other to fail.

The solution to such problems in the 1960s was acquisition and amalgamation of suppliers into vertically expanded groups. It is now, however, recognised that friendly association can produce similar systems benefits and retain the characteristics of enterprise and corporate identity that are vital to success.

The result of such close collaboration is to support the supplier, but also to place very clear requirements on it in terms of delivery, quality, price and specification. Such negotiations are frequently beyond the reasonable competence of sales representatives – they may need, and will frequently be required, to include industrial engineers, production managers and accountants in the negotiation team. Salespeople cannot be expected to make commitments for detailed aspects of other functions, except where the delivery specification is absolutely standard.

The second and third interfaces: inventory

There are two traditional views of inventory. The first is as a buffer to protect operations from the vicissitudes of the market and its own constraints by smoothing out the irregularities of supply and demand, imbalance in the production process and protection against natural and man-made disasters. The second view is as the independent variable in a mathematical function whose magnitude can be controlled by properly understanding the nature of the function. These may be described as the conservative and analytical approaches to inventory management. Both are valid.

It is useful, however, to take a broader, systems view of the function of inventory by looking at operations flows in a broad, although somewhat oversimplified way. We may regard the flow of activities in manufacturing as being from stock to operation and from operation to stock: S–O–S. This is the traditional manufacturing situation, where the factory uses both pre-process inventory and finished goods inventory to buffer itself from its environment.

There are occasions, however, when the two stock buffers disappear. Where a manufacturer has its own source of raw materials (not uncommon in pottery manufacture and with major steel producers), or a customer queue, other forms may be:

- direct supply from raw material source to operation and from operation to stock: D–O–S
- from stock to operation and from operation direct to customer: S–O–D.

Clearly, although the existence of stock buffers may have been developed principally for the benefit of manufacturing, the implications for marketing are equally significant. A finished stock buffer helps marketing and sales to offer independent delivery promises.

The absence of the finished goods buffer may result from a customer queue. Close collaboration becomes necessary, not only as to total capacity decisions, but also as to scheduling, priorities and lead time. It should also be noted by marketing managers that the form X-X-D does not prescribe the nature of the distribution channel, merely the absence of a stock buffer within it.

The absence of a raw materials buffer, similarly, may be created by shortage or rationing and has similar implications on the scheduling and control activities. Direct control of the supply of raw materials gives the manufacturer (the customer for its own supply facility) an extended scheduling problem, which is duly transmitted after modification or amplification by the production process, to the customer through marketing.

Critical changes occur when market or supply factors remove or return a queue to the supply chain. In these conditions the scale of the change can not be underestimated. It is no longer a change in magnitude of problem, but a change of order.

Currently there has been a great deal of interest in just-in-time (JIT) manufacturing management systems. These imply a flow direct from operation to customer (. . . O–D) and preferably also direct from the supplier: D–O–D. Manufacturing will not release goods from any stage in the process unless and until there is demand at the next stage. Simply put, this means no production until a sales order is received and no receipt of materials until a manufacturing order exists.

This concept, while possessing many advantages (release of working capital, reduction in obsolescence, concentration on methods and quality, etc.), is potentially also the greatest threat to marketing, and particularly sales. The nature of the threat lies in the ability to respond to fluctuations in volume, although there is a corresponding improvement in the ability to respond to changes in mix. Clearly, traditional methods are not capable of providing either type of flexibility and a major revolution in internal management methods is necessary before this new philosophy can be confidently embraced. The issue is discussed later in the context of world-class manufacturing, but it is important for marketing managers to note at this point that pressure to introduce JIT can easily be misplaced. Until manufacturing can cope with fast change-over and set-up times, without significant loss of efficiency, and move its culture away from the measurement of plant utilisation and towards customer service, JIT implementation should be deferred.

The fourth interface: the customer

It is not many years since the standard injunction to manufacturing was: 'Deliver the goods, but don't speak to the customer – that is sales' job.' This attitude has, fortunately, disappeared from most organisations. Where the customer has already introduced co-operative purchasing arrangements (as described above), it is likely that members of the manufacturing team will have met him or her before the contract was agreed. The trend towards job enrichment – giving a sense of meaning and purpose to operators' tasks – implies making them fully aware of the use and application of the work they carry out.

In many high-technology industries where orders are placed infrequently in relatively few large contracts, it has long been necessary for design and production personnel to play key roles in the negotiating and tendering team. In these industries the senior sales and marketing managers frequently have a production or engineering background. However, it is not being suggested that manufacturing should usurp the role of sales in contract negotiation. Generally, they have neither the time, the inclination nor the ability. Manufacturing personnel can, however, form a competitive advantage in selling (see Exhibit 3.2).

Customers need reassurance that the plant has the capability to deliver the goods that are being promised by sales. It is in this role that the manufacturing interface has most to offer. Visits by customers to the plant, meetings with key personnel, discussions about difficulties and mutual problem-solution are all ways in which the potential of the manufacturing function can be harnessed.

Exhibit 3.2 Manufacturing's role in sales negotiation

Butler & Newall, machine tool manufacturer, allocates a senior manufacturing manager to provide technical services to customers. This process includes confirming specifications (but not taking over the price and contracts negotiation from marketing), custom designing where necessary, supervising the installation and advising on the operation and use of the product, including designing parts of the supporting infrastructure.

There is another aspect of the customer interface which is often ignored. It is a sad fact that many firms still produce defective goods, or at least product that does not satisfy the customers' needs even if it meets their specification. It is important that all complaints, rejects, field failures, etc., should be passed to manufacturing as quickly as possible. The author functioned as production manager in a plant where all rejects and returns were held in the sales department for analysis and report, while being kept in ignorance of the fact that there was any problem at all. Except where they are highly trained and specialised, salespeople are not generally capable of making sound judgements as to all the possible causes of field failures or of making adjustments to the product to improve performance or rectify defects; they are never in a position to institute the necessary manufacturing checks and controls. It is vital for the most effective attention to after-sales service and rectification, either to have a dedicated team in full communication with manufacturing, or to have manufacturing members forming or participating in it.

The first uncertainty: forecasting

Manufacturing planning and scheduling depend on two factors. First, the relationship between the customer's lead time for delivery of the finished product and the supply and manufacturing lead time to produce it defines the inventory/production policy, as discussed above. Second, the accuracy and horizon of the prediction of customer demand determine all the decisions relating to the provision of plant, facilities and capacity.

Manufacturing managers inevitably demand accurate forecasts, precise by product type and variant over the longest possible period. This Utopian situation is recognised as unrealistic, but in the confrontational battle for resources is often used as a target or, in the event of failure, as an excuse. To manufacturing, the market forecasts are generally seen as optimistic or fictitious. The result is that manufacturing frequently apply their own rule-of-thumb modifier to everything emanating from the sales forecasting section, in order to establish their own planning criteria. If they are proved to have been pessimistic, there is a last-minute scramble for output and an increased emphasis on the reactive role described previously. If their pessimism is borne out by events, it reinforces the distrust and conflict between the two.

For new products, manufacturing are entirely in the hands of marketing in this respect. For established products, however, they have their own data of historical order intake, and frequently feel justified in carrying out a second forecasting activity using this history as a basis for predicting future trends. They do not, of course, use the results of marketing research activities, or take full cognisance of the potential of promotional activities. They do, however, through their own grapevine, frequently have knowledge of the performance and commitments of their competitors in the marketplace.

The issue of sales and production forecasts is seldom totally resolved and the pain of this interface continues.

Recent developments in organisational philosophy, which are discussed more fully later, both exacerbate and relieve the situation. Much has been made of the Japanese success with just-in-time (JIT) strategies. This implies no manufacturing until a customer has been identified. There is therefore no need for inaccurate short-term sales forecasts. Simultaneously, however, there is pressure for very short-notice delivery requirements. It becomes essential to establish a more flexible manufacturing facility and frequently to establish an apparent over-capacity in order to satisfy these short-term delivery requirements. The inevitable consequence of any plan to introduce JIT into a manufacturing/marketing company is the development of a close and trusting relationship between these two functions.

Brief mention should also be made of the trivial situation regarding forecasting. If the customer's lead time exceeds the time required to acquire capacity and materials and to complete the process of manufacture, the problem disappears unless it results in the permanent acquisition of capacity for which there will be no future demand.

The second uncertainty: product innovation

In the life cycle model to be discussed later, it is assumed that new products are available for development and innovation. At this stage the speed of introduction to the market could be critical, especially in view of the threat by competitors of 'leap-frogging' improvements and 'copy-cat' activities. A manufacturing involvement in and a rapid response to such product ideas are therefore essential. In most organisations, however, almost by definition, rapid new product innovation will be required to complement existing mature product manufacture. There is inevitably a need for a different kind of management system, including supervision, production and materials control, plant development and maintenance, and training for the innovatory product compared to the existing systems for established products.

Two solutions to this dilemma are commonly adopted and a third is becoming gradually accepted. First, the sales forecasts may be enhanced, giving indications of an opportunity to advance immediately into large-volume mature manufacturing systems. To achieve this it is necessary to lengthen the development period or to freeze the designs when further potential for product improvement still exists. The result could be late arrival in the market in high volume with an obsolescent product.

Second, a faster response could be achieved by the establishment of a separate small order unit with flexible tooling and methods and different operating systems. The result of this should be more rapid delivery, but at a very much higher cost. In a truly innovatory developing market, this may well be absorbed, but where the marketing strategy is one of substitution for existing products, the speed of entry may well be retarded by high unit pricing, or the whole enterprise may be threatened by unrealistically low margins.

The third approach is to attack the new product development cycle by using a set of techniques known variously as accelerators or concurrent engineering. The Rolls-Royce engine plant, for example, already specifies the requirements for sub-units of its product before the design to which they have to match has been completed. Provisioning and manufacturing planning also are initiated prior to finalising the 'sealed' design for other parts. The customer is in constant contact with purchasing and manufacturing engineering prior to the commencement of manufacture.

The issue highlights one of manufacturing's unsolvable problems: focus. Efficiency in production and control can be achieved by establishing a common purpose or focus throughout the organisation and especially within the manufacturing function. Traditionally, focus has been achieved through the use of common production technology creating the classical economies of scale. Focusing by product or design technology may produce conflicts in manufacturing – the same technology may be used for medium-volume commercial operations to a cost-based customer specification as for low-volume military operations based on maximum reliability in use in hostile field operations. Exhibit 3.3 provides examples.

Focus by management system creates the opportunity to match capability more closely to customer needs. It is probably the logical direction to move in the current market, but carries severe penalties in dual infrastructures and in conversion to mature market production systems when the time is right.

Much depends on whether the organisation has chosen to be an initiator or imitator. In the latter case it may well be necessary to extend development time in order to be able to enter the market with price and volume advantages over the existing leaders. Many techniques have been developed to shorten the new product lead time, discussed by Nayak (1991), Cooper and Kleinschmidt (1991) and others. Indeed, a new discipline has recently been developed to achieve this, variously called 'simultaneous' or 'concurrent engineering'. The concept of project teams has been used for years to give ownership to and obtain commitment from all those involved. This has been given a further boost by the 'World Class' concept, discussed later.

From the marketing point of view it is realistic to develop in many directions

Exhibit 3.3 Focus by technology: Louis Newmark and Fiat Auto

In the late 1970s Louis Newmark used sophisticated electronic technology to produce helicopter controls for the Ministry of Defence and commercial knitting machine controllers selling into a highly competitive domestic market – the result of a diversification programme. With both products being assembled in the same facility, different manufacturing standards reduced the flexibility of labour and equipment while competition for limited resources created the impression of a permanent 'poor relation' for one product group.

In an attempt to focus design and manufacturing technology on to the structural features of its vehicles, Fiat Auto produced a common angle for the rear windscreen for a number of different models. Although disguised by additional features of roof and boot, this profile produced a similarity detected by customers and hindered the company's attempts to maintain product discrimination. It was not until it used even more advanced computer-aided engineering and design systems that Fiat was able to introduce easily manufactured structural differences and restore the uniqueness of each model.

simultaneously, with a degree of confidence based on past success that some of the projects will be successful. Thus there may be a five-year plan showing, say, 25 per cent of business in five years' time coming from one of a selection of new products. This gives the opportunity for long-term decision-making in marketing, finance and strategic areas. However, if the ultimate selection is not made for three years, it leaves manufacturing once again in its reactive role struggling to survive in a two-year lead time.

The uncertainty of new product innovation is thus, first, 'Which product (and therefore which plant, technology and skills) will we be manufacturing?' and, second, 'Will the initial forecasts be accurate and will we be able to retain the existing focus within the organisation?'

MARKETING MODELS AS PERCEIVED FROM MANUFACTURING

There are many sophisticated analytical tools for examining the methodology and success of the marketing function. We discuss here three of these which have a direct impact on the manufacturing function.

Order winning

The familiar selling/marketing concept of the unique selling proposition is well developed and widely understood. As normally postulated, it is very much a proactive marketing tool and a reactive manufacturing response. However, with no change in concept and only a slight change in wording, it has been readdressed by Hayes and Wheelwright (1985) in the United States and by Hill (1985) in the UK as a definition of order-winning criteria. The emphasis is taken from the selling proposition to order winning, i.e. a company-wide dimension. Coupled with this is the acceptance of a distinction between 'qualifying' and 'order winning'.

A qualifying criterion is one which is an essential prerequisite to obtaining orders, but not one which will distinguish between one competitive product and another. In recent years some aspects of quality have ceased to be of any order-winning significance in many industries and markets. Without these defined quality aspects, customers will not even consider placing an order but, with them, they will still look for other distinctive order-winning criteria.

As perceived from manufacturing, the order-winning criteria are likely to include the following:

- product features
- delivery reliability
- delivery speed
- quality
- price
- design and product flexibility
- product reliability
- technical design
- form and aesthetic design
- after-sales service and product upgrading.

All of these can be influenced strongly or totally provided by the manufacturing function. Of course, there are other aspects over which manufacturing have no control, including the marketing and sales team and personalities, and the promotional package.

Although it is fair to say that without a marketing function manufacturing would have nothing to produce, it is also recognised, certainly within manufacturing, that their performance at the least constrains the ability of marketing to perform; at the most, it dictates the parameters within which marketing must operate.

This scenario, then, provides the background to conflict between the two key functions of business: marketing and operations. In its internal self-analysis, manufacturing has come to appreciate the importance of the value added concept. In this regard, it accepts that roles such as inventory management, production control, inspection and performance monitoring do not add value. Similarly, but controversially, manufacturing generally believes that marketing activities also fail to add value to the goods or service.

The interface in these areas is absolutely crucial to collaborative success. First, even the most blinkered pro-manufacturing devotee has to accept that for a clear understanding of the customer's view of order-winning criteria, the special knowledge of the marketing function is essential. The definition of the terms of reference of the criteria must be jointly established.

Carrying out an analysis of the profile of a product's position with respect to each of the potential order-winning criteria as perceived and provided by manufacturing and as perceived and expected by marketing can reveal areas of mismatch which could prove expensive to overcome in market terms and at the least would result in failure to conform to customer requirements. Indeed, extending such profiles to include both the customers' and suppliers' perceptions should complement the analysis and complete the chain.

If delivery speed is what the customer requires in a particular market, it cannot be provided without the active commitment of manufacturing. The inevitable corollary is that unless, and frequently even if, manufacturing are involved in making provision from the outset, there will be a trade-off between this criterion and other criteria. Short or instant delivery can be provided by distributing from stock, but this will carry a risk of obsolescence (affecting the product features offered) and stockholding cost (affecting the selling price) and will limit the flexibility to change or upgrade the product.

Thus conflict can and frequently does arise through the interface as a result of failure to communicate adequately the terms of reference or misunderstanding as to their bases. The excessive influence of manufacturing on the provision of the order-winning criteria can be frustrating to marketing and sales personnel. This frustration can lead to misplaced initiatives in varying the criteria. For instance, a responsible sales representative, sent into the marketplace with a price list which includes both high and low-volume items and with a knowledge of prime cost, factory cost and product margins, will expect to be allowed discretion in negotiating quantities and process. Exhibit 3.4's two examples from personal experience show the potential for conflict and its possible consequences.

The examples show the wisdom of further consultation with manufacturing, in the first case about actual manufacturing costs, and methods instead of theoretical prime costs and in the second case about total annual manufacturing budgets and utilisation. Joint development of future plans to the benefit of the company rather than the function could have achieved a more profitable result.

Product life cycle

We owe to marketing planners, Kotler (1991) and others, the understanding of the concept of the product life cycle (shown in Fig. 3.5) from introduction to growth to maturity to decline.

At the same time, strategic analysis has confirmed the importance of the experience curve, which shows that over a succession of progressive products and, to a lesser extent, within one product, the accumulated volume history of manufacture and supply can lead to a reduction in cost.

Exhibit 3.4 Conflict between manufacturing and marketing

AEI Switchgear (an old example, but still valid)
A high-volume range of switches selling at a price of approximately £2.50 in 1992 terms also had a special range with different terminations, involving slightly less material and labour and hence an intrinsically lower prime cost *when produced in volume*. Production was, however, carried out in a special, low-volume facility and the pricing decision had been to offer at a small premium of only 25p, pitched to appear credible to the customer and to indicate future opportunities. However, a representative obtained a large order on standard delivery terms at this price with a promise to renegotiate downwards to reflect the lower material costs. To supply the customer, the only choices open to manufacturing were to produce in the special facility at a realistic selling price of over £4 (no economies of scale); to integrate with the current high-volume line at a probable selling price of over £3 (interference with rhythm, additional inspection and defects and loss of performance); or to establish volume facilities, taking advantage of the learning process, and in about six months to offer the modified product at a price of £2.25 to £2.40 (after allowing for re-tooling and the conversion of other customers to the new product). This situation caused inevitable tension over the control of the delivery and price criteria.

ITT Components Group
An electronic component manufacturer, during the run-up to a recession, authorised the sales team to sell unused capacity on one production line, during the final three months of the financial year, at a minimal margin over prime cost. This was seen as a effective way to recover a limited amount of overhead cost and reduce potential losses to the business. However, armed with this knowledge, some of the sales force took orders against the core capacity for the new financial year and failed to prevent customer expectations of continued bargains. This clearly gave rise to under-recovery of overheads and a loss on that product group, jeopardising the job security of the manufacturing personnel involved.

An example from the computer industry is shown in Fig. 3.6.

The development of the product through the stages of its life is stimulated if not driven by marketing. The impact of these stages on manufacturing is a reaction to this development. With each new phase, the market definition changes and the qualifying and order-winning criteria change also. As the product develops, its demands on manufacturing change and the ability of manufacturing to produce and satisfy the defined order-winning criteria may also change. Manufacturing's tactical challenge (and in some cases its strategic challenge) is to maintain these criteria in pace with their development in the marketplace.

Although there are exceptions in specific industrial sectors, at the introductory stage with products made to order or for pilot marketing and a developing

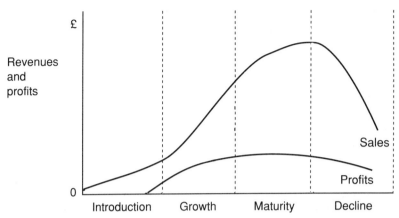

Fig. 3.5 The product life cycle

specification and technology, the emphasis for manufacturing will generally be on flexibility, technical and customer liaison and performance. This requires a flexible manufacturing control system, multi-purpose production units, self-inspection and the use of craft skills, innovative production engineering, low plant utilisation and a versatile labour force. This is summarised, with the other stages, in Table 3.1.

During the growth stage, with developing volumes and consolidation of ranges and designs, the manufacturing emphasis is on developing standards and quality, investment in volume production resources, reduction of delivery (and throughput) time in order to obtain new business, development of control systems and specification of all processes, materials and operations.

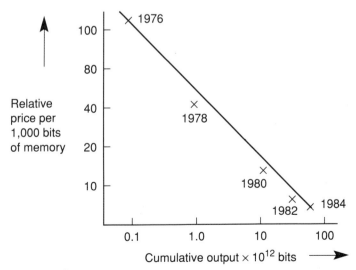

Fig. 3.6 An experience curve

Manufacturing will generally attempt to anticipate the move into maturity. It is a concept with which most production staff are comfortable, even though it may lead to further conflict about range, variety and volumes. The manufacturing effort is concentrated on increasing sophistication of systems and procedures, on cost reduction and quality, with limited flexibility, while the market may demand ever increasing flexibility in order to maintain market share in an ever more competitive environment.

In the decline phase, manufacturing will be directed at increasing quality and reliability of performance, flexibility to extend ranges and the development of unique product identities.

It can be seen from this that the emphasis on cost, on control systems and on flexibility and variety changes continuously throughout the life of the product. Perhaps the key interface with manufacturing is to ensure that they are kept informed on progress and life cycle development. Competitor research and summarised market research made available to manufacturing would enable strategic plans to be made in parallel with the reactive response to long-term sales forecasts.

The experience curve owes the steepness of its slope partly to improved efficiency of manufacturing methods but more to the development of new materials, technology and processes from one product family to its successor. Significant savings (of the order of 10 per cent per annum) can frequently be generated by the use of effective method study techniques both before and during manufacture. However, the real benefits of the experience curve phenomenon arise when the firm takes advantage of new developments in technology, whether developed in its own plant or elsewhere.

Although primarily a marketing approach, it must be recognised that the productive system develops along with the product through its life cycle, as shown in Table 3.1.

Table 3.1 Product life cycle

Phase	Volume	Focus	Controls	Flexibility	Investment
			Characteristic		
Innovation	Unit	Product	Project or job shop	High	Product technology
Growth	Batch	Delivery	Production control (e.g. MRP)	Moderate	Production
Maturity	High-volume	Cost	Systems and cost reduction	Low	Systems
Decline	Continuous	Stability	Systems and cost reduction	Little	None

Other models – product profiles and trade-offs

It has been quite common to develop product market profiles on a two-dimensional grid. An international television manufacturer presented its product profile to a group of managers as consisting of only two key factors: price and picture definition. All competitors were placed on this simple matrix and market positions were manipulated by product development reinforced by the promotional package. Similarly, manufacturing managers have been brought up to believe in simple trade-offs, for instance between cost and quality or between volume and flexibility.

The increasing sophistication of the market has proved the product profile model to be inadequate, while a better understanding of manufacturing strategy has rendered the trade-off model obsolete. However, both models still exist in the minds of managers and, more importantly, are attributed by managers in one function to their counterparts in the other as reasons for their lack of understanding of the competitive opportunities that are available.

Conclusion

As can be seen from the discussion above, the significance of both the order-winning criteria model and the product life cycle model to manufacturing differs from that for marketing. In a well-balanced and fully integrated organisation such divergence should not arise. However, in a traditional, functionally organised company, such identity of purpose is frequently achieved by accident rather than design. The development of a comprehensive corporate strategy should ease the problems of mismatch but, unless accompanied by further structural developments, may not eliminate it.

STRATEGY FOR MANUFACTURING

Generic strategies

Porter (1985) and others have identified three principal and different generic strategies for business:

- overall cost leadership
- differentiation (of product)
- market segmentation (or differentiation of customer).

These three strategies are generally mutually exclusive, except in special circumstances. For instance, cost leadership implies reduction of product unit cost to below that of any competitor in the market. To achieve this some economy of scale is necessary, with an accompanying loss of flexibility. It may be possible also to produce specials for individual customers or models, but they will not enjoy the same cost advantage and therefore the cost leadership will have been lost. Similarly, differentiation by product or market implies giving special consideration to individual characteristics and losing the cost advantage for the sake of establishing a specialist or 'niche' position.

Although all functions within the organisation have to work together to follow successfully any of the three strategies, the importance of manufacturing in achieving industry-wide cost leadership is paramount. However, cost leadership is not synonymous with manufacturing cost reduction. A large part of the cost improvement comes from following the 'experience curve'.

The experience curve identifies the rate of learning and the hypothesis is that the more manufacturing experience an organisation has accumulated, the lower will be its unit cost. The firm with the largest market share will produce the largest number of units and will have the lowest cost, *if all competitors are on the same slope of experience curve*. If, through knowledge of process technology, a firm can establish itself on a superior experience curve, it will have lower costs than its competitors *even if they all have the same cumulative experience*.

A firm with greater experience can use a more aggressive pricing policy to gain a greater market share because its existing experience has given it a price advantage. The greater market share should yield additional cash for investment in plant and this aggressive process technology policy can then be used to allocate resources towards mechanisation in earlier stages of product life and to automation in its later stages to maintain the position on the experience curve or to improve its slope. But the benefits will run out due to product obsolescence unless the firm can reinvest its advantage in the development of the next generation of products and processes, i.e. take advantage of its experience curve superiority. This moves the experience curve on to a new lower level and internal process cost-reduction improvements can then be used to gain further incremental improvements until the next substantial change can be achieved.

Manufacturing must then drive the improvements through a series of incremental and technological steps to maintain their competitive advantage.

In the face of a competitor with superior experience, most companies seek a position in a market or product specialism or have to accept lower operating margins and less reinvestment (see Exhibit 3.5).

If the product is set in an international market, the effects of exchange rate movements, where the cost of the factors of production is favourable to the international competitor, can mask the differential productivity advantage gained by the experience effect, or where the movement is favourable to the home producer, can assist it. Nevertheless, temporary exchange advantages have generally been overtaken in the long term by the inevitability of cost leadership experience.

If the firm has followed a cost leadership strategy, the implications of productivity improvement and cost reduction are especially crucial. The key platform of operations strategy thus becomes productivity improvement. The

Exhibit 3.5 The Canon/Xerox contest

Rank Xerox had a dominant position in the dry copier market and with it had acquired economies of scale and cost leadership. However, when Canon entered the market with a simpler product that permitted not only a lower cost but also different distribution channels (using retailer/distributor networks instead of in-house distribution and servicing), Xerox's position deteriorated in a very short time. It had not taken full advantage of its opportunities on the experience curve (the use of latest technology). It still dominated, through experience, its established market (customers who expect the entire supply chain to be dominated by the prime provider) but, by using experience to make only incremental improvements, it had missed the technological leap that allowed Canon's 'niche' (simple, open technology products) to become the new principal market. It now had to accept leadership of a delivery market or follow Canon on to a new experience curve for a new product and market.

experience curve will not operate unmanaged. The choice of productive system, control systems and technology must be consciously made.

Specific manufacturing strategies

Manufacturing decisions arise at a number of different levels. The first order of decision arises from the corporate mission and philosophy of the firm. This may frequently bind manufacturing (willingly or unwillingly) to employment or environmental policies, to the adoption of a quality philosophy (whether known as 'total quality' or by any other name) and to a technological goal.

On the basis of these overriding principles, the organisation then develops corporate marketing and financial strategies, and manufacturing integrates, feeds back and iterates its own strategic decisions. The manufacturing strategy decision areas (discussed in detail below) will generally include process choice, capacity, location and infrastructure.

The third level of decision (tactical or operational), which the chapter does not address in detail, includes scheduling, materials and inventory management, quality assurance, planning and performance and productivity. The following discussion relates only to strategic level decision-making, which must be carried out within the context of the corporate philosophies. Tactical issues, although having vital interfaces with marketing, are left to specific manufacturing texts, such as Buffa (1987), Hill (1991), Muhlemann (1992) and Schroeder (1989).

Process choice

There are four principal decision areas.

First, and perhaps simplest, is the selection of the appropriate technology. In innovative production this will have been part of the marketing/design/development process and should have been done jointly with manufacturing and with equipment suppliers. However, especially with mature products and processes, this decision involves matching the batch size requirements, the variability of output, the training needs of operators and setters, the availability of plant and personnel and the reliability of the equipment. This, in turn, depends on the market size and segmentation decisions, developed from marketing research and product concept evaluations. (See Exhibit 3.6.)

Exhibit 3.6 The Boffin approach

Until very recently, a major chemical manufacturer pursued its new product policy by encouraging laboratory and research-driven developments without market analysis. When a new chemical or drug had been produced, it was delivered to the marketing department to search for commercial applications. The 'solution looking for a problem' approach is still very attractive to inventors, especially those with high scientific and technical knowledge who see technology as the saviour of their industry. To this group can be added those who, like Sinclair with his electric tricycle, develop a product with an application, but without the necessary supporting marketing research.

Second is the decision whether to make or buy the component or product. This is a crucial issue of control as well as cost. In innovative or unique operations, it can make the firm vulnerable to have to depend on external suppliers for a part of the business that is crucial to success. In this respect, the decision is similar to decisions to delegate one's personal work to subordinates. The loss of control may be not only over the technology, but also over the prioritisation of production. In many cases, however, the process may be incompatible with current processes and skills, may impede harmonious relationships and may carry excessive needs for indirect support and overheads. The cost issue is also seldom as simple as it appears: costs of bought goods may be simply stated, even if they include contributions to tooling and establishment costs, but those of internal or domestic manufacture depend very much on the design of the management accounting system and, in particular, the allocation or absorption of overheads. The impact of this decision on marketing, and the contribution of marketing to it, are generally limited. However, where there is significant vertical integration of suppliers and customers, or where there is a brand or product image associated with the supplier which can be used either positively or negatively as part of the product package, the marketing interface may become acute.

The third area of process choice, and generally the most strategic, is that of organisational design. The choice of layout, management and system to support either a process-orientated structure, a product structure or a group cellular structure is both fundamental and crucial for success. The outputs from such organisations dictate in part the response to order-winning criteria requirements and must reflect these needs.

The fourth dimension of the process choice decision is positioning on the volume/variety matrix shown in Fig. 3.7. (See also Exhibit 3.7.) Although the position of the product on this matrix may heavily influence the choice of process, product or group management system, the two decisions are not consequential, and both must be made deliberately. Too often such decisions have been made by default.

Exhibit 3.7 Variety domain: Land Rover

The largest end of the variety decision is typified by Land Rover. Having lost the product uniqueness of the Range Rover to lower-cost models from the Pacific Rim and to rough, off-road vehicles, also based on military jeeps, it decided to introduce a new range of vehicles: the Discovery. This increased the range of products, and the volume, but capitalised on the product knowledge already existing in the organisation. However, most variety decisions are associated with additional variants within a range, rather than extra products outside it.

In general, the process of manufacture may be simplified to that of converting a set of inputs into a set of outputs. The inputs will be in the form of people, energy, materials, information and fixed assets of various kinds. The outputs will be in the form of goods and services.

In manufacturing industry, the mix of goods and services will be dominated by goods, but even here an element of service always exists in the output. The process choice decision must be confirmed after iteration with the other strategic manufacturing decisions and particularly with the infrastructure which pro-

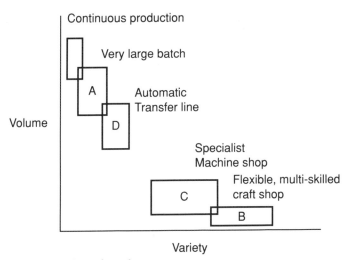

Fig. 3.7 Volume/variety domain

vides most of the service elements of the product package, before feeding back and iterating with other corporate decisions.

Capacity decisions

The determination of capacity comes at an early stage in the strategic planning of manufacturing. This has to be an early decision because capacity provision lead times tend to be significantly greater than any others. Incremental expansion can generally be organised at short notice but, even where only limited, its effect on the balance of workload and the use of the infrastructure can be significant. Large-step function changes in volume depend generally on the acquisition or extension of premises, where planning programmes tend to be in years rather than months.

The key decisions on capacity are whether to anticipate market needs or to follow them and whether to mirror the market forecasts or to prepare separate forecasts based on different assumptions. Following market growth means that at all times the capacity is insufficient to meet demand and has to be supplemented by subcontract work, overtime or partnership arrangements. Anticipating market growth means that, in general, the plant will be manufacturing at less than its full capacity and thus some economies of scale may not be deliverable. Figs 3.8 and 3.9 illustrate this point.

Production overload can produce problems with plant maintenance, pressures on output (at the expense of quality) and premium payments, with a risk of late delivery and deterioration of reputation. Production underload can produce, if not carefully supervised, inefficient working practices and negative production cost variances.

Location decisions

The strategic nature of this decision lies in two factors. First, relocation is an infrequent event, with a longer lead time than is involved in most other decisions. Second, apart from the distribution logistics implied by the decision, the

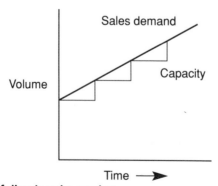

Fig. 3.8 Capacity following the market

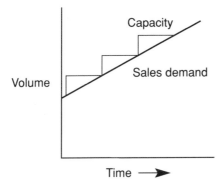

Fig 3.9 Capacity anticipating the market

nature of the premises acquired may constrain the process choice decisions to be made in the future or burden the final operation with unnecessary overhead and handling costs. Thus, it can have a massive influence on long-term profitability of the enterprise.

The traditional factors surrounding the location decision may be analysed as follows. First, the size of the facilities required can often be extrapolated from current performance (square metres per head or per unit of sales, etc.). The result of this analysis, when combined with market forecasts, is a need to establish additional capacity or to relinquish some of the existing. Second, the geographical logistics network is again, but even more sensitively, related to market forecasts, as it takes into account the potential distribution costs from manufacturing site to market location. In the case of national networks with multi-plant production, this is a particularly complex operations research problem. Introducing margins of error in each of the factors will produce the most robust solution, again dependent on forecasts, but also on operations performance in manufacturing and transport. Exhibit 3.8 provides an illustration.

Exhibit 3.8 A relocation decision

The decision of the Japanese motor manufacturers to locate in Western Europe, while dominated largely by political issues related to the European Community, also had a significant logistics element within it. The need to have manufacturing resource within one of its key markets was supported by the need to have an available workforce with an engineering background, but not possessing any of the entrenched attitudes of the established motor industry led them to establish plants in the North-East of England and the north Midlands. They now have access to component and service industries and a willing and trainable pool of skilled labour.

Focus decisions

One of the key side-effects of adopting either product differentiation or market segmentation as a principal generic strategy is the opportunity they both create for developing focus. The basis of facilities focus decisions may be a separation by volume (high or low) or by process (nature of technology involved). The benefits for improvement of manufacturing systems include concentration of skilled personnel, economies of scale, flexibility, standardisation, development of customised special-purpose plant and simpler infrastructural requirements. However, the organisation may decide to establish focus by market or even by customer which could produce benefits including responsiveness, new product introduction, quotation/pricing procedures and potential segmentation opportunities. Clearly, there is again a conflict of interest. Potential penalties also attach to focus decisions and the corporate dimension may overrule both manufacturing and marketing preferences (see Exhibit 3.9).

Exhibit 3.9 A focus decision: Raleigh

The introduction of the mountain bike was initially rejected by the UK brand leader (Raleigh). Apart from market opportunity myopia, the new product would have been seen to be substantially different in its manufacturing characteristics and therefore in its manufacturing focus. The product, if successful, would also have created a new market segment – of rough country users (adventurous children, hikers, etc.) in conflict with the road user (town children and serious cylists), purchaser of the existing product.

With the nature of much of modern manufacturing industry and its trend towards universal markets for high-technology products, rapid transport and delivery systems, reduced material content and high value added, many of the old location criteria are now obsolete. However, there are still a few situations where the nature of the raw material and its transportability constrain the choice of site to the regions in which the key resource is abstracted or manufactured. Similarly, fashion or obsolescence factors may dictate that the plant be relocated close to a critical mass of customers. These issues are, however, now rare.

Infrastructure decisions

The manufacturing infrastructure is the provision of indirect support in the form of production control, storekeeping, materials handling, inspection and test, cleaning, welfare services, etc. It is not proposed to expand on these in great detail at this point except to note their vulnerability to changes from strategic decisions. However, it is important to note the dependence of the infrastructure design on the nature of the market and its interface (see Exhibit 3.10).

Exhibit 3.10 An infrastructure decision: Direct Line Insurance

When Direct Line Insurance was launched by a major financial group without the traditional broker network, it was challenging the need for the existing infrastructure network. A different set of supporting services was created which Direct Line was able to use, not only to reduce the cost of its service but also as a feature in its promotional activities. Thus the selection of infrastructure benefited both manufacturing (in this case called, more generally, operations) and marketing.

Many infrastructural decisions are, however, merely tactical or operational – the result of cost-cutting measures or reorganisations driven by personal or political considerations.

The existence of a large number of small orders with individual customer requirements can demand the introduction of a sophisticated computer-based production control system where for steady volumes of standard products a simple manual scheduling procedure would have been adequate. Similarly, simultaneous manufacture of a wide product range can lead to low utilisation of equipment and facilities or significant maintenance and setting/resetting time. Frequent changes of delivery requirement or short-notice delivery requests may involve establishing overtime routines, evening shifts or duplicate production lines. Any of these can also lead to a significant increase in stores of both finished goods and work in progress, thus tying up capital which could otherwise be used to develop new markets, new products or improved processes.

A cellular or autonomous work group manufacturing organisation should minimise works paperwork and change the emphasis of inspection duties from monitoring to training. The adoption of product lines will reduce materials handling but put more pressure on urgent maintenance attention to plant breakdown and servicing. The concept of world-class manufacturing (discussed below) is aimed at simplifying the infrastructural complexities of the organisation. Even where this target is neither appropriate nor possible, some progress towards it may result in considerable benefits within a conventional organisation.

Thus the nature of the infrastructure depends heavily on the nature of the market and the customer response within it.

WORLD-CLASS MANUFACTURING

The concept

A traditional view of manufacturing is that it exists to provide a service which marketing can then offer in the marketplace, and that the pursuit of competitive advantage should rest with the design of the product and the elements of the marketing mix.

A new philosophy has been developed, however: that manufacturing can be a competitive weapon in business, not merely a tool to support the marketing initiative. The most cogent exposition of this philosophy has been developed by Richard J. Schonberger (1987), entitled 'World Class Manufacturing' (WCM). It encapsulates much that is best in current Japanese and British views of manufacturing excellence.

WCM's motto is 'Continuous and rapid improvement', and it replaces the pragmatic practice of trade-offs of success in one aspect of the manufacturing system against inadequate performance in one or more other aspects with the concept of excellence in all.

Management style was formerly one of 'managing by numbers' and was achieved by:

- supervision – to get more output from the same resource
- work study or industrial engineering – to carry out studies and analyses.
- operations research – to develop optimising practices encapsulating the trade-off principle
- systems – to manage by the establishment of standard, usually inflexible, control techniques and practices.

WCM aims for excellence by attaching attention to its three basic precepts:

(1) The smaller the batch size the better (JIT – just-in-time systems).
(2) Do it right first time (TQC – total quality control).
(3) Maintain so often and so thoroughly that equipment hardly ever breaks down (TPM – total preventive maintenance).

These are executed in the environment of employee involvement (EI).

The move towards WCM has come from two directions. In the 'Japanese culture' enormous progress has been made in the last two decades towards establishing the quality ethic, using as the principal engine of progress the collaboration and co-operation of all employees. Simultaneously, a number of firms followed Toyota's lead towards reduction of batch sizes. Thus, they achieved a standard of excellence which Schonberger's model to a large extent reproduced. However, this was completed largely in the environment of continuous or large batch production, using product management systems.

Meanwhile, the Western (primarily American) emphasis and world leadership lay in the improvement of 'job shop' or multi-product environments, where the rigours of independent demand procurement constrained many infrastructural activities. This inspired a philosophy of technological excellence and emphasised the need to implement trade-offs. Schonberger's genius was to recognise that the Japanese philosophy could equally be transposed on to his own industrial scenario.

Dedicated flow lines are natural JIT applications (but not the only way to achieve JIT). When capacity is cheap dedicated JIT lines make sense. The alternative task is to balance the inevitable mismatch between production schedules and customer orders.

The three precepts listed above are not seen as systems to be optimised, but as cultural styles and philosophies which should enable the organisation to satisfy customer requirements. Schonberger summarises this with the motto: 'If World Class Manufacturing effort fails to make it easier for Marketing, then something is wrong.' Consistent with the precepts, it is possible to define a set of subsidiary goals for WCM:

- reduce deviation from zero defects
- reduce deviation from zero manufacturing lead time
- reduce variability of product variables (dimensions, etc.)
- reduce variability of product attributes (finish, appearance, etc.)
- reduce variability of delivery lead time.

In order to appreciate the potential of WCM as a marketing advantage, it is important to understand how it affects the internal operation both of manufacturing and of the rest of the organisation.

Application of WCM to functional activities
Direct employee operations for WCM

Perhaps the single greatest impact of WCM on operations is the concept of 'no blame'. Research by Deming (1986) and others has identified that 85 per cent of shop-floor faults are caused by management, systems and external factors outside the operator's control. When this is accepted, it is a small (but difficult) step to move to an open relationship in which faults and errors are accepted without blame, and with a commitment to work jointly to remove or eliminate the cause.

The clearest demonstration of this application is the amount of control given to operators themselves over the rate of progress. They may have the power to stop the process of manufacture in the event of difficulties or defects, without sanction, and the entire operations team can use the incidents when such powers are exercised as a source of information leading to the analysis and elimination of the cause. Public display of this analysis can be used to focus attention, not on failures, but on achievements.

Implicit in this type of approach is the elimination of direct, volume-related incentive payment schemes coupled with an increased emphasis on other aspects of the performance of unit or team. The existence of the team and its members' pride in its achievement are the cornerstones of plant-level WCM.

A vital corollary to this is the communication system and employee involvement in communication. Schonberger quotes the example of a machine toolmaking plant, where an audit sheet on permanent (updated) display at each section shows the following factors rated according to agreed standards:

- the arrangement of operations in the workplace
- the management of stock (if any) at the workplace
- the management of equipment and tools

- inspection status and results
- systems of self-control and management of processes to guarantee quality
- manuals and notices.

This display is designed to develop a feeling of ownership of the process, pride in its achievement and involvement in the task.

Implementing WCM in the workplace also leads to a change in operator tasks and skills, as shown in Table 3.2.

Table 3.2 Skill changes

Old	New
Skill is in the set-up	Skill is in simplifying the set-up
Technicians and engineers involved regularly in action	Operators lead the actions, technicians help, advise and train
Operator watches the machine run	Operator thinks about next improvement
Assembly jobs simplified for unskilled labour	Assemblers acquire: • multiple skills • data-collection duties • diagnosis and problem-solving talents

In summary, the trend should be to take the skill out of the job and develop the skill of the mind. This should be contrasted with the simplistic interpretation of Taylor's (1911) 'principles of scientific management', which resulted in deskilling the operator but having nothing to substitute, i.e. leaving impotent, system-controlled machine minders.

Indirect staff in WCM

Consistent with the development of individual involvement and excellence, the emphasis should always be on carrying out skilful or thinking tasks, not on robotic or routine ones. Collecting data is a routine activity; analysis and decision-making are exciting and self-fulfilling.

Technical staff should be 'on call', preferably on the operating floor at all times and not shut away in executive offices. Operators are trained to carry out routine and simple non-routine tasks (for which they would otherwise have relied on specialists) and, more important, to know when to call in the specialist for assistance.

The objective is simplified manufacturing which requires better support from fewer people. The effects on key support staff include the following.

- *Maintenance* Operators are trained to replace maintenance in basic tasks, leaving the skilled personnel to analyse problems and carry out major overhauls only.

- *Management accountants* There should be no waste costs to collect and fewer indirect staff to account for. Therefore there would be smaller amounts of overhead to allocate, a simpler allocation procedure and fewer disputes (with smaller overheads, it matters less in which cost centre they are absorbed).
- *Quality assurance* Statistical process control can be carried out by the operators who are trained in analysis and interpretation. Thus, quality assurance personnel will be able to concentrate on audit and test.
- *Materials management* If the management system adopted is one of autonomous work groups, using the principles of group technology (Burbidge, 1975) and cell systems, there is no need (as in a continuous flow product line) for complex internal scheduling and progress. Ultimate targets may then be to eliminate handling, storage, counting and even, in some cases, conveyors.
- *Data processing* There willl be less data to collect and simpler systems of data analysis because of the lower needs of operations, accounts and materials.

Although these departments should see a reduction in their workload, a number of others may expand or develop in more positive ways. For example, industrial engineering should concentrate on work simplification and set-up or change-over time reduction; purchasing will be developing fewer but better suppliers; manufacturing will concentrate on developing improved processes and plant and design on product development instead of trouble shooting.

The result should be a significant transfer of effort from doing to thinking, a reduction in indirects, less emphasis on the allocation of overheads, reduction of trouble shooting from all departments and much less non-productive cost accounting and analysis.

Design and engineering for WCM

WCM requires full acceptance of the concept of design for manufacture. Industrial engineers, production staff, supervisors and operators need to be involved in the design process before, rather than after, implementation. This is consistent with the principles of employee involvement and total quality.

Good design requires investment in and knowledge of basic research into materials, technologies and products so that progress along the experience curve may be made without delay. It also requires detailed knowledge and collaboration with the customer. Jointly with the customer or the end user, we must determine what they really want. Manufacturing need to know whether it is a custom-made product, a guaranteed, fixed, standard, reliable product, or a standard product with a potential flexibility of features and design. WCM's two simple design concepts, to achieve JIT systems, are to reduce the part count and use modular designs.

World-class procedures apply to design and project offices as well as to the production floor. A key problem to be overcome is the tendency to reassign designers from detail design on existing contracts to initial quotation for future contracts (usually treated as higher priority) resulting in refamiliarisation by other personnel and revision at a later date.

Other management practices for design come from the same WCM methodology. Establish work teams with 'ownership' of specific products instead of tasks, leave detailed specification of components to the expert (i.e. the supplier, manufacturer, etc.), within general constraints, rather than a non-specialist from the assembly organisation, and where adequate, use sketches to reduce design time.

Other simple world-class design rules are to file by product type (classification), not by customer; use standard components and modules; use computers where possible including CAD/CAM and CAE systems; work on few jobs at a time, but complete each and avoid excessive work on unwinnable contracts.

Capital investment for WCM

An analysis of industrial capital investment shows preferences for heavy commitments to sophisticated computer-control systems, automatic materials-handling systems, automatic test and inspection (ATE) systems, automated stores, data-collection systems and accounting systems.

While these are all valuable, and many may be essential in certain circumstances, none creates any added value. The WCM philosophy is not to ignore these items, but to simplify the task so that massive investment is no longer needed.

Close scrutiny of the results of such system installations frequently reveals that a part of the benefit (sometimes a large part) has arisen from the redesign of operating procedures, data presentation, assurance procedures, etc., which would have been valid without the capital equipment and would have been more flexible to future changes in products and markets. Failure of such investments is almost always due to the preliminary system improvements not having been completed previously. Schonberger's advice when considering such projects is to plan for them in full detail and then to attempt to remove the capital element and reassess the cost/benefit calculation.

When justifying capital expenditure, it should be possible to consider, and evaluate, the costs and benefits of reducing the variability and flexibility which are frequently imposed by large investments in automation. Dedicated lines are not always simplest – they tend to be fixed in position, take time to install and are under-utilised or overloaded and expensive. The alternative may be to install several sets of unlinked equipment with proved high reliability to produce each separate model. As the price of marginal unit operating cost increases, we may gain flexibility, reliability and the ability to introduce new models at minimum cost and time.

The general principles of capital investment in manufacture thus are not simply to replace labour with equipment that cannot think or solve problems, but to recognise that the main advantage that equipment has over people is to decrease variability. JIT requires faster change-overs, which come from smaller machine units and simpler manual systems. Economies of scale are, however, real: by doubling capacity you can (nearly) halve unit cost. Take note, however, of Exhibit 3.11.

Exhibit 3.11 The supermachine cycle: a cautionary tale

- Market forecast is for massive growth over three years.
- Company decides to expand.
- The best machine for three-year growth is identified by engineers.
- Installation takes six months.
- Plant is under-utilised for two years until growth is achieved.
- Poor discipline for output and maintenance systems result from under-utilisation of plant.
- Plant is fully utilised by the end of the third year.
- At this stage, because of volume pressures and poor maintenance systems, it becomes undermaintained in third year.
- Reliability deteriorates, availability drops, capacity becomes insufficient and the machine is superseded by later models.
- The customer is dissatisfied.

All this assumes that a market forecast made three years in advance is actually attained. It might be more profitable to plan for three smaller machines, to be installed at twelve-month intervals, taking advantage of the latest technology and allowing flexibility for over- and under-achievement of market forecasts.

WCM as a marketing tool

WCM is designed to give the organisation a competitive edge. It is, however, also a marketing tool. WCM is already appearing as a slogan in UK corporate advertising (notably ICI's 1991 'World Class Solutions' campaign), but WCM's strength is greater than that.

A world-class manufacturer is proud of its business, its premises and its systems, and is prepared to use this in two ways. First, demonstrating competence by delivering the goods on time, to specification and in partnership with the customer. Second, demonstrating capability by showing customers how results are achieved. If operating in line with WCM principles there will already have been considerable interaction. A number of extra selling points for the product will arise, such as being able to show-how quality is achieved; process capability; how well trained operators are; regular use of preventive maintenance; etc.

The advantages of WCM can be encapsulated in its simplicity. It produces quick, visible results, involves low costs and releases working capital, while creating personal satisfaction for all employees, not just the directors.

FUTURE TRENDS

As discussed in the overview, the interface between marketing and manufacturing has never been constant. It must develop as the two functions develop. It is appropriate, therefore, to look briefly at the trends that may affect their inter relationship.

Developments within manufacturing

Two major developments within the manufacturing function appear likely to continue: management of the human resource and the use of information technology.

Since the heyday of scientific management, there has been a growing tendency to respect the abilities and strengths of employees. First, this was a recognition, through Elton Mayo and the human relations school, of the importance of people, followed by Macgregor's Theory Y which recognised that some people like work and gain satisfaction from doing a good job. However, a new dimension has been added with the trend to employee involvement enshrined in World Class Manufacturing. These have combined to lead to a philosophy generally called 'empowerment'. We can expect more and more employees at all levels to be given control of their own work, their own environment and their own strategic plans. Devolution of responsibility, autonomous work groups, management buy-outs, self-employed subcontracting and home- or teleworking are among the more formal structures that facilitate this. Internal practices include quality circles, team briefing, and upward and downward appraisal. Over all this is the concept of customer care, which is now extending from the field into the factory. Manufacturing employees are not only making direct contributions to the care of the ultimate customer, but they are increasingly regarding one another as customers of their internal processes.

Information technology (IT) has been making substantial advances in manufacturing for more than two decades. The use of computers for systems management is changing working practices and numbers in the infrastructure. The use of on-line data systems has effectively removed at least one level of management in many organisations, creating opportunities for greater employee involvement (as discussed above). The IT revolution is far rom mature. Although the Utopian paperless office and workerless factory are unlikely to arrive in the numbers predicted by the most enthusiastic supporters, there is no doubt that integrated systems in administration and computer-integrated manufacture (CIM) will continue to create large reductions in manpower, a change in the employee skills mix and a more flexible response to market and customer needs.

Richard Brooke (1988) in his analysis of the 'new marketing' proposed manufacturing as marketing's secret weapon. This was based on the concept of a totally integrated flexible system, managed by computers from the point of sale activity to the delivery of the finished product. Underlying this is the culmination of CAD/CAM's integration into the process of marketing and supply. The model assumes a totally flexible manufacturing system. The problem with fully integrated manufacturing in the past has been that it tends to be built round a series of machine centres that are highly flexible internally, but limited to the production of goods within a narrowly defined family. Brooke has addressed this issue by basing his flexibility concept around the organisational system and the supply logistics instead of around the production technology. With these revised constraints the idea gains considerable credibility. It should be possible for the customer to select design variants within a general specification of a product and the CAD system to prepare detailed CAM briefs, the MRP or JIT provisioning system to provide all materials, labour and machine resources and for customised production and delivery to follow automatically.

The success of early developments in this direction has yet to be established. Brooke has used the term 'leverage' to denote the benefits that manufacturing can bring to the operation – which is comparable to the 'competitive advantage' of Peters and others.

Developments in the international market for manufacturing

The future of manufacturing depends heavily on the future of the market. The trends appearing already in this decade and likely to be continued derive from two principal sources: demographic trends in (especially) the Western population and the economic emergence of the newly industrialised countries. The effect of demography is to create a customer base from a relatively wealthy ageing population, with greater expectations of quality, specification and individuality. This places demands on manufacturing for flexibility, reliability and availability. The emerging industrialised countries will increase the competition from regions with relatively low labour and land costs, capable of producing a wide range of standard products at competitive prices.

The consequence of these trends will be that cost leadership will be achieved only by well-directed research and development and relevant investment in manufacturing methods and processes. To obtain returns from this type of strategy, highly accurate market intelligence will be needed. Differentiation and segmentation strategies will require even greater flexibility from the manufacturing operation, again based on high-quality market intelligence.

The interface must become closer than ever before in order to achieve these results and survive. The future is positive but the road will be hard.

BIBLIOGRAPHY

Brooke, R. (1988) *The New Marketing*, Aldershot: Gower.

Buffa, E. S. and Sarin, R. K. (1987) *Modern Production and Operations Management*, 8th edn, NY: Wiley.

Burbidge, J. L. (1975) *The Introduction of Group Technology*, London: Heinemann.

Cooper, R. G. and Kleinschmidt (1991) 'New Product Processes at Leading Industrial Firms' *Industrial Marketing Management*, Vol. 20, p 137.

Deming, W. E. (1986) *Out of the Crisis*, MIT Center for Advanced Engineering Study.

Hayes, R. H. and Wheelwright, S. C. (1984) *Restoring Our Competitive Edge*, NY: John Wiley.

Hill, T. (1991) *Products Operations Management: Text and Cases*, 2nd edn, Englewood Cliffs, NJ: Prentice-Hall.

Hill, T. (1985) *Manufacturing Strategy*, Basingstoke: Macmillan.

Kotler, P. (1991) *Marketing Management*, 7th edn, Englewood Cliffs, NJ: Prentice-Hall.

Muhlemann, A., Okland J. and Lockyer, K. (1992) *Production and Operatios Management*, 6th edn, London: Pitman.

Nayak, P. R. (1991) 'Forces Driving Rapid Technological Development', *Market Intelligence and Planning*, Vol. 5, p. 29.

Porter, M.E . (1985) *Competitive Advantage*, NY: Free Press.

St John, C. H. and Hall, E. H. (1991) 'The Interdependency Between Marketing and Manufacturing', *Industrial Marketing Management*, Vol. 20, p. 223.

Schroeder, R. G. (1989) *Operations Management*, 8th edn, Maidenhead: McGraw Hill.

Schonberger, R. J. (1987) *World Class Manufacturing Casebook: Implementing JIT and TQC*, NY: Free Press.

Skinner, W. (1983) 'Manufacturing – The Missing Link in Corporate Strategy', *Harvard Business Review*, May–June.

Skinner, W. (1974a) 'The Decline, Fall and Renewal of Manufacturing Plants', *Industrial Engineering*, October.

Skinner, W. (1974b) 'The Focused Factory', *Harvard Business Review*, May–June.

Skinner, W.(1983) 'Operations Technology: Blind Spot in Strategic Management', Harvard Business School Working Paper, 83–85

Taylor, F. W. (1911) *The Principles of Scientific Management*.

CHAPTER 4

Marketing and Design: a critical relationship

Rachel Davies Cooper

INTRODUCTION

Design is something we are all aware of, either consciously or unconsciously. Our understanding of design and its contribution to corporate competitiveness varies significantly, however. This chapter aims to explain the role of design and its value to industry, to give an overview of design disciplines and how they operate and, finally, to focus on the interface between design and marketing.

THE MARKETING/DESIGN CONNECTION

Very little has been written about design in the marketing literature, and when it has, its relative contribution and value have varied. Kotler and Rath (1990) have identified design as a strategic tool, Service, Hart and Baker (1987) see it as part, albeit a significant part, of the product development process, and now there is a debate on how design should be managed, and whether it should be by marketing or whether design and marketing should be integrated (Bruce and Roy, 1991). It is worthwhile therefore to examine how design and marketing do interconnect.

Design and the marketing mix

Design has a connection with every one of the marketing mix tools.

In terms of *product,* as a tangible artifact, design is a major factor. It influences the quality, function, service, usability and appearance. It contributes to product features, which frequently add value to a product, in the eyes of the customer. Design has impact on all the features which differentiate one product from another as described by Kotler (1991), features such as performance, conformance, durability, reliability, repairability and style.

In terms of product, as a service, the design factors are only marginally less central. For instance, in such industries as insurance or banking, advertising and communications, design provides the information and evidence of the service, from policy document and chequebooks to the sales literature. In hotels and catering and the leisure industry, designers provide the environment for the service. Design also has a bearing on service differentiation, delivery, installation, customer training, consultation, repair, miscellaneous services and personnel and image differentiation.

In terms of *price*, effective design can save money for an organisation by designing products which are economical in terms of materials, energy and manufacture (Kotler, 1991). Design can also enhance a product and, therefore, its perceived value, enabling it to sell at a higher price.

Design has an impact on *place* or distribution, in that when they are designing a product designers can take into account the means of distribution, and will consider the nature of the packaging and storage.

Design also has a key role in *promotion*, packaging, promotional and sales literature, all forms of media advertising, and point of sale displays. Indeed, the whole retail environment is physically designed and specified by professional designers.

Without design most aspects of the marketing mix could not be put into operation.

Corporate communication

Current good management practice is for organisations to develop long-term goals, to share these goals with their employees through mission statements and develop strategies through which the goals can be achieved. Since the 1960s, and Levitt's (1960) 'marketing myopia', being market-orientated has been espoused as an essential strategy for companies. Indeed, it is increasingly important to develop and make explicit one's company philosophy and communicate this both internally and externally. Thus, to many companies the corporate image has become significant in accomplishing the corporate goals; this image involves design not only in the logo but also in all visual aspects of the company. This might include transportation, publicity and advertising, environment and architecture and products. As Wally Olins (1978) points out, the visual projection of a culture not only helps internal cohesion but also plays a large part in showing the outside world what the company is like and how it can be expected to behave.

New product development and innovation

New product development (NPD) is essential to any company; it must replace existing and dying products, or diversify into new markets. Marketing and design play key interwoven roles in the NPD process – studies of successful product development have shown that marketing and design professionals working in teams are essential to success. Designers are skilled in creativity and can contribute when idea generation is required. Innovation occurs when such new ideas are taken through to marketable products. Marketers and designers need to work together throughout product innovation, on idea screening and concept or product testing and launching. The development of an idea into a artifact or environment requires the design and visualisation skills of the designer.

Marketing, design and R&D

It is important here, to mention the interfaces between marketing, design and R&D, in particular in the development of new concepts and new products. Marketing provides the market pull in terms of their understanding of the customer and market trends, R&D provide the technology push in terms of their awareness of technology trends and their own research and development, and both market and technology trends are sources of innovation which design translate into products. The R&D function exists in its own right often only in the larger companies which can afford an independent R&D activity. Medium-sized and smaller companies must rely on the design or production function to monitor and develop new technologies. Others rely on independent research agencies or academic institutions for R&D knowledge. Whichever method is used, a company relies upon the communications link between R&D and marketing, both in terms of generating a balanced strategy for new products, i.e. technology- and market-orientated, and also in terms of feeding back to R&D product information such as customer needs and competitor product knowledge. R&D need market research information to provide guidance for their work, they need to identify problems with existing products and to know how they perform, so that they can improve upon them. Marketing need an understanding of the company's technological strength and future direction, to contribute to their product-planning process. This relationship is best built up formally through teams and project reviews and informally via newsletters, memos, workshops and team development. Management information systems provide the opportunity to communicate and share both market and technological data – however, it must be expressed in a language that makes it accessible to both functions.

Marketing functions and design

The many contributions to the company's activities that design makes mean that it is addressed separately by various marketing functions. For instance, corporate communications, promotions and advertising comes under the remit of marketing communications and advertising, buyer behaviour is often concerned with how the consumer reacts to the design aspects of a product, and idea generation under the remit of product development or marketing strategy. As Bruce (1991) suggests, 'as a result marketing academics and practitioners do not examine how design works and impinges upon marketing'. In addition, everyone assumes it is being covered by another marketing specialist.

DEFINING DESIGN

The definitions of design have been many and various. In its broadest sense, design is used as a noun relating to the structure, form, appearance and function of a product, a communication or a place: for example, 'the design of a Porsche is superb'. Design is also used as a verb, in terms of an activity which brings a plan or concept into reality: for example, 'they are about to design a new terminal', and latterly as an adjective synonymous with style, fashion, quality and expense, e.g. 'designer' jeans.

Many academics and professionals spend time trying to define what is meant by 'design'. Design can be all-encompassing: if we take the verb form, for example, everyone is able to bring a plan or concept into reality. Indeed, recent research (Gorb and Dumas, 1987) indicated that 'silent design' exists in every organisation, i.e. everyone was making design decisions of some kind. For the purpose of this chapter, however, we are concerned with the activity of designing as undertaken by professional designers, the process they follow and the skills they have. How companies and organisations use design, how companies manage design and the benefits gained from doing so effectively, will also be addressed.

The design specialisms

Traditionally, it was said that a skilled designer could design anything. This idea possibly originated as far back as Leonardo da Vinci, one of the greatest Renaissance painters and designers. He theorised on the circulation of the blood, he almost invented the first fighting vehicle, developed ideas for several aircraft and anticipated the submarine. In the nineteenth century William Morris was known not only for his book design but also for wallpaper, furniture and tapestries. Much of design, particularly in Great Britain, arose out of a strong arts and crafts tradition, yet over the last fifty years, with the increase in technology in all industries, design has become more complex and therefore more specialised.

The basic design process is the same for most design specialists. Design education develops the same basic skills, but designers tend to specialise early in their education, in order to develop the knowledge, skills and understanding necessary to be successful design practitioners. The specialisms fall into a number of categories, although there is overlap.

One of the most effective ways of categorising design was highlighted by Potter in 1969 (2nd ed, 1980), and his three simple categories – product design (things), environmental design (places), communications design (messages) – are still relevant today. Within each category, there is a broad spectrum of disciplines (see Table 4.1). At one end are those design disciplines that demand a large amount of aesthetic, visual and sensory awareness and input and resemble fine art. At the other end of the spectrum, the work more closely becomes a science, concerned with technology, manufacturing and architecture; these still demand aesthetic sensitivity, but their latitude for displaying aesthetics is limited. For example, an electric typewriter has an aesthetic component but many other factors influence its final form – unlike, for instance, a piece of jewellery or a vase.

Table 4.1 Design categories and disciplines

Product	Environmental	Communication
Studio pottery	Theatre design	Illustration
Industrial pottery	Exhibition design	Graphic design
Jewellery	Interior design	Packaging
Textiles	Landscape	TV film, photography
Fashion	Architecture	Advertising design
Furniture		Cartography
Retail products		Information design
Industrial engineering		
Engineering design		

Many of these disciplines have common skills originating from their craft origins; Walker's design family tree (Walker, Oakley and Roy, 1990) clearly indicates these roots and how, as they form new branches, they do so in the new technologies. This tree (shown in Fig. 4.1) also indicates the basic skills of perception, imagination, geometry, visualisation, dexterity, materials, etc. Common to most designers. Some design disciplines remain close to the craft roots, others become more specialised.

People who become designers have often done so because of their interest and ability in drawing or model-making, or visual problem-solving in one form or another. Most professional designers have also gone through an education system which develops those skills to a highly tuned degree in a particular specialism. For instance, a graphic designer will have a good sense of two-dimensional form, in space and colour, and an interest in problem-solving, which will be developed so that he or she is able to distinguish between typefaces, have an understanding of the mood a typeface may create and how letter forms relate to illustrations. Those at the more specialist, engineering end of design will have followed a different route entirely, with orientation towards scientific and mathematical problem-solving as opposed to a creative or visual approach.

In almost all design disciplines there is a shared language. Designers from allied disciplines do communicate with one another; they also frequently change specialisms. However, one of the major problems cited in current research is that the designers from an art/design background do not easily communicate with those from engineering and, as a result, problems occur in manufacturing and new product development.

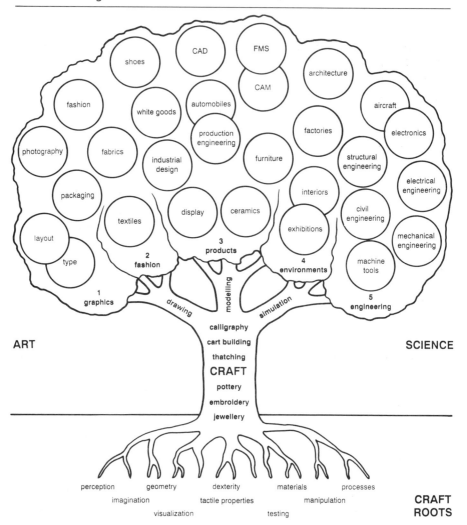

Fig. 4.1 The design family tree (the higher up the tree the greater the complexity)

Design techniques

To understand what designers can bring to the aid of marketing and management, it is worthwhile understanding some of the techniques they use in developing their design proposals. Throughout the design process, designers make use of a number of activities and skills.

Creativity

Designers skilled in creativity are taught techniques to enhance these skills. For example, they learn such activities as brainstorming, lateral thinking and morphological analysis. Creative problem-solving becomes second nature to most designers.

Making

Some designers, frequently known as designer/makers, actually make the finished article, either as they are designing it (a potter using a potter's wheel, for example) or from a paper design. Jewellery designers often make their own pieces, based on such designs.

Visualising

This technique is used by most designers to bring a concept or idea into a recognisable form, often employing drawings or diagrams of various types, depending on the specialism of the designer. A graphic designer will visualise a brochure by making a mock-up or facsimile using pen, ink, film and paper. A product designer will visualise a product by drawing it from a number of angles and using the most appropriate media to represent the look of the final product as closely as possible.

Model-making

For anything in three dimensions designers often make up or have made up models of varying complexity, for instance a sketch model, to give shape, form and size to their design.

Technical drawing and diagrams

Designers often produce detailed drawings to aid manufacture or model-making; these are more precise, giving dimensional and technical information.

Simulating/testing

Designers use all the technology available to simulate and test their designs. New technology, and particularly CAD, means that designers are now able to simulate a design and test it against operational criteria. They also use working models to simulate and test the design concepts.

THE DESIGN PROCESS

Academics and professional designers have spent a great deal of time trying to pin down a definitive model of the design process. Models which adequately cover the design process undertaken by every specialism tend to be so general as not to give any particular understanding of the activity involved. Oakley's (1984) model is an example:

Formulation → Evolution → Transfer of results to production and market
of model   of solution

Those which are more detailed may not be particularly relevant to more than one specialism or sector of industry (Hollins and Hollins, 1991).

Any model will have several forms depending on the perspective, that is, whether you are looking at just the design activity or the whole environment in which the 'design' is taking place. Most professional designers see their activity in stages. Many other factors surrounding the design process (see Table 4.2) are, however, linked to the industry sector, design specialism, etc.

In terms of using design effectively, it is important to understand a number of factors:

- how design fits into the specific business
- the activities of the design specialism you use
- what contribution they can make to your business environment
- what they need to understand to design effectively.

Asking designers to work out of context often means that they do not have all the appropriate information to bring to their design activity. Also, if the designers are not involved or have no understanding of peripheral activities, the creative contribution which they bring is lost.

Table 4.2 The design process as part of the product development process

Phase 1: Project initiation
- Analysis of business environment
- Formulation of corporate strategy, including marketing and design strategies
- Product idea development including contributions from design, marketing and production
- Idea/concept feasibility analysis including market research and production analysis
- Development of project plans
- Development of design brief, product specification, etc.

Phase 2: Design
- Stage 1: the design brief
- Stage 2: preliminary design work
- Stage 3: detailed design

Phase 3: Product introduction
- Production tests
- Fullscale manufacture
- Launch

Phase 4: The marketplace
- Customer appraisal and use
- Product appraisal and revision
- Disposal

It is impractical to highlight *all* design specialisms, and how they operate. Consideration will, however, be given to those most frequently used by industry. Walker (Walker, Oakley and Roy, 1990) relates corporate use of design to maturity, in that a firm usually starts with letterhead, sales literature and possibly a logo, and progresses later to some packaging design, perhaps, and then product design. Later still, the more sophisticated organisation may venture into examining its corporate image; its environment, buildings and interiors. Major companies such as Braun and Philips develop a corporate design policy that involves a number of design specialists, including architects, interior designers and corporate identity designers. Graphic, product and interior/environmental design are perhaps those most frequently used by companies.

Graphic design

Graphic designers are concerned primarily with two-dimensional images, although they do cover some three-dimensional design such as packaging. They are trained to be sensitive to word, image, communication and decoration, the use of colour, shape and layout. They should have an understanding of the psychological and perceptual qualities of the products they design. Some graphic designers specialise further into a particular sector: those skilled in developing campaigns and slogans for the print media, TV and radio, say, into advertising. Other designers specialise in corporate design: developing an image for all visual elements of an organisation from the letterhead and annual report to the lorries and signage. Designers must understand the media and materials they use: for packaging, the plastics, paper, or glass; for sales literature, a particular type of paper or printing method will be important.

The graphic design process, whether carried out within the organisation or by outside consultants, involves three stages:

(1) *Contracting:* agreeing with the client the brief; undertaking research (this could be market research if that has not been supplied); trying to understand the potential recipient of the design; analysing production feasibility and costs; redefining the brief if necessary, and obtaining approval.
(2) *Design research and preliminary proposals:* sourcing images, visual qualities, typefaces; developing preliminary ideas; screening potential proposals; presenting proposals as visuals/mock-ups at design review.
(3) *Design detailing:* design modification, detailed design development; specification and instructions to manufacturers for production; monitoring production (e.g. proof corrections, checking quality).

Product design

The breadth of activity of product designers is very wide, from designing a pair of glasses, say, to a photocopier or a hospital scanner. The specialist knowledge they develop as professionals will depend on the direction of their careers. Their training will, however, equip them with some basic skills and understanding: of three-dimensional form and space, of colour and texture, linked to the perceptual and psychological impact that these elements can produce on the end user; of ergonomics – human interaction with product form and function; of materials and manufacturing techniques.

This design specialism is often confused with engineering design. The distinction is that engineering design is concerned primarily with the function/operation and manufacture of the product; product/industrial design with the appearance and function/operation. However, neither engineering designers nor product/industrial designers can operate successfully without considering all three aspects of the product: appearance, function and manufacture. Sadly, a tradition has developed in British manufacturing industry of keeping these specialisms separate, through education, terminology and organisational structure. This has been shown (Cooper, 1992a) to be detrimental to new product development and research. Research has established that the most effective new product development occurs where NPD teams are brought together that involve marketing, product/industrial design and engineering design/technology. This is a method used most successfully by the Japanese.

The process a product designer follows varies quite significantly depending on the type of product involved, the complexity of the manufacturing process and how many other engineering and manufacturing functions are involved. That basic process involves four stages:

(1) *Contracting:* generation of design brief and product specification; undertaking research (which could be market research, if that has not been supplied); trying to understand the potential recipient of the product being designed; researching production feasibility and costs; redefining the brief if necessary and obtaining approval.
(2) *Preliminary design:* developing preliminary ideas, making visual models and testing them; producing good visual models of proposed designs and possible alternatives where necessary; consumer testing.
(3) *Detailed design:* detailed design, detailed drawings for production and specification for manufacture.
(4) *Introduction to production:* working model production and testing; supervision of product introduction to manufacturing.

Environmental/interior design

Designers involved in any aspect of environmental design must understand the use of space, light, colour, texture and scale. Their specific sphere of work will determine the particular specialist knowledge they develop. Retail environments demand an understanding of lighting, the control of customer flow, materials and display systems. Creating an atmosphere through the use of colour, texture, lighting, pattern and space is important to designers in the service industry for pubs, hotels and restaurants. Interior designers for the organisational environment should be skilled in space planning, organisational cultures and climates and the psychology of working environments, in addition to the general environmental design aspects. Again, there are four broad stages:

(1) *Contracting:* defining the brief, undertaking research, identifying user need, agreeing the brief.
(2) *Preliminary design:* developing ideas, producing sketches, sourcing potential materials and presenting proposals.
(3) *Detailed design:* design refinement; producing dimensional elevations, plans and sections; selecting fabrics, fittings, and furnishings; producing appearance model and presentations sheets for approval.
(4) *Implementation:* supervision of production/construction.

THE DESIGN INDUSTRY

The design industry in Great Britain grew considerably during the 1980s, much in line with the growth in the retail industry. The graphics and interior design specialisms grew more than product and industrial design. In 1987 the design consultancy industry in the UK was one of the strongest in the world (McAlone, 1987), but the recession of the late 1980s and early 1990s severely undermined it. Throughout the 1980s the British government promoted the value of design to industry. The DTI's Design Initiative encouraged industry to employ design consultants, by contributing to the fees through the Funded Consultancy Scheme, which began in July 1982 and continued (in various guises) throughout the 1980s. The DTI also promoted design awareness and design management education through its funded undergraduate, postgraduate and in-company training schemes.

A number of organisations represent design and designers, the Design Council being one of the most prominent. The Design Council selects and promotes good design through its design awards, advertises design to industry and offers companies an advisory service on design policy, training and design selection. Its head office in London holds exhibitions related to design, with regional centres providing consultancy and advice and promoting design in their region.

A professional body of UK designers is the Chartered Society of Designers (CSD). The CSD provides its members with advice on current issues – legal, business and environmental. The Design Business Association (DBA) is a satellite organisation of the CSD, and its members are design companies and groups who are concerned with the business of design. The DBA produces policy documents, supports research, promotes the design business and presents Design Effectiveness awards each year.

In addition to these national bodies there are professional associations for particular design specialisms, for example the Society of Illustrators.

THE VALUE OF DESIGN

There has been a gradual decline in British manufacturing industry over the last fifty years; exports of manufactured goods have declined and imports correspondingly increased. The situation has been debated by many academics, economists and politicians. Ivor Owen, the Director of the Design Council, suggested a very simple reason: 'much of British industry is making products that are just not good enough' (Roy et al., 1990). It has been suggested by Akio Morita, Chairman of Sony, and others that people simply do not want to buy much of what industry produces in the UK and in the US. Cost was traditionally thought to be the major factor; as the markets have become more sophisticated, however, consumers' expectations have risen both nationally and internationally. They are looking for differentiation, innovation, quality, etc., in addition to value for money – for the perceived additional value. Numerous studies have identified non-price factors, particularly design and quality, as crucial to market performance and the economy (Roy et al., 1990). A study in 1983 found that non-price factors accounted for 45 per cent of export behaviour, and for up to 80 per cent of British imports (Schott and Pick, 1983).

It is imperative, therefore, that industry use design to differentiate its products; that quality, reliability, product uniqueness and superiority, safety and ease of use be designed in. Used effectively, design can simplify manufacture and the use of materials, and so help keep prices competitive (Potter and Roy, 1991).

Despite the government's support and promotion of design since the Second World War, and particularly during the last decade, industry has adopted design very slowly. A reason for this may be the lack of real evidence that investment in design is effective. However, a study undertaken in the late 1980s by the Design Innovation Group looked particularly at investment in design (Design Innovation Group, 1992). The study found that :

- around 90 per cent of implemented projects which used design consultants were profitable
- where comparisons with previous, less design-orientated products were possible, sales were seen to have increased by an average of 41 per cent
- a quarter of the design-orientated products opened up new home markets and 13 per cent resulted in new or increased exports; a further 36 per cent had other international trade benefits, largely through strengthening British goods in the UK market against competition from imports
- other benefits of using design included reduced manufacturing costs, stock saving, increased profit margins and improvements in a company's external image.

Other less design-specific studies (Service, Hart and Baker, 1989; Johne and Snelson, 1991) have also cited use of design as a contributor to success, and argued that there must be a company-wide commitment to design, with design represented at board level. Research in this area has also identified crucial issues for maximising the use of design and being successful in new product design and development. The relationship between design and marketing has been identified as one of great importance in contributing to new product development and corporate success (Bruce and Howie, 1991).

WORKING WITH DESIGNERS

Three factors are essential to the efficient functioning of a business: identifying a market, developing a superior product for that market and delivering it to the market. The designer can contribute to all three, as can the marketing professional. It is crucial therefore that design and marketing communicate effectively with each other and understand each other's role.

Communications

In communicating with designers, one of the key components is the design brief. The terms 'design brief' and 'design specification' are often confused. Hales (1990) states that a design brief is usually concerned with the overall aspects of the project whereas the design specification is concerned with more detailed aspects. In addition, 'design brief' is used more by consultants and designers, 'design specification' by engineers.

Design brief

There are no rules governing the content of a design brief. In graphic and product design, the form the brief takes depends largely on the client (in this context any person or company responsible for contracting with the designer) and the designer. It also depends on when the designer is brought into the product development process. If, for instance, he or she is brought in at the idea generation stage, he or she will be working with the marketing and production team on the whole process. Specific design briefs will be written when alternative products or concepts need developing. This type of brief will arise from discussion among the team and probably be drafted by the designers themselves.

Where a product concept has been identified and the marketing strategy formulated, the brief may have been constructed by management, frequently by marketing itself. The brief is then communicated to the designer by the project manager. In this case, designers often question the brief in detail, to establish that they and their client have the same understanding of the problem, and that any alternative strategies have been considered.

Briefs should be relatively detailed, without being creatively constraining to the designer. They should give precise market details (size of market, consumer demographics, competitors, etc.), consumer needs, manufacturing and materials specifications, time and cost constraints. In many cases they are too short, because the authors have little understanding of the information needed by the designer. Design briefs are frequently given orally; this is inappropriate and often leads to failure, with misunderstanding between management and designers. Such briefs should always be confirmed in writing.

The most effective way of generating a design brief is to bring the designer in at the onset of the project – at the idea generation stage. Design knowledge and creativity can often contribute to that process. The brief can then be drawn up jointly by management and design. Many projects run into problems or fail completely because of poorly constructed project plans, and in particular a badly defined design brief. It is essential that everyone involved in the project be aware of the following five aspects:

(1) *Key personnel* This should include the major contributors to the product development and the key decision-makers.

(2) *Key tasks* Defining the key tasks and those responsible for carrying them out is essential. Too often this is not done thoroughly, resulting in problems later. Defining these tasks at the start of a project helps the team to define the problem and highlights hidden agendas, which may not have otherwise been discussed. Pahl and Beitz (1984) suggest some essential questions:
  - What is the task really about?
  - What implicit wishes and expectations are involved?
  - Do the suggested constraints actually exist?
  - What paths are open for development?
  - What properties must the solution have?
  - What properties must the solution not have?

(3) *Time scale* Designers will always want time scales to work to. It is important that the project is staged and that everyone is aware of his or her role and responsibility at each stage (i.e. who will do the work, who is to report to whom, who will make decisions).

(4) *Cost constraints* Even if all the relevant information has not been confirmed, cost boundaries must be defined for all stages of the project, in terms of human resources, time and product cost.

(5) *Product attributes* One of the most common complaints by marketing to design is that the design proposals bear no relationship to what marketing had expected. The designers respond that marketing did not clearly communicate their expectations or that the product design proposal accords the 'designer's understanding' of the brief. It is therefore essential that the product attributes are expressed clearly, and that all parties in the team understand what is meant. The list of attributes will of course vary with the product involved, but could include any of the following:
  - the targeted consumer and their lifestyle
  - product use, function or environment
  - operating requirements, ergonomics, safety, reliability
  - size, shape, colour
  - material
  - quality standards

- manufacturing constraints
- servicing and maintainability needs
- environmental concerns
- installation and assembly
- distribution and transport
- product life expectation.

Designers who have not been involved in generating a brief from the onset will, on receipt of one, analyse it and often revise it, based on their own understanding and discussions with the client. They will also schedule and estimate the fees for each stage of the work. When this is agreed in writing by the client it forms a contract, and any changes in circumstances subsequently, on either side, should be documented. Exhibit 4.1 shows the type of information a brief should contain, for designers external to a company. This is often relevant for internal designers too.

Exhibit 4.1 Design brief: summary of content

Background to company
Corporate strategy and relationship to the brief
The design problem
Design specification, product attributes
Consumer and market information

Product specifications

A product specification is used primarily to describe precise and detailed aspects of a product. It is most successful when developed after a product planning phase of a project, during which the design, marketing and engineering/technical functions have had time to develop their understanding of the product concept. If they have discussed preliminary design ideas, and undertaken market research and feasibility research, they will possess all the market, design and manufacturing information to write a detailed specification. The project is more likely to enter further stages of development without any major problems.

If product specifications are generated very early in the NPD development phase, when there is a chance they are ill-defined or have been poorly researched and tested, the later stages will involve random refinement and uncoordinated changes. This often results in numerous problems, leading to time and cost escalation.

Market intelligence

When working with designers, it is essential to be aware of the types of market intelligence that are most valuable to the design process. One must first understand that, in the act of designing, the designer is relying on information stored in the subconscious; information from all five senses, accumulated over time. Designers use this knowledge to solve both functional and aesthetic design problems. But they need the project information which will help them to understand the context in which their subconscious knowledge can be used to solve the design problem.

For example, a graphic designer asked to develop the image for packaging and advertising a new alcoholic beverage would need to know, among other things, where it is to be sold, to whom and how. In marketing terms, that information could be supplied as demographic, socio-economic, geographical and numerical data. Yet in order to develop an appropriate brand image, visual and lifestyle information would be more useful to the designer. Designers often do their own research to get such information, which they use to develop mood boards. Transmitting market intelligence through a mood board is a means of achieving an understanding between design and marketing and is useful to clarify aesthetic and functional attributes. A mood (or lifestyle) board is a presentation of images representing aspects of the consumers, their lifestyle and environment, texture, colours, etc. Mood boards are frequently used where design is a central feature of the product, for instance in fashion, textiles and small domestic appliances.

Another effective means of determining the product concept and conveying market intelligence is to use metaphor as a definition. Clarke (1991) gives an example used by Honda to describe the characteristics of its 1990 Accord: 'A rugby player in an evening suit'. This metaphor captured the 'personality' of the project, and was translated into key attributes such as 'rugged but fair', 'socially recognisable', 'polite, sportsmanlike', 'strong and secure', 'orderly', 'likeable', 'bright and elegant'. These were in turn translated into features: for example, 'friendly' became a soft-touch interior, 'tough' a larger engine and improved reliability in extreme conditions. Metaphor can be used to capture the feeling of the product throughout the development process, and to develop detailed specifications, which everyone in the development team can relate to, and which the designer can translate into aesthetic and functional design forms.

Setting the scene for the product, or developing scenarios, is another method of providing usable market intelligence to the designer. This method actually tells a story about people and the products, for instance describing fictitious couples or individuals, their daily lives, perhaps even their use of a product or behaviour in a situation (e.g. how they shop for groceries, the process they go through and what guides their decisions). This type of information helps the designer to focus on the sensory and function problems, and aids in forming creative and appropriate design solutions to the problem. It also guards against drawing too much from the designer's own personal experiences.

Designers also often look for analogies to help in communicating the desired attributes. When designing a stereo or video system, for example, a designer might ask: 'If this were a car, what would it be?' This question focuses the teams thoughts on the attributes and gives the designer a tangible form to relate to. It is, in effect, translating the marketing professional's knowledge into a form that enables the designer to use his or her own knowledge to solve the design problems.

It is well understood that conventional market research frequently reveals only what the consumer already likes, wants or needs, and indicates little about the future. It is therefore essential that the designer is provided with information from which to generate future perspectives. Understanding consumers' behaviour, in terms of how they operate from day to day, how much they spend, what make of car they drive, who makes dinner, who chooses the wallpaper, etc., what their tastes are and how they perceive the various design features, are important to designers. It is the cognitive and emotional issues, and their likely evolution, which are of interest to the designer (Woodhuysen, 1990). The designer can use these in conjunction with the data already in his or her subconscious to generate designs for the future.

Although the methods described above are valuable when communicating with designers, it should be said that most professional designers do find both the alphanumeric and traditional market research reports relevant to their work. However, the techniques used here aid understanding of such data.

Design proposals

Having briefed the designer, the next stage for management is to review the design proposals. Designers are asked to submit their ideas and design solutions. In most cases this involves a presentation, at which the designers reveal their proposals and explain the concepts behind them. One or more visual representations of the product will be included. Representation varies according to the demands of the design problem. Two main forms are used. *Two-dimensional work* consists of visuals or renderings (drawings of what the product will look like) and/or detailed drawings of specific elements or components and/or computer-generated drawings. *Three-dimensional work*, on the other hand, means mock-ups or models, sometimes block sometimes working prototypes, and/or computer-generated models.

The designer should also explain the reasoning behind the design development and the logic behind all details of the design. A written report containing this and design specifications should be included for future reference by the development team.

Presentations of design proposals may occur at various stages of the design development. Walker (1990) describes the types of proposals and the forms of communication for each fairly succinctly, as Table 4.3 shows.

To assess the presentations managers must not rely completely on their own intuition, however informed. It is wise to refer to the design brief as a benchmark, to the agreed statements of the desired product attributes and to the market.

Table 4.3 The categories of design communications

Who is it for? Audience	What does it show? Function	How does it communicate? Form
Concept		
Designers Design team	Trying out ideas Rapid changes Refining concepts	Sketchy, loose. Rough drawings. Lash-ups and mock-ups Private language
Embodiment		
Client/manager	Alternative models under development Main ideas Assembly. Seeking backing/investment Elementary costing	Clear presentation Non-technical drawings, models, working prototypes Public language
Detail		
Production engineer Producer Manufacturer Supplier	Details of components, finishes, etc. Instructions/prescription Evaluation of prototypes Detail costing	Technical details Detailed drawings and specifications Conventionalised language

Interpreting the visual submissions provided by the designer is another skill which the marketing profession needs to develop. When considering a presentation the marketer should not make any presumptions about the model or the image presented. If the colour is presented in a number of ways, obtain precise details about the use of colour; if the size in a drawing is not clear, ask the designer to give precise details of scale. Do not take for granted anything about size, layout, shape, function, use, manufacturability, etc. If the presentation does not make these aspects clear, make the designer be specific – before the decision to go into production.

Testing

Designers often feel that testing product proposals is not a valuable exercise, as most consumers base their judgement on their current perceptions of products, and there is only a small section of the population who are 'innovators', or even 'early adaptors' (Kirton, 1984). However, this is not always the case: if a product is being modified or developed for another market, testing might provide valuable information. Although it is up to marketing to decide on the testing process, it is valuable to involve designers in whatever testing is being undertaken. This helps them to develop an understanding of the consumer, and contributes to their understanding of the product and the design problems involved.

MANAGING THE PROCESS

The marketing and design relationship has been identified by numerous studies (Cooper, 1992b) as essential for successful product design and development in all sectors of industry. A need has been identified for marketing practitioners to be equipped with skills which enable them to prepare a design brief, evaluate the visual concepts presented to them, and communicate effectively with designers throughout the design process, to ensure that the brief is interpreted correctly within the budget constraints. This idea presupposes that marketing should manage design, but there is no evidence to support this supposition fully, and the preferred course of action is that they work together.

Marketing often initiates a design project, based on market knowledge: for example, it may identify a gap for a new or revised product, or the need for promotional or display material. Marketing professionals should, therefore, work with the designers to define the design brief, follow the design process and evaluate the results. To do this effectively the process must be managed. However, as Bruce (1991) suggests, if marketing adopts an autocratic approach and tells design what to do, design may be either too tightly constrained to come up with truly creative ideas or too inadequately informed about marketing's needs to produce commercially acceptable designs. Another approach to managing the process is where marketing acts as a consultant to design, supplying market intelligence and testing models. This is often found when the company has a strong design-led strategy.

A third approach, and one seen by many researchers (Bruce and Roy, 1991) as the most successful, involves a partnership between marketing and design, in a situation where they understand and respect each other's roles. Projects are managed by a project leader from each function.

Effective management of the process means that, once the design brief has been accepted, the designers and marketing professionals must work within the planned time scale undertaking their tasks, as identified at the onset. The design process must be phased and each phase reviewed, to assess achievements and to prepare for the next. The phases (or stages) will vary according to the project and the specialist design field, but the principles of review at defined stages, of targets being set, and of information and decisions being documented by the development team, are critical to the success of any design project.

CONCLUSION

It is important to realise that both design and marketing are essential to every organisation. Design is essential to the quality of the products or services it supplies, the environment in which its employees operate, and the way the organisation communicates internally and externally. The marketing function is essential: for early market recognition and understanding, product development testing, corporate communication and for product launch and sales.

The way in which both functions relate to each other, their communication skills, mutual trust and goal sharing are crucial to the success of the company. The marketing professional needs to:

● understand and value the role of the designer
● be able to collect and translate market intelligence appropriate to the design activity
● be able to communicate effectively market intelligence, e.g. in preparing design briefs
● be able to work in a team where design responsibilities are defined and market and design functions understand each other's contribution.

BIBLIOGRAPHY

Bruce, M. (1991) 'The Marketing and Design Seesaw', paper for the Design Management Workshop, Sweden.

Bruce, M. and Howie, A. (1991) 'Managing Design: A Task for Marketing', UMIST Working Paper.

Bruce, M. and Roy, R. (1991) 'Integrating Marketing and Design for Commercial Benefit' in *Marketing Intelligence and Planning*, Vol. 9, No. 5, pp. 23–8.

Clarke, K. (1991) 'Product Concept Development in the Automotive Industry', paper presented at the Third International Conference on Design Management Education and Research, The Design Management Institute, Harvard, May.

Cooper, R. D. (1992a) 'Diagnosing the Sources of Failure in NPD', paper presented at the Fourth International Forum on Design Management Education and Research, The Design Management Institute and London Business School.

Cooper, R. D. (1992b) 'Diagnosing the Success Failure Factors in New Product Development', *Proceedings of MEG Conference*, Salford University.

Gorb, P. and Dumas, A. (1987) 'Silent Design', *Design Studies*, Vol. 8, No. 3.

Hales, C. (1990) 'Proposals, Briefs and Specifications', in M. Oakley (ed.), *Design Management*, Oxford: Blackwell.

Hollins, G. and Hollins, B. (1991) *Total Design, Managing the Design Process in the Service Sector*, London: Pitman.

Johne, A. and Snelson, P. (1991) *Successful Product Development*, Oxford: Blackwell.

Kirton, M. J. (1984) 'Adapters and Innovators – why new initiatives get blocked', *Long Range Planning*, 17 (2), pp. 137–143.

Kotler, P. (1991) *Marketing Management, Analysis, Planning, Implementation and Control*, 7th edn, Englewood Cliffs, NJ: Prentice-Hall.

Kotler, P. and Rath, G. A. (1990) 'Design – A Powerful but Neglected Strategic Tool', *Journal of Business Strategy*, Vol. 5, No. 2.

Levitt, T. (1960) 'Marketing Myopia', *Harvard Business Review*, July–August.

McAlone, B. (1987) *British Design Consultancy Report*, London: The Design Council.

Oakley, M. (1984) *Managing Product Design*, London: Weidenfeld and Nicolson.

Olins, W. (1978) *The Corporate Personality*, London: The Design Council.

Pahl, G. and Beitz, W. (1984) *Engineering Design* (K. M. Wallace (ed.), London: The Design Council.

Potter, N. (1980) *What Is a Designer?*, Reading: Hyphen Press.

Potter, S. and Roy, R. (1991) 'The International Trade Impacts of Investment in Design and Product Development', paper for British Academy of Management Conference, Bath.

Roy, R , Potter, S., Rothwell, R., Gardiner, P. and Schott, K. (1990) *Design and the Economy*, London: The Design Council.

Schott, K. and Pick, K. (1983) 'The Effect of Price and Non-Price Factors on UK Export Performance and Import Penetration', Discussion Paper No. 35, Univeristy College London.

Service, L., Hart, S. and Baker, M. (1987) *Design for Profit*, London: The Design Council.

Service, L., Hart, S. and Baker, M. (1989) *Profit by Design*, London: The Design Council.

Walker, D., Oakley, M. and Roy, R. (1990) *Managing Design, Overview: Introduction*, Open University, Open Business School, OU Press.

Woodhuysen, J. (1990) 'The Relevance of Design Futures', in M. Oakley (ed.), *Design Management*, Oxford: Blackwell.

GRAPHIC DESIGN CASE STUDY

Highland Spring mineral water

This case study is taken from a report submitted by Michael Peters Limited for the Design Effectiveness Awards 1989, and is gratefully reproduced here by kind permission of Michael Peters Limited and Highland Spring.

The UK mineral water market grew throughout the 1980s. The fast rate of growth, combined with future prospects, made it one of the most competitive markets in the UK. By 1987, over 80 brands were jockeying for position.

Perrier had virtually created the UK market and held an almost impregnable position, with a 40 per cent share of 'sparkling'. Evian dominated the 'still' sector with a 30 per cent share. Most other brands (including Highland Spring) were available in both 'sparkling' and 'still'. It was thought that as the market matured there would be room for only two or three major brands besides Perrier and Evian.

Highland Spring was determined to be one of them. In the twelve months prior to October 1987, its share of the fast-growing mineral water market had declined. In the grocery sector volume share had fallen from 5.1 per cent in October 1986 to only 2.2 per cent in October 1987. Highland Spring needed to restore its growth. Design – in conjunction with the other marketing mix tools – was used to do this.

Marketing background

Prior to October 1987 Highland Spring was available as a brand in its own right, but also as a quasi-own-label: major multiples were selling the product under their own name, but still calling it 'Highland Spring'. This situation had arisen partly as a result of EC regulations which demand that the source of mineral water is described on the pack. The words 'Highland Spring' were being used to describe the source as well as the brand.

As brand share began to decline Highland Spring was becoming increasingly dependent on the quasi-own-label for survival and in a market where increasing competition was already exerting a downward pressure on margins (average price per litre fell from 65p in 1982 to 52p in 1985), Highland Spring Ltd was inevitably making even lower margins on quasi-own-label than their own brand.

A choice had to be made: either let the brand die and live off own-label arrangements or attempt to restore the brand itself via significant marketing investment. The company bravely (for by this time quasi-own-label made up the bulk of its business), decided on the latter course of action. It appointed the Cope Mathews advertising agency to develop advertising proposals and (at the agency's suggestion) Michael Peters Limited was briefed to look at the design of the Highland Spring brand identity.

At the same time, the company began negotiations with the major multiples to continue to supply own-label products, but no longer under the Highland Spring name. This in turn (to comply with the labelling regulations) meant that separate, dedicated bore-holes would need to be established for each of the major own-label customers, so that each would have its own 'source'.

Marketing objectives

Marketing objectives were set by Highland Spring's marketing group, as follows:

- to reposition Highland Spring as a premium mineral water brand
- to increase distribution of Highland Spring brand
- to increase margins of Highland Spring brand
- to reverse the brand's declining share-trend and restore it to growth
- to protect the position of Highland Spring Ltd as a major supplier of own-label product, but no longer under the Highland Spring name.

Relaunch design brief

In the context of the overall marketing objectives, the role of design was to create a stronger, more distinctive brand identity for Highland Spring, positioning it at the premium end of the market as 'the definitive Scottish mineral water'.

The target market was defined as ABC1 adults, aged between twenty-five and forty-four. Target Group Index (TGI) analysis and qualitative research (conducted by The Research Business) were used to help build up a picture of the target market's habits and attitudes relating to mineral water. In summary, Highland Spring had to appeal to health-conscious individuals who liked to think of themselves as sophisticated and discerning, motivated by 'quality of life' as much as by status.

Among mineral waters, Perrier was (predictably) the gold standard – but a slight undercurrent of (perhaps jingoistic) rejection of its overt 'Frenchness' was detected. More importantly, The Research Business found that Perrier's French origins (whilst undoubtedly endowing that brand with a chic, sophisticated personality) had very little to say about the product itself. The Scottish Highlands, by contrast, could – if treated in the right way – lend important credibility to communication of relevant product values (pure, natural, refreshing). Highland Spring's proposition would then be built around these core product values, supported by the product's origins in the Ochil Hills – a spectacular and unspoilt area at the foot of the Scottish Highlands.

The vital thing would be to get the brand's personality right – Scottish, but without being 'tartan-twee'; healthy and vigorous; but at the same time refined and civilised. Qualitative research was a vital tool in helping to define this brand personality. Consumers found the personality of the old Highland Spring design to be garish, loud, at best 'cheap and cheerful'. Using photo-collages, these findings were amplified by consumers' image-associations. It became clear that the old design – although communicating 'Scottish' – was associated with quite the wrong kind of Scottish image for a premium mineral water. Consumers were picking out images of Scotland 'as seen by Japanese golfing tourists'; loud, brash and invariably old-fashioned image of haggis and sporrans and tartan shortbread; 'Jock from down the road'; 'Scottish football supporters'. The Research Business concluded that 'Current Highland Spring has downmarket associations, which lack any connotations of freshness and undermine the product name.'

By contrast, when asked to select images appropriate to the 'ideal' Scottish mineral water, consumers put together a collage of clean air, salmon, lochs, malt whisky, subtle tartans and mountain streams.

The resulting image-boards were at the heart of the final briefing to the design team.

Research also found that Highland Spring's policy of colour-coding bottles according to the material used – green for glass and clear for plastic – was confusing to a market which associated green with sparkling water and clear with still water.

The creative solution

The design objectives were to:

- create a distinctive, aspirational brand identity
- differentiate still and sparkling water more clearly.

Six initial design concepts were created to the brief, and put into qualitative research to provide guidance for design development. These concepts reflected various approaches in terms of colour and typography, different aspects of Scottish imagery (some more overt than others), varying degrees of emphasis on the product's Ochil Hills source, and different positions and combinations of labels. The bottle shape itself was a 'given' (Highland Spring had already decided not to invest in new bottle moulds), but the various approaches to labelling created *apparently* different bottle shapes.

According to The Research Business, '*all* the new design concepts convey better quality'. However, one concept in particular stood out as best meeting the brief. It succeeded in conveying a 'Scottishness, class, sophistication and freshness', and in the words of one consumer, 'it looks elegant enough to bathe in' (prompted by which, an 'asses milk' NPD project was briefly considered, but wiser counsel prevailed). With minor modifications in the light of these research findings (for example, the original concept included long and detailed copy on the lower label, but this was felt to be 'over-the-top') the concept was developed and mocked up for a further stage of qualitative research, again conducted by The Research Business.

Included in a brand-mapping exercise, with no indication to consumers that this was a test design, it evoked a 'very positive reaction. Consistently positioned with Perrier in terms of quality and appeal.' It was 'seen to have integrity and individuality' and the minor negatives raised in the first research had now been eliminated. The developed concept was therefore progressed and became the new Highland Spring brand identity for the relaunch in October 1987.

The resulting design involved the label around the body being redesigned to show a panoramic illustration of the Ochil Hills, the source of the water. Positive images of the water's Scottish heritage were subtly integrated into an additional label around the neck of the bottle. A special tartan was created using a dark purple background and the shape of the label was based on a shield with crossed swords – replacing the swords with tartan. The cross symbolised the Scottish flag. See Fig. 4.2 for the old and new designs.

Evaluation

The new design was subjected to a quantified evaluation against the old design, on

Fig. 4.2 (left) Highland Spring before redesign; (*right*) Highland Spring after redesign.

criteria distilled from the brief. As Table 4.4 shows, the new design outscored the old by a significant margin on every dimension. Therefore, it *should* prove effective in helping to achieve Highland Spring's marketing objectives. Thorough qualitative research had helped to define the strategy and guide the design process. And quantified research confirmed that the new design was indeed 'on strategy'. But would it work in the marketplace?

In the months following Highland Spring's relaunch, competition in the mineral water market grew ever more fierce. Advertising expenditure continued to show dramatic year-on-year rises; new brands were launched at the rate of nearly one a month; and pressure on margins continued to bite as the major multiples' share of

Table 4.4 Highland Spring design evaluation
(Base = 145 Consumers ABC1 25-34 London area, 65% female, 35% male)

% agree strongly with statements	Old design	New design
A particularly refreshing mineral water	13	50
A high quality mineral water	15	62
Pure and natural	39	68
My friends would like it	17	52
For sophisticated people	7	39
A classy design	5	66
For health-conscious people	28	54
Looks cheap	62	6

Source: The Research Business

sales continued to grow. Despite this increased competition, every one of Highland Spring's marketing objectives was achieved.

Reposition Highland Spring as a premium brand

Average Highland Spring retail price per litre grew by 27 per cent between September 1987 and September 1988, despite overall market pricing holding fairly stable. Even market leader Perrier increased in price by only 5 per cent across the year (*source*: Nielsen).

Highland Spring's user profile moved from a down-market bias (compared to 'any mineral water') in 1986 to an up-market bias in 1988 (*source*: TGI).

In later qualitative research, Highland Spring packaging was again examined and 'received very positive reactions from all age groups (many even preferred it to Perrier packaging), communicating an *expensive, upmarket,* clean and natural drink' (*source:* The Research Business, August 1988).

Increase distribution

Distribution to retail outlets of Highland Spring water grew from 19 per cent of total market in September 1987 to 35 per cent in September 1988 (*source*: Nielsen).

Increase margins

Detailed margin information is confidential to Highland Spring, but the increases in average retail price mentioned above were profitable to Highland Spring as well as the retail trade.

Reverse the brand's declining share-trend

Share in the grocery sector grew from 2.2 per cent in October 1987 to 3 per cent in September 1988, giving a volume increase (allowing also for rising market size) of nearly 50 per cent. Due to the price increases, value share grew even faster (*source*: Nielsen).

In the smaller but nevertheless important specialist off-licence sector, volume share grew from 6.4 per cent in August/September 1987 to 9.1 per cent a year later (*source*: Stats MR).

Protect Highland Spring's position as a major supplier to own-label, but no longer under the Highland Spring name.

Design cannot, of course, claim any credit for this, but following the withdrawal of quasi-own-label, Highland Spring's share of own-label supplies nevertheless increased from 49.8 per cent in September 1987 to 55 per cent in September 1988 (*source*: Nielsen).

From these results alone, however, it cannot necessarily be concluded that the new design was effective in the marketplace. The brand might have succeeded *despite* rather than *because of* design's contribution. We need, therefore, to look at other variables in the marketing mix.

Product
There was no change to the Highland Spring product itself, only to the packaging design. There were no physical packaging changes which could have affected product characteristics.

Pricing
Highland Spring pricing after the relaunch grew dramatically, whereas competitors' pricing held stable or grew only modestly. Taken together with share data, these figures show *either* that Highland Spring is relatively price-insensitive versus the market-leader, *or* that pricing if anything will have depressed the volume share gains which might otherwise have been made. In any event, Highland Spring cannot be accused of having 'bought' volume share gains.

Sales force
There was no significant change in Highland Spring's sales force or distribution arrangements during the periods under discussion.

Market regionality
Significant changes in market regionality can sometimes distort overall UK totals. In this case, however, the regionality of the mineral water market as a whole has not changed significantly. There has been a slight shift in bias towards London and the South (where Highland Spring's share is below average) and Scotland (where it is above average). These effects virtually cancel each other out.

Market seasonality
There are two seasonal peaks in this market: one in summer (June to August) and a smaller one before Christmas (November and December). The degree of market seasonality, however, did not differ significantly between 1987 and 1988, and in any case would not in itself explain any differences in Highland Spring's *share*.

Sales promotion
There was no sales promotion behind Highland Spring at the time of the relaunch. From relaunch to September 1988, the only promotional activity was a low-key leaflet offer ('Buy 4 and send off for a £1 voucher') in Tesco, Gateway and CRS, which ran in May and June 1988. Consumer redemption was – as always with this kind of promotional device – low, although the promotion was undoubtedly helpful in consolidating distribution.

There has been no on-pack promotion of Highland Spring.

Advertising
Highland Spring advertised for the first time in November 1987, spending £411,000 (MEAL) in a four-week burst, followed by a further £665,000 (MEAL) in April–June 1988. This advertising ran in only two TV areas (London and South), and was effective in stimulating slightly faster share growth in these areas than in

Table 4.5 Brand ranking on 'quality'

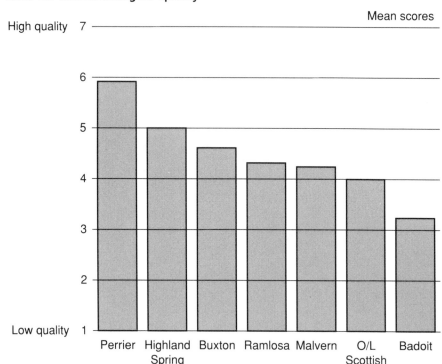

Source: The Research Business

others. However, there was also a healthy growth trend in the rest of the country where Highland Spring was not advertised at all, and had (prior to the relaunch) been declining at an alarming rate.

So, whilst advertising has undoubtedly contributed to Highland Spring's success, it cannot by itself explain all, or even most, of the gains which have been made. Further evidence of this is provided by analysis of changes in Highland Spring's regional user-profile. This shows that brand usership has strengthened between 1986 and 1988 in most parts of the country. There is certainly no bias here towards the advertised areas.

One further piece of quantitative research was carried out by The Research Business in January 1988. Two hundred and sixteen respondents who had *never seen* the commercial, but who were prompted only by the bottle designs, were asked to rank Highland Spring and six competitive brands in order, from 'high quality' to 'low quality'. Table 4.5 shows the results.

Conclusion

Highland Spring's relaunch marketing objectives were achieved. It is now, in the eyes of consumers, a premium brand, and this is reflected in its pricing. Distribution, market share and margins have all moved from a downward to an upward trend. All these positive changes demonstrably started with the introduction of the new design in October 1987.

Other elements of the marketing mix have also helped, particularly advertising in London and the South. But the overall improvements in Highland Spring's performance cannot be attributed to any significant degree to anything other than the new design. And both qualitative and quantitative consumer research support the view that the new design would explain these results. Moreover, it was an extremely cost-efficient marketing tool to use. Understandably, Highland Spring Ltd is not prepared to publish any detailed information on profitability or margins. It has, however, calculated that the entire design exercise (including the cost of new labelling machinery) paid for itself in well under a year.

The implication is clear. When used well, design works as a highly effective and cost-efficient marketing tool.

The marketing/design relationship

One of the key factors, Michael Peters Limited believes, in the development of a successful design for Highland Spring was the use of sensitive qualitative research before design work started, and in the early stages of its development:

> All too often in other cases, initial design concepts are hurriedly created to an imperfect brief, and research is used (too late) to 'pick a winner'. The trouble with this approach is that very often the 'winner' is merely the best of what may be an irrelevant bunch.
>
> In this case, good qualitative research early in the proceedings enabled us to understand the strengths and weaknesses of the existing design, and of the key competitors, as well as identifying the image-associations which would help position the brand correctly and give it the most motivating and relevant personality. From this, we were able to define the creative strategy very precisely, enabling us to focus all creative efforts on developing the optimum execution.
>
> The best advertising agencies have worked this way for years, but it is a relatively recent phenomenon in design. It is a way of working which is now the norm at Michael Peters Limited and certainly Highland Spring Ltd are convinced that this is the right way to approach design projects in the future.

This case clearly indicates the close relationship between efficient and effective market research and effective design. Highland Spring won the Design Effectiveness Awards for 1989.

PRODUCT DESIGN CASE STUDY

The Electrolux Contour vacuum cleaner range

This case study has been written with the help and co-operation of Electrolux Ltd and Fitch RS and is based on a combined report submitted to the Design Effectiveness Awards 1992. It is gratefully reproduced here with their kind permission.

The floorcare vacuum cleaner market is very competitive. Electrolux in 1986 prompted a major shift in the floorcare market with the 600 series, the first upright with integral tools. By 1987 Electrolux realised it had influenced the behaviour of its major competitors, Hoover and National Panasonic. Electrolux wanted to capitalise on this trend, to make a strategic move involving design to establish market leadership.

A new upright project had to succeed, but the risks were great. Electrolux's floorcare department based at Luton depended on the upright range for over 60 per cent of its business and failure in that sector might lead to losses of up to £120 million. The investment risks were also high, with development costs of up to £1 million and a similar cost for launch promotion.

Everything hinged on the designers developing an appropriate product which adequately met the objectives of the marketing and design briefs.

Market research

Consumer needs and requirements drive developments in this market. It is essential to monitor and interpret trends and changes which apply to vacuum cleaners. Electrolux's floorcare marketing group has a policy of continuous market research. It collects research as part of an ongoing procedure, which involves collecting information from the sales teams, qualitative consumer hall test programmes and post-purchase survey cards. From this can be built up a picture of trends in public perception, attitudes and needs.

The marketing team also works closely with product engineering, which provides information on technical developments or ideas that might be valuable to exploit in new product development.

Thanks to this ongoing research Electrolux did not have to undertake specific market research for this project.

Marketing objectives

Traditionally, Electrolux cleaners have attracted an older consumer, in the thirty-five to forty-five age bracket. Marketing wanted to widen the appeal of the brand with younger consumers, to include those aged nineteen to thirty-five. The team also saw the opportunity with the new product to simplify the production process and produce a more cost-effective, easier to assemble cleaner. Strategic marketing objectives were evolved from these locally recognised requirements and from the strategic group policies:

- to position Electrolux as brand leader in the upright vacuum cleaner market by the end of 1991
- to match the levels of innovation for the showroom model achieved by Electrolux in all areas of production development
- to incorporate a range of productivity improvements to reduce costs and therefore avoid eroding gross margins
- to broaden the appeal of the Electrolux brand to embrace a younger consumer profile, primary target women aged nineteen to forty-five
- to meet quality control requirements demanded by the global quality programme
- to develop and introduce a new range in which the design and overall impression give products a unique profile which is something retailers find important.

The design brief

The policy at Electrolux is that the new product development (NPD) team, which includes marketing, product engineering and industrial design, works through the product requirements. Marketing produces a design brief, and design responds to it to make sure there is formal understanding of the objectives. The relationship between the groups is good; they are located close to one another and have the opportunity for frequent informal and formal discussion.

However, at the time the in-house design team had not been built up to its current strength. It was therefore necessary to bring in external design groups to work on the project. Electrolux had used design consultants on other floorcare products and much of the NPD team's design awareness had developed as a result of such work. The design director for Electrolux Centre in Sweden also made regular visits to Luton, influencing the choice and use of designers. Fitch RS was chosen to work with the new product team at Electrolux.

The design brief given to Fitch was developed to reflect the strategic marketing objectives, with particular emphasis on adopting a radical approach to achieve results:

- to create a highly innovative product which establishes clear differentiation at the point of sale
- to consider identified consumer preferences for softer edges, power, durability and more up-front features in order to achieve mass market appeal
- to integrate a range of on-board tools
- to incorporate design improvements, which will enhance the productivity process
- to reflect ergonomic requirements in the design
- to develop a product which adequately reflects Electrolux's high-quality image and reputation as an industry leader.

The design development

During discussions over the brief, Fitch asked questions to gain an understanding of how the product fitted into the corporate strategy. It also conducted its own research into the company and its competitors, to gain familiarity with the area in which it was to work. Once this work had been undertaken, Fitch quickly began concept-generation, working in groups, conducting workshops and holding brainstorming sessions. A number of concepts were shown to Electrolux, a procedure that helps designers to focus in the right direction without discarding ideas too early in the development. This process also allows them to check their interpretation of the marketing brief.

Three-dimensional models were made as soon as possible. (Early ones are usually cardboard mock-ups a fifth of full size. It is essential that the product is handled to gauge the feel and spatial relationships.) Once the overall concept was decided the design detailing began: considering, for instance, the mechanical and electrical packaging, producing a more detailed model at full scale, and finally deciding upon graphics and colour.

CAD was used to speed up decision-making and modification procedures, and as a communication tool between the team. Marketing, engineering and design could all relate to CAD models and discuss proposals before prototype development.

The design solution

The Contour range of vacuum cleaners was the result of the design development. See Fig. 4.3 which shows the Contour model. The range had a number of innovative features.

Shape

The Contour ignores conventional wisdom on vacuum cleaner aesthetics by integrating the cleaner's body and handle, creating a smooth, slim silhouette that avoids the awkward 'shoulder' of traditional upright cleaners. The flowing sculpted moulding was inspired by the shifts in consumer preference to less angular forms, as reflected in the car market, for example, by Ford's introduction of the Sierra.

This distinctive, futuristic design ensures in-store differentiation, where it is clearly distinguishable from other brands and endorses Electrolux's commitment to design innovation. Its elegant form also counterbalances the width of the main body, which due to engineering constraints had to be sufficiently large to house the 800-watt motor. It is sleek, unobtrusive and sits well in the home, yet viewed front-on is sturdy and suggests power and durability – two factors of major importance to purchasers.

Productivity and quality assurance

The Contour design has totally integrated components: the handle with the main body and the base with the protection guard and wheels. This reduces the number of individual parts required and therefore enhances productivity and improves quality assurance.

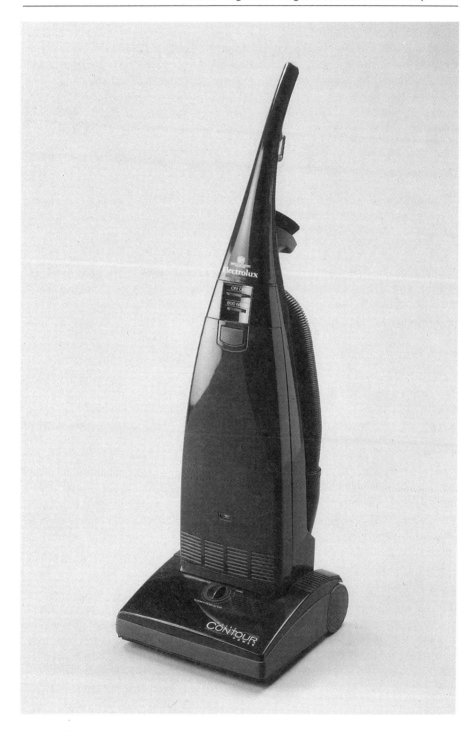

Fig. 4.3 Electrolux Contour vacuum cleaner

Tool storage and additional features

On-board tools are also totally integrated at the back of the cleaner for ease of access and so as not to impede visually from the front. A selection of extra features were included: fully variable floor-type selector, perfumed air freshener, and a 'bag full' indicator.

Ergonomic features

Ergonomic features were considered to aid the consumer at a practical level. These include a simple on/off switch and the bag-release button, a low-profile drop (operated with the foot by an anti-slip release pad on the base) to reach underfurniture, a textured handle-grip and a finger lip to assist when dragging, and a flush-finish rubber guard for easier cleaning at room edges.

Design to manufacture

Once the design was agreed and signed off with the client, Fitch continued the interface with Electrolux to ensure that the engineering and tooling drawings were correct, and that the product would meet the manufacturing budgets, which had been estimated during the detailed design.

Marketing/design success
Market impact

The Contour 1450 was launched in October 1990 and was the best-selling upright product on the market throughout 1991, beating Hoover's Turbopower Plus 2602. In December 1990 Electrolux's brand share of the upright market was 24.5 per cent (value) and 25.9 per cent (volume) on an annualised basis. By December 1991 it had risen to 30.6 and 31.7 per cent respectively, representing a swing away from major rival Hoover, whose share fell from 45.5 per cent (value) and 43.2 per cent (volume) to 40.7 and 36.5 per cent respectively. In April and May 1991 Electrolux became brand leader in the overall market for the first time ever.

In February 1992, in particular, the short-term trend indicator figure showed Electrolux outperforming the market by 20 per cent in volume and 27 per cent in value.

Pricing impact

Contour has also changed the whole structure of pricing brands in floorcare sales. At a retail price of £139.99, Contour sales have been at the top end of the market, with the result of pushing upwards the pricing bands of vacuum cleaners, generally. In the first quarter of 1990 sales of products in the £120–140 band accounted for only 7 per cent of the market and products above £140 for only 8 per cent. By the final quarter that had risen dramatically, to 22.9 and 11.2 per cent respectively.

Productivity impact

Contour's integrated components achieved productivity improvements, with savings made on handling and scheduling procedures estimated at 20 per cent. Quality assurance was enhanced by reducing the total number of items in the assembly procedure. The introduction of CAD technology cut lead times from eighteen months to a year.

Distribution impact

Electrolux's retail customers demonstrated their approval of the Contour by stocking both the 1410 and 1450 models, an initiative not always possible in this sector due to limited floor space.

Consumer perception

Evidence of a shift in consumer perception towards the Electrolux brand was registered through a tracking study conducted by a company called PHT research, which compared attitudes towards competitors' advertising. It indicated that the Contour is more visually attractive to a younger age group than Electrolux ordinarily enjoys.

Product development – the Airstream

 Electrolux followed very quickly by adopting the latest filtration technology and introducing a 1,000-watt motor (the first upright with such a motor) into the Airstream 1000. This was seen as the next stage in the product's evolution and was placed as a premium product selling for £189.99.

Electrolux estimated that they would sell 1,500 units a year. In February and March 1992 alone, sales exceeded 10,000 units. The Airstream also won Electrical Retail Trader's Product of the Year in 1991 for the innovation category, covering design and technology, and in February 1992 it received *Good Housekeeping*'s 'Best Buy' recommendation.

Conclusion

The Contour development demonstrates the good interaction between marketing, design and technology. Objectives were set; design development met them and as a result the product achieved market success and fulfilled the marketing strategy. This can be achieved only if the objectives are clear, the market is well researched, the designers are skilled in their use of market knowledge and the relationship between marketing, design and technology is close and each respects the others' roles.

Stirling Cooper

This case study has been written with the help and co-operation of David Quigley of David Quigley Architects. Their help and permission to publish is gratefully acknowledged.

Background

Stirling Cooper is one of the oldest names on the fashion high street, particularly in London where the company was established 25 years ago. The company is a small chain of medium to low price women's clothes stores. In 1992 Stirling Cooper were bought out by Bodybest, a small East End company, owned by the Dass family. Bodybest had previously manufactured about 80 per cent of Stirling Cooper's merchandise.

Bodybest noticed that Stirling Cooper were paying their bills late and assumed a problem with cashflow. They approached Stirling Cooper to buy the company; being their major supplier, they knew Stirling Cooper's market well. They spent a year negotiating the deal which included researching the company structure, investigating the finances and renegotiating the leases on some of the shops. They effectively bought the company, initially retaining the managing director, who was also a shareholder. However, shortly after the buy-out Bodybest also bought out the managing director who subsequently left the company. Paul Dass then took over as managing director and replaced all Stirling Cooper's management with new people. The initial aim was to get the financial business of the company under tight control.

At this point they also began to examine the company image. Stirling Cooper had some very good central London locations. However, it was felt the shop interiors projected an image of 'a slightly tacky, glitzy, black and chrome late seventies look'. Despite this image they had still managed to retain fairly good business and this is what Bodybest aimed to build on.

Business strategy

Stirling Cooper's main competitors were Top Shop, Miss Selfridge and Principles. Their merchandise was described as being for the East-End girl, who wishes to look fashionable on a limited budget.

The strategy for Stirling Cooper was to focus on this previously targeted market. However, given that they had existed for nearly two generations, they believed that both mothers and daughters could be targeted. In addition, in order to develop a slightly higher price point and promote a designer label to their customer, they negotiated a contract with Bella Freud. A range of Bella Freud merchandise was to be sold through Stirling Cooper shops, in the Autumn of 1993.

In terms of benchmarking themselves, Stirling Cooper's managing director (Paul Dass) and senior management team looked towards another clothing company, Jigsaw. Jigsaw had achieved success and expanded throughout the late 80s/early 90s recession, by carefully positioning themselves and choosing locations appropriate to their market. Jigsaw also focused on a mother and daughter market, selling high quality, fashionable, but simple, merchandise. They invested in well-designed shops and well-made merchandise.

In order to achieve their goals, Stirling Cooper needed to revitalise their image and therefore their shops. Paul Dass approached David Quigley Architects who had designed interiors for the Issue chain of middle-market women's wear. David Quigley subsequently accepted the contract to design the interior of Stirling Cooper shops.

The brief

There was never any form of written brief; rather a series of meetings with Paul Dass, with the public relations company working for Stirling Cooper, with the senior management and with the senior fashion designer. The aim was to establish what the company thought, how Stirling Cooper viewed the retail environment and what image they had of themselves. As David Quigley suggests, 'often clients tell designers what they think they need and miss out something vitally important.'

During these meetings the architects would walk down a high street with Paul Dass, look at images of garments and also at the manufacturing operations and the actual garments. The designers wanted to establish the culture of the organisation and, particularly, Paul Dass's values, whose management style was such that he would want to be involved in the detail of all major design decisions. Much of the company image would be a reflection of the manufacturing director's values, views and business strategy. From the designers' point of view, there is an analogy of the painter in this type of relationship, in that if you want to paint someone's portrait, you need to understand something of their character. In terms of designing shops it is necessary to thoroughly understand the character of the company and the people running it.

During discussions certain phrases were repeatedly used to describe the customer; 'East-End, streetwise girls', 'gutsy girls' with a lot of confidence. The clothes they sought were for nightclubs, discos, weekend wear, possibly for going to work in but not specifically office clothes – very much all round fashion-wear and street clothes.

David Quigley, when shown the merchandise and the promotional photography, immediately noticed that all fashion photography of the clothes was taken outside, in London. The photographs were located in markets, in the East End, against the river, by Tower Bridge. This indicated that not only were the clothes aimed at urban life, but they were set against an urban background. This became a catalyst for developing ideas.

Cost was considered a very important factor. David Quigley was told that Stirling Cooper had a very limited budget – £50.00 per square foot was the approximate budget to work to.

During the briefing discussions, David Quigley also wanted to establish how Paul Dass and Stirling Cooper viewed the role of the designer and what criteria would be used to judge success. David Quigley suggested that his job was to encourage customers to come into the shop and linger, while it was the company's responsibility to sell the merchandise.

In summary then, the briefing process was very interactive. Paul Dass had an open approach and the designers used persistent, subtle questioning to pick up views and cues of what was wanted. During these briefing meetings, the designers also explained how the work would be carried out, how contractors would be used and how the work would be charged to Stirling Cooper.

The design development

This partnership or team work between Stirling Cooper and David Quigley Architects continued through the design development. Initially the design team put together mood boards of urban imagery, of textures and colours, with materials such as rock, stone, concrete, chains, metals, barbed wire and rusty cans. They considered the degeneration and weathering of materials and the resulting textures and colours. The mood boards (see Fig. 4.4), together with physical examples of found materials, were discussed with the Stirling Cooper management to establish the visual and tactile quality required to support the marketing strategy.

Paul Dass and his team were led through the design experience, making design decisions with David Quigley. This assured Paul Dass that the designers were starting afresh and not mimicking work they had done for other retail chains.

Planning the interior

The designers' primary concern was to create a pleasant environment, an environment which enticed customers into the shop and encouraged them to stay. In the

Fig. 4.4 An example of one of many mood boards

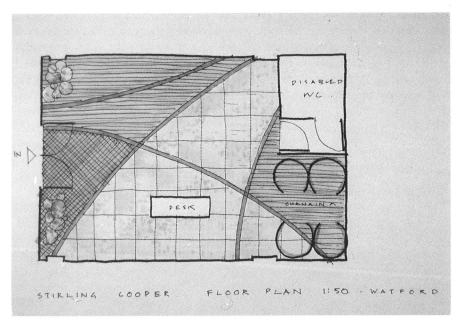

Fig. 4.5 A floorplan idea based on curves

Fig. 4.6 A floorplan idea based on geometric shapes

first instance, therefore, Quigley concerned himself with the feel of the interior, rather than more mechanistic issues of merchandising space and routes to the cash desk. City road layouts were used as references for the floor plan, creating avenues or streets of texture and colour (see Figs 4.5 and 4.6), some with more curved patterns, others with more formal regular plans. These ideas were discussed with Paul Dass and his management team – the more formal designs were felt to be too tight while the others lent themselves to the relaxed/informal approach that they were looking for.

The designers then turned their attention to the shop front. The aim was to achieve an uncluttered window through which one could get a deep view into the shop. The designer therefore had to create a minimalist effect using more glass and keeping all signage quite small (see Fig 4.7).

Using the most simple piece of metal that can be bought – the angle iron (used for everything from gates, fences to bed-frames) – the designers developed the basis of not only the shop frontage, but also a merchandising system. Again this was achieved through discussions with their clients and by showing them samples. They looked at the angle irons, deciding whether they should be stainless steel, mild steel, brass, etc. Through this process of finding materials and sharing them with their client, the designers assembled a palette of materials, textures and colours for use throughout the shops.

In order to develop the merchandising system, the designers spent some time analysing current systems used by other retailers, particularly Stirling Cooper's competitors. The aim in designing the merchandising system was not only to reflect urban life, but also to enable factory manufacture and ease of assembly. Angle irons were used to discuss floor hanging, side and forward hanging and shelving etc. Once decisions had been made, prototypes were built to consider usage, colour and texture. The system was tested through drawings and prototypes to examine the various conditions for which it would need to be adapted. The changing rooms (see Fig. 4.8) were developed from Parisian street cubicles, bringing elements of European culture into this urban environment.

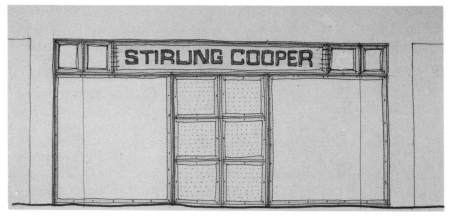

Fig. 4.7 The shop front elevation – one option

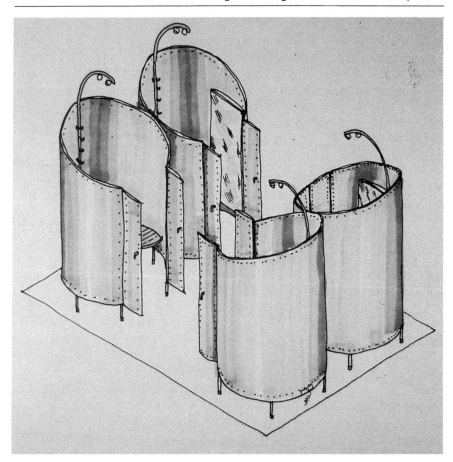

Fig. 4.8 Ideas for the changing rooms

Implementation

Before introducing the design into the main flagship store in Oxford Street, London, a test site was chosen in Kingston-upon-Thames. The designers commissioned and subcontracted the whole refitting project, managing and monitoring the work for Stirling Cooper. The finished shop was extremely successful (see Fig. 4.9), indeed the store doubled its turnover. The designers had achieved what they set out to do, which was to bring customers into the shop environment. Following on from Kingston, two more shops were opened in Watford and Lakeside, followed by the Oxford Street store in May 1993.

A roll-out programme, i.e every shop treated the same over a short time-scale, was not planned; rather David Quigley Associates decided with Stirling Cooper to identify sites and, whilst retaining a coordinated look, treat each site slightly differently in accordance with its location, introducing six or seven new shops each year over a two to three year period.

This project is an example of good communication between designer and client, the designers actively encouraging collaboration throughout the development and, as a result, able to correctly identify and interpret the clients' marketing needs.

Fig. 4.9 The finished shop front

CHAPTER 5

The Marketing/Finance Interface

Richard France

INTRODUCTION

Finance Manager: *'Why are we still planning on selling these sprockets? The last product contribution statements showed that they were not viable.'*

Marketing Manager: *'How was I supposed to know that? With the amount of information you sent me last month I could grow a beard a foot long before I deduced anything worthwhile.'*

How often have we heard comments such as this in corporate life? They underline one of the major problems in the marketing and finance interface: communication. Accountants communicate only in accounting terminology and marketing managers are tuned to receive information only in terms of advertising spend, sales volumes, differentiation strategies, etc.

The net result of this is that 90 per cent of the accountant's work is wasted and many of the marketing manager's decisions are based on minimal information. There must therefore be a detrimental effect on the efficiency and thus profitability of the company, in the long term at least.

Yet, over 70 per cent of study respondents (Ratnatunga, Hooley and Pike, 1992) in both finance and marketing functions stated that communication between the functions was adequate, whereas only 43 per cent of marketers felt that the *organisation* of accounting facilitated information flow to marketing (67 per cent of accountants felt likewise).

Problems

Perhaps if we look at the underlying causes of potential communication problems and then at the remedies we can move on to the positive benefits to be achieved by a close marketing/finance interface. The basic communication problem occurs where the information given to marketers differs from the information needed, or where the marketing department is unaware of the total information needed. Perhaps it is a little of both. Whether the information is transmitted through some sophisticated management information system or by word of mouth the principles remain the same, i.e. it must be:

- accurate

- relevant
- adequate
- on time
- understandable.

Let us look at the situation where a company is marketing drugs to pharmacists and the accountant sends the marketing manager monthly sales/contribution statements, on the 25th of the following month, breaking down the information by drug (there are 300) and by geographical area. We would start by assuming the information is accurate. However, if contributions are based on assumed margins and there has been a price-discounting promotion which has not been communicated to the finance department, the figures will be awry. If 90 per cent of sales are on four or five of the drugs, how relevant is the detailed breakdown of the other 295? If the geographical breakdown does not show how many health centres/hospitals are in the area it must be inadequate. Is the 25th of the following month really on time? It may well be too late for the marketing department to take any remedial action. Can the marketing manager actually understand the figures presented and find the information needed in the statement?

The problem therefore is often one of the accountant/financial manager deciding what sort of information the marketing managers need without first spending time with them to let them know what information he or she is capable of producing and in what format. This would avoid the too much/too little information syndrome.

Why does this problem occur? Simple laziness is often the reason given by senior management, but that is rarely as a result of deep analysis. The problem could be an organisational one in that if a company is run on a functional structure, the effect is to discourage the horizontal flow of information – sometimes because different functional departments are in different buildings!

Second, the corporate culture of the organisation could affect the problem, i.e. is the company strategically or financially controlled? The latter type of company tends to concentrate on results compared to budget whereas the former tends towards a more dynamic and creative approach to information needs relative to attaining its objectives as the environment changes.

Third, time is a major constraint on both sides but this is principally the financial manager's problem. Far too much time is spent by the accountant collecting data and subsequently converting it into information. Frequently, totally unrealistic deadlines are imposed on the accountant for producing monthly figures. For the last two or three weeks of the month the accountant is cruising and supervising the day-to-day routines of the office; then for the next ten days he or she is working flat out to produce the previous month's figures before the board meeting. As a result of this pressure and tight time scale, the figures are often not very accurate due to having too early a cut-off date for invoice processing, leaving some bills estimated or, indeed, not accounted for at all. Also, the figures end up being produced the day before the presentation and therefore little time is spent in interpreting them for non-financial departments such as marketing. Thus, a mass of financial information is produced and circulated to each department head; each divisional/functional head then has to decipher which parts of the information are relevant to him or her and extract from those the meaningful items. This should have been done, broadly at least, by the finance function.

Finally, there is often a significant age gap between marketing and financial managers. A financial manager is usually a qualified accountant which, after allowing for at least four years' post-qualification experience, will put the minimum age at twenty-eight or twenty-nine, but more often thirty or more. A marketing manager may well be only two years out of university and only twenty-three or so. The net result can be a totally unequal relationship, making one party unwilling to seek information from or give it to the other. Giving information can be seen to be a surrender of power and there is an instinctive urge for senior people to hold on to information for that reason.

Solutions

The solutions to these problems usually lie with the senior management.

First, there is a need for organisational change, usually moving from a less functionally directed to a more task-orientated organisation. This would mean, for instance, that an accountant could be employed as part of the marketing department to co-ordinate and interpret both the inflow and outflow of financial information.

Second, training is a key way of improving the communication blockage. If marketing managers are thoroughly trained in the work requirements of financial managers and vice versa it will have an unblocking effect. The two will exchange relevant and useful information and, hopefully, each will appreciate the other's information needs. Intensive short courses can help in this field but it is better if formal training qualifications such as DMS or MBA are pursued, certainly by the younger managers in the company. Unfortunately, UK companies tend to allocate too little finance to training budgets to do the job properly – due to the fear of training people to a level where they can earn a higher salary elsewhere and so losing them. This is an unfortunate legacy of the short-termism in management decision-making caused by the main stock market drivers being return on capital and earnings per share – and these *must* increase year on year. If a long-term training strategy is adopted it is frequently cut in times of recession without regard to the total waste of the previous training efforts (if not taken further) or to the future effect on employees' motivation and effectiveness.

Third, the accountant should produce more information and less data for the marketing department. This means much more time needs to be given to planning the information needs of the marketing department, by regular planning meetings and continually checking that information is being fed back effectively. For the accountant to have this time available there must be a total change in attitude by both the accountant and his or her seniors. The question is whether the accountant is purely a technician or a supplier of information. It has often been said that the UK is top heavy with accountants. This is merely a statement of how the roles in an organisation are defined. In Germany, for instance, there are far fewer qualified accountants. Rather than having, as the UK does, qualified accountants who collate and put the figures into financial statements and manage the financial function of the company, they have many more accounting technicians who collate all the figures, produce the statements and then pass them on to the financial managers, who interpret them and disseminate the information. These financial managers are, more often than not, trained in general management (MBA for instance) rather than purely in finance. The reasoning stands out clearly in that the information can be better managed by a manager with a handle on each aspect of business.

Fourth, the culture of the company could be changed so that it is driven by its own abilities within its environment rather than totally by the budget, often based on information that is twelve to eighteen months old. For instance (and going back to the functional roles), the accountant draws up a budget based on, among other things, the inclusion of £200,000 on new product development which shows returns of £400,000 the following year. A period of recession ensues and the new product development budget is cut by over half, midway through the year, as part of an overall overhead reduction made to achieve the budgeted profit. The move may well produce the results in the short term but what has happened to the strategic approach? What will happen to the market share next year? Instead of in-house development, the new products have to be bought in at what cost? Surely during a recession, if it is extended, although there is a tendency for buyers to stick with products they know, the only way of improving market share might be with new products. The company therefore needs to get away from the short-termist financially controlled culture forced on UK listed companies and move towards a longer-term strategic approach.

Finally, once the age-gap problem is recognised it can be tackled through joint presentations, meetings, courses and – hopefully – an open style of management which will decrease inhibitions.

BENEFITS OF A SUCCESSFUL FINANCE/MARKETING INTERFACE

There are two basic levels where the finance/marketing interface is most powerful – with, of course, significant overlap between them. The operational level has the management accountant feeding information to the marketing department. This would cover such things as contribution analysis, working capital management (stockholding, credit control), investment appraisal, product line management and scarce resource maximisation (see the Xenon Pottery case study at the end of this chapter for an example). There is then the strategic level, where the marketing and financial directors are liaising over corporate and marketing strategy covering such things as target profit, break-even price flexing, return on capital, return on investment, cash using and cash creating products.

OPERATIONAL LEVEL
Working capital

The first area of interface is in the management of working capital. By that we mean how we control the stocks, the debtors, the creditors and the bank balance. The management of creditors and bank does not directly affect the marketing department unless, of course, failure to pay bills on time results in non-receipt of goods which in turn creates a knock-on effect with poor delivery to the customer. It is not uncommon for marketing and finance to come to blows about this.

Stock management

The management of stock is an area of conflicting loyalties. The accountant requires all stock levels to be at a minimum to reduce the working capital needed to fund them, whereas the marketing manager requires a higher level of stock to ensure maximum service to the customer. There is therefore a two-way requirement: the accountant must supply information to the marketing manager on the amount of working capital available for stockholding and, based on this, the marketing manager must inform the accountant of the minimum month-end holding of different product lines needed to retain customer satisfaction.

In the late 1970s, one major UK fibres company bought out several well-run family-owned clothing wholesalers as a vertical integration strategy with a view to finding new channels of distribution for its clothing (and therefore cloth made with its fibres). It was at this time that major industries, being financially rather than strategically controlled, were suffering from an excess of accountants at the top. The acquired wholesalers had previously been profitable and reasonably efficient – but the accountants now became involved with them, with orders to increase the profits. The first thing they did was to take a financial view of the stockholding, which due to the low stock turnover ratios meant a stock reduction exercise. This was done successfully and achieved the objective of improving the stock turnover ratio (purchases/average stock). One by one the wholesalers went into liquidation. The reason was simple: in reducing the stockholding they had cut the primary service of the wholesaler – to carry stock and offer a choice. The customers therefore stopped buying. This was a classic case of non-communication between marketing and finance.

Managing the debtors

Also called credit management, this is another area of conflict. How often do we hear of accountants over-zealously chasing for payment, causing a lost account? And how often of weak credit control causing a build-up of debtors that results in cash-flow problems and an increased risk of bad debts?

The accountant is interested primarily in being paid as soon as possible for the goods supplied whereas the marketing manager is more concerned with customer satisfaction and increasing sales to that customer. There therefore needs to be a balance between the risk of giving increased credit to customers and the finance available to fund that credit. This in turn means that there must be a clear credit policy reflecting that balance. It must, however, be flexible: there will be occasions when a customer may require extended credit – not always due to an inability to pay. For instance, if a supplier to an expanding retailer were asked to give extended credit on all new store stocking, and refused, the business could well go to a competitor. Not only would the sale of the new store stock be lost but also all the future sales that stock could generate. Therefore there must be room for commercial views to be taken by the company outside the narrow priorities of either the marketing or the finance functions.

Capital budgeting and appraisal

All too often the investment appraisal of projects is done by the accountant solely on the basis of how much it will cost and the minimum return required to make the project feasible. This return is translated back into sales (for a sales-generating rather than cost-cutting project) and a judgement made on whether those sales are achievable. What *should* happen is that marketing be asked to forecast, with reasons, sales that can realistically be achieved out of a given project. This will then translate into cash flow generated and the figure used to compare with the project costs, using the internal rate of return, net present value, payback or whatever method is appropriate to judge the ranking or feasibility of differing projects.

An example of this is where company A was considering purchasing company B for £1 million. On simple analysis A would achieve a payback within five to six years as B was expected to make £200,000 profit a year. This was outside the company's present investment criteria, which required a payback in less than four years, meaning profits in excess of £250,000. The accountant went through an exercise of proposed cost cutting, particularly on overheads which could be saved if company B's manufacturing was done at A's premises. The result showed the project to be feasible. However, the marketing manager did an analysis of the products and markets and found that 50 per cent of sales were of products that were being superseded by a technologically superior competitor, which would reduce sales and margins dramatically on these lines. When translated into figures this again made the project unfeasible. This example, although simplistic, shows how the movement of information to the accountant from the marketing department and vice versa can be vital in making the correct investment decision. This is particularly important for some of those smaller investment decisions (e.g. a machine purchase) which, once taken, are rarely monitored due to the excessive costs involved. It is vital that investment decisions proceed with confidence rather than ignorance, for otherwise the same mistakes will be repeated without ever being recognised.

Another common investment decision is whether new product development or initial advertising costs are justified when measured against the expected return. This is commonly done by using a discounted cash flow technique, where the future net income streams are discounted back to present value and compared with the initial costs. For example, a company is planning the launch of a new product line and expects the net margin after ongoing promotional costs to be £500,000 a year for four years. The marketing director needs to know how much could be spent on pump-prime promotion to launch the product. If the company were borrowing the cost of this initial promotion from its bank at an interest rate of 10 per cent, that could be the discounting rate used. Table 5.1 shows the calculation.

Table 5.1 Discounted cash flow

Cash flow	Discount factor (10%)	Present value
Year 1 500,000	.91	455,000
2 500,000	.83	415,000
3 500,000	.75	375,000
4 500,000	.68	340,000
Total present value		£1,585,000

The company could therefore spend up to £1,585,000 on initial promotion before the project ceased to earn above the cost of the initial promotion of the project. Needless to say, this is a simplistic model and the detail of the cash flows, cost of capital rate, etc. would normally be more complex, requiring a close relationship between the marketing and finance departments. Additionally, in appraising an investment the accountant will have access to information on costs saved or incurred as a result of the investment other than capital costs. . This may well be of little interest to the marketing department unless they initiated the proposal, for instance suggesting a new machine to improve quality or achieve a given type of finish or design to a product. In this event, marketing has a vested interest in all aspects of the investment decision in order to justify the capital outlay, not least because any cost reduction could have an effect on the ultimate pricing of the product.

Product line management

It usually takes many years for product lines to evolve and it is the ability to control this evolution which produces a profitable company.

Product lines may increase due to new product development, whether a formal or informal process, or through a simple adjustment to the design of a product to suit a customer's needs. In other words, sales information is fed back to the design or production office, which in turn feeds the result to finance to cost the alterations. We therefore can end up with dozens of different models from one basic product and the result can be very inefficient production.

Frequently, a company can make more profit by dropping a product line than by creating a new one and we therefore need to examine the marginal or variable cost of a product in order to come to any decision about its future. Although the marketing department may already receive product profit statements these often contain, in the costs, elements of allocated fixed costs such as a proportion of the general advertising costs or sales force's wages. No product line decision can be made unless these fixed costs are stripped out. It is worth summarising the basic product line decisions and examining the financial influences on what is basically a marketing decision in each case: do we manufacture a product, do we buy it in or do we drop it?

Manufacture the product

The basic decision here is based on comparing the costs to the return. The marketing department recommends a price at which it can sell a product and the finance department analyses the costs of manufacture and distribution. Provided the sales price is higher than these costs, in simple terms it is worth manufacturing. These costs can be further broken down for other decisions. For example, the marketing department has analysed the feedback from the national sales force and found that by cutting the price of a given product by 30 per cent, it could compete with the company's rivals. The product profit after allocation of fixed costs is only 20 per cent of sales so a price reduction of this amount is, on the face of it, not feasible. However, if the costs are fully broken down, the marginal cost, i.e. the cost of making one more unit of product, can be extracted. Provided the marginal cost is less than 70 per cent of the current sales price, it could be worthwhile adopting the price reduction as contribution will be generated towards the overall profit which would otherwise be lost. The difficulty, of course, is trying to arrive at the marginal cost as many costs do not vary directly with sales. Needless to say, all pricing decisions cannot be taken on a marginal cost basis – if they were the factory would be working to capacity and still not making a profit due to not producing adequate contribution overall to cover the fixed costs. Marginal cost-based pricing should therefore be used only for short-term decisions such as filling a production gap.

Having decided whether or not it is feasible to make certain products or product ranges we then need to decide which products to make and which to drop in the profit-maximisation process of the product line management. Broadly speaking, it is fair to say that given unlimited capacity (or a capacity level which is nowhere near being reached, which has been a common problem in the UK for some years), any product producing a contribution should be retained, as dropping it will inevitably reduce net profit. However, this does not take into account the interdependence of products in the product line. For example, a company sells two wheelbarrows: model A, producing a contribution of £10 each, and model B, of £12 each. The company is selling five As and ten Bs a month. Dropping either model would appear to reduce profit. However, if it can be shown that to drop A would increase sales of B by five units a month, then for the £50 lost contribution on A, 5 x £12 = £60 is gained on B, thus increasing the overall profit. A reverse example would be a company manufacturing ballpoints and refills, the pens at a loss and the refills at a substantial profit. Dropping the production of the ballpoints will, however, inevitably lead to a massive fall in the sale of the refills – and thus profit.

It can therefore be seen that while there may be much pressure from the accountant to drop a particular product or range from a portfolio, the marketing manager also has relevant information on the market effects on other products.

One area of complication is where a company is working at capacity. In this case the decision whether to drop a product is not based on whether or not that product is making a contribution but whether by dropping that product it can be replaced with others which generate as much contribution. Once again a two-product company can demonstrate the decision process: it sells 50 of product A and 40 of B a month; A contributes £5 each, i.e. £250, and B £3, i.e. £120, totally £370. To drop B would reduce the contribution by £120. There are two possible courses. First, the lost contribution must be replaced by increased sales of A. B's lost contribution divided by A's unit contribution equals 24. Therefore if B were to be dropped A's sales would need to increase by at least 24 units so as not to reduce profit. Second, the lost contribution could be replaced by a third product (C) which produces a unit contribution of £10. The company would thus need to sell 12 Cs to achieve the same overall contribution. There is of course a risk factor to take into account when dropping a product in these circumstances: we are sacrificing *known* sales of an established product for *estimated* sales of a new product. The new product therefore needs to make considerable extra contribution to be worth the risk. In addition, potential growth of the new product as against the old must be taken into account (i.e. their relative stages in the product life cycle), so no sensible decision should be made on the basis of immediate effect although due to short-term pressures innovation in product line development is often slowed as product line profitability will often drop during the early stages of reorganisation.

Generally, if a company is trading below capacity it should not drop a product which produces a contribution. There is one instance, however, where this is not the case: when a product has *specific* fixed costs related to it which can be eliminated along with the product. If we revert to the previous example of product A contributing £250 and B £120, and suppose there are fixed costs of £300, the overall position would be: total contribution (£250 + £120) is £370; fixed costs are £300; thus profit is £70. Let us now suppose that dropping B would mean that a complete factory could be eliminated, i.e. no rates, rent, maintenance, etc. (or reassigned to another part of the company or group). The fixed costs associated with this factory are £180. If we now dropped B we would be left with A's contribution of £250 less fixed costs of £120 (£300 – £180), producing a net profit of £130. It can be seen that eliminating a product can actually increase the net profit where the attributable, or specific, fixed costs are greater than the contribution produced.

There are other financial implications to dropping or gaining products, not least from the production point of view. It is not uncommon for a company which is marketing-driven to go headlong for new product development and increase its product range from, say, twenty to ninety. The effect of this is to dilute the sales of any one product, which would basically mean much shorter production runs with the natural concomitants of increased wastage and production inefficiency. Similarly, rationalising a product range can have enormous production benefits which at the outset are not easily quantifiable and certainly not by the marketing department alone. In this instance we need a very close interface between the operations, financial and marketing managements.

Buy in the product

The final product line decision is whether to make the product ourselves or to buy it in. The rapid development of low labour-cost countries over the last ten years or so has meant that the UK as a nation has shed many manufacturing jobs, particularly in labour-intensive fields such as clothing and textiles. The basic reason is that imported items are cheaper than home-produced ones. We can translate this macro-economic effect into a micro-economic effect by looking at an individual company. Once again we have product A and product B, shown in Table 5.2.

Table 5.2

	Product A	Product B	Total
Total sales price	10	9	
Variable costs	5	6	
Contribution/unit	5	3	
Unit sales	50	40	
Total contribution	250	120	370

We now see that B has a much lower contribution percentage than A (33.3 compared to 50 per cent). We also find that we can source B abroad for £4 and drop our manufacture of it for £6 a unit. The effect of this is to increase the contribution of product B from £3 to £5 a unit, i.e. by £2 a unit, making £80 in total.

From a financial viewpoint we must have this product made outside if the buy-in costs are less than our own variable costs of manufacture. There are other considerations in this decision, such as buying lead times, delivery ability, and product quality control that will be lost if the product is subcontracted, but it is a common practice where companies wish to put all the bulk orders through their own factories and the smaller 'range enhancers' to outside contractors or vice versa.

Maximising scarce resources

All other things being equal, it is natural to assume that in the pursuit of maximum profitability a company will endeavour to sell the items with the highest gross contribution percentage per product. Let us take a company with the three products A, B and C, details of which are in Table 5.3.

Table 5.3

	Product A	Product B	Product C
Sales price	10	20	12
Variable costs	8	12	6
Contribution	?	8	6
Contribution (%)	20	40	50
Kg of material per unit	0.5	8	3
Contribution per kg	4	1	2

For a given sales value achievable our company should maximise its efforts on C up to its market potential, followed by B and, finally, by A, as C has the highest contribution percentage. On the other hand, if we are looking at a given number of *units* achievable across the whole company, we must surely maximise on the product with the highest unit rather than percentage contribution. In this event we need to concentrate on B, which yields £8 a unit followed by C (£6 a unit) and, finally, A (£2 a unit). Suppose the company has a production limit of 1,000 units and the market potential of A is 1,000 units, and B and C 600 units each. The company's result would differ with the prioritising factor chosen. If we took percentage contribution (priority C, B, A), we would make the maximum 600 Cs and devote the remaining capacity (400) to B. Contribution would be 600 Cs at £6, i.e. £3,600, plus 400 Bs at £8, i.e. £3,200, totalling £6,800. If we look at unit contribution, however (priority B,

C, A), the company would instead make 600 Bs and 400 Cs. Contribution would thus be £4,800 plus £2,400, totalling £7,200. In neither case would any units of A be made.

We can therefore see that by using contribution per unit for prioritising where there is a restriction on the number of units gives a higher return than by using contribution percentage.

To take the model further, let us suppose that the amount of material available was limited to 3,900 kg, and that A used 0.5 kg a unit, B used 8 kg a unit and C 3 kg a unit. The restriction on material means that we need to maximise our contribution per kg (see Table 5.3). We now need to prioritise as to A, then C, then B.

This now gives us the following, shown in Table 5.4.

Table 5.4

Priority	Units	Kg	Cont/Unit	Total contribution
Product A	1,000	500	2	2,000
Product C	600	1,800	6	3,600
Product B	200	1,600	8	1,600
				£7,200

This model assumes there is no additional restriction on the total number of units which can be manufactured. If there were no restrictions on any product quantities, all production would be on A which would not otherwise have been manufactured at all! The Xenon case study at the end of this chapter shows how a marketing decision can be affected by a further restriction on a key resource: in that case, skilled labour.

Budgetary control

Budgets are drawn up on the basis of the financial implications of the corporate plan. The financial objective is to achieve a given level of profit and the budgets are used to control the company and influence it towards the planned outcome. A master budget is produced and from that a series of departmental mini-budgets is produced. The overriding figure in the budget is the sales, which determines many of the costs as well as the amount and timing of the cash received by the company.

There clearly needs to be a close relationship between the marketing manager and accountant at two stages: in the planning stage liaison is needed on determining the level of sales anticipated and the credit given on average to each customer. Then, in the control stage marketing has to inform finance of any changes in sales projections during the year or likely bad debts or extended credit or discounts offered. Similarly, finance must inform marketing of any companies that are bad credit risks, perhaps with a view to withdrawing sales effort on those companies or using the sales force to collect outstanding debts.

In addition, the figures for the whole marketing mix need liaison at both the planning and control stages:

- *Product* – which products are being promoted and which are being dropped.
- *Price* – at what price the products are being sold. The interface here is important as the accountant and marketing manager can work together to determine which volume of sales at which price will generate the highest contribution.
- *Place* – what the relative costs of different distribution methods are and how a decision to take on a more expensive method will be justified.
- *Promotion* – what the anticipated costs of promotion are and the level of total costs within the promotional mix at which the business ceases to be worthwhile.

We are therefore looking at a close liaison between the marketing manager and the accountant across the whole range of costs associated with marketing a product or product line.

We need a detailed analysis of costs broken down by geographical area, product group and customer. This means there must be an adequate management information system to cope with this requirement because the breakdown of distribution costs and promotional spend must be allocated directly to the customer to which it relates rather than to some arbitrary allocation of costs across a customer group or geographical area. From this information channel profitability can be calculated and sometimes a channel previously assumed to be profitable can be shown to be a loss-maker. For instance, a salesperson makes ten calls on customer A to win a 1,000-unit order and two calls on customer B to get a 500-unit order. If the salesperson's time were apportioned equally between the two then, all other things being equal, A would appear more profitable than B. But in reality the salesperson is getting an average 100 units per call from A and 250 from B. As a salesperson is limited by the number of calls she or he can make in a given period, this would make customer B a more valuable customer during periods of heavy demand. Needless to say there are many other costs to consider but the principle remains that some form of activity-based costing needs to be applied in order to establish correctly the viability of a geographical area, product or customer. The accountant and marketing manager need to communicate on the budget not just because of the sales projections but also on promotional spend, capital expenditure on plant (for expansion), extra warehousing and cash-flow forecasting, to name but a few.

STRATEGIC LEVEL

At the strategic level the interface is between the finance and marketing directors. The areas of combined interest would be budget setting, brand valuations, product portfolios, target profit, strategic pricing and return on capital.

Budget setting

In drawing up master budgets two basic methods are used.

(1) The marketing environment can be analysed with the intention that the marketing department comes up with a level of sales anticipated for the ensuing year. This level of sales will then dictate the level of wages to manufacture the products, the level of purchases, finished stock levels, advertising and so on, down to the final profit which can be anticipated.

(2) The second method is less sensible but none the less common. The company decides what profit it needs to satisfy either the bankers or the shareholders or, for a listed company, the market and investment analysts. The profit figure is then extrapolated upwards to arrive at the sales figure needed to achieve this profit.

We therefore have a significant conflict at the strategic level because the marketing director is directly influenced by the environment in which he or she is operating, whereas the financial director is influenced by the stock market requirements, which in turn should be influenced by the environment or the internal requirements of the company for internal investment or expansion.

The question is how to resolve this conflict. The answer is that a combination of the two budgeting methods is used. First, the marketing department produces its anticipated level of sales for the company's products. This causes a cascade of budgets down to the final profit figure of £X. The finance department then reacts effectively by saying that this profit is not enough and needs to be increased to £Y. This is then conveyed back to marketing – hopefully, to say that with increased investment in a certain area sales could be increased enough to give a profit of £Y. The likelihood is that only marginal improvements in the sales estimate can be made, and so the only other strategy is to look at the company's costs. The costs of sales are presumably continually subjected to efforts to trim them, so the overheads are examined with a view to reducing them to ensure the ideal profit can be met. This is often done during the year in question when it is found that original sales budgets are unlikely to be met.

It is often at this stage (i.e. when profits are looking below market expectations) that companies are on the receiving end of hostile take-over bids. This threat has led to the creation of brand valuations to pump up the assets of a company.

Brand valuations

The valuation of brands on the balance sheet has caused a mass of controversy both within and outside the accounting profession. With no clear UK accounting standard (at the time of writing) it would seem that a company can place a value on its brands simply if it feels like it. (Under French company law brands may not be shown on the balance sheet.) This causes difficulty in making inter-company comparisons, primarily because it has the effect of increasing the intangible assets in the balance sheet and thus the reserves.

Brand values increase the balance sheet figure for capital employed, which in turn has a negative effect on the return on capital employed, a key ratio in determining relative company performance. If a company chooses to value its brands it will improve its assets and capital. This will also have the effect of reducing the company's gearing as its ratio of loans to total capital employed will decrease. This must be viewed as positive and so a great incentive to include brands. Similarly, it should improve a company's ability to borrow money.

The arguments currently raging about brands (and their valuation) are numerous, and many questions remain unanswered:

- Are they separately identifiable?
- Are they separately saleable?
- Are they internally generated or purchased brands?
- How are they valued (based on market sector, market growth, market share, advertising support, product margin, product life cycle, etc.)?
- How are they written off?
- Who values them?
- Why not value employees' skills and management skills as well?
- Does a balance sheet show a true and fair view if we do not value brands?

No doubt answers will be given in time, but meanwhile balance sheets are becoming increasingly three-dimensional when they are written in only two dimensions! More and more, therefore, brands are being managed according to how they can be incorporated into the balance sheet rather than from purely marketing objectives.

Target profit

Aside from the mechanistic aspects of budgetary control in arriving at a budget the strategic interface between marketing and finance comes through deciding what is an acceptable profit target and how to arrive at it.

The UK stock market is driven by maximising return on capital employed and, through that, earnings per share. These are maximised by striking a balance between safety and risk. If a company has few shares and high borrowing, for example, in periods of high profit the interest on the borrowed money is paid easily and the return on each share is high. In periods of low profit the interest might barely be covered. With low borrowings the return per share will be higher in periods of low profit. Thus a balance is required, and in recession sensible companies cut back on their borrowings.

A company making a profit of, say, 20 per cent on its initial capital of £10 million will earn £2 million. Assuming for the moment that it retains this profit, rather than paying a dividend, its capital will increase to £12 million; in order not to fall below a 20 per cent return on capital it must now make a profit of £2.4 million. So if the required return on capital is x per cent, the profit must also rise by x per cent in order not to show a decreasingly efficient use of capital.

The company can use a simple marginal cost structure to arrive at the target sales which will give the required rate of return on its capital. In the example above, let us say the profit/cost structure was as shown in column 1 of Table 5.5.

Table 5.5 Examples of return on capital

	1 (£m)	2 (£m)	3 (£m)
Capital (20% return needed)	10.0	12.0	12.0
Sales	20.0	20.8	20.8
Variable costs (50%)	10.0	10.4	10.4
Contribution	10.0	10.4	10.4
Overheads	8.0	8.0	10.0
Profit	2.0	2.4	0.4
As % return on capital	20.0	20.0	3.3

To arrive at the target sales we substitute the new amount of return on capital into the profit part of the model and work the model backwards (see column 2 in Table 5.5). We therefore have a sales target of £20.8 million as against the previous year's £20 million. In other words, we need a 4 per cent increase in sales. (In practice these figures would be flexed for alterations in projected contributions and the inflation and wage effect on overheads.)

A development of this model would be strategic pricing; perhaps the company would find that the overheads were going up to, say, £10 million. This would give us a new model as shown in column 3 of Table 5.5. To bring the return back to £2.4 million there has to be a price increase or a volume increase. In other words, the contribution must move up to £12.4 million from £10.4 million.

In this situation the flexible break-even chart shown in Fig. 5.1 could be used to arrive at the ideal volume/price mix. Here the demand for the products is plotted across differing price levels, so market research is obviously needed to substantiate the projections. The highest point on the demand curve will be the point of highest profit and this point may be under or over the total costs curve. Where the curve touches the total cost curve will be the price that will yield the required profit.

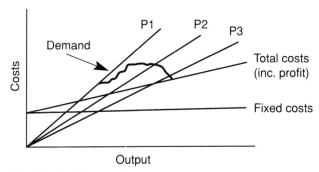

Fig. 5.1 The flexible break-even chart

Whilst one could question the feasibility of such an exercise at corporate level, it can be used readily at the operational level to maximise contributions from differing product groups.

Product portfolios

The final area of strategic interface is on the product range. It may be thought that the product range is totally a marketing decision, but clearly there are significant cash implications to product line management decisions. We will look at three basic marketing models used in product line management and examine the cash implications of each.

Product life cycle

Fig. 5.2 shows the product life cycle. Generally speaking, a product uses much cash at the development and innovation stage; many products also use cash in gaining a significant market share. It is therefore not until the maturity stage that significant cash is generated.

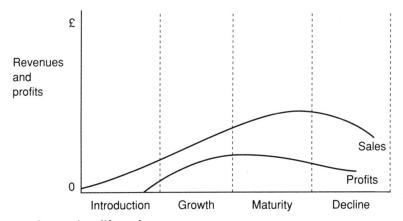

Fig. 5.2 The product life cycle

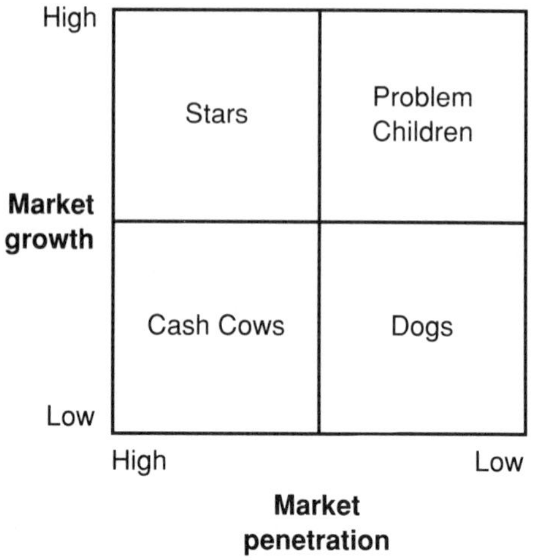

Fig. 5.3 The Boston matrix

If a company endeavours to develop and launch too many new products at the same time, their combined cash requirements can have a severe effect on the company's cash flow. On the assumption that cash resources are limited, the implication of this is that new product development needs to be staggered over a period so that the costs of developing one new product can be offset by the cash generated by a product in the mature stage of its life cycle.

The Boston matrix

This model, shown in Fig. 5.3, is used when looking at the company's portfolio of products. A product with a high share of a low-growth market is known as a Cash Cow. It spends just enough on the promotional mix to maintain its market share. It creates a lot of cash/profit and should be used for funding other cash-using products, such as a Problem Child – which needs to be taken from a low into a high market share, in a market with high growth, i.e. turn it into a Star. From a cash point of view it is best to have all products as Cash Cows or Stars and in recessionary times the companies with this mix are the ones which maintain their cash reserves and, of course, share prices. The strategy with a Dog (low share, low growth) is either to invest heavily to endeavour to transform it into a Cash Cow or, if the company is short of cash, to divest itself of the product, assuming it cannot just tick over without needing cash for investment or to support losses.

Ansoff matrix

The Ansoff matrix (see Fig. 5.4) is used for general product strategy where there is a mixed choice between the same products and markets or new products and markets.

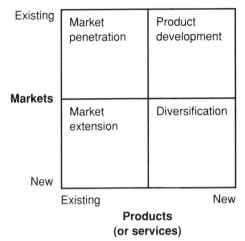

Fig. 5.4 Ansoff matrix

To pursue a new product into a new market is effectively total diversification, which is the most expensive product strategy decision. Pursuing the same products with the same markets is market penetration, the least expensive strategy. Between those stand product development (new products into the same markets) or market expansion (same products into new markets). Clearly, a cash-rich company can consider a diversification strategy which would not even be an option without significant finance. A company with little ability or opportunity to raise finance can consider only a market penetration strategy. It depends on the type of product/market involved whether product development or market expansion is the cheaper option.

Whether we are talking about the whole company or different product lines within the company, the principle remains the same. That is, there must be a balance between cash-creating and cash-using products. This creates a need for marketing and financial strategies to be closely linked as part of an overall strategic plan.

SUMMARY

In summary, we have looked at the problems of a poor marketing/finance interface: lack of mutual understanding, organisation and communication. The causes of those problems have been identified as lack of training, the differences between strategic and functional management-control approaches and the information flow and cultural problems.

The remedies have been identified as more training, organisational change and a corporate culture change. Finally, the benefits of close liaison have been highlighted from an operational viewpoint of working capital management, product line management, investment appraisal and budgetary control. From a strategic viewpoint we have examined targeting profit, targeting return on capital and product line strategies.

Overall, we must compare the actual costs of differing elements of marketing with the benefits, i.e. at what point does it cease to be sensible to spend further on marketing/promotion when that same money could be spent with greater return on product innovation, productivity improvements or, quite simply, be left in the bank?

BIBLIOGRAPHY

McLaney, E. S. (1991) *Business Finance for Decision Makers*, London: Pitman.
Mott, G. (1989) *Investment Appraisal*, MTE.
Ratnatunga, J., Hooley, G. J. and Pike, R. (1992) 'Marketing Finance Interface', *European Journal of Marketing*
Ward, Keith (1989) *Financial Aspects of Marketing*, London: Heinemann.

CASE STUDY

Xenon Pottery

Xenon Pottery is a small china-manufacturing company employing twenty-three staff. Its main products are Toby jugs and china teapots, which account for 25 and 75 per cent of turnover respectively. The staff comprises the Managing Director Mr Gilby, a part-time accountant Jenny Main, an assistant production manager and twenty employees on the shop floor:

- two casters
- one kilnman
- two spongers
- two aerographers
- two sorters/quality control
- one warehouseman
- ten hand-painters.

It is the hand-painters on whom this case study is based.

Xenon Pottery is very close to capacity for hand-painted products: 1,000 Toby jugs and 4,000 teapots a month. Mr Gilby has just received a large order from a customer with whom Xenon has been trying to do business for nearly a year. It is for a new product which Xenon has just developed: china lampstands. The figures are shown in Table 5.6.

Table 5.6 Xenon production and contribution data

	Toby jugs	Teapots	Lampstands
Monthly units anticipated	1,000	4,000	1,200
Sales value	8,000	24,000	12,000
Variable costs	2,000	8,000	6,000
Total contribution	6,000	16,000	6,000
Contribution %	75	67	50
Contribution per unit	£6	£4	£5

The highest unit and percentage contribution is on the Toby jugs. The new product range of lampstands gives the lowest contribution and is middle of the three in contribution per unit. As the Toby jugs and teapots are established lines and effectively taking up all the hand-painters' capacity, should this mean that the lampstands are not made or, if possible, subcontracted?

First, it must be established how a resource – in this case the hand-painters – comes to be scarce. It might be thought that in an area of Staffordshire where pottery has been a major industry for centuries there would be no shortage of hand- painters. This is true but, in order to employ more hand-painters, management must answer the following questions. Are there *unemployed* hand-painters?

(If not, *above* the average rate will need to be paid to tempt them away from other jobs.) If there are no hand-painters available what is the cost of training new ones and how long will it take? How long will the company be hand-painting its products? Will there be a change in demand for hand-painted goods (due to cost)? Will new technology replace hand-painting? Might the company change its product strategy (i.e. move away from labour-intensive products)?

A product can be scarce quite simply due to a managerial decision not to increase its quantity due to the extra risks involved. It is therefore not enough just to say that a resource is *not* scarce simply because it is available outside the company. Many companies operate with a scarce resource situation without really identifying it. To determine whether a resource is scarce it is necessary to look at the resource from two angles: in the event of need can the resource be increased without further increase in other costs? Second, if the resource can be increased, is management willing to increase it?

Having established that a resource is scarce the next stage is to establish a means of maximising the return from that scarce resource. This is done by looking at the contribution of each product and comparing it to the amount of scarce resource used by that product. Xenon's hand-painting times on each product are, per unit: Toby jugs half an hour, teapots and lampstands a quarter of an hour each. These times must be compared with the contribution for each unit so that the contribution per hour can be calculated, on the basis that the product which gives the highest contribution per scarce resource (in this case, hours) will be the one with most profit potential. The figures are as follows:

- Toby jugs – £12 per hour (two units at £6)
- teapots – £16 per hour (four units at £4)
- lampstands – £20 per hour (four units at £5).

So the lampstands produce the best return followed by the teapots and the Toby jugs – with a contribution per scarce resource just over half that of the lampstands.

The initial position taken by Gilby was to manufacture only Toby jugs and teapots as they give the best contribution percentage and would fully utilise the 1,500 hand-painting hours available. This would give a contribution of £22,000, as shown in the first part of Table 5.7.

The second position taken up was to maximise the sales in order of the contribution per unit. This would mean selling first the Toby jugs to capacity, then the lampstands to capacity, and finally the teapots. This meant that all the lampstands and Toby jugs were made, and the 700 remaining hours of hand-painting would be spent on the teapots. The figures are in the second part of Table 5.7. The total contribution is now £23,200 (£1,200 more than the initial position).

The accountant had a look at these figures and pointed to the flaw in the argument, which then highlighted the course of action to maximise the contribution: prioritise on the product with the highest contribution per scarce resource, in this case the lampstands followed by the teapots and finally the Toby jugs. The results are shown in the third part of Table 5.7.

Table 5.7 The different contribution calculations

	Toby jugs	Teapots	Lampstands	Total
Percentage				
Units	1,000	4,000		
Hours	500	1,000		1,500
Contribution per unit	£6	£4		
Total contribution	£6,000	£16,000		£22,000
Unit				
Units	1,000	2,800	1,200	
Hours	500	700	300	1,500
Contribution per unit	£6	£4	£5	
Total contribution	£6,000	£11,200	£6,000	£23,200
Scarce resource				
Units	400	4,000	1,200	
Hours	200	1,000	300	1,500
Contribution per unit	£6	£4	£5	
Total contribution	£2,400	£16,000	£6,000	£24,400

The total contribution is now £24,400 (£2,400 or 10 per cent more than the original position). This is achieved by selling the total market potential of the lampstands and teapots and using the remaining 200 hours on the Toby jugs: quite a change in strategy from Gilby's original position.

The accountant's work here was invaluable to the managing director as it provided the vital information with which to make a decision. However, the decision is not yet made as Gilby has to weigh up other marketing factors.

- The Toby jugs and teapots are certain regular business. Pursuing the lampstands beyond the initial order may prove prohibitively expensive, even though a new product is required and the initial order may give more short-term profit.
- There is little point in chasing the new business if there are further costs in promoting it. In this case, if the costs of gaining the new business are more than the extra contribution gained of £2,400 it will not be worthwhile.
- These are the ideal figures. Action is needed to make them happen.

Gilby finally makes the decision based on the following three points:

(1) There is a need to introduce new products that are not at the mature side of their product life cycle, in order to strike a balance across the range. The lampstands are a comparatively new product.
(2) As the lampstands are at the early stage of the cycle they would need promotion: he estimates this to be £1,000 a month.
(3) As the Toby jugs' manufacturing potential would be cut from 1,000 to 400 units, he estimates that the price can be increased by £2 to £10 a unit, and the anticipated sales will therefore drop from 1,000 to 400 units. This will generate an extra £2 a unit on 400 units, a contribution of £800 to offset the extra initial promotion on the lampstands.

In the event, Gilby's decision proves correct.

This short case study serves to illustrate how information is transferred between the accountant and the marketing manager. The marketing manager supplies the accountant with ideas and data, and the accountant then re-presents those ideas in a profit-related format. This information is used for decision-making and to produce an action plan to motivate the sales force in the direction that will produce the most profit. At no time at all is there conflict but, rather, a two-way flow of information, the main requirement being that the marketing manager is able to understand the accountant's logic and the accountant that the most profitable course on paper is not necessarily achievable in reality – so the marketer's judgement must have credibility and logic.

It should also be noted that where more than one scarce resource is identified (in addition to sales limits), the use of linear programming techniques on a computerised model would be beneficial. However, this is specialist work and therefore difficult to communicate!

CHAPTER 6

3D Forecasting

Gavin Dick

INTRODUCTION

Few would disagree with the desirability of accurate forecasting or the difficulty of achieving it in practice. Much is written in the literature of the effectiveness of specific techniques but less on the practical application of these methods. The problem is how to apply these methods to provide an unbiased projection of what can be expected to happen in a form which is useful to marketing, operations and finance.

This chapter seeks to address this problem by briefly reviewing the advantages and drawbacks of alternative forecasting methods and practices, within the practical constraints that are often found in companies. It will then develop a multi-disciplined approach to integrating a number of different methods, which should improve forecasting accuracy while encouraging team-work and commitment across functional boundaries.

To focus the analysis, we examine the situation that prevails in companies that have a wide product range and many customers. Space constraints require us to concentrate on short- to medium-term forecasting of the type normally associated with the monthly breakdown of annual sales and operational budgets. The wider application of the 3D method outside these limitations will be illustrated later by means of short case studies.

Marketing and operations: a conflict of interests

All too often distrust and scepticism are features of the relationship between marketing and operations departments. It is the failure of each department to satisfy the expectations of the other that underpins the relationship's problem.

The relationship can be characterised as reciprocal. Operations depend on marketing to supply information on forecast sales; both timing and type of product being critical needs. Marketing is dependent on operations as a supplier of product, or information on predicted delivery dates – the availability or reliability of which in turn depends on the quality and level of detail provided in the sales forecast. Any failure in this supplier–customer–supplier–customer loop will lead to claims that it is the supplier who is at fault. For instance, operations will blame marketing for failing to provide an accurate forecast, and marketing will blame operations for failing to satisfy sales that are on forecast (in the aggregate).

The root of the problem is often the sales forecast and can take a number of forms:

- marketing forecasts are at an aggregate level expressed in value terms: operations are expected to forecast the product detail from this, but find they cannot reconcile their forecast with the marketing one
- forecast volumes are consistently inaccurate at the individual product level
- lack of clarity as to the forecast's intended purpose, i.e. is it a sales target or a prediction of actual demand?

Examining the conflicting interests of marketing and operations helps to explain why the resolution of the forecasting problem is often intractable.

Marketing's interest lies with forecasting, which is relevant to measuring the success of their own function and with avoiding publishing product detail, which they know is open to criticism, because it is likely to be less accurate than aggregated forecasts. Aggregate forecasts are also required by the finance function, which supports this avoidance of product detail. Naturally their functional focus is customers, so detailed sales breakdowns (where they exist) are likely to be by customer rather than by product. Where marketing product forecasts exist they are likely to be confined to the aggregate level, avoiding the detail which is essential to operations.

Marketing will tend towards viewing the monthly breakdown of sales as a target, rather than the expected sales for that month. They are likely to remain optimistic that sales have only slipped if they are below forecast for the month, and can be recovered in future months. This in turn will lead to an unwillingness to reforecast sales.

Operations' interests are in direct conflict to these marketing interests. To plan materials and capacity, detailed forecasts month by month are required for all products. An unexpected change in product mix will find operations with target inventory levels, yet too little of what is now required to satisfy the orders received. The wider the variation of actual to forecast the larger the excess inventories and the cost of servicing the capital tied up in it. Products underselling will have surplus inventory and those overselling will need to have extra inventory to service the sale.

Operations will view sales slipping with concern: if they proceed on marketing assumptions that the slippage will be recovered, and it is not, operations will be caught with excess inventories and capacity. The longer the delay in downgrading the sales forecast the more severe the correction required to bring down excess inventories and capacity. For instance, if in a factory employing two hundred workers the sales forecast is belatedly downgraded by twelve per dent at mid-year, operations would have to reduce the workforce by 24 people which would damage internal morale. Also supplier confidence would be damaged by the cancellation of six weeks' purchase commitments. Operations cannot win – if they anticipate, by assuming that sales are lost and re-plan material and capacity to reflect this, they could find themselves unable to service the sales forecast. These concerns will lead to pressure on marketing to reforecast sales so as to avoid operations' responsibility for any corrections required.

With such diametrically opposed interests it is hardly surprising to find the marketing–operations interface characterised by interpersonal conflict and re-crimination. But how can it be avoided? The way forward must involve a process which satisfies functional interests while tackling the inherent conflicts. It should embrace the suggestions of academic research, on methods of improving forecasting accuracy while remaining practical in terms of resources and skills required.

FORECASTING METHODS REVIEWED

In this section a range of forecasting methods which address the interests of operations, marketing and finance will be selected and their advantages and drawbacks reviewed. This is followed by a review of the research, to highlight approaches that can be adopted to improve overall forecasting accuracy.

Selecting appropriate methods

Georgoff and Murdick's 'Manager's Guide to Forecasting' (1986) provides a matrix which allows selection of forecasting method on dimensions of time, resource requirements, and input and output characteristics. The matrix breaks these dimensions into sub-dimensions which can be used in selecting suitable methods.

Wheelwright and Clarke (1976) identified factors which companies considered important in selecting forecasting methods. They found a reluctance among managers to use techniques they do not fully understand. Companies' forecasting systems tended to evolve progressively from simple methods to more mathematically sophisticated ones. Methods should therefore be proposed that reflect this reality by limiting the selection of mathematical techniques to those that can be accomplished using simple formulae within spreadsheet programs.

Concerns that this limitation could compromise forecasting accuracy can be overstated. Makridakis et al. (1984) found that simple methods can in many instances perform better than more sophisticated mathematical methods. With these factors in mind the selection of methods needs to be considered from a functional perspective.

Operations

To satisfy the interests of operations, methods are required that:

- have a short- to medium-term time span
- are able to accommodate frequent revisions
- can achieve accurate detailed forecasts
- if quantitative, can be used within commonly available PC spreadsheet software programs.

The methods suggested by the Georgoff/Murdick matrix are described briefly and the advantages and drawbacks explained.

Jury of executive opinion

The consensus of a group of 'experts', often from a variety of functional areas within the company, is sought. This method is usually concerned with aggregate forecasts but can reflect on detailed forecasts which are components of the aggregate. Advantages are that the method can reflect changes and shifts in internal and external variables, making it accurate under dynamic conditions. Further, it achieves commitment across functional areas due to the collective decision-making process.

Moving averages

Recent values of the forecast variables are averaged to predict future outcomes. An advantage with this method is its universal comprehension. Drawbacks include the equal weighting given to recent and old information, which reduces sensitivity to recent changes, and its inability to reflect turning points in cyclical demand.

Exponential smoothing

An estimate of the coming period is made based on a constantly weighted combination of the forecast estimate for the previous period and the most recent outcome. Advantages with this method are its minimal data storage requirement and its ease of calculation. The only data required is the previous exponential prediction and the current actual to be able to calculate the new prediction. This method is also rated high in accuracy for short-term forecasts. Drawbacks include its inability to reflect turning points.

Other time series and causal methods

These have been examined and, although they satisfy the earlier requirements, have not been selected because they are found to require more sophisticated mathematical methods which are not commonly available as self-explanatory PC programs for use with spreadsheets.

Marketing

To satisfy the needs of marketing, methods are required that:

- have a medium-term time span
- are able to achieve accurate aggregate forecasts

- can detail how the aggregate forecast relates to customers and/or sales area targets
- if quantitative, can be used within commonly available PC spreadsheet software programs.

The methods suggested by the Georgoff/Murdick matrix are described briefly and the advantages and drawbacks explained.

Sales force composite
A compilation is made of estimates by salespeople or dealers of expected sales in their territories, adjusted for presumed bias and expected changes. This method can be very accurate or subject to substantial bias. Its advantage is its ability to provide information which is essential to sales force management and performance targeting. Drawbacks include its inability to handle wide variations in demand adequately.

Jury of executive opinion
This is the same as for operations.

Delphi technique
A successive series of estimates is developed independently by a group of 'experts', each member of which, at each step in the process, uses a summary of the group's previous results to formulate new estimates. This method's advantage is that it reflects change well and can usually predict shifts. Its drawback is its lack of accuracy unless the time horizon is extended. It is also expensive if outside 'experts' are used.

However, the technique can be used successfully with company executives as the 'experts', as described by Basu and Schroeder (1977) in their study of American Hoist and Derrick. Here the method was used to produce sales forecasts which were accurate within a third of 1 per cent in the first year and within 4 per cent in the second year. The study suggests that combining the Delphi method with the jury of executive opinion gives results superior to those obtained by use of the individual methods in isolation.

Market surveys
Attitudinal and purchase intentions data is gathered from representative buyers. An advantage of this method is its application to special cases such as new products or markets. In these cases there are few alternative methods unless there are substantial similarities to existing products or markets. Drawbacks are the high cost and the relatively low accuracy.

Time series methods
These are as for operations, but looking at customers and often products at the aggregate level.

Finance

To satisfy the needs of finance, methods are required that:

- have a short- and medium-term time span
- are able to achieve accurate aggregate forecasts
- can detail or group the aggregate forecast in a way that allows the analysis of cause and effect relationships between cost and revenue
- if quantitative, can be used within commonly available PC spreadsheet software programs.

Finance's requirement to detail or group the aggregate forecast in a way that allows the analysis of cause and effect relationships between cost and revenue is often avoided by the use of established ratios. This assumes, however, that the aggregate groupings are relatively static.

It can be seen that finance and marketing interests are closely aligned where the product range and customer base does not change significantly. As this is often the norm little support for the operations perspective can be expected from finance.

The methods that satisfy marketing interests can therefore be viewed as satisfying the interest of finance also and so do not require further detailing.

The assumption that cost and revenue ratios remain static is unsound over any extended period, and warrants at least annual review. To achieve this review the detail at the product level will be required to establish the cost of sales.

Improving forecasting accuracy

A comprehensive selection of academic research studies can be found that support the view that a simple or a weighted average of forecasts out-performs most or possibly all the individual methods (Makridakis and Winkler, 1983; Essam, 1984; Lawrence, 1986; Makridakis, 1986; Russell and Adams, 1987). As Makridakis and Winkler say, 'Combining forecasts seems to be a reasonable practical alternative when, as is often the case, a true model of the data gathering process or a single best forecasting method cannot or is not, for whatever reason, identified.'

This suggests that greater accuracy will be achieved by finding a way of combining the methods that were selected earlier. And that, where there is a choice between alternatives, consideration should be given to choosing those that have discrete and complementary origins, as this broadens the overall database considered in arriving at the finalised forecast.

Finally, it is necessary to consider what weighting should be given to intuition. The implication of many studies is that human predictive judgement is frequently less reliable than the predictions of simple quantitative models (Ebert, 1976; Hogarth and Makridakis, 1981). This suggests that preference should be given to quantitative predictions. The positive benefits of judgement methods should also be considered, however. Such methods have the ability to:

- predict turning points and step changes, a feature not found in simple quantitative techniques
- combine quantitative methods by evaluating the inconsistencies and establishing a best forecast
- establish a commitment among the participants to the agreed forecast.

In the next section these suggestions and ideas will be put together, into an integrated system of forecasting known as 3D forecasting.

THE 3D METHOD

In this section the principles of the 3D forecasting method are given, and the individual models for the marketing, operations and finance dimensions detailed. This is followed by an explanation of the method used to integrate the individual methods in a way that provides an opportunity to utilise informed judgement to improve the quality of the forecast further.

3D method principles

The underlying principle of the method is that each function has unique perspective and hence knowledge that can be harnessed to improve overall forecasting accuracy. The individual functional forecasts can be viewed as three dimensions which, when compared, give the forecasters valuable insights into the cause and effect relationships which drive, or will drive, changes in the structure and volume of sales demand.

Marketing are required to predict demand by customer, operations demand by product, and finance the value of orders received. Each function uses its own resources to derive these forecasts, using appropriate methods to do so.

A method similar to the Delphi technique is then employed. The individual forecasts, together with assumptions and explanations, are published to the other functions. Successive rounds of independent forecasting follow, taking into account the information supplied in the previous rounds. Explanations are requested to elucidate the differences between the individual dimensions, if these have not been provided. This is illustrated in Fig. 6.1, where the input from the three dimensions and their progressive convergence through the use of the Delphi technique can be seen.

The last stage is the use of a jury of executive opinion to discuss the remaining differences and agree the final forecast.

Focusing on the essential few

The prospect of the mass of work involved in deriving detailed forecasts is

Finance

Marketing   Operations
Fig. 6.1 3D forecasting dimensions showing progressive convergence

daunting. There are ways of avoiding this volume of work which will still give the forecasters sufficient detail to know the origins of the majority of the demand.

The Pareto principle (named after a nineteenth-century Italian economist), or 80–20 rule as it is sometimes called, states that if the components of a distribution are ranked by cumulative value, approximately 80 per cent of the value of the distribution would be derived from 20 per cent of the components of that distribution. My own experience suggests that in a wide range of industries, wholesaling and retailing this principle holds good, within plus or minus 10 per cent. This principle will allow the forecasters to concentrate their attention on detailing demand for a relatively few customers and products, those top 20 per cent of customers and products that represent approximately 80 per cent of the value of the demand. The balance of 80 per cent of products and customers, which represent only 20 per cent of the value, will be forecast in the aggregate only. This has the advantage of not only reducing the workload but also concentrating our attention on the vital few which represent the organisation's core activity.

Identifying the vital few customers and products from the trivial many can be done by a full Pareto analysis or by a more limited approach of drawing on common knowledge of the significant major customers and products. The two approaches are described below.

Full Pareto analysis: products

Enter into the columns of a spreadsheet program the following detail for all products sold the previous year. Price should be average price achieved rather than list. To make data entry an easier task ignore products with less than 0.1 per cent of total sales.

- product code
- quantity sold
- unit price

and then calculate:

- sales value
- cumulative sales value
- sales percentage.

Then use the spreadsheet's sort function to reorganise the rows by ascending sales value. The percentage for the cumulative sales value can now be calculated. Products below the 80 per cent cumulative value can now be aggregated as a single 'other products' category and, with those above the 80 per cent value, make the forecasting list. Recently introduced products should be kept on the short-list, obsolete products deleted and obsolescent products noted.

Full Pareto analysis: customers

A similar process can be used for customers. Enter customer code and sales value and calculate cumulative sales value and sales percentage. After sorting customers by ascending sales value, customers below the 80 per cent cumulative value can now be aggregated as a single 'other customers' category and, with those above the 80 per cent value, make the forecasting list. Keep new customers on the short-list and delete lost ones.

Intuitive Pareto method

Where the data to allow a full Pareto analysis is not available an intuitive approach can be used to arrive at a list of the top 20 per cent of the products and the customers. The method will be illustrated by using customers as an example.

Obtain informed opinion on who are the most important customers and prepare a spreadsheet as in the full Pareto method above, listing only these customers. Compare the cumulative value with the full year sales value for all customers. If this is in excess of 80 per cent, delete the customers with the lowest sales value until the short-list is close to 80 per cent. If, however, the list falls short of the 80 per cent, note the sales value of the lower customers and search for other customers with similar or higher values than these, and add them to the list until an 80 per cent cumulative value is achieved.

The lists generated can now be utilised by operations and marketing to detail their forecasts.

The operations model

Before forecasting can commence the appropriate interval for the detailed forecast must be decided. This is essentially dictated by the lead time and order frequency and so will vary from firm to firm. For illustration a monthly time interval will be used.

For each of the short-listed products the monthly demand for the previous twelve months needs to be entered into a spreadsheet as a quantity, the demand for all other products being aggregated as a value for each of the twelve months. The demand pattern for each of the products now needs to be examined. Is there a trend or a seasonal pattern or is the demand stable? (Using the spreadsheet's charting capabilities to view the demand for each product as a line graph can be a great aid in this analysis.) Where the demand pattern is relatively stable, simple time series methods can be used to calculate the forecast. If there is a distinctive trend or seasonal pattern, correcting factors can be calculated to modify these to reflect the pattern. (This will be discussed later.)

As was explored earlier, there are a number of time series methods that can be used to satisfy operations' interests. Exponential smoothing has been selected for illustration as this responds well to recent changes in demand. The method is much easier to use than its title suggests. Only two items of information are required: the last forecast and the actual demand in the period. These are added together in proportions which are calculated by using a smoothing constant called *a*. This constant represents the time period (as will be explained later) over which the forecast will consider demand.

This method gives a progressively greater weighting to recent demand, and hence is often known as the exponentially weighted moving average method. The calculations are surprisingly easy to use despite the forbidding title of the method and are explained in Exhibit 6.1.

Exhibit 6.1 Exponential smoothing explained and illustrated

If	Xt	is actual demand in the previous period
	Mt^{+1}	is forecast for the next period
	Mt	is forecast for the previous period
	a	is an exponential smoothing constant

$$Mt^{+1} = (Xt \times a) + (Mt \times (1-a))$$

To illustrate: if

34	is actual demand in the previous period
38	is the forecast for the previous period
0.2	is the exponential smoothing constant

The forecast for the next period would be

$$(34 \times 0.2) + (38 \times (1 - 0.2))$$
6.8 + 30.4
= 37

The quandary of a value for the smoothing constant *a* is similar to the one posed for normal moving averages. How many periods should one average over? Too few periods will cause a rapid response to change in the mean level of demand but will also produce instability in the forecast due to the reflection of random variations. On the other hand, too many periods will cause the average to lag too far behind current changes but will smooth out random changes well. Table 6.1 indicates approximately the number of months moving average that different smoothing constants are equivalent to.

Table 6.1 Months represented by smoothing constants

Smoothing constant	Moving average equivalent
0.05	37
0.10	19
0.20	9
0.30	6
0.40	4
0.50	2

As only a twelve-month history is available in our example, a smoothing constant a of 0.4 is suggested for the first four months followed by 0.2 for future months. The next step is to set up the exponential smoothing formula in the spreadsheet and calculate the monthly forecasts. Experimenting with alternative a values will be much easier if the forecaster sets up the formulae to refer to an absolute cell where the a value for a specific product line can be stored.

It is suggested at this stage that the forecasters use the graphics charting facility in their spreadsheet package to view the results graphically to satisfy themselves that each of the forecasts predicts a credible demand pattern. Looking at the forecast for the second six months and comparing it with the actual demand during this period is recommended. However, forecasters will need to accept the fact that any forecast based, as this is, on history will always lag behind increases or decreases in demand. Forecasters should experiment with different smoothing constants if they find the forecast consistently over- or under-reacts, to see if they can improve the accuracy. Where there is a growth or decline trend in the pattern, forecasters should calculate the average period percentage trend and adjust the formulae to compensate for this. (See Vollman et al. (1988) to explore more sophisticated methods of trend and seasonal time series forecasts, but remember the research reviewed earlier suggests that sophistication does not necessarily imply greater accuracy.)

This process is then repeated for each of the short-listed products and the aggregated value of the balance of the products. The final forecast can now be extrapolated for each product to cover each month of the budget period and extended by the average price per product. The monthly forecasted value and the total value for the year for each product can now be calculated. These computer predictions should be modified individually where there is specific knowledge of changes which affect the future demand: for instance, non-availability of a product due to rationalisation of a supplier's product range. Notes should be made of all the general assumptions that have been used as well as specific assumptions for individual products. This is essential to allow other functions to understand the logic that has been used in deriving the forecast when the integrating process takes place.

The marketing model

For each of the customers listed the monthly sales for the previous 12 months need to be entered into a spreadsheet as a value of sales orders received. These will need to be scheduled where necessary to take into account phased delivery requirements. The sales for all other customers are aggregated together as a value per month. The sales pattern for each of the customers now needs to be examined. Is there a trend or a seasonal pattern or is the demand stable? Again, the spreadsheet's charting capabilities can be most helpful in this analysis. Where the demand pattern is relatively stable, forecasters can use simple time series methods to calculate the forecast. If there is a distinctive trend or seasonal pattern, they can calculate correcting factors to modify these to reflect the pattern.

The detailed method of deriving a time series forecast for each customer is identical to that described earlier for each product in the operations model. However, there is no need for the marketing model to choose an identical time series method: moving averages may be preferred to exponential smoothing for their simplicity, for instance.

Choosing the best number of periods to average over can be established by experimentation. It is suggested that forecasters use the graphics charting facility in their spreadsheet package to view the results of alternative averaging periods graphically, as was discussed earlier for operations. They should experiment with different numbers of periods to average over, until they are satisfied that the forecast predicts a credible sales pattern. Where there is a growth or decline trend in the pattern forecasters need to calculate the average period percentage trend for each customer and adjust their formulae to compensate for this.

Marketing forecasters can improve on this time series forecast by providing the historical information and the calculated forecast to the salespeople or dealers responsible for these customers and asking them to provide a forecast. Salespeople or dealers do not always see this as a part of their job and so they may have to be persuaded of the importance of their participation.

This 'sales force composite' forecast will have the advantage of drawing on specific local knowledge while being based on a historic trend which should represent the no-change base. Where there is a change it should be examined and justified by an explained cause and effect relationship. Increased sales could be justified, for instance, by the salesperson's explanation that the customer intends to cease dual sourcing of supplies and consolidate sales in your favour.

Notes should be made of all the general assumptions that have been used as well as specific assumptions for individual customers. This is essential to allow other functions to understand the logic that has been used in deriving the forecast when the integrating process takes place.

The financial model

The emphasis in the financial model depends on the nature of previous management accounting reporting in the firm. Historical information for monthly sales by product group and/or major customer accounts could be used. Where both are available the model can usefully be developed for each. However, here the minimum case will be assumed where the model derives its information from an analysis of the sales ledger.

A forecasting method similar to the marketing one can be used. Alternative methods should not be discouraged, however, as the diversity of methods is likely to improve overall accuracy – as was noted in the research earlier. For instance, if the accounting function has available the skills to use causal mathematical methods to derive a forecast, encourage it.

As with operations and marketing, notes should be made of all the general assumptions that have been used as well as specific assumptions for specific items. This is essential to allow other functions to understand the logic that has been used in deriving the forecast when the integrating process takes place.

The integrating mechanism

The integrating mechanism has two stages. The first involves a method similar in principle to the Delphi technique. The individual forecasts are published to the other functions together with assumptions and explanations. Successive rounds of independent forecasting follow, taking into account the information supplied in the previous rounds. The last stage is to use a jury of executive opinion to agree the final forecast.

The Delphi method

As was noted earlier in the review of appropriate forecasting methods, the Delphi method uses a successive series of forecasts independently developed by 'experts', each member of which, at each step in the process, uses a summary of the group's previous results to formulate new estimates. The role of experts here is taken by the functional forecasters. Their individual functional expertise and knowledge of their own data and analysis give them this status, and each brings his or her own perspective and forecast which looks at a different dimension.

Operations provide the product dimension, marketing the customer dimension, each having built-in adjustments based on known changes or actions planned and how they will affect demand in the future. These adjustments are based on assumptions about cause and effect relationships. As was noted earlier, these assumptions must be made explicit. Finance provides an alternative dimension which, because of its remoteness from the knowledge of detail of changes to customers and products, provides a sound no-change scenario. It is the anchor dimension against which the others can be compared.

The first phase of the integration process is the publication of the three dimensions. Operations, marketing and finance each study the forecasts for the other dimensions, and particularly consider the assumptions used. Where there is insufficient information an explanation is requested as part of the output of this round for a response in the next round. It is important not to hold up the preparation of the current round forecast by requesting additional information before completing it.

It is vital for the chief executive of the business unit concerned to lay down the timetable and progress the process, while at the same time avoiding becoming personally involved. The danger of personal involvement is the bias it can bring to the process: the dimension in which the chief executive is involved can become the one the others converge on. This unintentional signal is best avoided if the technique is to achieve a balanced forecast.

A time period must be specified for each round. At the end of the round a new forecast is expected from each of the functions, with modified assumptions noted. Less than a week is suggested – it is important to keep the detail in the forecasters' minds fresh.

The number of rounds required depends on the degree of convergence which is achieved between the three dimensions. Moves towards convergence tend to be greatest in the earlier rounds. It is likely in practice that no more than three iterations are required to achieve a high degree of convergence. It is suggested that the chief executive's timetable includes three rounds and that he should review progress towards convergence at the end of the third. If there is still a wide disparity between dimensions, sounding out the forecasters on whether they are likely to amend their forecast in the light of the last published forecasts of the other dimensions will suggest whether another round is worthwhile.

Jury of executive opinion

When the chief executive believes a reasonable degree of convergence has taken place, a meeting should be called to discuss remaining queries and differences between the functional dimensions. This jury of executive opinion can reflect on the merits of the individual dimension and reach a consensus on a final forecast.

The process which encourages convergence needs to be examined. The knowledge of the general assumptions used by the other forecasts leads to a re-examination of assumptions and the realignment of these and the forecast particularly when the rationale in the other dimension or dimensions appears stronger than the original one. The knowledge of specific assumptions by product or customer which significantly increase or decrease the overall forecast can persuade the alternative dimensions to review their own forecasts, in the light of this new insight.

This structured approach has considerable advantages over the alternative of a meeting to discuss the forecasts and their merits.

- The knowledge that the forecasts will not be viewed as alternatives but as input to the forecasting process avoids the 'turf patch' issue of whose prerogative it is to forecast sales demand.
- The process allows time for detailed reconsideration of the assumptions used and the consequences for each dimension of the forecast. Meetings tend to avoid this detailed consideration and consequently tend to arrive at agreement on totals without consideration of the way they will be made up in terms of specifics by product and customer.
- The requirement to provide detail of the assumptions used where the forecast varies from that predicted from past experience of demand ensures that 'gut feel' is avoided, or at least kept in check.
- The iterating process with its emphasis on improvement rather than the defence of the forecast avoids polarisation, and encourages convergence.
- Because the process encourages more participation, more commitment to the agreed outcome can be expected, as well as a more accurate forecast.

To understand fully how this 3D forecasting integration process works, the Powertech case study at the end of this chapter needs to be followed through its stages and dimensions.

THE 3D METHOD: THEORY AND PRACTICE

The Powertech example at the end of this chapter is based on the situation that prevails in a manufacturing company with a wide standard product range and many customers. It assumes short- to medium-term forecasting of the type normally associated with annual sales and operational budgets. That is not to suggest, however, that the method is valid only in these circumstances.

Longer-term forecasts can equally benefit from the method, as can forecasting in firms in widely different sectors of the economy. The initial forecasting methods will need to be altered, (Georgoff and Murdick, 1986) suggests suitable methods for most circumstances) to reflect the altered time frame and the nature of the product, etc. This is illustrated in the two short case studies that follow.

Case study: a regional trade distributor

Wessex Tile Ltd sells British and European ceramic tiles to trade tilers and independent retailers, and direct to the public. The range of products is broad with a need to offer a corresponding level of stock.

Although the company has a less clearly differentiated marketing and operations function, the 3D forecasting method can still be used. At Wessex Tile the customer forecast was prepared by the sales manager, who is also responsible for marketing and inventory management decisions. The product forecast was prepared by the buyer, and the financial dimension prepared by the chief executive. Interdepartmental co-operation is poor and a considerable degree of rancour is evident in the relationship between purchasing and sales in particular.

Although an integrated computerised accounts, sales and order-processing system is used by the company, there is a lack of personal computing skills, so all forecasting was done manually.

The operations forecast

Products were forecast as product groups, a style of tile in a range of colours from a specific manufacturer. The buyer used his stock and buying records as his historical data for forecasting.

A rough Pareto analysis identified the fifteen product groups that represented 81 per cent of demand. Monthly demand over the last twelve months was established for each of these groups in money terms, the balance of demand being aggregated under a miscellaneous heading. Simple moving averages were calculated, it being decided to use a three-month average as this seemed to predict actual demand adequately when adjusted for a trend factor on an individual basis.

The marketing forecast

The marketing forecast used the sales ledger as its source. A rough Pareto analysis identified the twenty-five customers that represented 78 per cent of sales, one of these being retail sales. Monthly sales over the last twelve months were established for each of these customers in money terms. The balance of sales were aggregated under a miscellaneous heading.

Simple moving averages were calculated. It was decided to use a three-month average, which seemed adequately to predict actual sales demand when adjusted for individual trend factors for each customer.

The finance forecast

The chief executive calculated the financial forecast (the method was described by him as 'taking a view'). No detail of how this was built up was given and no assumptions were noted when the forecast was published.

Integration

The integration process was carried out in a similar way to that described in the Powertech case study. From an early stage the operations and marketing forecasts converged, while the finance forecast difference remained higher and showed little convergence in later rounds.

The difference was resolved at the jury of executive opinion stage. The chief executive was so surprised at the agreement and mutual support of his marketing manager and buyer (when in the past it was unusual to find any common ground between them) that he found his view of the forecast difficult to justify and agreed on the marketing and operations forecasts.

The 3D method had the added advantage at Wessex Tile of allowing a less biased contribution to the forecasting process despite the status differences of the participants.

Case study: major capital goods

Maxtel designs and manufactures complex data communication equipment. Each system is unique but consists of a combination of existing system modules with modules and software designed specifically for the customer. There are few customers but the average system value is in excess of £500,000.

As some of the components have a purchase lead time of nine months, and it takes up to a year to design, build, test and install a system, the overall lead time for a system is in excess of eighteen months. A key order-winning criterion for the company is its shorter delivery lead time, which drives the need to purchase and manufacture in advance of order being received. To do this, accurate forecasts at a detailed level up to three years in advance are required to allow purchasing and the planning of manufacturing capacity.

Budgeting for actual sales for the next financial period is not seen as a major problem as nearly all of them will be met from the existing order book.

Marketing forecast

This long-range demand forecast is derived by reviewing all live prospects for systems. These prospects are then given an 'expected value' derived by judging the probability of the order being won, which is entered in the forecast in the quarter in which the order is expected to be received, with a note of the planned installation live date and the system reference code. (This defines the system design configuration which was last quoted for the customer.) This information is then aggregated and added to the order book to give an expected value of demand by quarter for the next two years.

Design engineering develop from this information a schedule which breaks down each prospect into common modules and details of long lead time components which are unique to the prospect, by quarter, for the next two years.

Operations forecast

The operations forecast is based on historical records of past usage of common modules in previously manufactured systems and the usage rate of extended lead time components. Forecasting is done by the exponential smoothing method, using a low smoothing constant with a freak demand filter (this removes demand input that is way out of the expected range of demand).

Spreadsheets are used for these calculations. The graphics charting facility in the spreadsheet package is used to view the results graphically, to test that previous forecasts have reasonably predicted the actual demand pattern and that the new forecast extrapolates the past demand trend.

Operations have calculated that the common modules in systems represent 60 per cent of the average work content of a system and that this ratio has been reasonably static. The forecast results are published as an expected usage by quarter for all modules. Ratios are then used to convert this into an average system value by quarter.

The finance forecast

Finance's forecast uses the sales ledger as its source. The forecast is at the aggregate level only and is derived from studying the trend graphically. The finance forecast by quarter for the next two years is published along with the marketing and operations forecasts.

Integration

The integration process is carried out in a similar way to that described in the Powertech case study. The initial difference between the functional dimensions was very large. But the information provided with the forecasts made each function significantly reappraise their assumptions and adjust their forecasts accordingly.

At the next round the finance and marketing forecasts converged; the operations forecast difference remained high but was adjusted to convergence in the final round when the shift of mix in future systems towards less standard module content was accepted. The final round results were so close that the jury of executive opinion stage was omitted.

At Maxtel a major benefit of employing the 3D forecasting method was a new openness between functions gained from an appreciation of how other departments were affected by and coped with a difficult forecasting problem.

CONCLUSION

The 3D method is flexible in its application because it does not depend on elaborate or complicated forecasting models. It is robust because it draws on the theory that averages of forecasts produced by simple forecasting models are more accurate than those produced by a single sophisticated method. The integrating methods suggested draw out the underlying cause and effect assumptions which underpin the dimensional forecasts, and give the opportunity for these to be questioned in a way which minimises conflict and avoids polarisation.

Although it has the disadvantage of being time consuming, particularly in the first instance, the 3D method does offer the opportunity to achieve a far greater degree of accuracy, with the level of detail required to plan and control functional activities effectively. Without this detail there is no true link between the forecasting process and the actions the organisation takes to achieve it. The initial time investment required to achieve 3D forecasts is low compared to the benefit that better interdepartmental integration and use of assets bring; both in terms of returns of capital employed and productive utilisation of the organisation's most important resource – the people who work in it.

The cost to an organisation of poor planning can be very high. Without accurate detailed forecasts by customer and product the integration of marketing and operations information and activities becomes an impossible task, with mutual recrimination an inevitable consequence.

Piercy (1987), quoted in Ian Wilson's chapter (1), emphasises the central importance of sales demand forecasting to the organisation:

> if the marketing department (or, it should be noted, some other subunit) does not convert the uncertainty of the marketing environment into a sales forecast, there is no basis for planning production, manpower or the financing of operations. In this sense, the management of information is the very centre of the status of marketing management and the implementation of the marketing concept in the company.

The 3D forecasting method manages information and the process of integrating it into a forecast that satisfies the needs of each function in terms of detail. In this sense the 3D method can be viewed as a vehicle for realising the marketing concept in practice. The external customer cannot be satisfied effectively and efficiently without also satisfying the needs of internal customers. The 3D process recognises this need to satisfy the diverse and at times conflicting needs of internal customers and provides the mechanism for achieving it in the contentious area of forecasting.

BIBLIOGRAPHY

Basu, Shankar and Schroeder, Roger G. (1977) 'Incorporating Judgements in Sales Forecasts: Application of the Delphi Method at American Hoist and Derrick', *Interfaces*, Vol. 7, No. 3.

Ebert, Ronald J. (1976) 'A Comparison of Human and Statistical Forecasting', *AIEE Transactions*, Vol. 8, No. 1 etc, pp. 120–7.

Essam, Mahoud (1984) 'Accuracy in Forecasting a Survey', *Journal of Forecasting*, April–June, p. 139.

Georgoff, M. David and Murdick, Robert G. (1986) 'Manager's Guide to Forecasting', *Harvard Business Review*, January–February, pp. 110–20.

Hogarth, Robert M. and Makridakis, Spyros (1981) 'Forecasting and Planning an Evaluation', *Management Science*, Vol. 27, No. 2, pp. 115–38.

Lawrence, Michael et al. (1986) 'The Accuracy of Combining Judgemental and Statistical Forecasts', *Managerial Science*, Vol. 32, pp. 1521–32.

Makridakis, Spyros (1986) 'The Art and Science of Forecasting: An Assessment and Future Directions', *International Journal of Forecasting*, Vol. 2, pp. 987–96.

Makridakis, Spyros and Winkler, Robert (1983) 'Averages of Forecasts: Some Empirical Results', *Management Science*, Vol. 29, No. 9, pp. 987–96.

Makridakis, Spyros et al. (1984) *The Forecasting Accuracy of Major Time Series Methods*, New York: John Wiley.

Piercy, N. (1987) 'Developing Marketing Information Systems', in M. J. Baker (ed.), *The Marketing Book*, London: Heinemann, p. 205.

Russell, Thomas D. and Adams, Evert D. Jr. (1987) 'An Empirical Evaluation of Alternative Forecasting Combinations', *Management Science*, Vol. 33, pp. 1267–76.

Vollmann, Thomas E. et al. (1988) 'Enhancing the Basic Exponential Smoothing Model to Incorporate Trend and Seasonal Factors', in *Manufacturing Planning and Control Systems*, Dow Jones Irwin, pp. 685–92.

Wheelwright, Steven and Clarke, Darral G. (1976) 'Corporate Forecasting: Promise and Reality', *Harvard Business Review*, November–December, pp. 120–7.

CASE STUDY

Powertech

Powertech manufactures and markets a specialised range (approximately 900 lines) of electronic components. The products are sold direct by technical sales representatives to major customers, who incorporate these components in their products. Smaller volume customers are serviced through national distributors. A growing proportion of sales are overseas through independent distributors. Product prices range from £1,000 for multi-output power supplies down to £5 for power converters. The company has been growing steadily, increasing its share in a growing market. In sales value 70 per cent of the products are manufactured by the company, the remainder being subcontracted or factored.

The company organisation is conventional, with all marketing activities and sales management being the responsibility of the marketing director. The operations director is responsible for all manufacturing, purchasing and despatch, including the management of finished goods stocks. Financial and cost accounting responsibilities are covered by the company secretary.

Forecast round one at Powertech

Using the methods illustrated in the chapter, each function has prepared its own annual forecast. The marketing forecast detailed by customer or distributor is £15 million. The operations forecast, detailed by product, is lower at £14 million. The lowest forecast is finance, at only £13.4 million. Each forecast includes details of the assumptions used and an explanation of any decline or increase outside the norm for individual product or customer cases. Powertech's first round forecasts for the three dimensions are shown in Fig. 6.2.

The first phase of the integration process at Powertech is the publication of these three dimensions. Operations, marketing and finance now each study the forecasts for the other dimensions, and particularly consider the assumptions used. The process

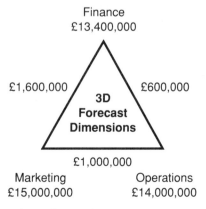

Fig. 6.2 Results of round one forecast

of reforecast for each function will now be expanded upon using a limited number of illustrations. In practice the process would be considerably more complex.

Finance reforecast round two

Finance review their forecast by considering the difference between it and operations' – £600,000. They examine the assumptions and explanations that accompany the forecast and note that for most products the expected growth in demand is 2 per cent above the level which they have allowed for. The detail offered by product looks convincing, and would increase their forecast by £268,000. They also note that the operations forecast allows for the full-year sales demand for 'Quaser', a product that was introduced part way through last year, which represents an additional £110,000. Taken together these lead finance to consider a revised forecast of £13,778,000.

Finance now need to examine their original difference with the marketing forecast (£1.6 million). They examine the assumptions and explanations that accompany the forecast and note that for most customers a growth of demand of nearly 6 per cent above the level they have allowed for is expected. The explanation offered – increased advertising and a fully staffed sales force – is what finance would expect, but lacks sufficient detail on cause and effect relationships to convince the forecaster to alter the forecast at this stage. A note is made of this lack of cause and effect explanation in the marketing forecast and this will be requested when the forecasts for finance are published at the end of this round.

Finance note that marketing are expecting sales demand to increase dramatically with two customers, representing an increase of a further £750,000. The first, accounting for £350,000, is Whybark, a successful customer whose new product incorporates a number of Powertech's in its design. The other is Barr International, an overseas agent under new management who is expected nearly to double previous sales demand, an increase of £400,000. Marketing justify this increase by the size of the market in the country in question, Powertech's small share of it, and the lack of interest in promotional activity by the previous management of the agency.

Finance consider this and take the view that these increases could be realised in the longer term but are unlikely to have the dramatic effect predicted in the twelve months of the forecast. They modify their forecast by £350,000, to take into account these two customers.

Consideration of the merits of the two modified forecasts are needed now to arrive at a revised finance forecast. The first had information which they accepted as adding £378,000, the second in their view justified an extra £350,000, a total of £728,000, leading to a revised forecast of £14,128,000. They decide to publish this as the revised finance forecast, along with their request for additional information to justify the marketing growth rate. Notes to explain how the revised finance forecast has been calculated are also included.

Operations reforecast round two

Operations may reconsider their forecast by reviewing the difference between it and finance's: £600,000. They examine the assumptions and explanations that accompany the forecast and note that for most products they have forecast a growth in demand 2 per cent above the level finance have allowed for. They check the detail of their product forecast and remain convinced that their forecast increase is realistic.

They now examine the marketing forecast to seek an explanation for the £1 million extra forecast. Like finance they are concerned by the lack of a convincing cause and effect relationship to support the increases in sales and note this for a request for more information for the next round.

They note with interest that marketing are expecting sales demand from two customers to increase dramatically. The first is Whybark (£350,000). Operations examine the recent demand trend and their forecast for the particular products and note the very recent increase in demand, which has not been reflected in the forecast. Changing the exponential smoothing factor from 0.2 to 0.4 in their spreadsheet better reflects this recent trend. This increases operations' forecast by £280,000.

The second is Barr International, expected to increase by £400,000. Marketing justify this increase by the size of the market in the country in question, Powertech's small share of it, and the lack of interest in promotional activity by the previous management of the agency. Operations examine the mix of products that this agency has sold in the past and find it is very broad based. If the £400,000 were spread across all products they calculate it represents just under a 3 per cent increase. This size of increase as the result of one agent's efforts has not been accomplished in the past, which leads to operations downgrading the effect to 1 per cent. The formulae are adjusted in the spreadsheet for this and calculate an extra £140,000. The revised operations forecast is thus £14,420,000.

This is published with the request for additional information from marketing and notes to explain how the revised operations forecast has been calculated.

Marketing reforecast round two

Marketing may reconsider their forecast by reviewing the difference between it and operations' – £1 million They examine the assumptions and explanations that accompany the forecast and note that for many products a growth in demand 4 per cent less than their forecast is expected. They know of Barr International, their overseas agent who under new management is expected nearly to double previous sales demand, an increase of £400,000, which represents an approximate 3 per cent increase to overall sales, which helps to explain this difference. When the detail offered by product in the operations forecast is examined it looks convincing, with a few important exceptions.

On examining the products affected by Whybark, it becomes clear that the operations forecast does not include the increased volumes. Marketing have forecast an increase for this customer of £350,000, but when they examine how much the individual product forecasts would have to increase to match this, they realise it could be overstated. Not enough allowance has been given for the ramp up to full volume. They decide to reduce the forecast for this customer to £200,000.

The other exception is the 'Quaser' product that was introduced part way through last year, and shows only an additional £110,000 in the operations forecast. Marketing are expecting to target most of their promotional activity on Quaser. They are expecting it to achieve additional sales of £450,000 in a full year, £330,000 more than allowed for in the operations forecast.

They feel that they can now adequately explain the remaining difference of £520,000 (£1 million minus £150,000 minus £330,000) by the increased sales expected from the full-year effect of a fully staffed and trained sales force. Marketing decide to submit a revised forecast of £14,850,000. They annotate their forecast to indicate the specific effect they expect on product demand of their promotion and increased sales activity, to ensure that the other dimensions are aware of its planned impact.

The results from this second round are shown in Fig. 6.3, where a considerable move towards convergence can be seen. All the dimensions have closed their differences. The maximum divergence remains between finance and marketing, but even this has reduced by over half, from £1.6 million to £722,000.

Finance reforecast round three

Finance may reconsider their forecast by first reviewing the significance of the differences that remain between it and those of marketing and operations. The difference between finance and operations is the smaller, at £292,000. That between finance and marketing is significantly larger, at £430,000.

They study the explanations for the revisions in forecast and note that operations have forecast £70,000 more than finance for the effect of the new agent Barr International. The explanation suggests finance have perhaps been too pessimistic, and they decide to adjust their forecast to include the extra £70,000.

Finance also note the extra £330,000 that marketing have explained is expected from promotion targeted on the 'Quaser' product, and adjust their forecast to

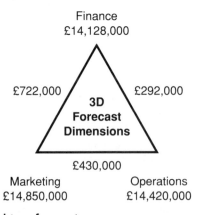

Fig. 6.3 Results of round two forecast

incorporate this as well. The adjusted forecast of £14,528,000 is published along with the explanation of the adjustments.

Operations reforecast round three

Operations note the fact that marketing have downgraded their forecast for additional sales from Whybark (the new customer who is incorporating Powertech's products) from £350,000 to £200,000, £80,000 less than the operations forecast adjustment. Operations reduce their forecast to reflect this reduction.

They also note the extra £330,000 that marketing expects from the 'Quaser' product, and adjust their forecast to incorporate this as well. The adjusted forecast of £14,670,000 is published along with the explanation of the adjustments.

Marketing reforecast round three

Marketing review the comments made by operations and finance concerning the forecast from Barr International, the overseas agent. After discussing the matter with the agent they decide to downgrade their forecast to £200,000. This reflects what can be achieved in the forecast period given the lag between market prospects and demand. The adjusted forecast of £14,650,000 is published along with the explanation of the adjustments.

The dimensional forecasts converge

At the end of round three the differences between the individual dimensions (shown in Fig. 6.4) have closed to under 1 per cent and that between operations and marketing is insignificant, at a fraction over 0.1 per cent. The chief executive is satisfied with the degree of convergence achieved and now moves to the next stage. He arranges for the senior functional managers to meet as a jury of executive opinion to decide on the final forecast.

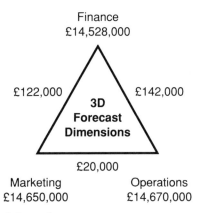

Fig. 6.4 Results of round three forecast

Jury of executive opinion

The jury in this example have an easy task as two of the forecasts are so close. Each function is asked if they have any outstanding questions on the other dimensions which may alter their forecast. When these questions are answered, the views of each executive on the merits of their forecasts are requested. Marketing and operations both put forward the view that they feel the detail that each has on the other's forecast reinforces their confidence in their figures. Finance are asked to put forward a case for their forecast. They decline and agree to the marketing and operations forecast of £14,650,000.

Final consensus has been achieved at Powertech, with little difficulty. The earlier effort in forecasting and reforecasting has been rewarded, by each function at Powertech having:

- a forecast which satisfies their functional objectives
- a commitment to the forecast due to their participation in the decision process
- a knowledge that the accuracy of the final forecast has been greatly improved by the variety of forecasting methods used and the effort that all have put into the 3D method.

The process of periodic revision

During the year there is the need to update forecasts, to provide revised and rolling budgets. The 3D method used in formulating the original functional forecasts can be easily updated to provide a revised set of functional forecasts. A truncated version of the Delphi method is used, and a single round could provide sufficient convergence. A jury of executive opinion is then used to reach final agreement on the revised forecast.

CHAPTER 7

The Marketing/Information Technology Interface

Michael Carter

INTRODUCTION

This chapter concerns the interface between marketing and the areas of management information and information technology. Examined in the chapter will be the way in which information management and information technology can provide marketing management with information to allow them to react quickly to changes in the marketplace. This will enable organisations to create a competitive advantage using information more effectively. More general ways of creating a competitive edge using information technology will also be considered.

The chapter is organised by first considering the organisation of marketing information. The information will be dealt with in a series of profiles: customer profile, product profile, competitor profile, industry/environment profile and market profile. The first four profiles will feed information into the market profile (see Fig. 7.1). Each profile will be examined in detail and they will be integrated together in the market profile. The market profile may also contain further information from, for example, market research.

The final part of the chapter will consider more general ways in which information technology can be used to create a competitive edge.

It is important to consider the organisation of the information needs of marketing first. Information technology can mean more and more data being provided to management more economically. This does not mean more information; in fact it is possible to swamp management with this excess of data. Infor-

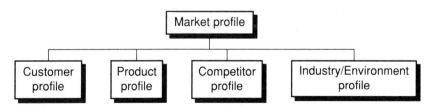

Fig. 7.1 Relationship between profiles

mation is produced out of the data by understanding the data and it is important that the marketing information system starts this process. It has always been possible to specify a marketing information system into a series of profiles that will enable marketing management to take effective decisions in changing conditions. Now with the recent advances in information technology it is possible to deliver such marketing information systems at economical costs, thus more readily bringing a significant competitive advantage to organisations using them.

The profiles will be developed and then examples of their use to give competitive advantage will be given later in the chapter.

CUSTOMER PROFILE

An important area of information gathering must concern the customer. A record of customer information can be used by sales management for planning or as a valuable customer information resource for sales personnel. By carrying out analysis work on the customer information records it will be possible to build up customer profiles which will be very useful when planning and controlling the business, especially when expansion is being considered. Virtually all organisations will have customers – whether the product is a car, an industrial pump, health care or an insurance policy. The term 'customer' should therefore be taken in the widest sense.

In information management terms the different types of customers can be split into two groups. First, those that can be identified and kept track of, for example a company selling machine tools to a number of engineering companies. The second group of customers are those who cannot be identified, for example customers shopping in a supermarket. The Pareto principle will almost certainly apply to most organisations' customers. That is to say that 20 per cent of the customers will account for 80 per cent of the business of the organisation. It is important in many cases to build a detailed profile of this 20 per cent of large customers. To reduce cost it is normal to build detailed profiles of only a sample of the remaining 80 per cent.

The traditional way of recording customer information is the card index. However, such an approach will be very limited because of the cost of collecting and collating information. Information technology can significantly reduce collecting and collating costs. Giving management a greater understanding of customers can also give a competitive edge. It is likely that some form of database or database management system will be used to create customer profiles.

Identifiable customers

Within this group of organisations are ones that can identify their customers and can track them through the organisation's records. Examples of this group are patients in health care, telephone subscribers, car manufacturers, etc. The detailed customer profile can be split into five segments: identification, contacts, customer sales, customer sales reports and customer intelligence.

Identification

This segment will be needed in the case of all customers and will contain the physical information of identification. It will contain, for example:

- name
- address (this may be split into delivery address, invoice address, parent company address,etc.)
- telephone number
- fax number
- approximate size
- type of customer (subsidiary, private company, etc.)
- customer's market(s).

It is important that these records are kept up to date and accurate. In terms of information technology it should be the ultimate aim of the organisation to use the name and address from this file when sending invoices, writing letters, etc. and not have to re-enter them. This approach can significantly reduce the costs of the organisation.

Contacts

This segment will be needed by organisations only where there are specific contact people in the customer organisation. It will contain, for example:

- contact name (including preferred first name if normal practice)
- position in organisation (title)
- address in organisation (if different from that in the identification segment, above).

Again, it is important that these records are kept up to date and are accurate. Few things upset people more than continually getting their name and/or position wrong. Like the previous segment it should be the aim by using information technology not to keep re-entering this information but to draw it directly from a database.

Customer sales

In this segment of the profile will be recorded the orders placed by customers. It needs to be recorded in as much detail as possible, for example dates, types and amounts of product(s). This information is best stored on a database on a computer, often a personal computer. However, the data should be directly downloaded from the organisational computer into the personal computer. It would be far too expensive to re-input the data a second time.

Information in this segment of the profile can be of great use to sales and marketing management. It is information technology that makes the analysis possible at a reasonable cost. There are a number of ways that the information from such an analysis can be used, for example:

- A picture of the type of products and quantities bought by customers can be built. By using the identification data the buying patterns of different types of customers can be identified. Such information can be extremely useful and valuable when developing product strategy.
- This segment of the profile can also be used to keep track of significant changes in customers' buying patterns. The computer can be programmed to flag significant changes in the size of orders or the product make-up of the order. Such analysis would highlight customers requiring extra attention and changes taking place in the product-buying patterns.
- With some customers it may be possible to identify buying patterns. These may be regular time slots when purchases are made and the information can ensure sales visits or mail shots are made at the most effective time. If regular product-buying patterns can be identified (particularly in a large customer) it can be valuable to the salesperson and to operations' scheduling in planning the product.

Examples of this type of customer information gathering will be found later in the section on competitive advantage.

Customer sales reports

The vast majority of the customer profile so far outlined has been hard (reasonably accurate), formal information. This next segment contains quite different information – softer, subjective and its source external. It is not possible to produce this segment for all organisations in the identifiable customer group. To carry out this form of analysis, direct contact with the customer (usually via a salesperson or sales staff) is needed. The information for this segment is collected in the form of a report when contact is made with the customer. This has been a practice of a number of organisations, but it was difficult and expensive to collate and analyse such reports. Information technology can now make such an analysis more effective, and at a reasonable cost. The data can be collected by the computer. The salesperson enters the report on to the computer. The report should use a number of multiple choice questions and scoring scales. There should be a minimum of written input. Multiple choice questions and scoring scales will ensure the efficient collation and analysis of the data. There are also now packages that will search the written parts of the report for particular words and phrases, allowing the written parts of the reports to be analysed efficiently.

The types of information that can be collected are, for example:

- customers' attitudes to the product (quality, delivery, pricing, etc.)
- comments on competitors and their products
- customer attitudes to new products
- assessment of potential growth in the customer account
- assessment of the changes in the product mix of the customer account
- customer comments on competitors.

This information is much more speculative than the rest of the customer profile and should therefore be treated with care; nevertheless it is still of great value in forecasting, product planning and customer care.

Non-identifiable customers

This section considers the type of organisation whose systems cannot identify or track customers. A good example of this type of organisation is supermarkets. There have been exceptions: the share account used by the Co-operative Society made it possible to track a customer's purchases. For most large retail outlets the only way to find out about customers was to carry out expensive market research.

With the use of information technology many large retail outlets have found a way round this problem. Sainsbury was one of the companies to lead this development. The key to the solution lies in capturing the data for the computer where the transaction takes place. In the retail trade this data capture hinges on bar codes and the technology of reading them by laser.

Prior to this technology the data on customers' purchases was lost – the till recorded only prices and totals. With the new technology the bar codes allow the complete set of purchases to be recorded in detail. This process adds little to the normal transaction costs and in fact, given the more efficient way of checking out, often reduces costs. One large supermarket chain used the slogan 'Check out at the speed of light'. The system does not allow the tracking of individual customers but by examining the shopping baskets does build a picture of different purchasers. Different buying patterns can be identified at different times and under different conditions, for example on different days of the week or in times of recession. Information of this type can be extremely valuable in deciding stocking policy, reducing waste and increasing customer satisfaction.

There are additional benefits to these point of sale systems. They keep stock records, being able to notify store management when items on shelves need replenishing or when orders need to be placed to bring fresh products into the store. Such information has also been used to ensure products are positioned in the right place in the store to gain the maximum chance of sale. The information on customer buying behaviour is also a valuable commodity: some stores have sold this information to their suppliers. The benefits and savings from the operational efficiency and from a greater understanding of customer and marketplace have proved to be considerable.

It is often difficult to identify and track the type of customer discussed in this section. However, with careful use of information technology it is still possible to extract information that will allow a greater understanding of the customer and hence the marketplace.

PRODUCT PROFILE

It is very important to know how the products of the business are performing. The term 'product' needs to be taken in its widest form, to include service organisations. Virtually all organisations have some form of product. This may be a physical product, like a car, or a service, like health care and financial services. Building a product profile is important to any organisation to enable it to respond to changes taking place in its product base. The basic principles in building such a profile are similar across all types of organisation, although the final format will differ. By using up-to-date information technology and modern information management is be possible for organisations to create a competitive advantage by being responsive to change in the product base. This section will explore in detail how a product profile can be built to aim for a competitive advantage. The product profile is split into two parts: sales analysis and product costing. It must be remembered that strategies will be made not simply by using the product profile but by integrating all the profiles.

Sales analysis

Past sales figures provide one of the main sources of information within the business. These figures are likely to be an accurate representation of the sales of the business, but may not be representative of the market in which the business is operating. The sales and the market are two different factors and must not be confused. They may behave in a similar manner but it is possible to find them completely opposed. It is important in the planning and control of any business to know the relationship between the two. Over the past few years information technology has significantly changed the amount of information that can be extracted from the sales analysis.

Measurement of sales

Although past sales will not necessarily represent the market within which the company is operating, they will provide an important and vital measure of how the company's organisation and products are performing.

Care should be taken in the collection and collation of sales data so as to enable reasonable forecasts and decisions to be produced from it. It is important that the sales analysis is used to its best advantage in making decisions and planning the business. The choice of units should be given careful consideration. A common mistake is to produce sales data in monetary units. In this form the data is useful for working out cash flows and other accounting modelling approaches; unfortunately, it is not very stable for the production of reasonable trends for use in decision-making and planning. The problem lies in money itself. It is not a stable commodity: at home inflation is but one factor constantly affecting its value; in the export market fluctuating exchange rates are a further complication.

This leads to two major problems when money is used as the unit of sales data. First, it can give a false impression of growth. For example, if sales volume in money terms has increased by 3 per cent over a particular year this may appear to be a healthy growth. However, if inflation for that year was 4 per cent or greater the company will in fact have seen a contraction in real terms. The second problem can occur when a business is achieving growth in real terms: coupled with inflation it can give an apparently astronomical growth rate. This can give a false picture of the company's potential if it is not corrected. It can also provide an unstable relationship between time and sales, which can make it difficult to produce realistic trends.

Given that monetary units of sales are not very useful in determining trends, what units should be used? The best for use in forecasting is some physical measure of sales, i.e. number, weight, volume sold, etc. These measures do not suffer from the unstabilising influences of inflation or fluctuating exchange rates and therefore provide a stable set of figures to determine trends from. Most businesses find it possible to use such units but some may face problems. Those companies dealing with products that are one-offs or small specialised batches will have most problems. The problem lies in the apparent incompatibility in the comparison of the products. In most cases some common unit can be found, for example production hours, or some commonality between batches. In a small number of cases it may not be possible to find a suitable physical unit and in these cases monetary units will have to be used, with care.

In cases where monetary units have to be used, the monetary values first need to be stabilised. This is done by removing the effect of inflation. There can be problems in actually determining the rate of inflation. If asked, most managers would quote the government's figure for inflation, the Retail Price Index (RPI). Unfortunately, this figure may not be relevant to the company in question. The RPI gives a weighted average inflation for a 'typical' family budget in the country; it includes things like food, mortgage payments, electrical consumer goods, etc., all given a weighting to reflect the average shopping basket. In any particular business the figure may be totally different, reflecting higher increases in fuel charges, raw materials, etc. The inflation rate will therefore need to be determined for each company by the accounts section, having regard to all the price rises for the previous year. Having achieved this difficult task, the effect of inflation is removed and the trend produced; to make this trend meaningful it must be used in planning the future. This leads to another formidable task: forecasting the inflation rate for the future. For these reasons this approach should be used only as a last resort, if no suitable physical measure can be found. It will always be easier and more sensible to use some form of unit measurement.

Format of the sales analysis

The units the sales are to be measured in having been determined, the format of the sales analysis now needs to be considered. Time is the first consideration in this. The time scale of reporting in the analysis and the time split in measurement will depend upon the business and products. It may be daily, weekly, monthly, quarterly or yearly. In extreme cases it may even be hourly. Many sales analyses will contain more than one time scale: produced weekly, for example, but containing monthly, quarterly and yearly figures. Special reports should be produced at month-, quarter- and year-end. The example just given is probably the most widely used time scale. However, the final time scales chosen will depend on the level of sales; the greater the sales volume and activity, the smaller the split in the sales analysis can usually be. The sales analysis will be of more value in terms of reading the sales pattern for future trends if it has a history and contains a reasonable number of time periods. But when trends are produced they should take more account of the most recent data.

The middle level of the analysis will depend upon the size and type of business and in small businesses may not exist at all. At this level will be factors like geographical split, sales personnel split, unit or divisional split. This will be of advantage in determining future trends. It will also be very powerful in the control and planning of the sales force, units and divisions of the company. The exact use will be determined by the structure of the company and the type of product or service.

The final level of the analysis will be the actual products or service. At its base level the sales analysis needs to be split into, in most cases, separate products or services to give product class, line, item, etc. At this base level it will give a very large table with the many combinations of time areas, products, etc. From this the products part of the analysis needs to be drawn together into generic groups. The Pareto distribution will almost certainly apply to product range: approximately 20 per cent of products will account for approximately 80 per cent of sales volume. When deciding on the grouping this analysis should be taken into account, i.e. alongside unit values for trends we also need the sales volume. It is important that large sales volumes do not swamp or obscure other small but important sales volumes. The number of groups in the sales analysis will depend upon the product range, the number of items sold, sales volume and the planning use being made of the analysis. The analysis should have sufficient detail divisions to make it a useful planning aid but not so many that it becomes too complicated or meaningless. This is not an easy balance to achieve and will vary from business to business.

Against the actual sales figures the sales analysis also needs to show what happened in previous years (one or more years' data depending on the stability of the products). This will be needed to produce trends into the future. It is also useful to show the forecasts, targets or budgets, thus showing progress against what was expected. To help this monitoring process it can be very useful to show the previous sales, actual sales and forecast sales as cumulative-to-date values. It is far less serious if an under-sale one month balances against an over-sale the next month than where a series of months show under-sales. Cumulative figures will illustrate the serious situations more effectively than will mere monthly differences.

Given the analysis so far produced it would be an understatement to say that most businesses will end up with a very large table. We have taken time scales against geographical splits, etc., against products, and then grouped products. For each of these we have listed previous, actual and forecast sales, both in unit terms and in sales values, and cumulatively. How do we use this very complex table to its best effect in planning and controlling the sales and marketing effort of an organisation? Again, it is the information technology advances of the last few years that enable managers to extract the maximum information from the raw data.

Presentation of the sales analysis

The sales analysis so far described will be too complex to give a great deal of information to sales management. The first stage of the presentation will be made on this full breakdown. It will be analysed by the forecasting and control mechanisms, using information technology. Reports to sales management at this stage will be exception reporting. The computer-based control system will flag only where product, area, group, etc., sales are changing significantly. These flagged products can then be examined using other information (particularly informal information) to decide if a real change in the product is taking place.

With this type of analysis it will enable companies to identify quickly the products that are in the ascendant and those coming to the end of their life cycle. It can also identify products that need some extra promotion to revive them. This type of control analysis can also identify regional changes that are taking place, and changes in the performance of sales personnel, etc.

Using control analysis in this manner will enable companies to gain the maximum competitive advantage. A company which can react quickly to changes that are taking place will survive in an ever changing environment. The modern sales environment tends to favour such companies. The important part of the process is to have the product sales analysis in sufficient detail to enable the analysis to be carried out. However, it should always be remembered that the identification of changes should not be carried out in only a numeric way. The numbers and control system will flag significant changes, but these must be considered along with other information to flag up real changes. Changes may be identified from other information sources than the sales analysis, as will be shown later in this chapter.

The first part of the sales analysis produced exception reporting. We now need to consider the main reports. This stage will not give a single sales analysis report but a series of reports for a variety of purposes. The full detailed analysis, due to its size, will be unlikely to be produced as a single report unless there is only a small range of products. Even then, this analysis will be for senior sales management only. Sales personnel performance measures should not be put into general circulation.

The first set of full reports should be for each product or service group, giving the sales of each product within the group and the group sales total. These should be measured in unit sales and monetary value and give a comparison with previous sales and predicted sales. This set of reports will be completed with a summary report of the sales of product groups. The summary will be for general circulation, the detailed product group reports more limited. These reports will be used to plan products and the product splits. The information contained in these reports will be important to planning in parts of the business other than the sales department.

The next sets of reports will depend on the specific business for their exact detail. To some organisations geographical split can be important. This can be extracted from the full analysis. In most cases it will be sufficient to split out the product or service group totals. If products are changing within a group it may be necessary to produce a more detailed product against geographical area. Again these should be given in monetary and unit value and provide a comparison with previous sales and predicted sales. Such reports will be important in determining, for example, the regional strategies of the organisation and in conjunction with other information.

Many companies have a series of sales outlets, whether retail stores, a number of sales personnel operating from the main office or a series of branch offices. Like the geographical reports the sales outlet report for general strategic and market planning will in most cases be sufficient if it splits out product or service group total. Again these should be in monetary and unit values and give a comparison with previous sales and predicted sales. This information can be used in the control and planning of the sales outlets. Further reports split down into more product detail will be needed by each sales outlet for its product planning. These reports will be vital to both the sales outlets and the main organisation in the planning and control of these outlets.

In any particular organisation there are likely to be further splits that will be required at varying levels of detail. These will be specific requirements for many companies and it is beyond the scope of this chapter to cover all the possible levels of reporting. The key to a successful sales analysis report is to consider it not as a single report but as a series of reports with different purposes.

Information technology has now made such a detailed sales analysis possible. The analysis can be carried out on mainframe computers but this often creates problems of scheduling the work on such machines as they are usually busy with real-time data processing. This problem becomes worse when non-standard analysis or 'What if?' calculations are required. With the recent significant increases in personal computer capacity and speed it is now possible to carry out such an analysis on a PC using the latest spreadsheet packages. To do this efficiently it is important that the data for the analysis is downloaded directly into the spreadsheet and not re-keyed in. It is also important to store the data to be analysed in its most detailed form. The spreadsheet can then be used to generate the standard reports, i.e. collating and forming the data into information. The advantage of keeping the data in its most detailed form is that it gives management maximum flexibility when carrying out *ad hoc* analysis of the data. The ability to carry out exception reporting, searching for changes in trends, can also be built into the spreadsheet.

The final part of this section deals with the physical presentation of the reports. The basic choice is between some form of tabular or graphical presentation. This choice will depend on the use to be made of the reports. If the figures are required to be read from a particular presentation then some form of table will be needed. If the particular presentation is to demonstrate trends or relationships then some form of graphical or pictorial presentation will be needed. This will almost certainly mean that the sales analysis will need both tabular and graphical presentations. Line graphs and bar charts can be used to present sales trends and pie charts to show how a market is split into its segments. It is also possible to use pictograms to good effect when presenting the sales analysis. In an important presentation Mr Kipling's Cakes used a pictogram based on a pie chart. A picture of the different cakes the company made was used and cut into slices to represent the market segments. This added a new meaning to pie charts and they became apple pie charts. Modern graphics packages can produce pictograms cost effectively.

Information technology can be of great value in presenting the information. It is likely that the final part of the sales analysis will be carried out on a spreadsheet package. Latest versions of industry-standard spreadsheet packages, like Lotus 123, Excel and Supercalc have excellent facilities for producing tables and graphs. If these packages are operated within the Windows environment then all the tables and graphs can be easily imported into a word processing package to produce sales reports. If higher-quality tables and graphs are required one of the specialised graphics packages such as Harvard Graphics and Freelance can be used. These types of package will produce very sophisticated tables and graphical presentations. It is easy to import the basic tables directly from the spreadsheet package into the graphics package. An added advantage of the graphics package is the ability to produce sophisticated slide shows for use in overhead projection presentations. The personal computer and the graphics package are now an important part of the marketing presentation and their falling cost and rising power now mean they are within the reach of the smaller organisation.

Product costing

When considering the sales analysis an important factor is still missing. It is not sufficient simply to identify patterns of sales, it is also vital to know how much the product has cost to 'produce' and therefore the margin. 'Produce' needs to be taken in its widest context to cover manufacturing and service industries.

Traditional costing approaches will not identify the cost in sufficient detail to give accurate costing down to product level. Again, information technology can help with the collection of accurate costing data. The use of bar code readers and hand-held computers makes it possible to record the resources needed to 'produce' the product. With such detailed information it is possible to arrive at a detailed product costing and therefore a reasonably accurate view of margin.

It is important to examine the product mix of an organisation in terms of margin. Loss leaders are a strategy used by some organisations; what is very dangerous is where traditional costing systems are hiding products with very low or negative margins. Margins are likely to be different across the product range of an organisation. It is important to match this true reflection on margins with the sales analysis. The changes taking place in the product mix need to be mapped carefully on to the analysis of margins. It is important to know when high-margin products are moving into decline and to know the margin on growth products and new products. High-margin products in decline and new growth products on a low or negative margin are a dangerous combination. An organisation using traditional costing methods could find that by the time this is discovered it is too late. By using information technology and good practice in information management, forewarning of these events could be obtained and strategies to counteract them developed.

Margin analysis should also be applied to other parts of the sales analysis. It may also reveal interesting information if applied to different divisions of the organisation or different sales personnel.

Information technology has made both the detailed product costing and the detailed sales analysis possible. By using this information to best advantage at both operational and strategic levels it is possible for an organisation to gain a competitive edge over its competitors.

COMPETITOR PROFILE

The analysis of competitors is an important part of developing a market strategy. In most markets there are likely to be many players but the Pareto distribution will apply and a small number will account for the majority of the market. The key competitors in the market are likely to be the larger players who in many cases dominate it, but the perceived key competitors identified by sales personnel and customers should also be considered. If the organisation operates in a segment of a market, its key competitors are likely to lie mainly in that segment. For example, Morgan Cars' key competitors are not Ford or Vauxhall but manufacturers of other specialist traditional sports cars. It is likely that there will be too many competitors to carry out a full analysis on all of them, hence the need to identify the key ones.

The purpose of a competitor profile is to allow management to estimate the effects of competitors on the marketplace. There will be a variety of sources of information on competitors. Financial information and general information can be obtained from company accounts and reports. This information will be held on a computerised database in any good business library, and is produced by organisations like Dun and Bradstreet. Further information can be found in trade journals, the local press, etc., indicating and reporting on the future intentions of competitors. Again, a good business library's database will produce abstracts of articles written about organisations.

Details of competitors' market shares for many products and services can be purchased from market research consultants. It is usual for a particular consultant to concentrate on different markets; information about total markets can often be obtained from government statistics. Less formal information on competitors can often be collected by sales personnel using their experience of the marketplace and the views of customers.

The information needs to be collated and analysed to estimate the competitors' effect on the market. One of the simplest and reasonably effective devices for carrying this out is to undertake a SWOT (strengths, weaknesses, opportunities, threats) analysis.

- List the strengths of the competitor and ask questions like: How can we counteract these strengths? Are there any we would like to develop?
- List the weaknesses of the competitor and ask questions like: How can we take advantages of such weakness? Are the weaknesses common across all or the majority of competitors?
- List the opportunities open to the competitors and ask questions like: Are these opportunities open to all players in the market? If not, what makes them open to the competitor and can it be replicated in our own organisation?
- List the threats to the competitor and ask questions like: Are these threats to all players in the market? If not, what effect could they have on the competitor?

The simple SWOT analysis can be a most effective way of positioning competitors in the marketplace. It also allows an organisation to position itself against its competitors.

It is also possible to use some of the more sophisticated corporate modelling devices like company capability profiling. It may also be possible to use strategic position and action evaluation (SPACE) analysis to show the likely strategies competitors may pursue.

INDUSTRY/ENVIRONMENT PROFILE

This profile will contain principally information concerning and from the external environment. This information comes from both official sources (government statistics) and non-official sources (trade associations and professional bodies, market research consultants, banks, stockbrokers, local authorities, private companies, computer databanks and libraries).

Official government statistics

The government is the main producer of statistics in the country and these are varied and comprehensive. Statistics are produced to cover the general economy and there are series covering industrial production and sales, imports and exports, employment and earnings and population. Such statistics can be most valuable to business. The general economic statistics can give an overall guide to the direction of the economy. The statistics are important to put the sales and market forecasts into the context of the general economy. Another important series could be industrial production and sales. Within this series are included over 200 producing sectors which are covered by individual reports and within these sectors information on a variety of products is also given. This series will give the overall market position for a wide range of businesses. The population figures could be useful if a business is considering expanding into a new area for they could give some idea of potential new markets. These are just some examples of the multitude of government statistics. To help find the particular statistics applicable to the market of the individual small business two guides are produced by the government. *Government – A Brief Guide to Sources,* produced by the Central Statistical Office, is a free booklet that describes the main publications. It also provides a useful list of telephone numbers and points of contact for further information. It is limited by its size and provides only a brief guide. *Official Statistics* published by HMSO is the principal guide to government statistics. This guide is a substantial volume and so is probably best examined in the larger library. It provides useful descriptions of all the official publications. A subject index can direct the user to published sources on a particular area.

An important point to remember about government statistics is that they provide a relatively cheap form of market information. The government publications themselves are not that expensive and it may be possible to look at them in the larger reference libraries. Government statistics are under-used by British business. Many businesses succumb to the myth that government statistics are either too high powered for or of no use to them. Neither belief is true. Government statistics can provide a considerable amount of information about the market in which the business is operating and about potential markets, and they provide it at a reasonable cost.

Other government agencies also produce market statistics. The National Economic Development Office (NEDO), for example, produces some very good market sector reports either free or at a very reasonable price.

Non-official sources

There are many non-official sources of market information. The main ones are listed below with comments on their usefulness to business.

Trade associations and professional bodies

There are several thousand trade associations and professional bodies in the UK and their output of useful market information varies considerably. It must be remembered that the associations will provide the information they produce only to members; thus membership is essential. The association may produce information of two types depending on how good they are. First, they provide statistical information on the overall market. This may be a reproduction of government statistics but in the better associations will include extra information collected from members. Second, they may produce a journal or a newsletter with news of members of the association. This may provide useful market intelligence information concerning customers or competitors.

Market research consultants

Many of the market research consultants produce market reports (other than specific market research briefs). Examples are the one-off industry and market reviews published by organisations such as the Economist Intelligence Unit, Keynotes, Gower Press and Jordans. Like all products some of these reports are better than others and some are quite expensive for what they give.

Banks

Banks provide general economic statistics usually summarised from government figures. They also provide for customers reports giving general economic statistics for other countries. Such a source can be of limited use to the small business though is usually free of charge. An example of this is the ABECOR Country Report Series distributed by Barclays. Regular reports on every country in the world are issued free of charge. They provide, among more general matters, information on exchange rates, difficulties with payments, inflation rates and sectoral trends. These could be a useful starting point for the company considering exporting to a particular country.

Stockbrokers

Stockbrokers' reports can be a useful source of market information – assuming access can be gained to them. Many of the reports have a limited circulation, not always because they are confidential but, in some cases, simply because they are not widely publicised. Some stockbrokers have realised there is a market for their publications and now make them available on subscription. For example, Wood Mackenzie and Co. offers an annual subscription to its reports on the oil industry and Vickers de Costa has a similar facility for its quarterly reports on the leisure industry. Some stockbrokers, for example Phillips and Drew, produce more general reviews of the economy as a whole and its future prospects. The reports from stockbrokers can prove very useful to business, again for information concerning the market they are in, although some of the published reports are expensive.

Local authorities

Some of the larger local authorities regularly publish statistics on social and economic trends in their area. These may be of limited use to the small business when setting their forecasts in the context of the economy as a whole. The advantage is that the information is more localised. Local authorities and to some extent central government have set up a number of agencies to help business, although in many cases concentrating on small business. However, the majority of them do not provide market or sales information and data.

Private companies

Some of the larger companies, as part of a public relations exercise and as corporate advertising, produce statistical reviews of their industry. These can give a very good picture of the total market in the industry. A well-established example is BP's annual *Statistical Review of the World Oil Industry*. These reviews can be a very useful source of market information if you are lucky enough to find one for your industry.

Computer databanks

A fast-growing source of market information is the on-line statistical databases. These are large databases of market, economic, population, etc., information stored on a mainframe computer. Users of the system link into the computer via their own terminal and telephone line. They can interrogate the databank and carry out a wide range of analysis work on the data. Unfortunately, such systems will almost certainly prove to be too expensive for the smaller business at present, but with the fast falling cost of computing and the greater use of such databases this could change in the not too distant future.

Libraries

Libraries can provide a very useful service to business. Most large public libraries take the main UK government sources and some material from international organisations and they will probably be able to obtain the less popular material as well. A growing number also provide access to on-line services which may provide a suitable way for businesses to access such services. Librarians can and in most cases will help in the search for market information sources but do not expect them to do all the work unless you want to alienate the librarian completely from your cause. Most university and college libraries allow access to the general public and this can be of advantage because of the specialist business sections that most of them contain.

Profiles

The information from the various sources including the competitor analysis needs to be collated into the industry profile. The industry profile needs to contain, for example:

- *The competitive structure of the industry*
  Barriers to entry
  The type and intensity of competition
  Relative bargaining power
  Pricing policies in the industry
  Strategic positioning of competitors
- *Products and services in the industry*
  Medium- and long-term trends in demand
  Stability of the market
  Stages in the product life cycle of the industries
  Technology employed in the product/science
- *Capacity and supply in the industry*
  Industry capacity
  Technology employed in the industry
  Resource availability
  Supplier strength
  Social constraints
  Environmental factors
  Government legislation and policy
- *Economic and political factors (national and international)*
  The economy (growth, inflation, economic activity, cycles, etc.)
  Political power and influence (stability, fiscal policies, etc).

This profile will be contained in a series of reports. Some of these may use corporate modelling devices like industry profiles. It will also be possible to use decision support systems like Stratpac.

MARKET PROFILE

There is some overlap between the four profiles considered above. It can be dangerous to take just one element of these profiles and then build strategies or take operational decisions. There is a very apt saying from Confucius in connection with these profiles: 'The essence of knowledge is, once you have it use it.' It is possible to gain a significant competitive advantage from the information in profiles built using the latest ideas in management information and information technology. At the operational level cost reductions can be achieved and at the strategic level a greater understanding of products, markets, competitors and environments can be gained. This greater understanding can ensure that an organisation reacts in the best way to changes taking place in the market. This is important. The modern sales environment tends to favour companies that can respond to change in the best way and quickly. The profiles will indicate the direction to take. It is important, however, to take a holistic view of the market, paying regard to product/service, competition and the wider environment. Modern information management and information technology provide the ability to carry this out.

COMPETITIVE ADVANTAGE

The idea of competitive advantage was first put forward in the 1980s, by Michael Porter from Harvard Business School. There now exist a number of organisations which by a strategic and planned use of information technology have achieved a competitive advantage. It is possible to transfer the idea behind these competitive advantages into an industry in which they have not yet been considered. The examples of competitive edge can be considered in four main groups: customer links, other links, communications and market information. These different types of competitive advantage will achieve one or more of:

- cost reduction
- product/service differentiation
- greater understanding of the markets.

Customer links

One of the best and earliest examples of this type of competitive advantage is shown by Kodak. Kodak achieved a competitive advantage by using information technology to link its major customers into its origination. Kodak provided for its major customers a computer-based stock control scheme. The system gave good stock control balancing cost for the customers. It orders automatically when stocks fall to the re-order level. The link occurs because the order is sent to Kodak. This gives Kodak a number of advantages. First, it links its customers directly into its systems, a form of differentiation not in direct product terms but in the quantity of service. Second, it reduces cost: the cost of order collection is significantly reduced. Finally, it increases Kodak's knowledge of the market.

Kodak applied its competitive advantage within the film and film processing market. There are still many markets and market segments where it is possible to link in customers by using computer systems. They are waiting for an organisation to exploit such an advantage.

Other links

There can be more general links than the one-supplier dedicated link. American Airlines developed an airline seat booking system called SABRE. This system now dominates bookings throughout the airline industry. This gives American Airlines a number of advantages. First, a cost reduction: the development cost of SABRE can be spread among many users. Second, a product differentiation is created: the basic product of American Airlines is providing air transport, but it now has a second major product – providing information technology systems. This example also shows how a new business can grow out of existing players in a marketplace. This has been created by providing a service to the rest of the market. There are a number of markets where creative use of information technology could be used by a player in the market to provide such a service.

Communications

Information technology can provide very sophisticated communication systems for organisations and taking full advantage of them can provide a competitive edge. The systems can reduce costs, by increasing the speed of communications within the organisation. The modern systems also lead to flatter organisational structures. This again reduces costs and usually also makes the organisation more efficient and able to change direction. These computer-based systems also make communications with customers faster and more efficient, thus improving quality. This can be a way of product differentiation through significant improvement in quality of service.

IBM is a good example of using such techniques, although the rate at which electronic mail and communications systems are spreading through organisations and industries makes it difficult to create new competitive advantages with this technique. Such communications are fast becoming necessary in business.

Market information

The improvement of market information by using information technology has been dealt with in the bulk of this chapter. The key to this type of competitive edge is the ability to read changes in the market and to react to these changes. Examples of this type of competitive edge are Sainsbury and the larger supermarkets, but it is open to many organisations. Most organisations have considerable potential information about all aspects of their market they can tap into and use to advantage.

A number of organisations are now using highly targeted mail shots. They buy a series of mailing lists and then target common names. This allows a sophisticated level of targeting which significantly increases the chances of success from the mail shot. Successful exponents of direct mailing include Reader's Digest and the Automobile Association.

Hotels are a further sector where masses of potential information exists, but with many hotels it is lost within the organisation. This information can be concerned with the type of service customers require or their likes and dislikes. If this information is retained using information technology a hotel could gain a competitive advantage by providing an increased level of service to its regular customers. Holiday Inns have their 'Priority Club', Hyatt Hotels 'Hyatt Gold Passport' and Four Seasons their 'Greetings' system. All these developments use customer information to improve customer service.

Most organisations will find information being discarded within their operations. With the use of information technology it is now possible to retain this information and create a competitive advantage.

SUMMARY

This chapter has presented the interface between marketing and modern practice in both management information and information technology. It demonstrates how a competitive edge can be found by achieving a greater understanding of the market. This understanding is facilitated by the construction of a series of profiles: the customer profile, product profile, competitor profile and the industry/environment profile. All these profiles integrate to form the market profile. This then allows the organisation to build well-founded and realistic market strategies to take advantage of changes taking place in the market.

The chapter also considers other ways in which information technology can give a competitive advantage. This can be by linking the organisation into its customers and so forming 'golden chains'. It can also be achieved by providing a communication service across a complete industry. The final approach is to use the advantages of computer-based communications within the organisation. This will give more efficient communications and also achieve cost reductions.

CHAPTER 8

Marketing and Human Resource Management: a relationship of interdependence

Ann Hollings

INTRODUCTION

This chapter examines the relationship between marketing and Human Resource Management (HRM). It aims to explain the development and role of the organisational culture in establishing a value system conducive to the achievement of organisational aims and objectives, and the fundamental role of Human Resource Management initiatives in securing the culture. Inevitably, many features of Human Resource Management are not addressed, or are left to inference; it is not the purpose of this chapter to describe Human Resource Management in total. It is hoped, however, that the reader is convinced of the critical nature of the relationship between marketing and Human Resource Management and is encouraged to delve deeper.

CORPORATE CULTURE

Peter is the managing director of a small, low-technology, highly successful organisation specialising in the grinding and milling of powders. The organisation has built its reputation on the basis of good quality, good service, a recognition that the customer pays the bills and, above all, an ability to respond to the demands of the market. The environment in which Peter operates is simple, with the customer being relatively easy both to identify and to predict product requirements for, but at the same time is volatile. There is no room for complacency and no assurance that a job well done will bring repeat orders. Furthermore, operating on a jobbing basis leads to peaks and troughs in production; there is little opportunity for steady drip-drip products – that flow of continuous orders which provide a bed-rock of security. The atmosphere is tense, charged with the accompanying behaviour of people permanently on 'standby' and yet it works. Why? It is no accident that has led Peter to create an organisation which is continually looking for new opportunities and translating those opportunities into organisational realities and firm contracts. Indeed Peter's philosophy is based on his belief that there are no 'problems', only 'opportunities'. His *modus operandi* is one of 'can do' and his employees have no illusion as to what is expected from them and how they are expected to behave. Perhaps more crucially, they are also aware of what is likely to happen if they cannot (or will not) fulfil their side of the bargain. Peter has spent considerable time and money in creating a work environment and workplace culture which reflects his preferred approach to the achievement of corporate objectives.

In short, if we examine the vignette, Peter has made at least one strategic decision in an attempt to bring about the successful achievement of his corporate objectives. That strategic decision concerns his employees. It is a decision which encompasses a variety of issues, but in general it is one that addresses the organisational culture and, because it involves directly his employees, one that comes under the broad heading of human resource initiatives. Perhaps what is more significant, however, is the relationship between this human resource initiative and the type of organisation which Peter controls. The company is in manufacturing and has a 'product' which must be marketed, or in this case a production capacity which offers customers a customised service to produce that which they want.

Peter relies on his ability to sell the company on the basis of its production capacity, which is its unique selling point. But, in order to fulfil this task, he relies on his employees to perform that which is required to produce goods to the customer's satisfaction. So although the primary task is clearly market-orientated (and customer-driven) Peter is totally dependent on the human resource factor within his organisation. He can achieve his corporate objective only if his employees perform to a very high standard which is implicit in the sales contract. It needs his employees to embrace the sales philosophy if he is to succeed. Furthermore, Peter needs to have a high level of conformity reflected in the way that his employees perform their jobs if he is to meet the tight operational constraints caused by his customer-driven sales generation strategy. That level of conformity conveys the strength of the organisational culture. The greater the degree of conformity the 'thicker' the culture and the more goal-directed towards the achievement of corporate objectives, the more functional the culture. Peter's success depends not just on his productive capacity and marketing strategy, but on his workforce's willingness to perform.

What is beginning to emerge is that there are a variety of interfaces between different facets of the organisation relating to both its external reference points and its internal activities. The integrating factor between them all is that of the human resource. Just how well the interfaces themselves merge, dissolve and coalesce to present a corporate operation (which is effective and efficient) depends to a large extent upon the cohesiveness of the human resource and the strength of the sense of commitment (stemming from common interest) to collaborate in furthering the organisation's goals. After all, it does not matter how brilliant a strategy is on paper, if it cannot be implemented it becomes nothing more than a good idea.

As Ahmed and Rafiq (1992) point out, successful competitive advantage is often the result of the success in implementation of strategic policies precisely because it is these internal operations which are elusive to imitation. Where there is a contingency between, on the one hand, the way the human resource adopts and makes operational a strategic initiative and, on the other, the goals of the organisation, there is a greater likelihood of the organisation retaining its competitive edge.

Clearly the cultural imperative, and the way a culture is preserved or changed as is seen fit, are key issues in the attempt to establish corporate dominance, both internally and externally, and have been the subject of extensive research and commentary over the past decade.

So what is corporate culture? How does it emerge? How is it learned by the employees? And perhaps the most interesting question, how is it managed? Throughout the last decade, the 'culture' of corporations has emerged as one of the central themes in the field of management and organisational studies. As a theme its attraction has had a lot to do with the assertion that organisational performance can be enhanced by the establishment of an appropriate corporate culture. Indeed a prevailing theme of the 'Excellence literature' so predominant during the mid-1980s was explicitly based on that assumption as exemplified by what Peters and Waterman (1982, p. 51) say:

> The top performers create a broad, uplifting, shared culture, a coherent framework within which charged-up people search for appropriate adaptations. Their ability to extract extraordinary contributions from very large numbers of people turns on the ability to create a highly valued sense of purpose. Such purpose emanates from love of product, providing top-quality services and honouring innovation and contribution from all.

From this the message is clear. Corporate culture is not something that can be imposed and acted upon without question. For culture to become something which shapes and guides the behaviour of organisational members in a desirable way, there must be a willing investment by individuals into that very culture. For culture to make meaning of employees' actions it must have meaning, relevance and value to them. It becomes a mutually supporting relationship.

But what constitutes corporate culture? In what are employees investing? To Handy (1976) culture represents 'a set of values and norms and beliefs – reflected in different structures and systems'. Furthermore, he recognises that organisations have different cultures, making each organisation an idiosyncratic entity, not surprisingly because 'the cultures are affected by the events of the past and by the climate of the present, by the technology of the type of work, by their aims and the level of people that work in them'. Like people, no two organisations can ever have experienced the same life and development.

More simply, corporate culture has been described, for example, as 'the way things are done around here', 'the dominant values espoused by an organisation', 'the philosophy that guides an organisation's policy towards employees and customers'. And, more perceptively (Schein, 1984, p. 3), as:

> the pattern of basic assumptions that a given group has invented, discovered or developed in learning to cope with its problems of external adaptation and internal integration, and that have worked well enough to be considered valid and, therefore, to be taught to new members as the correct way to perceive, think and feel in relation to those problems.

Taking these ideas together it is possible to establish an understanding of what corporate culture is, how it emerges, why it emerges and how it is sustained (and, if necessary, how it can be changed). The final piece of the culture jigsaw is 'How can it be identified?' Schein (1985) offers this as an answer: 'Organisational culture provides a system of shared meanings which represents a pattern of beliefs, symbols, rituals, myths and practices that have evolved and been transmitted over time.'

This could be represented as in Fig. 8.1, in which there is a bed-rock of shared meanings comprising the underlying values, beliefs and feelings which generate attitudes; these in turn lead to assumptions and expectations about what will be experienced. On this bed-rock of shared meanings float cushions of behaviours (that which people do), practices (guidelines as to how people should do things), symbols and sayings (artifacts and expressions representing the value system), heroes and baddies (people who are 'in' and 'out'), rituals (ceremonials and set-pieces which take place) and myths and stories (tales of how the company has survived and tackled difficult moments).

For the culture to be sustained requires that an employee's experiences are consistent with that which the employee wants and expects to experience. As

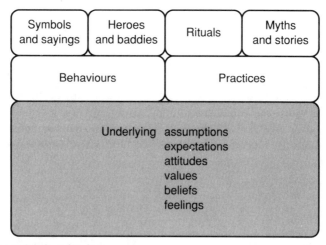

Fig. 8.1 Organisational culture

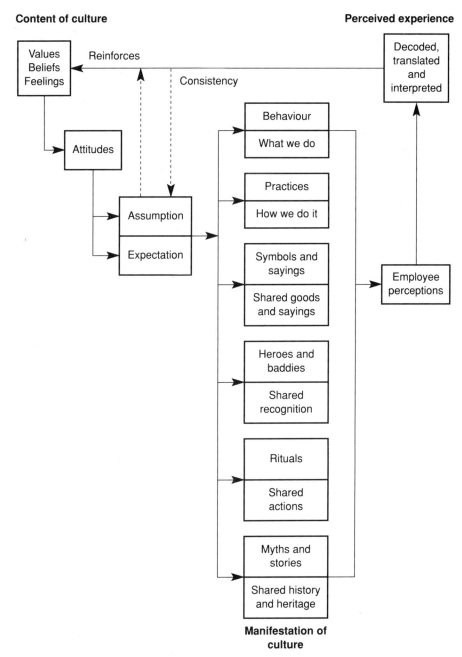

Fig. 8.2 The balance between attitudes and experiences

such, there is the need for employees to experience a balance/consistency between their attitudes and experiences (see Fig. 8.2). The diagram in Fig. 8.2 begs the question: 'Well, what happens if there is an inconsistency between the perceived experiences and what was assumed/expected?' In practice the employee will experience cognitive dissonance (Festinger, 1957) and will attempt to bring about consistency through a variety of possible strategies. From a management perspective, however, the important objective is to attempt to ensure that what the employee experiences is what the employee assumed and expected he or she would experience. This objective is firmly within the arena of the HRM practitioner, who can apply the techniques and tools of his or her trade to attempt to generate congruence between experience and expectations which in turn generates a commitment and loyalty to the organisation and a desire to help the organisation achieve its goals.

The culture and HRM

Michael Armstrong's (1990, p. 1) description of human resource management explains:

> Human Resource Management (HRM) is an approach to the management of people based on four fundamental principles. First, human resources are the most important assets an organisation has and their effective management is the key to its success. Second, this success is most likely to be achieved if the personnel policies and procedures of the enterprise are closely linked with, and make a major contribution to, the achievement of corporate goals and strategic plans. Third, the corporate culture and the values, organisational climate and managerial behaviour that emanate from that culture will exert a major influence on the achievement of excellence. This culture must therefore be managed, which means that organisational values may need to be changed or reinforced and that continuous effort, starting from the top, will be required to get them accepted and acted upon. Finally, HRM is concerned with integration; getting all the members of the organisation involved and working together with a sense of common purpose.

This description makes an explicit link between culture, HRM and the achievement of high performance and quality (excellence), whilst emphasising the holistic approach of HRM. It is this strategic emphasis which is critical to the issue of organisational interfaces because the focus is now one of assertive HRM strategies to enable the achievement of corporate objectives through the establishment and sustainment of a co-operative corporate culture. Only by providing the blueprint to enable employees to discover what is required of them and how this can be achieved (as well as persuading employees that what is 'on offer' is better than what they have now) will the organisation achieve its objectives. In particular, any corporate initiative which relies on behavioural changes must also come to terms with the crucial involvement of HRM in the strategic design for bringing about such change. As Piercy (1992, p. 26) proposes in his rationale of market-led organisations emphasising the primary pursuit of customer satisfaction: 'being market-led may require substantial and painful upheaval in the way our organisations are structured, the way decisions are made, the key values we communicate to employees and managers, how we all do our jobs and how we look at the outside world'. He goes further (ibid, p. 7) and suggests that the achievement of the marketing process may have less to do with specialist marketing and sales executives and more to do with those who operationalise the activities of the organisation, including human resource managers.

If the role of the HRM practitioner is to ensure employee allegiance to the corporate culture by applying appropriate HRM strategies, what are the key characteristics of corporate culture upon which such strategies are applied and what are the HRM strategies and their constituents? Robbins (1990, p. 439) suggests ten key characteristics of corporate culture:

- individual initiative
- risk tolerance
- direction
- integration
- management support
- control
- identity
- reward system
- conflict tolerance
- communication patterns.

Key characteristics of corporate culture!

All of the key characteristics require employees to know how they are expected to behave, why they are expected to behave in that way and what they will gain for appropriate behaviour. They include both structural and behavioural dimensions and depend on the organisation being well designed and structured with effective job design and work allocation; having the appropriate people doing relevant work for which they are properly rewarded; having an effective control system which allows employees to experience self-direction, albeit within the parameters of the organisation's preferred behaviour; having employees who are properly trained and developed so that their personal competence can lead to competent work; having a supportive management system which displays effective leadership and employs appropriate procedures and practices to develop and extend conducive employment relations. In short, a fundamental underpinning of HRM initiatives.

To leave all of these to chance and *ad hoc* development denies the organisation the opportunity to achieve its potential. Organisation success requires a fully integrated and coherent approach to all of these features affecting organisational performance. There needs to be a high degree of congruence and empathy between the policies designed to fulfil these objectives. Without them, piecemeal development is likely to degenerate into ineffective and inefficient

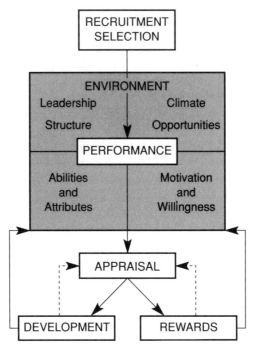

Fig. 8.3 The HRM cycle (adapted from Devanna, Fombrun and Tichy, 1984)

practices, which in time could lead to internal conflict and reduced goal fulfilment.

The HRM approaches which can be implemented to secure organisational effectiveness can be represented by the adapted model of the cycle of HRM developed by Devanna, Fombrun and Tichy (1984) (see Fig. 8.3).

But before proceeding with the main body of information about HRM in theory, let us first consider HRM in context.

CASE STUDY

Transferral Ltd

Transferral Ltd is a wholly owned subsidiary of a large international conglomerate. Left largely to its own devices in terms of its preferred operational strategy, the company enjoys a high degree of autonomy. It is a specialist operation, unique in the overall organisation profile, with no other subsidiary manufacturing anything similar. The conglomerate is UK-led, with its head office in London. The customer base is very specialised, there being only seven major users of the products in the UK. Worldwide opportunities have been developing but so has the competition. Two years ago the company recognised a major threat to its dominant market position from a French-based company which had already established a reputation for prompt delivery and high-quality products.

The senior management team recognised the need to address the threat posed by the French competitor and suggested that the introduction of new working practices, coupled with a commitment to Total Quality Management (TQM), should ensure that Transferral would sustain its market position. The decision to change working practices was not taken lightly. Many of the workforce were long-service employees, with several able to boast twenty years' with the company. Their commitment to the way things were done was significant and was not easily ignored; particularly as all were in charge of fairly large groups of people and in a position to influence many other employees within the company. The main thrust of the changes reflected the board of directors' belief that flexibility was the key to improved performance. This required a number of employees to become multi-skilled and the rumour went round that a large number of people would be losing their jobs because of the company's insistence on all employees learning new methods of work.

The implications of the board's decision were particularly significant for the HRM team. TQM, whilst a commonly used phrase in today's organisations, required Transferral's management team to address exactly what it meant to their company and what it was to achieve in specific terms. It was decided that as a market-driven organisation the emphasis should be on customer satisfaction with a full appraisal of the way all employees had to become aware of, and fully conversant with, the values and attendant behaviours of an organisation committed to a marketing orientation value system. The HRM team created a major programme for change, concentrating both on communications and on developing new skills and practices. It was anticipated that the main part of the programme would extend over nine months – in fact it took thirteen months and in parts of the company is ongoing. But perhaps of greater significance is the continued emphasis on changing people's values. Many employees are still not fully committed to the new-style organisation. They keep referring to 'the way things were'. The culture of Transferral is still in transition.

Communications and skill development were not the only activities for the HRM team. Performance was being affected by the rumours abounding, motivation was falling and something needed to be done if the company was to be able to maintain its service to existing customers. The head of HRM set up three special project groups. One was to address the issue of falling performance and the likelihood of a new reward system, one the issues associated with new skills and knowledge acquisition, and the third to address the full implications to the workforce in terms of transfers and promotions, recruitment and redundancies. All three teams liaised regularly as the activities of each impinged on those of the others.

Although the experience was fraught with tension, the general feeling is that the change programme has been successful. The market position has been sustained and the company is much more confident about the impact of the French competitor. It is also much more aware of its vulnerability to other aggressive competitors and is convinced that next time it will not be so slow to respond.

The management team is satisfied with the new working practices which are in operation, and the new reward system appears to be successful in terms of employee satisfaction and organisational objectives. The employee development programme is ongoing and support and monitoring systems, not least the appraisal system, are in place. The company also has a very coherent human resource plan that has addressed the workforce needs for the next five years. It has been accepted by the board that without the strategic response of the HRM team, Transferral would not be in the position it is now; rather, there would probably have been a large-scale redundancy programme to respond to decreasing sales and market share.

Devanna, Fombrun and Tichy suggest that four generic processes take place in all organisations: selection, appraisal, rewards and development – although it must be accepted that these processes may be fairly basic and informal in some organisations. The four processes are designed to impact on performance, which is the key dependent variable. But, whereas performance is assessed through the appraisal process, it too is subject to other influences such as how motivated the individual is, what abilities he or she has and how conducive the environment is in which the individual is operating (Cummings and Schwab, 1973).

To achieve high levels of performance employees should be exposed to good performance management, defined by Armstrong (1992, p. 162), as being 'a process or set of processes for establishing shared understanding about what is to be achieved and of managing and developing people in a way which increases the probability that it will be achieved in the short or longer term'. The corporate cultural link is again paramount. The design, implementation and management of effective employee resourcing, human resource development and employment relations policies and practices should provide the base from which the corporate values can be espoused. HRM can provide the mechanism through which commitment to, and mutuality between, organisational goals and individual aims can be achieved.

The Devanna, Fombrun and Tichy cycle will provide the model for the rest of this chapter as we explore more precisely what HRM entails.

THE SELECTION PROCESS

The aim of the resourcing strategies should be to select the people who are best able to perform the jobs (as defined by the organisational structure) and whose attitudes and behavioural characteristics will fit well into the culture. Resourcing depends on seven questions being properly researched and answered:

(1) What constitutes our existing human resource?
(2) What constitutes the human resource required for us to operate successfully in the future?
(3) What is the gap between (1) and (2)?
(4) What kind of people do we need to attract/release?
(5) How can we best secure the right people for our organisation?

(6) What can we do to develop existing employees?

(7) What do we need to do to retain those employees we want/need to keep?

What constitutes our existing human resource?

A prerequisite for any strategy is to establish the present position. Consequently, the starting point is an inventory of the existing workforce. The inventory involves establishment and classification of the profile of the present human resource expressed in statistics such as age mix, length of service, gender mix, organisation mix. An analysis must be made of the qualifications employees possess. What experience in terms of skill and knowledge do they have? What is the potential for promotion and advancement? All need to be related to an employee classification in terms of the occupation analysis. Alongside the inventory an attempt should be made to predict attrition, i.e. to project the likely reduction of the present workforce due to turnover, retirements, deaths and dismissals. The projection can be based on both factual data and historical trends.

What constitutes the human resource required for us to operate successfully in the future?

This requires an establishment of the workforce profile in terms of the experience and expertise needed in relation to the jobs which people will be doing. This assumes that the jobs people will be doing have been properly analysed and designed (see later for the development of this point).

What is the gap between the existing resource and the required one?

The answer to this establishes the basic demand for people: the analysis of what we have, who we have available and who has potential compared with what we need for successful future operations. It provides the skeleton upon which other decisions regarding resourcing can be built. It is at this point that a clear idea of what is needed in terms of skills, knowledge and experience is established. Further refinement can be made to ensure that factors which reflect best practice in employment philosophy, such as equality of opportunity, are also taken into account. Such factors could consider, for example, sex, race, disability and age distributions. From this point strategies for fulfilling the demand can be initiated.

What kind of people do we need to attract/release?

From the preceding question a statistical breakdown has been established in terms of factual and objective information. What has not been addressed is the overall person specification in terms of the human characteristics that an individual should possess in order to do the job and fit in with the organisation's value system. Consequently, as Townley (1989) suggests, the aim will be to recruit employees whose attitudes and behaviour will support the achievement of corporate objectives because they will more readily adopt and adapt to the corporate culture. This requires a clear understanding of what the corporate values are and what attitudes employees should express. Two well-used human attribute classification systems are Rodger's (1951) seven-point plan and Fraser's (1958) fivefold grading. Whilst it is suggested that both attempt to prevent concentration on subjective feelings the information they seek to elicit is based (in part) on abstract features such as disposition and special aptitudes (Rodger) and innate abilities, motivation and emotional balance (Fraser). However clearly the criteria are specified, there is an inevitable reliance on subjective judgement. This is further compounded by the overriding culture to which these relate and reflect which, in itself, is value-ridden and therefore exposed to subjective assessment.

The replies to this question and that in the preceding section provide a clear description of the criteria that need to be met to develop the workforce required for the organisation of the future. An assessment then has to be made whether that demand can be fulfilled internally or is a recruitment process which trawls the external labour market necessary? It will also become apparent that some existing employees will not fit into the future organisation and a decision has to be made as to how to deal with these.

How can the organisation best attract and secure the right people for it?

This question addresses the labour supply from the external labour market. Only through establishing exactly what type and kind of potential employee is being sought, can the recruiter work out an appropriate campaign to attract those people. This process relies on good marketing practices as the job is the 'product' being sold, and how best to promote the job becomes a critical question in an effective recruitment campaign. Decisions must be taken on five matters.

(1) Where to promote – locally, regionally, nationally or internationally?
(2) Using what media – newspapers, trade publications, professional journals, education establishments, job centres and government agencies, word of mouth, head-hunters, specialist recruitment agencies?
(3) When to promote, to take account of the expected difficulty in finding the right person and of notice periods?
(4) How to construct the promotional literature including the job advertisement? This will take account not only of information such as the job itself, the organisation and the type of person but also of the reward package. The reward package reflects both where the job fits into the recruiting organisation's structure and also what competitors are providing for similar jobs. This requires continuous market research to ensure that the organisation remains competitive and attractive to the right calibre of potential employees.
(5) In what form should applications be sent and by when – an application form (assuming that the application form provides relevant information), a curriculum vitae, a letter, examples of work?

Once the applications have been received a short-list of candidates needs to be drawn up. These will be those people who most closely match the criteria established in the preceding section. It is essential that good practice is exercised throughout the selection process in the search for the most appropriate person. If the criteria have been established properly and arbitrary criteria are not applied to sift out 'unsuitable' applicants, e.g. those who write in 'odd colour' ink, anyone over the age of forty five, single parents, then there is no need to fear legal redress. Aikin (1988) makes salutary reading to those who choose to flaunt the conventions of fairness and objectivity.

Selection

The next stage is the actual selection of the employee from the short-listed candidates. The selection techniques used need to take account of many factors, such as:

- job position within the organisational structure
- number of other job-holders in that or a similar position
- scarcity of experience required
- level of skill and/or knowledge required
- degree of organisational influence the job-holder could wield
- the colleagues the job-holder will be working with.

For the more influential/senior and individual jobs, it is likely that more sophisticated selection techniques will be used in an attempt to identify the person best matching the specified criteria.

Lewis (1985) suggests that the selection criteria can be considered from three levels or aspects: organisational, functional/departmental and individual.

Organisational criteria are those which reflect the organisation's overall strategic expectations. For example, the culture is something which will be expressed at this level and the selectors will be looking for an individual who indicates a match with the cultural value system and appears to be more 'comfortable' within the organisation. Often these organisational criteria are not explicit and the selectors are aware of them through intuition. Sometimes they relate to a particular strategic response such as organisation growth and diversity, in which case selectors will look for people who can demonstrate flexibility and creativity as specific attributes. Miles and Snow (1984) identified three types of behaviour and supporting organisational characteristics so that if an assessment of the organisation's characteristics had been conducted and classified according to whether it was a 'defender', 'prospector' or 'analyser', then the most suitable managerial characteristic could be correlated. Kochan and Barocci (1985) provide a useful approach to relating human resource management activities to the organisational life cycle. Their approach relates not only resourcing issues but also rewards, development and employee relations characteristics.

Functional/departmental criteria are those which are pertinent to belonging to a particular department/function and reflect a generalised expectation of what those functional specialists will display. As an example, human resource specialists will display different characteristics from finance specialists and, perhaps more subtly, different criteria will be applied to sales specialists and marketing specialists. This level of criteria relates to general technical competence in a chosen field, and also to the micro-culture of belonging to that specialist group. Individual job criteria are highly specific to that job and are contained in the job description and person specification – if these exist. It follows, therefore, that these criteria can be much more easily identified and described and tend to be the ones more often used in the selection process.

Selection techniques themselves cover a wide range of activities. The objective is to use the combination of techniques most appropriate to that job. The most common method is that of the selection interview, which itself has many variations on that single theme; increasingly, however, employers are prepared to adopt other supporting techniques in their attempt to identify 'Mr/Ms Right' and reduce the cost implications of employing the wrong person. These other techniques include exposing the candidate to some form of selection test (of which thousands are available, but a few tend to predominate). A good test displays four characteristics:

(1) It can *discriminate* between subjects by being sensitive to the person to whom it is applied.
(2) It has to be *standardised* to represent properly the population to which is to be applied.
(3) It is *reliable* in that it always measures that which it is intended to measure regardless of to whom (in relation to point (2)) it is applied.
(4) It is *valid* in that it measures the characteristic which the test is intended to measure and not some other characteristic.

The main types of test which are used are those designed to measure:

- aptitude – an individual's potential to develop to achieve competence
- intelligence – an individual's overall mental capacity (usually related to verbal and abstract reasoning)
- trainability – an individual's ability to be trained to perform (usually) craft-type work
- attainment – an individual's skills that have already been acquired
- personality – an individual's personality characteristics such as motivations, interests, attitudes and values. Whilst these are often the most controversial of the test types it is easy to see why they may be popular in helping identify the right 'person' for a specific organisational culture.

Assessment centres are also popular in some organisations. These use a range of assessment techniques in an attempt to ascertain a candidate's suitability.

They are also useful in establishing development needs. Armstrong (1992, p. 149) suggests that assessment centres provide a good opportunity for identifying the extent of the match between candidate and culture because the assessment technique used will relate closely to the cultural values and preferred ways of doing things. Whilst tests are likely to play a part in the assessment centre programme, other techniques often include things like situational analysis, role-play, group activities and simulations, all of which will highlight the considerable closeness to or distance from the organisational preferred behaviours.

Other less common selection methods may include such things as graphoanalysis, which is an analysis of an individual's handwriting in order to identify personality characteristics. Graphoanalysis has proved to be more popular in France. In the US an article in *Business Week* (28 May 1990) suggests that genetic testing is becoming more popular as attempts are made to link genetic characteristics with workplace health hazards.

All these techniques should be used in conjunction with the selection interview. The interview should be in-depth and be designed to integrate all the information from the application form and any other technique used to generate evidence in support, or otherwise, of the candidate. Because the interview offers a face-to-face opportunity and everyone has some sort of experience of interviewing, there is a tendency to disregard the level of sophistication of this process. If it is to be done properly great care needs to be taken to ensure that the interviewer is capable of making such an important decision.

Sadly, interviews are often a very bad experience and do nothing to provide selectors with any substantive evidence on which to base a reasonable prediction about the suitability of a candidate for a particular job. As Plumbley (1986, p. 115) notes: 'In practice, many so-called interviews consist of untrained employers talking generalities about jobs they have not analysed to would-be employees about whom they know little, and then deciding whether or not to offer them the job.' Unless adequate preparation has taken place and the interviewer knows what criteria need to be matched, and why, the face-to-face meeting becomes little more than a 'chat'. Research by Wiesner and Cronshaw (1988) has shown that even well-prepared interviews have only low to moderate validity. Interview validity can be improved depending on the type of interview used and the capabilities of the individual interviewers, but it would appear that the predominant view is that, for many people, the interview experience is a 'hit-and-miss' affair.

The right person

It is necessary to secure the *right* person. That can be achieved only if the person is persuaded that the job being offered provides a satisfactory reward package. Although the details regarding rewards will be dealt with later, it is worth commenting on the issue of job value and the problem this presents. Essentially there are three levels of perception of job value: that held by the job-holder (or potential job-holder), which gives one reference point on what the individual expects to receive in rewards; that held by the organisation, which indicates the value of the job in relation to other jobs in the organisation; and, third, the perception based on the general labour market, which indicates the value of that job from a much wider reference point. All three levels of perception need to be reconciled in an attempt to present the job as being both fairly and properly rewarded.

Retention

The sixth and seventh resourcing questions are to do with existing employees, although how people are selected for development and how they are selected to be retained pose many of the same problems as those identified in relation to the first five. Whereas development will be dealt with in much greater detail in a subsequent section it is valuable to consider the importance of retention.

People leave organisations for one of two reasons: the individual is either dissatisfied in some way with internal employment factors or is no longer required by the organisation and needs to be released. For the organisation the second reason is often the more straightforward to deal with (although if handled badly the law can pose some embarrassing penalties) and is certainly within the organisation's control. Furthermore, it is reasonable to assume that because the organisation is the primary mover, the individual does not pose a 'retention' problem. It is the first reason which causes concern because the decision control-point is with the individual. If a person chooses to leave, the organisation is forced to react to the vacuum that is created. The vacuum is made more serious if the individual was performing a job which carried a high job value to the organisation. The loss value and replacement cost become very significant. Obviously it is impossible to create an organisation from which no one wants to go, but, particularly in the case of key staff, a fully coherent and integrated approach to HRM and especially individual career management and succession planning will create a workplace environment in which a larger proportion of key staff will be retained because they want to stay.

As Walker (1992) suggests, to fail to plan ahead for recruiting, promotions, training and development, and other career management actions is a failure to manage a critical business resource. The consequences of failing to manage key staff retention will result in key staff loss, placing an extra burden on recruitment and selection requirements.

As organisations face change that happens at an ever increasing rate, they find themselves operating in an increasingly competitive market. The ability to hold on to highly competent staff is becoming a main factor in the war to gain competitive advantage. Creating the workplace environment in which people want to stay is a major management skill and requires a full appreciation of the benefits of the effective management of people, either as individuals or in groups.

PERFORMANCE

The second box of the HRM cycle (in Fig. 8.3) focuses on performance. The diagram shows several aspects of organisational life impacting on performance and each of these will be described as they relate to the Cummings and Schwab (1973) equation:

Performance = f (function of = motivation, ability, environment)

Each of these elements needs to be improved if performance is to be positively affected. The usefulness of this equation is that it draws attention to the need to have more than motivation in order to achieve higher levels of performance. If the environment is not conducive it does not matter how motivated an employee is, performance will be only marginally improved, if at all.

The environment

A good starting point is the environment factor in the equation, and in Fig. 8.3 four variables have been included as making an impact: leadership, climate, opportunities and structure.

Leadership

Good leadership has always been a much sought after asset in managers. Mintzberg (1973) identifies the leader role as being one of the ten most often played by managers. With the emphasis on culture and excellence a prominence has been given to leadership within the organisational context and in particular its role in creating a culture of excellence. Whereas Mintzberg presented a set of roles, the importance of which would vary depending on 'who', 'where' and 'when', leadership is now seen as the critical factor in gaining employee commitment to organisational goals. Effective leaders create the environmental dynamics that cause people to want to follow their example and direction; stimulate motivation to achieve and improve; provide the mechanisms through which people can accomplish; empower (and inspire) people continually to improve and provide people with a sense of emotional stability as the organisation offers security and a sense of belonging to those who adopt and fulfil the organisational aims. The more able an individual is at influencing others to subscribe willingly to the organisation's goals and values, the more highly prized that individual. As a commodity being hawked around the market in the bags of the management development specialist, 'leadership development' carries a very high price.

The ability to gain such high levels of commitment and enthusiasm to helping the organisation achieve its goals has been described in several ways. Burns (1978) distinguishes between two types of leaders: *transactional,* who are compliance-oriented and use (largely) financial rewards as an incentive to conform; and *transformational,* who are inspiration-oriented and seek to raise the consciousness of followers to higher level values which can be achieved.

Bass (1985) describes transformational leaders as those who can generate trust, admiration, loyalty and respect from their followers, but at the same time enable the follower to develop by serving as a coach, teacher and mentor. The development (or identity) of managers who have the ability to display such leadership attributes is seen as an essential ingredient in the pursuit of performance improvement.

According to Bennis and Nanus (1985) effective leaders are those who can articulate the vision so that it can be understood by those whose commitment is being sought, is appealing enough to evoke that commitment and credible enough to be accepted as being realistic and achievable.

Another factor often seen as desirable is that of charisma and Conger and Kanungo (1987) provide a useful set of features of charismatic leaders which they suggest followers attribute to this type of leader:

- the presentation of a vision which is at variance to the status quo but viewed as being attainable
- a high personal risk factor – as these leaders appear to make self-sacrifices in their pursuit of the shared vision, this tends to invoke trust in their motives
- the display of unconventional and innovative strategies as the leader appears to be different
- the ability to assess accurately the situation and outsmart the competition
- the ability to draw together disenchanted followers of the 'old way'
- an air of self-confidence which is communicated to the followers and engenders trust and confidence in the leader's activities
- the use of power based on their expert ability and their personality which tends to inspire others to trust their judgements and to want to model themselves on the leader.

Also on the point of charisma, Bass (1985, p. 31) says: 'Charisma is a necessary ingredient of transformational leadership, but by itself it is not sufficient to account for the transformational process.' Strength of personality is not enough. Leadership involves much more than the establishment of a strong leader–follower bond.

Komaki (1986) established research findings that suggest that the more a leader monitors performance and indicates knowledge of that person's performance (performance consequences) the more likely he or she was to be effective. Her research indicates the need to record leaders' actual behaviours and not simply subordinates' perceptions of them.

All those theories tend to isolate the leader role from any other context, suggesting that a leader who adopts certain behaviours will be effective. This is too simple a proposition. Effective leaders are those who can change their style to match the requirements of the situation. Biddle and Evenden (1989) report on research conducted by Roffey Park Institute which suggests that managers who modified their approach to their subordinates in accordance with peaks and troughs in workload pressures were not likely to be associated with lower-performing groups.

It would seem safe to conclude, therefore, that effective leadership does not depend on the individual merely performing behaviours that are assumed to bring about improved follower performance. Leadership is contingent upon the situation the leader finds himself or herself in and his or her ability to analyse the situation and respond in a way which leads to optimum leader behaviour. Clearly this is an extremely sophisticated process.

Feidler's (1967) contingency theory of leadership classifies leaders according to how positively they view the least preferred co-worker (LPC). A high LPC score signifies a positive view. The suggestion is that the high LPC leader is far more able to distinguish between bias based on his or her personal dislike and the individual's potential inherent worth. The high LPC leader is also assumed to be more person-orientated and much more likely to involve people in the general running of their job functions. Low LPC leaders are considered to be more task-orientated, preferring to retain direct control over what others do. Feidler then proposes that different situations will present more favourable opportunities for leaders depending on whether they are high LPC or low LPC. The key aspects of the situations are:

- leader–member relations: the degree of trust and liking between the subordinates and their leader
- task structure: the extent to which tasks, goals and performance levels are clearly defined
- position power: the extent to which the leader exercises control over rewards and punishments.

These three key aspects combine to provide eight different situations in which the leader can operate. The most favourable situation is where the leader–member relations are good, the task structure is high and position power is strong. The least favourable is where leader–member relations are poor, the task structure is low and position power is weak. Feidler proposed that in highly favourable and unfavourable situations, group performance was better if the leader displayed a low LPC score. In situations of moderate to low favourability high LPC scores were better. Or, to reinterpret this, in situations where everything is good, spending time on interpersonal relationships is unnecessary and therefore the leader can get on with the task; in situations where everything is bad it is pointless to spend time on interpersonal aspects so the task becomes the focus of control; but, where the situation is neither 'one thing nor the other', time spent on the interpersonal aspects of the group dynamics may bring dividends.

This now introduces a new dimension: the impact of the group on performance and the group's relationship with the leader. An extension of the group is the team, although the two are not necessarily synonymous. Not only is team building another highly popular strategy to bring about higher levels of work performance, teams can play a major part in establishing a positive and conducive climate.

Climate

The climate of an organisation describes the working atmosphere, which itself is a feeling an individual has about the degree of co-operation which exists in the workplace, the air of friendliness, how much tension is felt and friction sensed; in short, how well people 'get on' with one another. It follows that the more they do get on the more likely they are to experience enjoyment from being in the social environment of the workplace, and with enjoyment comes a sense of satisfaction. Clearly the emphasis is on interaction and the quality of that interaction for the parties involved. However, organisations are not designed on the basis of individuals milling around interacting with other individuals in an *ad hoc* manner, organisations are designed on the basis of work groups. The work group is a very significant feature of organisational life and the better the dynamics in the group and between groups the more conducive the climate is for potential optimum performance.

The task of management is to try to make groups more effective and move more towards team operating. Groups form for a variety of reasons but they all have one important feature, that of a common purpose. In the pursuit of that common purpose group members interact, establishing what expectations they have of one another in terms of group norms and conventions and individual roles. Depending on the level of commitment each member has to the common purpose and to the other members, members will exhibit behaviours which conform to a greater or lesser degree to the group norm. The greater the degree of conformity of behaviour and the higher the sense of value each member experiences by belonging to that group, the more highly cohesive that group is likely to be.

Teams develop when members experience a high level of satisfaction from being a member of a group. Teams exhibit high levels of co-operation as members work to ensure success. Members collaborate as they develop the skills, ideas and energies necessary to solve problems and respond to competitive challenges – both internally and externally. As individuals become more committed to the team, so their individual goals and needs become subservient to those of the team. The greater the congruence between team goals and organisational goals, the greater the potential for higher performance at all levels.

The roles of teamworking and HRM pose an interesting dilemma, the solution to which lies in the strength of the culture operating in the organisation. HRM operates on two levels as far as the individual is concerned: on the individual himself or herself and on the individual as he or she operates in groups.

In the pursuit of the organisational goals, conformity to group purpose, values, vision and ideals becomes expected and is expressed through the ability of the leaders to gain commitment to these ideas. However, whilst a sense of shared commitment and belonging is considered essential, often HRM practices are related more to the individual as competence and ambition are recognised and rewarded through such features as individual, performance-related reward systems. Legge (1989) suggests that the cultural emphasis not only aims to give a sense of vision but also reconciles the tension that exists between the two opposing ideals of individualism and collectivism. In HRM collectivism is given credence through the establishment of joint commitment and the sense of the 'happy family'; individualism is valued because it allows the individual to develop skills and grow and pursue continued improvement in his or her performance. The latter cannot, however, be allowed to flourish unchecked and the former serves the organisational goals by presenting a set of 'unobtrusive controls on attitudes and behaviour' as the individuals are 'socialised into a strong culture' and therefore behave in accordance with the organisation's preferred behaviour.

The role of HRM in establishing the right climate relies on the ability of practitioners to create optimal working groups, which display the characteristics of teamworking, whose direction is articulated through the ability of transformational leaders to gain willing commitment to organisational goals and a belief in their attainment, thus engendering mutual support, trust, esteem and work.

Establishing the 'happy family' does not guarantee higher levels of performance, and the work of Krech, Crutchfield and Ballachey (1962) provides a useful framework on which to consider this relationship and build a strategy for more effective group activity. The main feature of their work is that member satisfaction and group productivity are not directly dependent on the variables controlled by the design of the organisation. It is the interaction between the dependent variables (structural, environmental and task) which leads to emergent (or intermediate) variables including leadership style, group task motivation, friendship between members and membership participation. It is these variables which affect group productivity and member satisfaction. For HRM specialists the message is an interesting one: only by giving emphasis to the emergent variables and providing opportunities for them to emerge, will the organisation gain the potential benefits from teamworking. The starting point of this process is effective organisation design and appropriate structure.

Structure

In designing the organisation managers take account of the need for order and co-ordination of the activities of employees in achieving organisational goals. Organising the workplace involves decisions about the division of work, the allocation of authority and responsibility, and the co-ordination of tasks. The organisational structure is the formal system of working relationships specifically designed and imposed by management not only to distinguish tasks from one another but also to integrate them into a meaningful and coherent whole.

The formal structure representing command and control provides a useful mechanism for getting things done but it does not explain *how* things get done. A pattern of relationships is fine as a bureaucratic exercise designed to represent people on paper, but may not reflect how those people actually interrelate and collaborate. The latter is a response to the adequacy of the structure in providing individuals with the resources necessary for them to fulfil their workplace role. Various attempts have been made to establish useful ground rules for designing the best structure, particularly in response to rapid change.

Mintzberg (1991) describes the 'right' organisation structure as the one which best fits the situation in which the organisation is placed. This is clearly an external reference point, but he also recognises the need to provide enough stability and consistency within the organisation to enable people to continue operating in the way they know how. By meeting the demands of the situation the organisation should remain a viable entity. However, recognising the demands of the situation is not a simple exercise in observation. It requires a sophisticated analysis to establish what factors are relevant and to what extent, and then to proceed to modify the structure accordingly.

Several contributions have been made to the body of literature on organisational structural design. Some are considered to be 'land mark' contributions and include the work of Burns and Stalker (1961), Emergy and Trist (1965), and Lawrence and Lorsch (1967). Burns and Stalker draw conclusions about how structure and managerial practice should change according to environmental conditions.

They described two types of structure:

(1) Mechanistic structures, characterised by formalisation, centralising and complexity. They tended to be routinised with procedures and rules to programme behaviour and were relatively slow to adapt.
(2) Organic structures, characterised by an ability to respond to change by being flexible and adaptable. The emphasis was on internal communications rather than hierarchical relationships and influence based on expertise and knowledge rather than position and authority.

Burns and Stalker proposed that the most effective structure is that which adjusts to the requirements of the environment, so in the more stable environment the best fit will be achieved by a mechanistic structure. When the environment is more susceptible to change and turbulence an organic structure would provide the best fit.

Emery and Trist identified four kinds of environment in which an organisation could be operating: (1) placid-randomised, (2) placid-clustered, (3) disturbed-reactive and (4) turbulent field. The four types increase in complexity from (1) to (4). The placid-randomised environment is the least threatening of all. It has a low uncertainty and therefore provides opportunity for reasonably accurate predictability. Management decision-making is made less risk-orientated because change is slow and random.

The placid-clustered environment offers more challenge because threats to the organisation are clustered rather than random, that is, the threats are related in some way and need a carefully planned strategic response. Organisations operating in this environment tend to show centralised structures which engage in long-range planning.

The disturbed-reactive environment is much more complex. The organisation is faced with many competitors and attempts are made continually to secure the competitive edge. Management decision-making centres around tactical initiatives, predicting the competition's next move and developing counter-strategies. Survival is the critical issue and these organisations tend to decentralise in their attempt to remain responsive and adaptable.

The turbulent field is the most dynamic and most uncertain environment of all. Change is a constant phenomenon and the elements in the environment become increasingly related and therefore highly threatening to the organisation. The management response is one of continually trying to anticipate what is likely to happen and to develop a strategic response. Long-term planning is seen as pointless, but some planning is necessary for otherwise the organisation loses control of its own destiny.

There is a clear relationship between Emery and Trist's work and that of Burns and Stalker, with the first two types of environment being responded to with a more mechanistic structure, whilst the other two demand a more organic/flexible one.

Lawrence and Lorsch focused their attention on the nature of the environment and its relationship to the degree of differentiation among departments within the same firm and on the degree and type of integration required across departments. Differentiation refers to the degree of specialisation into different functional units accompanied by managers holding different attitudinal and perceptive responses according to their specific goal perspective. Integration refers to the way in which departments collaborate in order to achieve unity of effort. The research concluded that the more uncertain the environment in terms of the relative difficulty managers had in analysing it, the more success was achieved when organisations were more highly differentiated with more sophisticated integration processes. Where the environment was more stable, less differentiation was required and less sophisticated integration processes. However, what was also significant in the research conducted by Lawrence and Lorsch was that structural differentiation was not the main key success factor. They found that even if the organisation had responded correctly to the environment in terms of its degree of differentiation, if the organisation had not responded with appropriate integrating mechanisms and processes, it would be at a disadvantage in terms of performance.

Fig. 8.4 shows how the ideas of Burns and Stalker, Emery and Trist, and Lawrence and Lorsch are related.

Whilst these ideas have presented important contributions to helping decisions regarding more effective organisational design, the environmental imperative has not secured universal support. Weick (1969) suggests that because environments are perceived by managers on site, the environment will reflect the structure for which it is perceived. Pfeffer (1978) points out that not all environmental change can be called uncertainty because some change can be predicted and is not therefore uncertain. John Child (1972) found that in reality there was no clear pattern to support the assertions. His research showed that organisations operating successfully in similar environments displayed different structures and that organisations having similar structures were operating effectively in different environments. Furthermore Child (1984, p. 9) proposes that these approaches do not go far enough. The change of structure also 'incorporates the preferences which decision-makers and other influential groups have for a particular approach to management'. These preferences will reflect their values, principles and self-interests and will also relate to how much influence particular individuals wield within the decision-making arena.

Questions regarding organisation design and structure have gone further, however, with some writers suggesting that structure itself inhibits organisational potential. Mintzberg (1981) refers to 'ad hocracies', fluid structures which allow the organisation to respond to change and challenge. In this type of or-

Environmental uncertainties

LOW			HIGH
	Mechanistic	Organic	
Task definition	Rigid	Flexible	
Communication	Vertical	Lateral	
Formalisation	High	Low	
Influence	Authority	Expertise	
Control	Centralised	Diverse	
Decision-making	Directive	Participative	
Simple integration	Moderately complex integration		Sophisticated integration
Low differentiation	Moderate differentiation		High differentiation
Placid/ randomised	Placid/ clustered	Disturbed/ reactive	Turbulent field

Fig. 8.4 Integrated model of organisational structure response to environmental uncertainty

ganisations power is based at the focus of knowledge and skill, not on position; progress is made through the use of project teams and task forces which are created and disbanded according to need. Stewart (1990, p. 27) talks about busting bureaucracies, and creating 'enabling systems', which represent a:

> redirection of the controls so that they form a framework rather than a cage. Just as, on a micro-level you can replace rules by principles, on a macro-level you replace the controlling systems which support rather than restrict; which give people not a ceiling above which it is difficult to rise, but a floor below which they have no excuse for falling.

Handy (1985 and 1989) describes two types of organisation design to respond to new ways of work, new technologies and new attitudes. In referring to automation and information technology he argues that 'we still imprison ourselves in organisational forms and shapes designed when none of these things were possible'. He advocates urgent revision of the literature of management theory to take account of new demands. He suggests reorganising work along the lines of the shamrock organisation which contracts out that work which is not core to workers who are not essential because their work could be done by someone else, or the federal organisation, which requires a centre to co-ordinate, advise, influence and suggest but with units operating round the centre controlling the initiative, drive and energy. It is these units in which the main power is based, the centre having a relatively low profile. Federal organisations operate on the principles of subsidiarity because 'the federal on-going action will not work unless those in the centre not only *have* to let go of some of their power but actually *want* to do so, because only then will they trust the new decision-makers to take the right decisions and only then will they enable them to make them work' (Handy, 1989, p. 100).

The idea of flexible small units, generated on the basis of needs, operating with a high power base and considerable authority, is a recurring theme in recent literature. Described by Walker (1992, p. 134), 'flexible organisations are characterised by dual or triple reporting relationships, lateral relationships, increased teamwork and empowered employees. A flexible structure can drive traditionally oriented managers crazy.' But another recurring theme is that of empowerment. Stewart (1990, p. 61) makes the point that empowerment is more than redrawing the lines on the organisation chart because, as Stewart's law of reorganisation states, 'structural solutions to functional problems don't work'. Empowerment requires that power and authority are relinquished from those at the centre and given to those who are operating at the interfaces with clients, suppliers, customers, etc. It is these people who see new things for the organisation and need to have the authority and trust in them to act. There is a very close correspondence between Stewart and Handy on this, but both make the point that it is easier described than done. However, what is also apparent is that for these new types of organisation to succeed, the values, beliefs and attitudes of the management group have to change.

Opportunities and job design

The culture has to be based on a high information-sharing norm, trust, commitment and a divestment of power, control and authority. It relies on people being able to perform by being provided with the resources to do so and knowing how to use them; it is not simply a case of providing a mechanism through which they can perform.

Opportunities to perform are, however, an essential part of the performance equation and this relies on good job and task design. David Buchanan (1989) argues that 'effective work design strategies for the future need to be more radical in their organisational effects and need to be formulated as part of an integrated employment and rewards package'.

The aim of job design is to create jobs which both serve the organisation's requirements and satisfy the individual's needs. The organisation requires high levels of productivity, commitment, operational efficiency and quality. The individual needs to have a job that gives a sense of achievement, challenge, interest and scope for development. Whilst the process of job design starts with a micro-analysis of what tasks need to be performed, the skill is in putting the tasks together so that they form a job which is intrinsically motivating for the job-holder, achieves the optimal level of productivity for the organisation, but

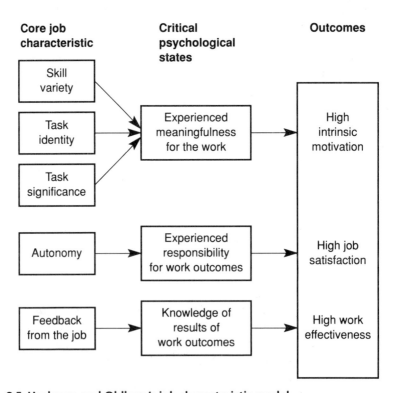

Fig. 8.5 Hackman and Oldham's job characteristic model
Source: Hackman, J. R. and Oldham, G. R., *Work Redesign,* © 1980 Addison-Wesley Publishing Co. Inc. Reprinted by permission.

also is related to other jobs in a meaningful way that assists the social lubrication of the organisation and leads to a sense of belonging.

In an attempt to provide a useful framework on which to base good job design Hackman and Oldham's job characteristic model (1980) has provided a valuable contribution to making job design a more coherent exercise. The model relates core job characteristics with critical psychological states, and these lead to outcomes for and from the individual. The model is represented in Fig. 8.5.

The three core characteristics – skill variety (the extent to which the job offers an opportunity to use a range of skills), task identity (the extent to which a job provides the holder with a 'whole' piece of work) and task significance (the extent to which the job provides worth to others inside and outside the organisation) – all create a sense of meaningfulness in the work. With meaning comes value and that in itself is a major source of motivation.

Autonomy describes the extent to which a job allows the job-holder to exercise discretion and control over his or her work and is a primary contributor to job satisfaction, allowing the individual the opportunity to affect the outcome of his or her efforts. Gaining feedback from the job creates the provision for individuals to learn from reinforcement, generates knowledge of the results of work undertaken and work done well and provides recognition of that achievement, leading to a greater potential for improved work effectiveness.

The design of jobs to ensure that the organisation has a skilled, motivated, committed and flexible workforce necessary to cope with the increased competitive nature of organisational life is not a feature to be left to whim or drifting evolution. Organisations which cannot fulfil customers' expectations for price, delivery and quality will find their business lost to their competitors. In today's increasingly quality-conscious environment, the emphasis on quality is paramount. Quality not only reflects quality of production and service, it also transcends the organisation as part of the 'quality experience'. Employees are encouraged to affect the 'quality environment' in which the workforce is operating. As a factor in the generation of the 'quality workplace' job design has a major part to play. Whereas, traditionally, jobs have been designed simply to lead to higher levels of productivity, the emphasis is now on providing people with jobs that allow them to grow and develop. Rather than constraining people within jobs which minimised skill requirements, maximised management control and minimised the time required to perform the task (Taylor, 1979), good job design is seen as that which builds increased challenge and autonomy into the work for the people who perform it – to empower employees to act (Walker, 1992). This requires that jobs are considered in terms of value to both the organisation and the individual. The greater the sense of value in the work being done the greater the sense of self-worth felt by the individual. Through a process of continually reviewing the work that is done managers can redesign work so that employees are much more effectively utilised. Effective employee utilisation requires that an attempt is made to match individual talents and aspirations with cost and contribution to the organisation.

Taking account of individual aspirations demands that job design is not considered in isolation from career development. According to Gutteridge (1986), more organisations are giving thought to career development systems; this entails managers providing for growth in a job and growth between jobs as individuals progress and are promoted or redeployed. Good job design enables managers to help employees perform effectively and provide an environment for personal growth and satisfaction. As Arnold, Robertson and Cooper (1991, p. 279) note, 'satisfaction and commitment are not the only desired outcomes of career development systems. Others include a good match between people and their jobs, and an improved pool of valuable skills and experience within the organisation.'

Stress

Before moving on to the ability factor in the Cummings and Schwab equation, it is worth considering an increasing cause for concern in organisational life: workplace stress. Over the past twenty years greater consideration has been given to the impact of work and the workplace on the physiological and psychological well-being of organisational members. As greater expectations are made of, and by, employees, so greater pressure is placed on individuals to fulfil these expectations.

The organisational environment is now a 'hot-bed' for ill-health and workplace stress is now recognised as a primary contributor to the number of working days lost through absenteeism and falls in performance. Whilst it is widely accepted that increased pressure can lead to increased job performance, sustained or added pressure can cause individuals to experience stress. Conversely, too little pressure can also be stressful. The important point is that in designing jobs and development opportunities, managers must be aware of the implications of stress and consider jobs from an 'optimum pressure' perspective. Cooper, Cooper and Eaker (1988) have identified six sources of stress, their relationship with two different types of individual and the likely consequences of stress being experienced. These are represented in Fig. 8.6.

Ability

Being able to do the job is obviously an important source of confidence, or, if not able to do it, having the confidence in the system to know that with proper training and socialisation, learning the job should prove no obstacle to achievement. Although the model in Fig. 8.3 recognises both appraisal and development as separate boxes for discussion, it is worth reflecting on abilities at this point, in relation to performance. Having the abilities to perform is no guarantee of performance, but they do help!

Ability is a term which encompasses more than possessing the skills and/or

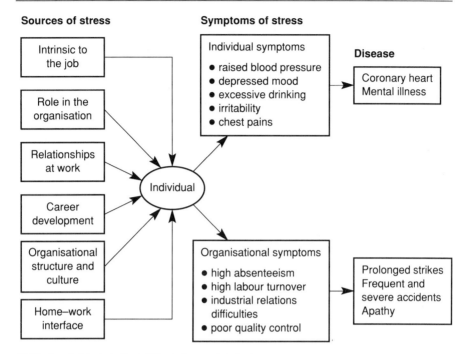

Sources of stress

Symptoms of stress

Intrinsic to the job

Role in the organisation

Relationships at work

Career development

Organisational structure and culture

Home–work interface

Individual

Individual symptoms
- raised blood pressure
- depressed mood
- excessive drinking
- irritability
- chest pains

Organisational symptoms
- high absenteeism
- high labour turnover
- industrial relations difficulties
- poor quality control

Disease

Coronary heart
Mental illness

Prolonged strikes
Frequent and severe accidents
Apathy

(1) Factors 'intrinsic to the job' include poor job design.

(2) 'Role in the organisation' considers such features as role conflict and role ambiguity.

(3) 'Relationships at work' consider the quality of the social environment and interpersonal dynamics.

(4) 'Career development' refers to the opportunities for personal progress and growth.

(5) 'Organisational structure and culture' refer to the opportunity for individuals to belong and contribute.

(6) 'Home–work interface' considers the impact of home life and aspirations on work activity and vice versa.

(7) The 'individual' refers to whether the personality reflects Type A or Type B as described by Rosenman, Freidman and Straus (1964), with the suggestion that Type A personalities are more likely to exhibit stress-inducing behaviours and experience their consequences.

Fig. 8.6 Sources and symptoms of stress at work

knowledge to do a job. It also includes qualities, power, proficiency and talent. It is a description of what a person can do now; there is no expectation of further training needed to bring the individual up to the required standard. This distinguishes it from aptitude, which is an individual's potential for performance, or the possibility of an individual being developed up to a specified level of ability. This distinction between the two is important because ability is, in many instances, an assumption made of the job-holder and performance is monitored against that assumed ability.

It is also something which is becoming increasingly stated as fact and the move towards competence-based qualification is an attempt to define more accurately an individual's ability to perform. To specify competences requires that the job be broken down into its generic key skill elements. This is forcing all aspects of work to be subject to a critical analysis, as the jobs that people have been doing are expressed in clear terms of what needs to be performed, to what standard, to enable the job-holder to be assessed as 'competent'. An emphasis is given to transferability (the assertion that competences are not organisationally bound, but are equally applicable anywhere), which raises an interesting question in relation to the unique nature of all organisations and the cultural influence of 'the way things are done here'. The competence movement, with its attendant qualifications, states categorically that the individual who has been assessed against the criteria and has been acknowledged as meeting the criteria has the ability to perform. It does not, however, guarantee that the individual will be able to perform.

Motivation

This leads on to the last part of the equation: motivation. Steers and Porter (1975, p. 406) define motivation as 'that which energises, directs and sustains human behaviour'. It is composed of three characteristics: the amount of effort an individual is willing to exert; that the effort be directed towards some goal or target, i.e. is focused; and that the level of effort will be continued over an extended period. To this definition should be added the important aspect of choice, because motivation is also governed by the individual choosing to put in motion behaviours which will help achieve the desired outcome. This means that motivation is something which affects and is controlled by the individual, which poses some problems for managers who tend to base decisions about how to manage on people collectively rather than as individuals. Motivated behaviour is what all managers hope for from their subordinates. The more effort people put into achieving something for which they are striving, provided that the personal goal is related to the goals of the organisation, the more managers can anticipate improved individual performance. The problem, though, is trying to identify what individuals will want to achieve and then providing the opportunity for achievement.

The purpose of motivation theories is to help predict behaviour, thereby allowing managers a better opportunity to design jobs and create the most appropriate environment in which employees will choose to exert greater effort. By providing opportunities through which employees can gain a sense of fulfilment through the achievement of work, managers should be able to sustain the continual drive for improved performance. This poses several questions, such as: What is it that people want? How badly do they want it? Can work help them achieve their wants? Does the organisation benefit through helping people achieve their wants? Do people experience the same wants? Why will some things lead to motivated behaviour and others not? Do the things that cause motivated behaviour change? If the answers to these questions were straightforward there would not be the multiplicity of motivation theories that abound. Motivation is a very complex feature of organisational life; it depends on the individual, and his or her particular situation, subject to whatever circumstances arise. Yet to leave influencing motivation to chance would almost certainly leave the organisation floundering with very little sense of purpose and little directed behaviour.

In order to bring about some control and a sense of direction managers need to be aware of the contributions made from, at least, the main themes of motivation. There is no single generalised theory of motivation. None of the theories offers a complete understanding of the subject but all have something to offer. The more the manager knows and understands about what influences an individual to choose to work willingly and effectively, the better able he or she is to judge the relevance of these theories to particular work situations.

The theories fall into two groups: content theories and process theories. Content theories attempt to describe the specific constructs within the individual that energise and sustain behaviour. Process theories explain how or why an individual is motivated. Together they provide a reasonable understanding of motivated behaviour in the workplace.

The content theories

Four content theories are those of Maslow (1943), Herzberg, Mausner and Snyderman (1959), Alderfer (1969) and McClelland (1965). Each describes a specific set of needs held by individuals. Each of the theories presents different needs and each offers a different interpretation of the way the needs affect motivation. Despite their differences they do display a strong relationship and it is the strength of this relationship, coupled with their essential pragmatic attraction, which makes them so popular with managers (see Fig. 8.7).

Maslow's 'Hierarchy of Needs' established a way of thinking about people which recognised both their dignity and worth and also that each person is striving to achieve his or her full potential. The school of psychology to which this view of the self-actualising person is attributed is *humanism* and its significance in respect of the popular approaches regarding Total Quality Management initiatives cannot be ignored. Maslow stated that each person experiences five general needs which are hierarchical in terms of their prepotency, that is, the needs are arranged in an order in which basic needs take precedence and prevent higher-level needs emerging until lower-level needs have been satisfied. Motivated behaviour occurs as an individual attempts to satisfy an unsatisfied need, which, once satisfied, no longer motivates. As a need becomes satisfied so a person moves his or her attention to satisfying the next level of needs. Unfortunately, people will not be on the same level of the hierarchy nor will they experience a sense of a need being satisfied at the same time. Consequently, organisations must present a range of incentives, experi-

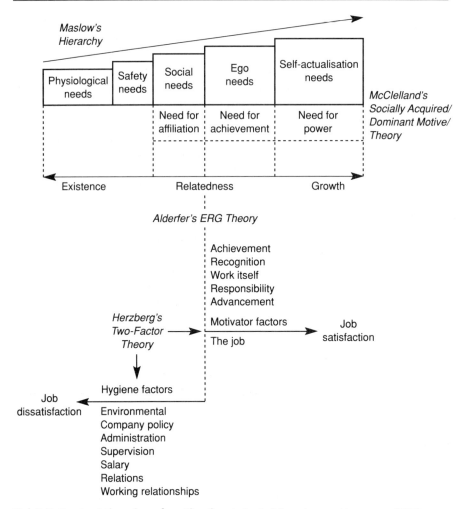

Fig. 8.7 Content theories of motivation (adapted from Lee and Lawrence, 1991)

ences and opportunities to enable employees to meet their unsatisfied needs.

Although popular, this theory has been widely criticised and research does not support the idea of five levels of needs, expressed in that particular order, with the described relationship between them. But as a starting point to the consideration of motivation its apparent logic and simplicity are hard to match.

The ERG Theory presented by Clayton Alderfer is an attempt to refine Maslow's Hierarchy of Needs by collapsing the levels into three needs: existence, relatedness and growth. Although there is a very close correspondence between Maslow and Alderfer, Alderfer differs in his view of prepotency. He believes that progression through the hierarchy does not depend on the lower-level needs being satisfied, and that people can experience all three needs simultaneously. He also differs in another respect, concerning the deprivation or frustration of a need. For Maslow, if a need was threatened the person moved back down the hierarchy, became motivated to achieve satisfaction of the threatened need and did not experience the high-level need until lower-need satisfaction had been achieved. Alderfer places a more interesting interpretation on this. He suggests that the more existence and relatedness needs are deprived or frustrated, the more they will be desired. However, if growth needs are frustrated the individual compensates for their lack of satisfaction by demanding more in terms of existence or relatedness needs and not by desiring more personal growth and development. This interpretation offers some possible explanations of human behaviour, demands and expectations in relation to job design and opportunities – in particular why some people appear to be continuously dissatisfied with rewards that are considered by managers to be adequate.

Explaining motivation from a different perspective, David McClelland presented his Socially Acquired Dominant Motive Theory, which is closely associated with learning theory since he believed that needs were learned, or acquired, through social experience. He believed that having experienced events individuals learned needs, which represented behavioural predispositions, that then influenced the way they perceived situations and motivated them to pursue particular goals. McClelland was particularly interested in three types of needs: the needs for achievement (nAch), for affiliation (nAff) and for power (nPow). McClelland's theory argues that by identifying an individual's dominant motive, it is possible to predict the likely behavioural response to particular stimuli because of the different characteristics possessed by those responding more strongly to one need than to the others.

Individuals with a high nAch display behaviour which attempts to accomplish and demonstrate competence or mastery over tasks. They tend to be competitive and respond to high standards of excellence. McClelland also showed that high nAch people like to have a moderately high level of responsibility for their work, like tasks for which they are reasonably confident of success and like to have a good flow of feedback on their progress.

Individuals who have a high nAff are those who have a desire to establish and maintain strong interpersonal relationships with others. These individuals tend to be characterised by a strong desire for approval and reassurance from others, a tendency to conform to the issues, norms and expectations of others, particular those whom they value as friends or whose patronage they are seeking; they display a genuine and sincere interest in others. It follows, logically, that high nAff individuals need to work with others and their performance will be enhanced if they are engaged in work in which co-operation and support are important.

People who display a high nPow are usually found at the high levels of management, if only because, as McClelland suggests, these needs are learned and power tends to be unevenly distributed towards higher managerial levels. These individuals tend to display a desire to be 'in charge', to influence the behaviour of others and to be responsible for their actions. They gain their satisfaction from seeing others achieve the goals and objectives that they have identified and set. High nPow people seek positions of leadership and influence, they tender their views and opinions readily and attempt to bring others round to their point of view. They are likely to display considerable personal confidence and self-assuredness. McClelland distinguishes between 'personal power' and 'social power', with the latter considered to be the more important determinant of managerial success. Personal power is that which is wielded for personal gain, and whilst those who are motivated to achieve self-gain may be charismatic, they may also tend to be dominant and highly political. Social power, on the other hand, is power that is exercised in pursuit of organisational gains and effectiveness. The individual uses his or her ability to influence others for communal satisfaction rather than satisfying egotistic desires.

In a further attempt to identify what actually caused motivated behaviour, Frederick Herzberg and his colleagues established the Two-Factor Theory. In this theory two groups of factors are delineated, each group affecting differently the way individuals feel about their job. Herzberg's theory is most controversial in the assertion that dissatisfaction and satisfaction are not on the same continuum. He points to the difference between the factors based on 'context' and 'content'. Those factors which relate to the context in which the job takes place lead people to experience a sense of less dissatisfaction if they are improved but will do nothing to enhance performance. These factors he terms 'hygiene factors' and include such things as supervision, working conditions, relationships with others, company policy and administration and pay. These are useful in terms of basic maintenance and have the potential to make people feel unhappy. On the other continuum are the factors related to the 'job content' and are much less easy to measure and identify. They include such things as achievement, recognition, job challenge and responsibility, opportunities for growth and advancement. These are described as being important to establishing job satisfaction and, if present, will enhance performance; they are called the 'motivators'. Herzberg believes that both sets of factors are qualitatively distinct, often referred to as intrinsic (satisfiers) and extrinsic (dissatisfiers) with each operating in its own domain. For the organisation this means that excessive attention to pay rewards will not influence performance, but only reduce the sense of dissatisfaction and that managers should therefore concentrate on those aspects of the job itself.

Table 8.1 provides examples of how the organisation could respond to the range of needs as identified in the various content theories. The intention is that by supplying the general rewards and opportunities, employees are provided with factors which should satisfy some needs for the majority. The organisation can then reasonably expect motivated behaviour as the workforce strives to meet those needs which are pertinent (and available) to each of them.

Table 8.1 Ways of satisfying needs in the workplace (adapted from Gordon, 1987)

Need	Organisational response
Physiological	Pay
	Pleasant working conditions
	Cafeteria
	Toilet facilities
	Rest rooms
Safety	Company benefits
	Job security
	Safe and healthy environment
	Child care
	Medical facilities/benefits
Social affiliation	Cohesive work groups
	Break periods
	Sports clubs and social societies
	Social events
	Professional associations
Status	Social recognition
	Job title
	Prestige location
	Material artifacts of status
Achievement	Autonomy
	Responsibility
	Feedback on job success
	Job challenge
Power	Leadership positions
	Authority
	Control
Self-actualisation and growth	Opportunities for development
	Opportunities for creativity
	Autonomy
	Achievement in work
	Advancement

The process theories

Whilst the concentration has been on identifying what motivates people there has been no attempt to suggest how motivation occurs. The theories which deal with the process of motivation are also referred to as cognitive theories because they assume that the decision to exert effort is based on rational thinking. The three process theories which will be addressed are equity theory (Adams, 1965), expectancy theory (Vroom, 1964; Nadler and Lawler, 1977), and goal-setting theory (Locke, 1968).

Equity theory

Equity theory evolved from social comparison theory and assumes that individuals compare their performance and attitudes to others'. Rather than focus on objective measures, the focus is on the feelings and perceptions of individuals. The key point of address is 'Am I getting fair treatment?' The comparator base is the individual's inputs to the job relative to the outcomes he or she receives, on one level, and then a further comparison between the individual and another person or group of people. The process is one of individual A comparing the value of the outcomes he or she receives for doing the job against what he or she believes the inputs are worth in terms of such factors as effort, experience, qualifications, importance, difficulty, scarcity, age, length of service, sex – in fact anything which the individual chooses to introduce as being a variable worth considering. The outcomes (often easiest if thought of as rewards) again include those factors and variables which the individual recognises as being of value to him or her and will consist of both extrinsic and intrinsic rewards, the proportional value of the factors being made at the individual's discretion. The principles behind the theory are that, if the individual perceives that the outcomes relate fairly to the inputs, behaviour will be sustained at that level to ensure equity remains. If, however, the individual perceives an imbalance, the individual is motivated to reduce any perceived inequality by changing either the inputs or the outcomes until a state of equity is reached. Obviously this could mean that the individual's effort is reduced, indicating a demotivated person. The individual will also make the comparison with others, assessing inputs and outcome ratio for self against the input–outcome ratio for the comparison person. As Huseman (Huseman, Hatfield and Miles, 1987) suggests, the greater the inequality the individual perceives, whether the perception is one of over- or under-reward, the more distress and discomfort the individual feels. As individuals feel distress the harder they will work to restore equity.

The techniques used to restore equity include changing input behaviour, changing or distorting the valuation of inputs and/or outputs or changing the point of comparison, several of which are within the domain of the individual's perception and are not apparent to observers. Whilst the theory has an intuitive appeal the empirical evidence is mixed. It does offer an explanation, however, of why an individual can change significantly in a very short space of time. It also makes the point that it is important for managers to realise that individuals do notice and care about what happens to others, and will quickly respond to what they believe to be 'unfair treatment'.

Expectancy theory

Expectancy theory asks 'What's in it for me?' It aims to explain how people choose which of several courses of action to pursue. Originally the theory addressed three questions in relation to the components of the theory:

(1) E (expectancy) refers to the person's perception of the probability that effort will lead to a particular performance or action being achieved.

(2) I (instrumentality) refers to the person's perception of the probability that an outcome will be attached to that performance.
(3) V (valence) refers to the person's perception of the value of the outcome to him or her.

The idea is that people will choose to put in the effort if they can answer the three questions positively:
(1) E: If I put in the effort will that make the difference in my performance that I'm looking for?
(2) I: If I gain the new performance level will I be rewarded?
(3) V: Is the reward that I'm likely to receive something that I want?

$$\text{Motivation} = E \times I \times V$$

Nadler and Lawler (1977) followed this formula with a more complex model:

$$\text{Motivation} = [E \rightarrow P] \times \Sigma [(P \rightarrow O)(V)]$$

This allows multiple-outcome formulation, with each outcome being attributed a different valence. The individual is then able to assess the likely consequence of his or her action on a much wider decision base.

Although support is again mixed, the message is useful to managers by getting them to consider whether the individual can influence his or her performance; whether outcomes for that performance are recognised and easily attributable; and whether the outcomes are likely to be valued. Assessing these three questions allows a manager not only to make some judgement as to the individual's level of motivation but also to decide whether job design, environmental influences and reward policies are appropriate.

Goal-setting theory

Goal-setting theory has enjoyed increasing attention and support since it was first introduced by Ed Locke and his associates in the 1960s, although there are still areas for concern. The basic principle is that an individual who has a goal, in attempting to achieve that goal, is likely to display both focused and motivated behaviour. Several variables, such as 'specificity', 'difficulty' and 'acceptance', can affect the goal.

Specificity, or clarity, refers to the extent to which the goal is measurable and observable. Difficulty is based on the individual's perception of ease of goal attainment. Acceptance refers to the degree of ownership the individual extends to the goal and is likely to affect the levels of commitment extended to that goal.

It is also important that the individual receives feedback as a condition for continuing to work towards goal achievement. Mento, Steel and Karren (1987) reinforce the point by suggesting that there is clear support for the efficacy of coupling feedback with hard specific goals and that both knowledge and motivation are necessary for enhanced performance.

From a managerial point of view the importance of this theory is to recognise that goal statement is not enough. The individual will make many evaluations of the goal before committing effort to achieve performance. Consideration will be given to such factors as ability, complexity, situational constraints, priority, enjoyment, interest, rewards, feedback, involvement. A manager perceiving a level of effort below that which is expected can examine the factors which affect the individual's perception of the goal.

APPRAISAL

The next process on the human resource management cycle is that of appraisal. Appraisal (or performance assessment, performance review, individual assessment) is a major component of performance management and should, therefore, be considered in this context. According to Torrington and Hall (1991) appraisal is more than an organisational process, it is an attempt to formalise the conscious or subconscious activities in which we are all involved, by which we seek to establish worth, usefulness, contribution, qualities, strengths and weaknesses, personality, behaviour and value of ourselves, of others and the systems through which we operate.

There are two types of appraisal: one based on 'control' and the other on 'development'. Torrington (1991) believes that the 'control' approach is more common in practice and is likely to engender reduced co-operation, a more negative attitude to the actual process, and lower trust. Control approach systems tend to be seen as being imposed by those in authority and are based on judgement and probably are most effective in organisations which have a culture emphasising competition. The development approach is seen as being much more orientated towards the individual with an emphasis on collaboration and co-operation. The approach seeks to enhance the individual's contribution to organisational goals through his or her growth and development.

Bevan and Thompson (1991) noted the emergence of performance management systems as integrating processes providing the link between various human resource management systems and the business objectives of the organisation. They identified two thrusts: reward-driven integration, which emphasises the role of payment systems in changing employee behaviour; and development-driven integration, which focuses on the need to have appropriate human resource development initiatives to ensure a competent workforce for the future. It is reasonable to envisage the control approach to appraisal featuring as a central activity within an organisation emphasising 'reward-driven integration'. George (1986) suggests that an effective appraisal scheme depends on ensuring that the style and content of the appraisal process do not conflict with the culture of the organisation, and, if properly designed and implemented, should help socialise employees into the prevailing culture. George also suggests that appraisal could be used to change a culture.

A good appraisal system, which is both respected and considered to be credible, can be used to:

- assist the human resource planning process by providing information on promotability and potential of employees
- provide information to enable better recruitment and selection of future employees
- identify training and development needs so the contribution of employees can be enhanced
- enable individual career plans to be developed
- provide a mechanism upon which individual compensation can be calculated
- give feedback on performance to improve current performance levels
- motivate and stimulate behaviour to secure higher future performance levels
- identify individual targets and objectives linked to departmental and organisational goals
- identify and solve job problems and opportunities
- provide a framework in which individuals can monitor, and have monitored, their performance and contribution.

Clearly, some of these potential uses are in conflict and their emphasis within a system will depend on the preferred objectives of the system by the management of the organisation. The assumption, then, is that in designing an appraisal system the designers know what culture, mission and organisational goals the system is intended to support.

That purpose then needs to be communicated to all appraisers and a programme of education and training needs to be introduced to ensure that all those who will conduct appraisals do so in the spirit in which appraisal is intended. It is also just as important to ensure that all those who will be appraised are equally aware of the purpose so that they know what to expect and can contribute accordingly.

Randell, Packard and Slater (1984) suggest that if appraisal is to be effective it should not attempt to satisfy all the potential uses. They propose that the uses of appraisal fall into three broad categories – reward reviews, potential reviews and performance reviews – and that a system should attempt to satisfy only one of these. The implications of this are significant because it proposes that, in an attempt to fulfil the potential gains from appraisal, employees need to be exposed to more than one review process. In their discussion on employee self-appraisal Taylor, Lehman and Forde (1989) make the recommendation that performance development and performance pay reviews should be separated in time.

Perhaps the most important feature of appraisal within the context of performance management is that it is seen as an essential process of management. Its philosophy is holistic and links individual performance to desired organisational outcomes. Consequently, it is not something which is performed periodically as a discrete exercise related to the individual at an operational level. It is an ongoing activity in which all managers need to make a major investment if they, their staff and the organisation are to achieve the potential benefits.

Philpott and Sheppard (1992) suggest four factors that can be assessed: the achievement of objectives, observing core values, personal qualities and potential. To assess effectively they propose a range of 'core skills' which need to be developed: communication, motivation, objective setting, assessment, coaching, delegating and supporting. These core skills reflect the view of Handy (1989) that performance management systems make managers become more supportive in their role as counsellors and mentors, rather than commanders and judges; more able to trust their staff to take initiatives and manage their own tasks; and more effective as leaders, empowering their staff to handle problems and issues, becoming more transformational in their style.

If appraisal is to be effective it must provide the individual employee with a meaningful and valuable experience. If the employee is to benefit, the targets for achievement, the mechanism through which targets can be achieved, the feedback process and the outcomes received for achievement must all be integrated to produce a coherent message to which the individual can subscribe.

The individual should feel part of and have a sense of ownership of the process. In setting objectives individuals need to agree jointly both content and degree of challenge, and to understand how they will be assessed, against what criteria and in what form. The feedback process needs to be one of mutual involvement in which the individual can contribute on the basis of his or her own assessment. Feedback should seek to take advantage of the benefits of reinforcement theory, which applies the behaviourist learning theories to motivation and is based on the work of Skinner (1938, 1974). The feedback should also address the impact of what has been achieved by the individual's performance, not just on his or her own work activity, but how he or she has contributed to the performance of the team, department and, wherever possible, the organisation.

Before leaving appraisal, one final point: there is, perhaps, no other Human Resource Management process that engenders such negative feelings. Despite the fact that, in theory, appraisal is designed to serve both the individual and the organisation, writers continue to describe the actualities of appraisal in dismal terms. Armstrong (1988) says that 'there is no other aspect of managing human resources which is generally done so badly', Walker (1992) that 'the results of this sometimes tortured and damaging ritual are not particularly beneficial to the company' and Torrington (1991), quoting from statements written by students of the Institute of Personnel Management, that 'our scheme is not objective and becomes a meaningless ritual'.

To force people to continue experiencing appraisal as an activity which is worthless, meaningless and often intimidating, is not only a waste of time and money but is also potentially damaging to all other Human Resource Management processes, however well designed and good intentioned they may be. As Philpott and Sheppard (1992) point out, 'performance management is potentially the area of Human Resources Management which can make the most significant contribution to organisational performance'. Performance management is therefore a fundamental process of effective Human Resource Management and should be used as an essential component of the process of managing human resources towards strategic objectives.

The links between performance and the last two boxes in Fig. 8.3 are now obvious. Performance management concerns both rewards and development, although emphasis will vary from one organisation to another. To appreciate fully the complexity of each and the impact on the way that people behave and work, both need to be addressed separately. Hopefully, it is now recognised that reward management is not simply a case of linking a payment system to a strategic direction based on employees' contributions. It is far more sophisticated and subtle, recognising both intrinsic and extrinsic rewards, financial and non-financial. The non-financial rewards will be accounted for largely by the incorporation of good job-design techniques, involving more autonomy and objective setting by the individual – ideas that have been introduced earlier.

REWARDS

The financial rewards will be communicated through the remuneration policy. The policy will reflect the relationship between pay and individual contributions, performance and potential. If the policy is to be credible and acceptable, it must take account of expectancy theory, which identifies the link between effort, performance, rewards and value, and equity theory, which requires pay levels and awards to be both comparatively fair and commensurate with effort.

Writers such as Crowe (1992) suggest that the problem with most reward schemes is that they are not considered from an overall organisation-wide perspective. More often than not they are piecemeal and unco-ordinated. Such *ad hoc* approaches leave what is, potentially, the most powerful communicator of an employer's intention and obligation to his or her employees exposed and open to rejection and systematic abuse. A reward strategy that embraces the organisation as a whole provides the opportunity to communicate well beyond its purely tangible purpose. Holistic strategies underpin and sustain the culture, particularly core values relating to performance, quality, teamwork and competition. The reward strategy will also convey to external agents the strength of the organisation's commitment towards its human resources. If properly designed, reward schemes will encourage behaviour that will contribute directly to the organisation's performance and will aim to give value for money.

The most significant change in reward philosophy over the past decade has been in the recognition of individual contribution as a factor on defining pay. One of the most important design decisions is that of striking a balance between rewarding individual performance and trying to develop more effective teamworking. The problem is that teams are the critical work unit, yet recognising and rewarding high levels of individual contribution are both morally justifiable and also likely to lead to improved performance levels by other members of the team. Furthermore, as greater emphasis is placed on resource management in general, differential payments for differential rates of return from different individuals would reflect the 'hard' version of Human Resource Management as identified by Storey (1989). This move towards paying for performance is reflected in the rise in the number of performance-related pay schemes which are becoming increasingly a feature of reward strategies.

If performance-related pay schemes are to be successful, several features need to be present (Armstrong, 1992, p. 184):

- targets and standards of performance to be attained should be clear
- fair and accurate measurement of performance should be possible
- individuals must be able to influence their performance
- there must be a clear link between performance and reward
- the rewards must be meaningful and valued to make the input effort worthwhile.

The five criteria for success need to be considered against other questions, such as (Crowe, 1992):

- Do individuals perceive and believe the relationship between performance and pay?
- Does the scheme encourage desired behaviour or does it produce disfunctional activities which are against the interest of the collective action?
- Does the scheme encourage co-operation and collaboration between members of the organisation?

  And, lastly,
- does the scheme assist or hinder organisational change? Is it flexible enough to allow the organisation to respond to the challenges of the environment or is it too rigid to allow individuals to grow beyond the structural boundaries imposed by a tightly defined system?

Whereas performance-related pay is seen as one approach which addresses the issue of a payment system designed to meet the important issues of contemporary organisations, there are other innovative approaches. Two broad types are emerging: a total remuneration package approach, or a 'cafeteria' approach. The former identifies a cash equivalent ceiling for a total package the employee can expect to receive. The individual then chooses to take the amount wholly in cash, or partly in cash and partly in fringe benefits. The 'cafeteria' approach incorporates a specified base salary and a 'menu' of fringe benefits from which the individual can choose those most appropriate to him or her. The attraction of these schemes is that they allow the individual to reflect on those rewards that are pertinent, which inevitably means that they will represent a higher intrinsic value too. Consequently, by individualising the reward package the organisation has the potential to gain more in commitment and loyalty and (hopefully) performance.

Another basis on which to reward employees is that which reflects acquired skill and personal development. This approach is becoming more relevant with the increasing emphasis on competence at work and qualifications to reflect competence. Skill-based reward schemes can also cater for the demands for a more skilled and flexible labour force that can respond to new technologies and changing job demands. This type of reward approach does not reflect the job itself but the abilities of the job-holder and therefore encourages the individual to seek growth and development opportunities. Training and development become key features of the support system.

If full advantage is to be gained from a reward system it must not be designed in isolation from other human resource initiatives. The system must support the strategic intentions of the organisation and must reflect the culture and core values. If changes are to be made in the way the organisation is operating and the value system it reflects, the reward system needs to be able to facilitate such change – not cause the organisation to be dragged backwards and lose competitive edge. The individual must be able to relate to the reward system, and the reward system must be able to relate the individual to the organisation. The individual must be able to understand how his or her input, in terms of effort, abilities, attitude, skills and experience, achieves a particular reward; how he or she can influence that reward; how his or her reward relates to other people's rewards, and the value of that reward as an expression of the contribution being made to the overall organisation performance. Given also that reward strategies should also encourage growth and development, each individual needs also to understand how to progress through the pay structure.

DEVELOPMENT

The final part of the model shown in Fig. 8.3 is development. Perhaps no other aspect of managing people has experienced such a meteoric rise in profile as that of Human Resource Development (HRD). The nature of change in the organisation's environment, whether it be technological advancement, economic decline and growth, greater and more aggressive competition, changes in consumer tastes and demands, changes in societal values and expectations, and changes in knowledge and skills requirements, all place pressure on the organisation to respond. Senior management is becoming increasingly aware and appreciative of the need to ensure its human resources are both able and willing to cope with the challenges of organisations in a competitive and volatile environment. As such, they are focusing on the benefits to be gained from assertive and holistic employee development interventions.

There have been a few signals which have indicated the need for a major focus on developing people to ensure a ready supply of the right people – ready developed and acculturalised. Externally there was the dramatic castigation of British industrial training and development commitment raised in 'A Challenge to Complacency' (Coopers Lybrand, 1985) and 'The Making of Managers' (Handy, 1987), which led to a reassessment of the way the workforce as a national entity was being developed.

Initiatives such as the Management Charter Initiative, which aims to recognise competence in management practice; National Vocational Qualifications, which seek to ensure that all people at work or eligible to work have the opportunity to have workplace competence recognised and standardised to nationally prescribed descriptions and levels; Investors In People, emanating from the 1988 White Paper *Employment for the 1990s,* which requires those organisations seeking the award to make a public declaration of their commitment at the most senior levels to develop all employees to achieve their business objectives; open competition from the Single European Market, which raised questions as to whether the UK labour force could compare with their European counterparts as well as pressure to extend the principle of a common vocational training policy; the consequences of the 'demographic time bomb', which suggested that there would be a shortage of potential employees entering the labour market, have all emerged in response to criticism of the UK workforce.

Lastly, but by no means least, there was the move to a change in management philosophy following the ready acceptance of the excellence movement and the popularity of the Total Quality Management initiatives which aspire to endless improved performance. All these triggers pointed to a necessary organisational response, a coherent approach to employee development if the organisation was to succeed.

There were internal pressures too. Difficulty in recruiting skilled managers and technical specialists placed a requirement on developing and retaining 'home-grown' employees. Rapid changes in the environment meant a need for a more flexible and adaptable labour force. The insecurity of market position and future existence made it more imperative that employees and organisations moved together in the same direction, entailing an alignment of employee potential with organisational objectives, planning individual careers and development to ensure continuous growth and development and a much more holistic view towards performance assessment and management. Again, the key feature to fulfil the organisational demands was an organisation-wide response to the total development provision concerning all types of employee at all levels.

The emphasis is one which is clearly strategic, a move away from the fragmented *ad hoc* tendencies towards training at operational levels and a conscious attempt to link the full range of employee learning to corporate aims. The integration of HRD with organisational mission and goals is a key characteristic. Human resources are seen as an essential contributing factor in business planning and a fully developed workforce as a necessity in corporate goal achievement. With the HRD planning process analysing and responding to both external and internal triggers it is, according to Higgs (1989), Hales (1986) and Hendry and Pettigrew (1986), a strategic function and not simply a service function putting into practice the requirements of others.

This change in focus requires a different set of responsibilities for managers. Top management must display its commitment to developing its employees not solely through a statement of intent but by being seen to be wholly embracing the concept and practice of HRD. Line management also has a vital part to play: line managers become key deliverers of programmes and suppliers of information on which to base decisions. The line manager is seen as being best placed to assess the training and development needs of his or her staff, well placed to provide a major input into each subordinate's development programme and advice to those who may be delivering special programmes. This raises a question about the ability of the line manager to take on and fulfil this responsibility. Identifying training and development needs requires a manager to know how to appraise performance and identify the skill gaps – that requires him or her to know what skills are needed. Effective performance appraisal needs sensitive and empathetic interpersonal skills. It would appear that the starting point to a fully integrated HRD programme is management development. If managers themselves are not competent as managers of people, HRD initiatives will have only a marginal impact. As Keep (1989) says, 'Actions speak louder than words and employees have normally not been slow to notice inconsistencies in the messages emanating from management.' Consequently, development is not something which is simply done to others, it is something in which all members of the organisation are involved. Twigg and Albion (1992), reflecting on the Reg Revans belief that, for organisations to survive, the rate of learning by employees must be at least equal to the rate of change, and preferably greater, propose that 'learning' and 'development' should be part of every employee's expectations about organisational life and should not be seen as the responsibility of specialist trainers and developers and/or managers.

When HRD is linked to organisational survival it becomes easier to view the development process as an investment rather than a cost. Unfortunately, training has tended to be seen as a cost, a drain on financial resources and therefore one of the first 'luxuries' to be axed when organisations face adverse economic conditions. Bentley (1991) argues that developing employees is an investment for the organisation and can be appraised using the same techniques as those used to appraise investment in capital equipment. He makes the case for managers being able to assess how the improvement of individual performance affects profits, which then provides the basis for measuring the effects of training on profit. If every individual is linked to organisational performance improvement, the organisation must provide the opportunities for individual growth and development. Two concepts which have become popular recently are now relevant. The first is the establishment of the 'learning organisation', in which 'continuous development' (the second concept) will take place naturally.

A 'learning organisation' is one which has established a culture of continuous personal growth, development and performance improvement. Pedlar, Boydell and Burgoyne (1989) define the learning organisation as 'an organisation which facilitates the learning of all its members and continually transforms itself'. The relationships are of mutual interdependence and benefit. Individuals are empowered to learn actively, seeking opportunities to explore, experiment and challenge the old ways in their pursuit for performance improvement. By allowing individuals the freedom in which to take advantage of learning opportunities, the organisation is able to become more flexible and thus able to cope with environmental challenges. The process of continuous development is achieved if certain conditions are met. These conditions are outlined in the Institute of Personnel Management's 1987 code of practice and propose the introduction of employee knowledge and skill requirements in the strategic plan, the integration of learning and work, managers who are able to recognise and define learning needs as they emerge and the commitment and involvement of the top management team. But putting these conditions into practice requires a change of attitude for many key people in the process, not least of whom are the individual learners themselves.

People will commit time and effort to the learning process only if the learning outcome is something that is valued. 'Learning', therefore, has to be seen in conjunction with the reward system, something that is both recognised and seen as desirable by the organisation and which is reflected in the individual's value system. The match of values strengthens the culture and the momentum for learning is increased. But what benefits accrue to the individual? The most obvious link with rewards is that of personal growth and development achieving, those higher-level needs identified in the content theories of motivation. Improved performance can be rewarded through other needs too, such as performance-related pay and better career prospects. HRD initiatives can relate to all levels of needs depending on how the individual chooses to interpret the impact of the intervention. An investment in HRD can also bring about job redesign, enabling people to experience greater job satisfaction through improved job requirement.

What is becoming apparent is that HRD should not be viewed as an isolated function operating at the periphery of management thinking and decision-making. It is central to the achievement of organisation objectives and totally integrated with other Human Resource Management initiatives. Keep (1989) asserts that for effective HRD there must be a coherent package of complementary initiatives which relate to the other three key constituent elements of HRM – selection, appraisal and rewards. It is the integration of the four that has the greatest impact on performance and organisational success.

CONCLUSION

In this chapter we have examined the link between Human Resource Management and organisational effectiveness, arguing that if organisations are to succeed consideration of the human resource at strategic level is critical. For many organisations business success is a reflection of client satisfaction whether it be for goods or services obtained. The marketing imperative in the judgement of what constitutes business success is patent. So too, therefore, is the interface between marketing and Human Resource Management. The relationship is not simply one of providing suitable employees to resource the marketing function, it is much more fundamental to the whole purpose and operation of the organisation.

If marketing's role is to define properly what customers require and then to deliver it to ensure business survival in the long term, then HRM's role is to ensure that those employed by the organisation know what is required of them, why it is required and what they must do to fulfil that requirement. HRM places the management of people into the general business perspective of strategic development, ensuring that the plans and actions necessary to gain and sustain the competitive edge though the proper management of people at work are aligned with corporate objectives. Whilst it is reasonable to subscribe to the view that marketing is essential for the establishment of organisational purpose and direction, providing the interface between the organisation and its environment, the relationship is not sufficient to assume success. Marketing can succeed only if those in key positions subscribe to the view that it is people who make things happen and embrace wholeheartedly the vision and potential for Human Resource Management.

BIBLIOGRAPHY

Adams, J. S. (1965) 'Inequity in Social Exchange', in L. Berkowitz (ed.), *Advances in Experimental Psychology*, NY: Academic Press.

Ahmed, P. K. and Rafiq, M. (1992) 'Implanting Competitive Strategy', *Journal of Marketing Management*, Vol. 8, pp. 49–67.

Aikin, O. (1988) 'Subjective Criteria in Selection', *Personnel Management*, September, p. 59.

Alderfer, C. P. (1969) 'An Empirical Test of a New Theory of Human Needs', *Organisational Behaviour and Human Performance*, Vol. 4, pp. 142–75.

Armstrong, M. (1988) *A Handbook of Human Resource Management*, London: Kogan Page.

Armstrong, M. (1992) *Human Resource Management Strategy and Action*, London: Kogan Page.

Arnold, J., Robertson, I. T. and Cooper, C. L. (1991) *Work Psychology, Understanding Human Behaviour in the Workplace*, London: Pitman.

Bass, B. M. (1985) *Leadership and Performance Beyond Expectactions*, NY: Free Press.

Bennis, W. G. and Nanus, B. (1985) 'The Four Competencies of Leadership', *Training and Development Journal*, Vol. 38, No. 8, pp. 14–19.

Bentley, T. (1991) *The Business of Training*, London: McGraw-Hill.

Bevan, S. and Thompson, M. (1991) 'Performance Management at the Cross Roads', *Personnel Management*, November.

Biddle, D. and Evenden, R. (1989) *Human Aspects of Management*, London: IPM.

Bower, M. (1966) *The Will to Manage*, New York: McGraw-Hill.

Buchanan, D. A. (1989) 'Principles and Practice in Work Design' in K. Sissons (ed.), *Personnel Management in Britain*, Oxford: Blackwell.

Burns, J. M. (1978) *Leadership*, NY: Harper and Row.

Burns, T. and Stalker, G. M. (1961) *The Management of Innovation*, London: Tavistock.

Child, J. (1972) 'Organisational Structure, Environment and Performance The Role of Strategic Choice', *Sociology*, January, pp. 1–22.

Child, J. (1984) *Organisational: A Guide to Problems and Practice*, London: Harper and Row.

Conger, J. A. and Kanungo, R. (1987) 'Toward a Behavioural Theory of Charismatic Leadership in Organisational Settings', *Academy of Management Review*, Vol. 12, pp. 637–47.

Cooper, C. L., Cooper, R. D. and Eaker, L. H. (1988) *Living with Stress*, Harmondsworth: Penguin.

Coopers Lybrand (1985) 'A Challenge to Complacency'.

Crowe, D. (1992) 'A New Approach to Reward Management', in M. Armstrong (ed.), *Strategies for Human Resource Management. A Total Business Approach*, London: Kogan-Page.

Cummings, L. and Schwab, D. (1973) *Performance in Organisations, Determinants and Appraisal*, Glen View, Ill: Scot Foresman.

Deal, T. E. and Kennedy, A. A. (1982) *Corporate Cultures: The Rites and Rituals of Corporate Life*, Reading, Mass: Addison-Wesley.

Devanna, M. A., Fombrun, C. J. and Tichy, N. M. (1984) *Strategic Human Resource Management*, Chichester: John Wiley.

Emery, F. E. and Trist, E. L. (1965) 'The Causal Texture of Organisational Environments', *Human Relations*, February, pp. 21–32.

Feidler, F. (1967) *A Theory of Leadership Effectiveness*, NY: McGraw-Hill.

Festinger, L. A. (1957) *Theory of Cognitive Dissonance*, Stanford, Calif: Stanford University Press.

Fraser, J. M. (1958) *A Handbook of Employment Interviewing*, London: Macdonald and Evans.

George, J. (1986) 'Appraisal in the Public Sector: Dispensing with the Big Shock', *Personnel Management*, May.

Gordon, J. (1987) *A Diagnostic Approach to Organisational Behaviour*, Boston: Alyn and Bacon.

Gutteridge, T. G. (1986) 'Organisational Career Development Systems: The State of the Practice', in D. T. Hall and associates (eds.), *Career Development in Organizations*, San Francisco: Jossey-Bass.

Hackman, J. R. and Oldham, G. R. (1980) *Work Redesign*, Reading, Mass: Addison-Wesley.

Hales, L. D. (1986) 'Training: A Product of Business Planning', *Training and Development Journal*, Vol. 4, pp. 65–6.

Handy, C. (1976) *Understanding Organisations*, London: Penguin.

Handy, C. (1985) *The Future of Work*, Oxford: Blackwell.

Handy, C. (1987) *The Making of Managers*, NEDO: London.

Handy, C. (1989) *The Age of Unreason*, London: Hutchinson.

Hendry, C. and Pettigrew, A. (1986) 'The Practice of Strategic Human Resource Management', *Personnel Review*, Vol. 15, No. 3.

Herzberg, F., Mausner, B. and Snyderman, B. (1959) *The Motivation to Work*, NY: John Wiley.

Higgs, M. (1989) 'A Strategic Approach to Training and Development', *Training and Development*, November, pp. 11–14.

Huseman, R. C., Hatfield, J. O. and Miles, E. W. (1987) 'A New Perspective on Equity Theory: The Equity Sensitivity Construct', *Academy of Management Review*, Vol. 12, pp. 222–34.

Keep, E. (1989) 'Corporate Training Strategies: The Vital Component', in J. Storey (ed.), *New Perspectives on Human Resource Management*, London: Routledge.

Kochan, J. A. and Barocci, T. A. (1985) *Human Resource Management*, Boston: Little Brown.

Komaki, J. L. (1986) 'Toward Effective Supervision', *Journal of Applied Psychology*, Vol. 71, pp. 270–9.

Krech, D., Crutchfield, R. S. and Ballachey, E. L. (1962) *Individual in Society*, Maidenhead: McGraw-Hill.

Lawrence, P. and Lorsch, J. W. (1967) *Organisation and Environment: Managing Differentiation and Integration*, Boston: Division of Research, Harvard Business School.

Lee, R. and Lawrence, P. (1991) *Politics at Work*, Cheltenham: Stanley Thornes.

Lewis, C. (1985) *Employee Selection*, London: Hutchinson.

Legge, K. (1989) 'Human Resource Management: A Critical Analysis', in J. Storey (ed.), *New Perspectives on Human Resource Management*, London: Routledge.

Locke, E. A. (1968) 'Towards a Theory of Task Motivation and Incentives', *Organisational Behaviour and Human Performance*, Vol. 3, pp. 157–89.

McClelland, D. C. (1965) 'Achievement Motivation Can Be Developed', *Harvard Business Review*, November–December, pp. 6–24.

Maslow, A. H. (1943) *Motivation and Personality*, NY: Harper and Row.

Mento, A. J., Steel, R. P. and Karren, R. J. (1987) 'A Meta-Analytical Study of the Effects of Goal Setting on Task Performance, 1966–1984', *Organisational Behaviour and Human Decision Processes*, Vol. 39, pp. 52–83.

Miles, R. E. and Snow, C. C. (1984) 'Designing Strategic Human Resource Systems', *Organisational Dynamics*, Summer.

Mintzberg, H. (1973) *The Nature of Managerial Work*, NY: Harper and Row.

Mintzberg, H. (1991) 'Organisation Design: Fashion or Fit?', *Harvard Business Review*, January–February.

Nadler, D. A. and Lawler, E. E. III (1977) 'Motivation: A Diagnostic Approach', in J. R. Hackman, E. E. Lawler III and L. W. Porter (eds.), *Perspectives on Behaviour in Organisations*, NY: McGraw-Hill.

Pascale, R. T. and Athos, A. G. (1981) *The Art of Japanese Management*, NY: Simon & Schuster.

Pedlar, M., Boydell, T. and Burgoyne, J. (1989) 'Towards the Learning Company', *Management Education and Development*, Vol. 21, No. I.

Peters, T. J. and Waterman, R. H. (1982) *In Search of Excellence: Lessons from America's Best Run Companies*, NY: Harper and Row.

Piercy, N. (1992) *Market-Led Strategic Change*, Oxford: Butterworth-Heinemann.

Pfeffer, J. (1978) *Organisational Design*, Arlington Heights, Ill: AHM Publishing.

Philpott, L. and Sheppard, L. (1992) 'Managing for Improved Performance', in M. Armstrong (ed.), *Management Strategies for Human Resource Management: A Total Business Approach*, London: Kogan Page.

Plumbley, P. (1986) *Recruitment and Selection*, London: IPM.

Randell, G., Packard, P. and Slater, J. (1984) *Staff Appraisal*, London: IPM.

Robbins, S. P. (1990) *Organisation Theory Structure, Design and Applications*, Englewood Cliffs, NJ: Prentice-Hall.

Rodger, A. (1951) *The Seven Point Plan*, London: National Institute of Industrial Psychology.

Rosenman, R., Freidman, F. and Straus, R. (1964) 'A Predictive Study of CHD', *Journal of the American Medical Association*, Vol. 189, pp. 15–22.

Schein, E. H. (1984) 'Coming to a New Awareness of Organisational Culture', *Sloan Management Review*, Vol. 25, Part 2, p. 3.

Schein, E. H. (1985) *Organisational Culture and Leadership*, San Francisco: Jossey-Bass.

Skinner, B. F. (1974) *About Behaviourism*, NY: Knopf.

Skinner, B. F. (1938) *The Behaviour of Organisations*, NY: Appleton.

Steers, R. M. and Porter, L. W. (1975) *Motivation and Work Behaviour*, NY: McGraw-Hill.

Stewart, V. (1990) *The David Solution*, Aldershot: Gower.

Storey, J. (1989) *New Perspectives on Human Resource Management*, London: Routledge.

Taylor, G. S., Lehman, C. M. and Forde, C. M. (1989) 'How Employee Self Approvals Can Help', *Supervisory Management*, August, pp. 33–41.

Taylor, J. C. (1979) 'Job Design Criteria Twenty Years Later', in L. E. Davis and J. C. Taylor (eds.), *Design of Jobs*, 2nd edn, Santa Monica, Calif: Goodyear.

Torrington, D. (1991) *Management Face to Face*, Hemel Hempstead: Prentice-Hall International.

Torrington, D. and Hall, L. (1991) *Personnel Management, A New Approach*, 2nd edn, Hemel Hempstead: Prentice-Hall International.

Townley, B. (1989) 'Selection and Appraisal: Reconstructing Social Relations?', in J. Storey (ed.), *New Perspectives on Human Resource Management*, London: Routledge.

Twigg, G and Albion, P. (1992) 'Human Resource Development and Business Strategy', in M. Armstrong (ed.), *Strategies for Human Resource Management: A Total Business Approach*, London: Kogan Page.

Vroom, V. H. (1964) *Work and Motivation*, NY: John Wiley.

Walker, J. W. (1992) *Human Resource Strategy*, Englewood Cliffs, NJ: McGraw-Hill.

Weick, K. E. (1969) *Social Psychology of Organising*, Reading, Mass: Addison-Wesley.

Wiesner, W. H. and Cronshaw, S.F. (1988) 'A Meta-Analytical Investigation of the Impact of Interview Format and Degree of Structure on the Validity of the Employment Interview', *Journal of Occupational Psychology*, Vol. 61, p. 275–90.

CHAPTER 9

Case Study: Snacks and Nibbles Ltd

Keith Moreton and David Williamson

INTRODUCTION

The case of Snacks and Nibbles Ltd examines the management of the supply/
demand interface of a company engaged in marketing, developing and manufacturing fast-moving consumer products in an extremely competitive and volatile environment. The case investigates the problems and opportunities facing a
company which has been bought out by its management, who are attempting
to turn the company round and create a success story.

'Snacks' – as we have affectionately abbreviated the company name – is
based on our research of the food industry; particularly biscuits, confectionery,
snack foods and food retailing.

The case contains substantial information relating to manufacturing, manufacturing logistics, human resource management and financial data in addition
to marketing and competitive data. A large proportion of the information may
appear to be technical, i.e. manufacturing related. It is, nevertheless, essential
to the case and enables it to be used in various ways. It can be used as an
integrative case study in corporate strategy; it can be used to study marketing
strategy and the rationale for maintaining a consistent, or symbiotic, interface
between marketing and operations, finance and other functional areas of a
business or it can be used to examine functional strategy and tactics separately.
'Snacks' raises a variety of questions and issues at all these levels. These are
generically framed by the consultant, 'John Ashworth', in the final section of
the case.

In addition to Ashworth's questions, however, we wish to raise a much more
fundamental one. We have developed a dismal general hypothesis of organisations in the UK (particularly manufacturing businesses, but it also extends to
service industries and the public sector) and it is this:

In reality most organisations do not understand how to manage functional
interfaces. More particularly they do not have any (or have very little) knowl-

This case study is based upon a number of companies within the food industry. Although all names
have been altered to ensure anonymity, the information contained within the case study is factual.

edge of the 'mechanisms' and 'bridges' which enable business and marketing strategy to be operationalised effectively. A 'credibility and communications gap' exists between what is intended in a business strategy and what can actually be achieved and this we believe is most prevalent between the marketing and manufacturing functions. We suggest that the following factors partially explain this organisational incompetence.

1   Too much vision, too much rhetoric and not enough definition of language.
2   Obsession with process.
3   The perpetuation of functional archipelagos.
4   Inability to understand key constraints.
5   Inability or reluctance to communicate in a common language.

You will see that these factors are all related, but are not exhaustive.

1 Too much vision, too much rhetoric and not enough definition of language

There is a history in the UK of the inability of companies to operationalise 'big ideas'. During the 1960s and early 1970s the strategic apex of organisations were unable to comprehend the 'scientific manager' who believed that the panacea for success was the application of multiple regression analysis, linear and non-linear programming and a 'toolbag' of miscellaneous hard mathematical and statistical processes.

However from the mid 1970s up to the present day the situation has gradually reversed. The language of the strategist has become esoteric to the point where it is nearly incomprehensible to the managers who are charged with getting things done. It is the language of the visionary who has no functional competence. Contemporary 'management speak' is permeating corporate strategy, marketing strategy and manufacturing strategy and is saturated with 'guru' hyperbole, superlatives and rhetoric which masquerade as self-evident reality and action. Listed below are a few examples of this language (with our comments). These terms are regularly used by managers and students on postgraduate programmes without resort to definition.

'Manufacturing excellence'	Measured against which yardstick(s)? Kaplan (1990) has attempted to address this deficiency.
'Competitive advantage' or 'Competitive edge'	This 'advantage' or 'edge' is seldom defined let alone measured, without which these superlatives are meaningless. There is ample evidence that managers who have read Porter (1985) texts have not proceeded beyond the first chapters.

'Continuous improvement'	How measured and where measured?
'Premium customer care'	An anecdote: There is a blue chip electronics company with a comprehensive 'customer care mission statement'. However, in one of its major divisions the rework in its operation exceeds 40 per cent and delivery performance is unmeasured. How does *your* company measure 'customer care'?
'Management commitment'	Commitment = dedication or obligation to (a) particular action (Oxford English Dictionary). How is this dedication measured? Does it mean managerial involvement and, if so, how many managers are involved and to what depth? Does it mean financial commitments?

There are many more of these terms which remain meaningless until defined.

2 Obsession with process

During the 1980s a legion of business acronyms were imported into the lexicon of manufacturing strategy. They were supposed to shock 'western manufacturers into a new paradigm for competitive success' (Kaplan, 1990). Here are a sample: Zero Defects (ZD); Just in Time (JIT); Optimised Production Technology (OPT); Manufacturing Resource Planning (MRPII); Total Quality Management (TQM). Many refer to optimal conditions and some, such as JIT and MRPII, are referred to as ideologies, philosophies or methodologies. Unfortunately many organisations have been unable to proceed beyond the philosophical stage and there is a strange belief that these ideologies can be implemented by exhortation. This is a pity because they do provide mechanisms to bridge the marketing/operations interface. There is also an unfortunate tendency for manufacturing managers to regard them as new panaceas (MRPII and BS 5750 Quality Accreditation are examples). They are then bureaucratised by managers as they become obsessed with 'process' or technology rather than the beneficial outcomes. This proposition is partly supported by recent research by Voss (1993) who, for instance, discovered that BS 5750 neither improved the quality of products/services nor enhanced the customer focus of manufacturing businesses.

3 The perpetuation of functional archipelagos

Despite the ideology in favour of organisational integration, the flat organisation and the 'organic organisation', segmentalisation, as described by Kanter (1983), is the norm rather than the exception even in small/medium size organisations. We prefer to describe this segmentalisation as 'functional archipelagos'. Each island in the archipelago has a name, of course, be it marketing, finance, design, R&D, manufacturing, planning and control, etc.

These islands are both mutually exclusive and mutually incompatible. They are also 'islands of philosophy' which are intended to prevent both integration and transparency. They exist in order that the status quo may be maintained.

4 Inability to understand key constraints

It is in the nature of business that marketing is a 'probabilistic' activity. Manufacturing on the other hand has some inbuilt determinisms: 'we have X capacity'; 'we can produce to Y quality'; 'we can produce at Z cost'. These represent major constraints. These manufacturing parameters may be changed, of course, but at a cost and over a time that is positively correlated with the magnitude of change required. Manufacturing, therefore, can present a major barrier to marketing opportunities. In short manufacturing, to use Skinner's (1978) terminology, can easily deteriorate from ' . . . a corporate asset to a corporate millstone' when the manufacturing infrastructure can no longer support the organisational task competitively. The problems of task vs infrastructure are not going to ease for two key reasons:

(1) Markets and buyers are becoming increasingly discriminating because there is more choice and expectations are continually being raised.
(2) Product life cycles will continue to shorten in all sectors, not only in fast-moving consumer goods.

Marketing and manufacturing, therefore, have to adapt in the following ways. Marketing must become more effective in environmental forecasting and the definition of future opportunities whilst simultaneously understanding, in detail, the constraints in manufacturing which are potential barriers to opportunity. Manufacturing must be capable of responding to change faster in order that the business can be 'there when the bell rings'.

5 Inability to communicate in a common language

All of the above factors highlight barriers to communication. These barriers are not easily demolished and they tend to perpetuate the 'ancient' stereotypes and antagonisms which have characterised the marketing/manufacturing interface. The hubris generated contributes to the inability of the two functions to communicate in a common language.

There are a variety of techniques and methodologies available to breach the language barrier. The most obvious is the business plan, which is useless if confined to the boardroom. The business plan defines the financial objectives of the business in detail and is a document to which both marketing and manufacturing have major inputs. It contains marketing assumptions in respect of revenues and manufacturing assumptions in determining the cost of earning these revenues. It also provides a 'broadbrush' benchmark for production planning and, as such, it also represents an opportunity for making the supply/demand interface effective. However, there are three prerequisites if business planning is to be an effective means of communication:

- the plan must be realistic over its time span;
- it must be achievable, and
- it needs to be communicated beyond the boardroom to the people who get things done.

At lower levels there are a variety of techniques which facilitate the use of a common language, in detailed product terminology. Most of these techniques are the result of developments in manufacturing planning and control systems (MP&CS). These have been incorporated to ensure that there was substantial marketing, design and financial inputs to MP&CS as well as manufacturing inputs. These techniques are all, to some extent, related to the function of master production scheduling (MPS). The MPS is a statement, in detailed terms, of what will be produced, rather than what management would like to produce. This does not mean that it is set in granite; MPS is an interactive process and must be reviewed regularly.

The major inputs to MPS are the business plan and the 'demand management' process. The latter requires a variety of marketing/sales planning and manufacturing inputs amongst which are the time-phased order backlog (or order book), forecasts of future demands and inventories. The MPS process can enable the sales function of marketing to operate order promising procedures which, over short time periods, can be effectively synchronised with manufacturing capability.

In addition to all this, these techniques usually require organisations to structure bills of materials in such a way that they reflect the way in which the product is sold rather than how it is designed or manufactured. Planning bills of material, as they are known, provide a powerful language laboratory for marketing, manufacturing and financial personnel at middle and junior management levels.

Some of these integrative 'techniques' are reviewed in the case, but for the reader who wishes to know more we would suggest an excellent and comprehensive text by Vollman, Berry & Whybark (1992).

Now to the 'fundamental level': marketing is as much a component of the 'value chain' and operations logistics of a business as, say, manufacturing, distribution or service (Porter, 1985 and Christopher, 1986). Of course, one of the primary tasks of marketing is to understand the sociological profile, demographics, economics, buying patterns, even the psychology, of target markets – it is an 'external' task. This task requires great skill and even greater judgement. Why then aren't these same skills applied internally to an organisation, as well as externally? After all, business organisations consist of people, not abstract concepts. These people have social and educational backgrounds; they have perceptions of what constitutes business success and varying levels of understanding of the business mission. They also have skills and competences which are not always recognised, let alone utilised. These human characteristics need to be known, otherwise a common language of understanding is impossible and functional xenophobia will flourish. This is the major reason for deliberately adopting the dialogue or storytelling narrative in this case study. (The style was popularised by Goldratt (1984) with great success.) We suggest, therefore, that you study the characters in 'Snacks' with the same zeal that you apply to the analysis of the more formal information provided.

SETTING THE SCENE

John Ashworth was in that sort of 'limbo' time between jobs, with the last assignment nicely working itself out of his system (but not his bank account), yet with the thought of a new one refusing to register any interest or adrenaline at all. His telephone rang.

'John Ashworth of Ashworth and Dean Consultants.'

'James Hobart, the Managing Director of Snacks and Nibbles, speaking. I am currently reviewing the company from a number of different angles, and I was wondering if you might be interested in assisting in one or two ways?'

'Yes, certainly. What is it you want me to do?'

Ashworth noticed a momentary pause before Hobart replied: 'The background to the problem is rather long, it might be a good idea if we could perhaps have lunch together, so that I can fully explain it. Could you make it to Swans on Friday of this week, at say 12.30?'

'That sounds like a good idea. I look forward to seeing you then. Cheerio.'

Well, that's the end of the easy life, thought Ashworth, as he pondered over the unexpected request. Three days later, on Friday, he arrived at Swans. Hobart was at a table and, as he introduced himself, Ashworth was struck by both his physical size and the air of authority and assertiveness he exhibited. After the pleasantries Hobart began to outline the nature of his request.

'As you may know, John, Snacks and Nibbles has been operating for a little more than two years as an independent company. It had been a subsidiary of Conglomerate Holdings for the twelve years before, but the business hadn't really performed well during the 1980s. In 1990 they decided that the company wasn't really part of their core business and put it up for sale. I was invited, by two existing executive directors, to join them in putting together a management buy-out bid and turning the company round. They, the existing managers, convinced me there was a future for the business. I have had some experience with the food industry and corporate financing. I was eventually convinced it had a chance. I put a business plan together very quickly and together with our own equity and City finance we completed a deal with Conglomerate Holdings within a month.

'But first let me provide you with a brief overview of the recent history of Snacks and Nibbles Ltd. I'll just refer to the company as 'Snacks' for simplicity. Anyway, Snacks was in very poor shape. In my first two months there I began to wonder if I had made a serious error in attempting to turn it around. I can tell you I had some sleepless nights.'

'That bad?'

'Probably worse, because the snack food business is highly competitive and there are some very effective "big players", the entry barriers for new blood are small and the City, which financed 80 per cent of the buy-out, are obsessed with positive results – fast. There were, therefore, a number of overriding priorities to be tackled.'

'And what were they?'

'Well, first I had to strengthen the management team. Marketing and finance directors were in place, but I had no manufacturing director or any real expertise in middle management in either manufacturing or marketing. I virtually conned a long-time friend, Michael Hoylake, who had a reasonably secure post in the manufacturing food industry, into taking the position. He's also a shareholder.

'He in turn recruited a bright young MBA with ten years' experience in the food industry. He's very good, especially in the areas of manufacturing planning, control and QA. They've worked very effectively together in building a real team in manufacturing.'

'And what about marketing?'

'That brings me to the next priority. The company was not really marketing-led. The company had a "turnover at all costs" policy and a close scrutiny of our product portfolio revealed that less than 10 per cent of the product range was contributing. This had to be rectified.'

Ashworth was growing interested: 'How are you progressing on that front? I would imagine that would take some time to rectify.'

'Yes, it does – and it has. About half our product range is now "performing". I must add that contribution analysis and budgetary control are quite recent innovations, believe it or not. Another priority (actually one of the earliest) was to reduce our cost base. This required rationalisation.'

'Workforce?'

'Not only the workforce, but the total overhead. You see, we operated on two sites five miles apart. This contributed to a lot of duplication and confusion in the operation and it was decided at an early stage to have our administration and production on one site only.'

'That must have reduced your turnover considerably.'

There was more than a hint of satisfaction in the reply. 'Not on your life. Hoylake and I judged that there was a tremendous amount of slack that could be taken up – we've maintained the same level of output with much reduced direct overheads, but we had to invest.'

'In new capital equipment?'

'Yes, but also in new administrative systems which, hopefully, will effectively integrate the functions of marketing, manufacturing and finance. Employee facilities such as toilets and cafeteria have also been completely upgraded. The previous working environment could only be described as atrocious. The company didn't have a particularly good track record as an employer. There was a lot of dissatisfaction which manifested itself in high absenteeism rates.

'The improved workforce facilities were as much a goodwill gesture as an improvement in working conditions *per se*. We believed that "putting our money where our mouths were" had to be the first step in establishing our credibility, especially after a significant reduction in headcount.'

'But improving physical facilities, the hygiene factors, won't completely solve the HRM problems will it?'

'No it certainly won't, but we're getting into too much detail. My manufacturing manager David Laker will provide you with far more information, particularly about how we're attempting to change attitudes and improve flexibility in the plant. The main point is that now, despite interest charges, we're making a reasonable after-tax profit from a slightly increased turnover.'

'Can you give me a rough idea of the bottom line?'.

There was no hesitation 'Certainly. You would have no problem finding out anyway, it's on Extel. Our turnover for this financial year was £20 million and profit after tax £2 million. At the time of the buy-out, Snacks was the same amount in the red.'

'Well,' said John, 'you seem to have doctored the business into a fairly healthy position and, implicit in what you've told me so far, you're attempting continuously to improve its economic performance and you've got a "handle" on the control of the business. My question for you is – How could I possibly contribute to an improving situation?'

Hobart replied, 'This issue was raised at our last board meeting. In the last couple of years we have implemented some drastic improvements in all functional areas. We have significantly reduced our cost base. And we have the confidence of the City, as our first year's results were slightly better than expected. Briefly, we are solving all the short-term problems. We have, if you like, made good progress in tuning the company engine; now we need to decide the direction we want to drive the company car. I mean strategic direction, and for that, I believe we need an unbiased analysis of our current position and the options we need to consider, not just to survive, but to thrive in the long run. Would you be interested?'

'Yes,' said John, 'but before we firm anything up can I leave this business questionnaire with you?' (See Exhibit 9.9 at end of case study.) 'Don't attempt to answer all the questions in any detail. It's primary purpose is to provide an *aide mémoire*, when I meet your colleagues and the middle management of your company. I want to know as much as possible about your company, within the boundaries of commercial confidence. It doesn't address any single function, such as marketing, but the operation of every function in the business. You will also see that the first set of questions refer to "Industry profile". These are strategic in nature, but they beg other questions about both the industry in general and your operation in particular.'

'How much time do you require to provide recommendations to our board?'

'Approximately two to four weeks to undertake an in-depth evaluation and provide the board with options you can all live with. That time frame, of course, depends upon my access to your board colleagues and other senior management. By the way, you may even arrive at the same conclusions as me at the end of the process, but you must remember there will be no *right* answers. Snacks Ltd, not I, will be responsible for making a preferred strategy operational. This is not meant to be a caveat or disclaimer from me. It's a fact of business reality.'

'When could you start?'

'When we've agreed on specific terms of reference and settled the contractual formalities, I'll need two days to research the snack food industry independently. When can you introduce me to your colleagues?'

'As soon as you've completed your research. You'll also need these.' Hobart produced the company accounts for year ending June 1992 and the formal organisation chart. These are reproduced as Fig. 9.1 and Exhibits 9.1 to 9.3.

Exhibit 9.1 Snacks and Nibbles: Management accounts

Note: These accounts do not constitute statutory accounts within the meaning of Section 240 of the Companies Act 1985.

At the 30 June 1992 the following had substantial interests in the Ordinary Shares of the Company.

Directors and Employees	33 per cent
Snacks and Nibbles Pension Fund	5 per cent
City Bank International	28 per cent
Sprogett and Silvestor Ventures Ltd	15 per cent
Amiable Life Assurance plc	10 per cent
Ogden Holdings	6 per cent
City Capital Nominees	3 per cent

Accounts approved at a board meeting on 4 August 1992.

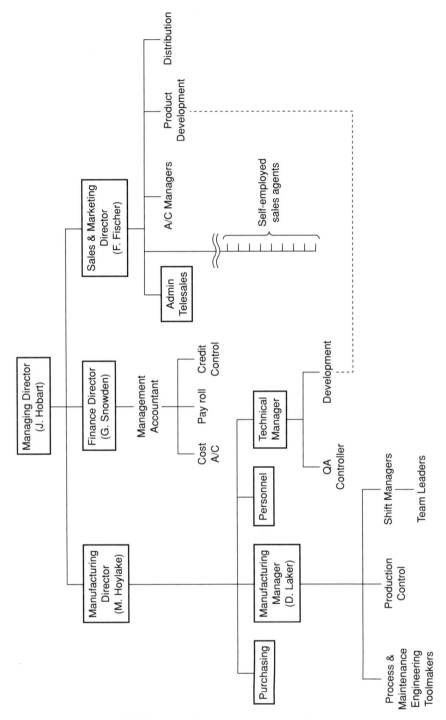

Fig. 9.1 Snacks and Nibbles Ltd: Functional organisation chart

Exhibit 9.2 Snacks and Nibbles: Profit and loss account

	30 June 1992	30 June 1991
	£000s	£000s
Turnover	19700	18900
Discounts and allowances	1005	992
Net Turnover	18695	17908
Cost of Sales		
Ingredients	4950	4600
Packing	2800	2650
Factored	620	280
Total	8370	7530
Value Added	10325	10378
Direct Labour Costs	1780	1960
Gross Margin	8545	8418
Factory Overhead		
Labour	696	690
Other	950	920
Factory Contribution	6899	6808
Sales Overheads	1070	900
Administrative Overheads	560	550
Distribution Overheads	800	1420
Warehouse Overheads	300	630
Depreciation	550	300
Total Earning before Interest and Tax	3619	3008
Profit/Loss on Sale of Assets	(100)	–
Interest	(544)	(495)
Net Profit before Tax	2975	2513
Tax	745	728
Profit after Tax	2230	1785
Dividends Paid and Proposed	1204	980
Transfer to Reserves	1026	805
Number of Employees	330	390

Exhibit 9.3 Snacks and Nibbles: Balance sheet

	30 June 1992 £000s	30 June 1991 £000s
Fixed Assets		
Buildings	3540	3150
Plant	1500	300
Vehicles	–	250
Intangibles	500	1500
Total	5540	5200
Current Assets		
Stocks	900	1080
Trade Debtors	1720	2040
Other Debtors	230	210
Cash on Hand and at Bank	1000	1600
Total Current Assets	3850	4930
Current Liabilities		
Trade Creditors	1500	1650
Loans/Overdraft	1300	1600
Others	50	100
Total Current Liabilities	2850	3350
Net Current Assets	1000	1580
Total Assets minus Current Liabilities	6540	6780
Creditors Falling Due after More than **One Year**		
Finance Debt	3400	3575
Provision for Liabilities and Charges	40	300
Capital and Reserves		
Called up Share Capital	2100	2100
Reserves	1000	805
	6540	6780

THE SNACK FOOD INDUSTRY
Market growth

From his research, Ashworth defined the snack food market as packeted and tinned snacks falling into three categories:

(1) savoury snacks;
(2) crisps;
(3) nuts.

The total snack market had a very attractive growth rate, with a sales value in 1990 of over £1.3 billion (see Table 9.1). Sales were expected to reach £1.5 billion in 1992. Although the information was a little dated, other data such as company turnover in 1991 indicated that an aggregate annual sales growth rate in the region of 8–9 per cent was still being sustained despite recession.

Table 9.1 Growth in UK snacks market

	1985 £m	1990 £m	Annual growth %
Savoury snacks	228	439	14.0
Crisps	556	741	6.0
Nuts	100	137	6.5
	884	1,317	8.4

The fastest growth rate was the savoury snack market, with 14 per cent annually. This market included all sales of snacks by manufacturers, of own-brand and private branded products – retailers' brands (e.g. Sainsbury, Tesco, Morrison, etc.). Savoury snacks were defined as 'puffed' (extruded) products or products fried from pasta pellets and artificially flavoured.

The market for savoury snacks was segmented not only by brand type, but also by price (see Table 9.2).

Table 9.2 Price segmentation of savoury snacks

Segment		Price range per packet (includes individual and multi-packs)
Economy	'Cheap & cheerful'	5–10p
	Upper economy	15–25p
Mid-range		25–40p
Top range*		45p–£1

*Top range products not all in packets but in plastic or cardboard cartons (includes dip snacks).

The annual market growth rate of the economy segment was in excess of 18 per cent. This was interesting: Snacks Ltd served a large part of this market and it was evident that there were many players, but of most significance was the fact that very large organisations such as Dalgety (Golden Wonder, Sooner Snacks), United Biscuits (KP) and PepsiCo (Walkers, Smiths) had moved into the market in a large way.

The potato crisps market could be similarly segmented by price, and although crisps had the lowest growth rate in the snack market, the economy end (10–

15p per packet) was much higher, at approximately 14 per cent per annum. The large players were also in this market too, with their own brands and retailers' brands.

Another important feature of the economy market was the fast growth (approximately 15 per cent per annum) of multiple packs of savoury snacks and crisps. Multi-packs accounted for approximately 15 per cent of sales, most of which were sold through the larger multiples. Ashworth (a natural cynic) decided that the multi-pack products gave the consumer a perception of economy.

The players

Most of the large players in the industry had diversified, with apparently synergistic operations and products. United Biscuits was by far the largest organisation, with operations worldwide. Its share of the total biscuit market in 1992 was nearly 25 per cent and it had a similar share of the total snack food market through its leading brand KP. John had previously associated KP with nuts but the brand also incorporated middle and top range potato crisps and covered the major price points in the savoury snacks market.

Dalgety was represented by several prominent brands in the snack food market, the major ones being Golden Wonder and Sooner Snacks. Sooner Snacks (a recent acquisition) were extremely active in the economy range, being sold through both large and small retailers and franchised chains such as Londis and Spar. Both United Biscuits and Dalgety manufactured for private labels.

Redmill, a subsidiary of Portfolio Foods Ltd, was of a similar size to Snacks Ltd in the UK. However, the company also had operations at two sites in Holland, which served not only the Dutch market but also neighbouring Belgium, Germany, and France. Redmill products were nearly all extruded savoury snacks and Portfolio claimed 62 per cent of the economy snack market in the UK. Redmill accounted for approximately 25 per cent of Portfolio's turnover in 1992. The largest proportion came from confectionery, and the company owned some well-known brands, several being recent acquisitions, e.g. Butterkist (toffee popcorn), Cravens of York, Keiller and Milady.

Other major players in the snack food market were Bensons, Walkers and Smiths Crisps (subsidiaries of PepsiCo Inc.). Walkers was probably the largest potato crisp manufacturer and was beginning to penetrate the savoury snack market. Smiths Crisps, the brand leader in savoury snacks before the Second World War and through the 1950s and early 1960s, had made a dramatic comeback as a brand under the ownership of PepsiCo.

All the major companies had a broad national customer base through all the major retailers and/or the multitude of local corner shops and franchised chains. There were, however, an even larger number of regional manufacturers and brands, with an individual turnover of less than £10 million. These smaller enterprises were niche marketers, focusing their sales and marketing efforts in the regions where their operations were located. For example, Seabrook, a

Bradford-based company, had channels throughout West Yorkshire and East Lancashire. Tayto, a Northern Irish company, targeted Northern Ireland, the Republic of Ireland and the West of Scotland.

Ashworth consolidated this information into a brief summary of 'Who owns who' in the snack food industry (Table 9.3). He also jotted down brief financial data of some of the major and minor players (Exhibit 9.4). He noted that, in terms of return on capital employed, the snack food industry was the most profitable sector of the food industry after the large food retailers.

Table 9.3 Who owns what brands in the snack food industry?

Company	Core Brands	Marketing Brands (Snacks)	Other Businesses and Brands	Notes
United Biscuits	KP Derwent Valley (Snack Foods) – still independent but acquisiton by KP almost certain.	KP Nuts Hula Hoops Brannigans Phileas Fogg Tortilla chips Peking Noodles	Biscuits – McVitie's Frozen and chilled foods Confectionery (Terry's)	KP leads the extruded snacks and nuts sector. It has at least 60% of nuts sector - sells 40–50% as private brand.
PepsiCo	Walkers Smiths Tudor Planters (Nuts)	Walkers Crips Smiths Quaver Smiths Crisps Walkers Monster Munch French Fries (Walkers) Planters Nuts Frazzles (Smiths)	Pepsi Cola Fritolay Kentucky Fried Chicken Pizza Hut	PepsiCo is recent entrant to snack food market (acquired Smiths and Walkers in 1989). Very close number two to UB in snack market.
Portfolio	Redmill (Snacks) Butterkist (popcorn) Confectionery: Craven; Keiller; Barker & Dobson	Redmill (Snacks) Supa Krunchie Thinga-me Jigs Onion Rings Pork Scratchings Yankee Stars	See Core Brands	Redmill is in direct competition with Snacks Ltd. However, it has a larger operation and has European manufacturing capabilities.
Dalgety	Sooner Snacks Golden Wonder	Rileys (Crisps) Grocers (Crisps) Wheat Crunchies (Snacks) Nik Naks (Snacks)	Food Distribution Agri Business Food Ingredients – incl. Homepride Spillers Food – including petfoods.	Golden Wonder is number three after KP and PepsiCo. Golden Wonder has only a small share of extruded snacks.
Burton Snacks	Seabrook (Crisps)	Seabrook (Crisps) Fish'n'Chips (Ex. snack) Potato Puffs (Ex. snack)		
Bensons	XL Crisps Ltd Hedgehog Foods Ltd	XL XL Crinkle Cut Mammoth Bites Chinese Crackers		

Exhibit 9.4 Extracts from consolidated accounts for major and minor players in the snack food industry (£000s)

Company	Bensons Crips plc	Dalgety plc	Portfolio	Walkers Crisps (subsidiary of PepsiCo)	
Date of accounts	Nov. 1990	June 1992	March 1992	Dec. 1991 (18 months)	1990 (12 months)
Turnover	21,968	3,982,400	85,281	247,054	146,303
Profit before Tax	1,361	116,800	2,139	71,014	37,011
Current Assets	5,667	497,000	21,331	84,610	48,865
Current Liabilities	5,906	513,000	22,167	70,532	33,844
Fixed Assets	3,739	425,000	15,639	56,951	45,641
Number of Employees	600	16,073	1,130	1,722	1,713
Stock Turnover (Times/year)	N/A	22.00		13.44	50.87
ROCE %	38.9	36.5	40.9	66.7	61
Advertising Expenditure on snacks	N/A	6,000 Golden Wonder	N/A		7,000

Company	Derwent Valley Foods	United Biscuits (Holding) plc	Seabrook	Smiths Crisps (subsidiary of PepisCo)	
Date of accounts	March 1991	Dec. 1991	Sept. 1991	Dec. 1991 (18 months)	1990 (12 months)
Turnover	18,269	2,979,100	13,404	243,720	161,263
Profit before Tax	1,726	211,300	909	(4,679)	13,892
Current Assets	4,231	704,200	2,626	47,107	42,245
Current Liabilities	4,245	565,500	2,022	58,355	33,122
Fixed Assets	3,900	939,900	4,385	45,385	41,574
Number of Employees	195	40,226	320	3,149	3,434
Stock Turnover (Times/year)	28.7	13.9	33.5	14.25	16.46
ROCE %	44.4	19.59	18.2	(9.1)	27.4
Advertising Expenditure on snacks	1,400	5,800	N/A		4,500

Exhibit 9.4 cont.

Company	Sooner Snacks Ltd (wholly owned by Dalgety)	Tayto (NI) Ltd	RTP Crisps
Date of accounts	December 1991	?	?
Turnover	56,645	Approx. £10m	N/A
Profit before Tax	1,525	N/A	N/A
Current Assets	20,072	N/A	338
Current Liabilities	30,493	N/A	161
Fixed Assets	N/A	N/A	524 (Capital Employed)
Number of Employees	1,100	270	17
Stock Turnover (Times/year)	N/A	N/A	N/A
ROCE %	26.4	N/A	N/A
Advertising Expenditure on snacks	N/A	80	N/A

Source: Company accounts

Brands and channels market shares

Ashworth found manufacturers' brand share claims in specific segments of the snack food industry a little too confusing to be read straightforwardly. He therefore decided to analyse the data in aggregate, i.e. *all* snack foods as he had defined them earlier. This was a useful starting point. The approximate proportions of UK turnover held by each section were as follows:

- savoury snacks: 33 per cent
- crisps: 56 per cent
- nuts: 11 per cent.

By comparing company market share claims with manufacturers' turnover he arrived at what he thought was a satisfactory ranking of own-brand and private label market shares (see Table 9.4). The most significant facts to arise were the dominance of the United Biscuits, PepsiCo and Dalgety brands and the high proportion (approximately 16 per cent) of private retailers' brands. The latter takes on added importance when one considers that in 1992, 80 per cent of all snack food sales were through twelve major grocery multiples in the UK. Sainsbury and Tesco alone accounted for more than 30 per cent of sales and these two retailers not only had nationwide coverage but most sales of snack foods were private label.

Table 9.4 Approximate brand shares of all snacks in packets/cartons (all price points)

Brand Share by Value	1991 %	1992 (estimates) %
Manufacturers' Brands		
KP (United Biscuits)	29.3	31.0
Walkers (PepsiCo)	18.5	18.6
Smiths (PepsiCo)	14.5	14.0
Golden Wonder (Dalgety)	9.8	10.0
Sooner Snacks (Dalgety)	3.3	3.0
Bensons	1.4	1.3
Redmill (Portfolio)	1.1	1.2
Derwent Valley Foods	1.0	1.1
Snacks and Nibbles Ltd	1.0	1.0
Seabrook	0.8	0.8
Tudor (PepsiCo)	0.8	0.7
Others	1.2	1.2
Subtotal	**82.8**	**84.0**
Retailers' Brands		
Sainsbury	5.1	4.9
Tesco	3.3	3.1
Asda	1.8	1.6
Safeway	1.3	1.4
Co-op	1.7	1.4
Gateway	1.4	1.1
Marks and Spencer	1.1	1.0
Other private labels	1.5	1.5
Total	**100.0**	**100.0**
TOTAL VALUE	**£1400 million**	**£1520 million**

Sources: Trade Estimates/Euromonitor and Extrapolation by J. Ashworth

Superficially the savoury snack food market looked very attractive with its high growth rate, but there were lots of competitors, and at the top end these had substantial resources and there were many powerful buyers. Ashworth tried, for a while, to place himself in Hobart's shoes: Snacks Ltd served the whole of the UK but it not only had major competition and the large national buyers to deal with, it also had to compete regionally with niche marketers. The industry certainly did not have 'five star' attractiveness unless you had 'mass' – was Snacks Ltd big enough? This was a question for which he did not have a ready-made answer. He needed to discuss the sources of competitive advantage with Hobart and his managers.

THE SNACKS AND NIBBLES MANAGEMENT TEAM

Hobart had assembled a cross-section of the Snacks management team in the boardroom and, after outlining Ashworth's brief (which everyone present appeared to be aware of), he introduced each of the managers present.

Michael Hoylake, the Manufacturing Director, was in his forties and had been associated with the food industry for most of his working life.

David Laker, Manufacturing Manager, had also made his way through the food industry, in Northern Foods and United Biscuits before joining Snacks.

Frank Fischer, the Marketing Director, was in his mid-fifties. He had been with Snacks for fifteen years, starting as an sales accounts manager. Before that he had worked in several sales/marketing posts including one at Walkers Crisps.

Gillian Snowden, Finance Director and one of the buy-out team, had arrived by an entirely different route: she had spent most of her career in banking before joining Snacks.

Stephanie Kenworthy was the youngest in the group. She was a shift manager, reporting to Laker. She had graduated with a BSc in Food Technology and had been on a two-year teaching company scheme with Sainsbury before joining Snacks.

'These are your "facilitators", John,' Hobart announced. 'They all have a copy of your questionnaire and, so far as I'm aware, they've all had a shot at answering it. So I'll leave you to their tender mercies.'

MANUFACTURING AT SNACKS AND NIBBLES

Hoylake told Ashworth that he'd delegated the task of explaining the operation to Laker, who had been responsible for some significant changes in manufacturing in order to meet Snacks' business targets. As the two of them walked down to the plant, Laker gave a warning: 'The smell from the flavouring process will put you off crisps and snack food for ever.'

They entered the plant.

'It is rather overpowering isn't it!'

'Just wait until we've got a large batch of salt and vinegar.'

Laker explained in detail every process during their tour. Beneath the smell of flavours the production environment was spotless and extremely well ordered. There were at least fifteen production lines, organised in a cellular arrangement. The manufacturing process, albeit hectic, was relatively straightforward. There were two basic sequences: one for extruded products and one for fried products. (See Fig. 9.2.)

Extruded products

Extruded products form approximately 90 per cent of turnover, and the five-stage process described below is used for the production of all the porous snacks.

Stage 1

Maize and water are mixed in stainless steel containers to form a paste.

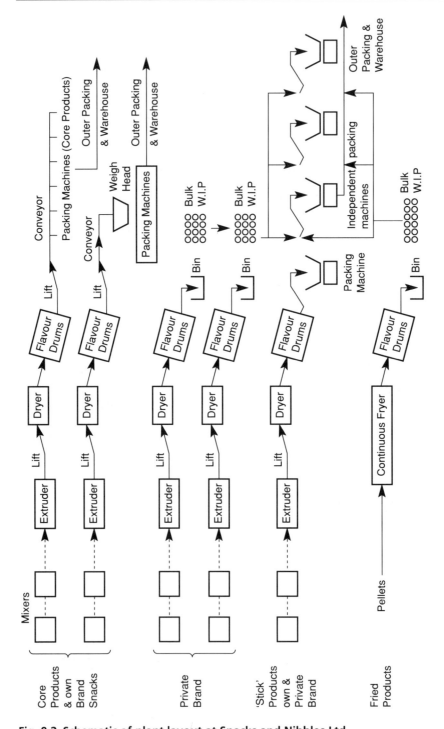

Fig. 9.2 Schematic of plant layout at Snacks and Nibbles Ltd

Stage 2

The maize paste is 'extruded' at high pressure and temperature through dies to form various snack shapes. The extruding process partly cooks the paste into a crisp honeycomb. The product leaves the extruder in a continuous stream, but almost immediately it is cut to length by a rotating blade, rather like an aircraft propeller.

Stage 3

The extruded snacks are dried in a continuous oven to remove residual moisture.

Stage 4

Once the product has been dried completely (it is not cooked at the drying process, that occurs at the extruder) it is flavoured. The flavour that is applied to the product comes in the form of a powdered concentrate. The powder is mixed with edible oil in a 'flavour kettle' or a flavour machine, both of which produce a 'slurry' that is sprayed into a revolving drum in a steady stream, coating the internal surface of the drum. The unflavoured product is fed through the drum. It becomes coated in the slurry as it passes through the drum. The product, being porous, absorbs the slurry and takes on the required flavour.

At first sight this appears to be a relatively simple process, but it raises several important quality issues. The flavour level must be sufficient to ensure good taste. If the flavour level is too high the density increases and the amount of product in the finished packet will be too low in which case customers would perceive they *weren't* getting value for money. Conversely, if the flavour level is too low, causing overfilling (due to lower product density), packets could split or the product quality would be perceived as poor due to low flavour levels.

After this operation, on half the production lines the product is bagged in bulk for the next operation. The other half carry the product automatically to Stage 5.

Stage 5

The product is automatically weighed and bagged in pre-printed packing film and the bags loaded into cases (almost in a despatch state). There are additional bagging operations for products which have been individually bagged, but are required for filling variety multi-packs.

Additional quality issues arise at the bagging operation. Average weight legislation specifies that individual packets, on average, have to contain a minimum stated weight. Any more than this weight and the company is giving product away, any less and the company is liable to prosecution. Product 'give away' is typically less than 1 per cent.

Fried products

The other method of manufacture is to fry products. This involves frying dehydrated pellets of corn, pasta or potato. The fryer is a continuous flow process and so the cooking time for the pellets, the degree of cooking and hence the expansion which takes place in the product are proportional to the temperature of the oil in the fryer and the speed with which pellets move from start to finish of the process (speed is controlled by a belt mechanism). The degree of expansion and the amount of oil absorbed will then govern density as the product leaves the fryer. Controlling density is as important for fried products as it is for the extruded products.

The fried product is then flavoured. The concentrated flavour powder is applied to fried products in a dry state by an electrostatic applicator.

The product is then weighed and packed on machines similar to those used for extruded products.

Although products manufactured from fried pellets account for only 10 per cent of turnover, the margin on them is better than on extruded products because there are fewer operations, i.e. there are no mixing or drying operations.

Laker appeared intimately acquainted with the 'sharp end' of production. On two occasions during the tour he was able to provide rapid advice to technical queries posed by first line managers.

When back at the office Ashworth commented favourably on Laker's technical 'know-how'.

'Look John, in my job and in this business you can't sit back in a plush office pressing delegation buttons in the fond hope that there is always an appropriate person to whom you can delegate responsibility.'

'Doesn't that kind of approach absorb an awful amount of your time?'

'Time well spent I'll tell you. I firmly believe in Tom Peters' (1982) advice on management by wandering about. However, you have to possess a time management strategy to make it work.'

'What's the basis of this strategy?'

'That's a secret, but generally speaking a strategy of unpredictability.'

'Unpredictability?'

'Sure – knowing when it's important to get involved and get your hands dirty, knowing when to delegate down and, more importantly, when to pass the "buck" up.'

The 5 Ps at Snacks and Nibbles

After the tour of the plant, Ashworth and Laker discussed what they had seen. 'Did you notice the rate of production?' Laker asked.

'Yes, it's quite fast.'

'Well, this type of production could be classified as VFMCG – very fast moving consumer goods. We produce, on average, 20,000 cases of snacks each day, six days a week and each case contains 50 bags of snacks, i.e. 120,000 cases and 6 million bags of snacks a week – varies of course.

'So it's essential that we take care of the sharp end almost continually. Short-interval control, whether it's quality control, short-term scheduling, technical issues, such as preventive maintenance, have to be effective if we are to meet the aggregate objectives of the business plan. There must be highly defined and workable linkages between the front end of the business and its sharp end. However . . .', and Laker started to change the subject: 'I've read your business questionnaire by the way. (Exhibit 9.9.) Very operations/manufacturing-orientated isn't it?'

'It's really only an *aide mémoire* and it does address more strategic issues as well.'

'Manufacturing's a strategic issue as well. Anyway, it's a fairly comprehensive questionnaire and I have studied it from start to finish and I have a lot of answers prepared. However, I have slightly rearranged it.'

'Whatever have you done to it?'

'I've used what I consider a simpler framework for addressing the issues in your questionnaire. Nevertheless it doesn't leave a stone unturned. I've used Lockyer's (1974) 5 Ps – elements of production. You know: product, process, plant, programmes and people. I'll deal with each element discretely, but obviously they are all interrelated. Let me start with the product element.'

Product

'The product element contains a load of decision variables, most of them driven by marketing, that have a direct impact on the effectiveness with which production meets profit objectives, customer requirements and specification. You might even say that "product" is pivotal in determining the hard and soft systems and resources in manufacturing.

Volumes

'As I've already pointed out we produce 6 million bags of snacks each week, but the necessity of meeting cost criteria and due dates in this kind of environment places everyone in manufacturing under a great deal of pressure.

'We operate a three-shift system six days a week and we could, if necessary, increase volume by 20 per cent at this moment in time without encountering any major bottlenecks. We also operate a "chase strategy", that is, we use a pool of temporary labour to tackle peaks in demand. It would be nice to level out production, but that would not only incur unacceptable stockholding costs but also give rise to problems associated with shelf life. Retailers want a maximum period of safe shelf life after manufacturing. Nearly every organisation in the food industry operates a similar policy in terms of capacity management. However, the product mix and variety on offer provide an additional complicating dimension.'

Variety

'There are approximately forty different basic shape/flavour combinations in the product portfolio: varying combinations of sticks, rings, puffs, pellets and shapes combined with about twelve flavours. However, we don't market loose snacks; they are bagged and this increases variety to about 150 different products. Actually it might not appear to be a large variety compared with the total volume, but there is a wide range of demand across the product range.

'Our policy, again to minimise inventory, is to produce on a lot for lot basis, i.e. we principally make to order. Sixty per cent of our production is "own brand" Snacks Ltd, the other 40 per cent for private brands such as Morrison, Sainsbury and the other large and small retailers. All own brand and some private brand (about 80 per cent of turnover) is manufactured to order. The other 20 per cent is for stock and that's all private brand.'

'What's the frequency of order receipt then, David?' Ashworth broke in.

'Let me put it another way; our order size varies between 200 and 1,000 cases. That's an order value between, say, £500 and £4,000.'

'That's a fairly wide variation. Do you have an approximate distribution of work order size or customer order size?'

'No, but I have a copy of last week's product margin analysis. (Table 9.5.) This will provide you with a reasonable indication of the products manufactured in any one week – of the 150 I mentioned we probably produce 70 varieties each week – but it varies.'

'Do you receive any forecasts from your customers?'

'You might be quite surprised when I tell you that all we receive is an "indication" of requirements – but no comprehensive forecasts are provided by the customers. The large multiples (e.g. Sainsbury) give no indication of forecast requirement – no, forecasting is absolutely minimal.'

'That has the potential to destabilise your delivery performance.'

'In this environment there is no real connection between forecasting and delivery performance. The key element to delivery performance, as I will explain later, is a combination of rapid response and very short overall lead times.'

'What is your delivery performance then?'

'We have two measures: aggregate and disaggregate. The aggregate measure is based on what are termed "cross-offs", i.e. product not delivered on promise date. I have set a maximum of 1,400 cases of cross-offs each week, about 1 per cent of production. That was set as a benchmark six months ago and it's never been exceeded. It's usually in the region of 0.5 per cent.

'The disaggregate measure is defined as "customer service" – it is calculated on a customer by customer and order by order basis – so a delivery before due date or by due date is classified as 100 per cent customer service. At the moment the customer service level is running at 97 per cent. A year ago it was only 82 per cent.'

Table 9.5 Snacks and Nibbles Ltd: Selection from product range with contribution analysis for the two-month period ending 28 August 1992

Product	Labour per case	Mtl cost	Net sales price	Agent comm	Rebate	Margin	Sales volume cases	Contribution rate	Contribution
	£	£	£	%	%	%		£/hr	£
CORE 10p Snacks Ltd									
10p Cheesy Whirls	.1911	.77	2.3	1.93	6.48	54.4	47850	70	54812
10p Salt'n'Vinegar Whirls	.1977	.70	2.33	1.93	6.48	57.9	34798	75	43024
10p Indian Chiefs	.1889	.80	2.31	1.93	6.48	53.2	99325	68	111825
10p Monster Teeth (cheese)	.2111	.85	2.26	1.93	6.48	48.7	32625	61	32912
10p Monster Snacks (salt/vinegar)	.2722	.85	2.28	–	2.5	49.5	12397	51	13647
10p Animals (pickled onion)	.3044	.79	2.28	–	2.5	50.8	13919	52	15710
10p Animals (tomato)	.1882	.82	2.28	1.93	6.48	51.8	24650	78	26673
10p Sharks Teeth	.1736	.87	2.29	1.93	6.48	50.2	74675	76	78696
10p Monster Daleks	.1700	.82	2.23	1.93	6.48	51.5	196475	76	206783
Total for 10p Range						**46.7**	**740002**	**56.5**	**760320**
(some products not included)									
CORE 5p Snacks Ltd									
5p Cheesy Whirls	.2518	.66	2.12	1.93	6.48	53	52181	44	53743
5p Indian Chiefs	.2580	.60	2.12	1.93	6.48	56	43643	46	47295
5p Monster Teeth (cheese)	.2506	.64	2.1	1.93	6.48	54	43643	44	45073
5p Monster Daleks	.2504	.67	2.07	1.93	6.48	52	38707	42	37758
Total for 5p Range						**53.5**	**178174**	**44.2**	**183667**
50 gramme Snacks Ltd									
50g Puff Balls	.1828	1.16	3.39	1.93	6.48	57.4	7500	166	13367
50g Whirls	.1597	1.11	3.42	1.93	6.48	59.5	12450	174	23190
50g Cheese 'n' Garlic Sticks	.1843	.94	3.4	1.93	6.48	63.9	18750	186	37309
50g Chilli Mexican Sticks	.1954	.99	3.4	1.93	6.48	61.9	36225	180	69864
50g Cheese 'n' Fibre	.2528	1.53	3.73	1.93	6.48	47.8	12500	143	20422
Totals for 50 gramme						**58.1**	**87425**	**170**	**164152**
Dip Snacks									
Snacks Prawn Dip	.1308	2.37	4.73	1.93	6.48	42.3	0	320	0
Snacks Chilli Dip	.1285	2.57	4.53	1.93	6.48	35	14078	254	20421
Tesco Prawn Dip	.2206	3.68	6.73	–	–	42	2016	330	5704
Tesco Chilli Dip	.2185	3.81	5.9	–	–	32	2166	218	4054
Totals for Dip Snacks						**37**	**30490**	**270**	**47540**

Table 9.5 cont.

Product	Labour per case	Mtl cost	Net sales price	Agent comm	Rebate	Margin	Sales volume cases	Con tribu tion rate	Con tribu tion
	£	£	£	%	%	%		£/hr	£
Multi-pack									
Mixed Whirls	.4451	1.51	3.88	–	–	49.6	1097	93	2112
Mixed Monsters	.4631	1.51	3.88	–	–	48.6	7740	91	14605
Totals for Multi-pack						49.1	8837	91.7	18718
SPAR									
Spar Cheesy Puffs	.1609	1.13	3.5		4.5	61.4	10925	191	22414
Spar Crinkle Chips	.2004	.90	3.57		4.5	67.7	7481	215	17273
Spar Spicy Pasta	.1952	1.06	3.57		4.5	63.2	3741	201	3059
Spar Prawn Dip	.1411	2.27	4.85		4.5	47.9	3741	388	8307
Spar Peanut Butter	.1344	2.52	4.39		4.5	36.7	4138	269	6365
Spar Multi-pack	.6835	1.78	4.44		4.5	47.8	1841	69	4150
Total for Spar						56.5	58746	246.3	120764
SAFEWAY									
Safeway Puffs	.2252	1.74	4.26			54	11872	161	27244
Safeway Rings	.2432	1.60	4.26			57	11234	169	27150
Mickey Mouse Pack	.2750	1.46	4.26			59	15511	177	31590
Fred Flintstone Multi-pack	1.0414	3.73	7.25			34	2453	56	6080
Safeway Sweet'n'sour	.8875	2.49	7.33			54	2183	92	8629
Safeway Dip Snack	.3603	3.12	6.64			47.5	981	236	3100
Safeway Chinese Crackers	.4598	2.19	6.04			56	0	253	0
Safeway Valentines	.3527	3.17	4.83			27	1228	98	1605
Totals for Safeway						48.5	42462	155	105388
SAINSBURY									
Sainsbury Chip Sticks	.2850	1.66	5.7			66	6640	263	24933
Sainsbury Prawn Cracker	.2500	2.63	6.99			59	9505	359	39065
Sainsbury Prawn Dip	.2928	4.76	9.09			44	1900	353	7671
Sainsbury Monster Multi-pack	.8480	2.14	7.36			59	9505	101	41568
Total for Sainsbury						57	27550	269	113237
LONDIS (All 50 gm)									
Londis Curls	.2091	1.41	3.69		3	55	1875	146	3657
Londis Sticks	.2612	1.18	3.68		3	60	1250	159	2661
Londis Onion Rings	.2612	1.33	3.68			55.5	2184	148	4332
Londis Prawn Cocktail	.2438	1.33	3.68		3	56	1875	149	3742
Total for Londis						56.5	7184	150	14392

Table 9.5 cont.

Product	Labour per case	Mtl cost	Net sales price	Agent comm	Rebate	Margin	Sales volume cases	Con tribu tion rate	Con tribu tion
	£	£	£	%	%	%		£/hr	£
OTHER PRIVATE LABELS									
Morrisons						46.3	29774	64.1	40178
NISA					3	56	15346	151	30745
Littlewoods						62	2031	249	6531
ASDA						52	11875	227	23350
Others						44.5	99636	112	141456

'How often do you monitor delivery performance then – once a week?'

'That kind of frequency would be of no value to us at all. We measure delivery performance every day as part of our short-term control regime. Anyway, let's move on to processes.'

Processes

'As you may have observed, the production logistics are quite straightforward – in fact very simple. If you had the inclination you would have very little difficulty in starting up your own plant if you could gain customer acceptance of your own snack food brand. However, the static simplicity of the process sequence disguises the complexities that volume and production velocity create. That complexity cannot be eliminated by equipment alone. Let me start there, however.'

Investment programme

'Until eighteen months ago there had been no new equipment for five years. The company had been starved of capital investment. That accounts for the age profile of the production equipment (six to eight years). Since the buy-out, however, we have a capital expenditure commitment of £3 million for the first two years and £2 million of that has been budgeted for new process equipment and improvements to plant layout. However, the planned investment is not yet complete.'

'Have you targeted any particular area?'

'Not particularly, but you could say that some emphasis has been placed on wrapping machines, which do create bottlenecks and are most prone to breakdown. Most of the equipment is standard. Nevertheless, we do have some new equipment which, I suppose, could be classified as approaching state of the art.'

'At what stage of the process is that then?'

'Flavouring, believe it or not. Monitoring flavour injection rates to the flavouring plant used to be a manual procedure. The flavours used, by the way, are not an important cost component of the product, but there is a quality dimension. We used to receive a lot of customer complaints about over-flavouring. The most persistent complaint was the discovery of congealed product which consisted mainly of flavour concentrate. It has a dreadful taste, you can imagine, and it cost us a lot of money both in wastage detected here, and, more importantly, in discontinued accounts. We've also managed to reduce WIP by installing new conveyor systems, but you could hardly classify those as revolutionary or even state of the art.'

'You said earlier that you had made improvements to plant layout.'

'Yes, in terms of "process" this has been the area of most significant benefits. We've created dedicated lines which have been designed around product groups. This GT (group technology) approach has substantially reduced lead times and halved waste product. However, we haven't totally completed planned improvements to layout or flow. You will have noticed some work in progress being bagged in bulk and manually transported to the wrapping operation. We want to eliminate that type of product handling during the next year, but this will only marginally reduce the level – and at some expense.

'I wish that I could convince some of our people that lead time doesn't start and end in manufacturing. Sales order processing, for instance, takes far too long, it accounts for 25 per cent of total lead time, but no one believes that it's significant enough to investigate, let alone spend money to reduce it.'

'Does it cause a problem?'

'Of course it does. It adds lead time to the product and it fouls up production planning – just remember 80 per cent of what we produce is for firm orders. Sales have to realise that, internally, I'm their customer and at present they aren't providing me with good customer service. But time's running out – enough to have a brief glance at "programmes" and then I'll have to dash off.'

Programmes

Laker explained what he understood by 'programmes': 'Basically they're the routines, procedures and controls, from top to bottom of the business, that ensure that the whole is at least equal to the sum of its parts. In the first place the "sharp end" of the business must deliver the business plan every hour, every day of the month – not just at the end of the month or week – otherwise we don't get any shredded wheat for breakfast. Secondly, we have to meet the established platitudes of marketing: deliver the right product to the customer at the right quality and price at the right time.

'Problem is – every word in that statement needs defining. Let me give you an example: the customer. The customer in this business, to a very large extent, defines the "manufacturing task" *and* the breadth and depth of control that's required in the operation. For example, the private brands – Sainsbury, Tesco,

Safeway et al. – are very fussy about quality and specification not to mention delivery lead time, delivery reliability and shelf life available after manufacturing. On the other hand, small corner shops who buy our "own brand" aren't half as fussy. This is a simplistic categorisation of customers, but they are distinct areas of business and a major problem I have at the moment is a result of indecision in this area.'

'What kind of indecision?'

'The company has been unable to make up its mind which to target – private brand or own brand. Last month it was private brand, but the emphasis dissolved after we discussed the quality implications and had a closer look at the margins we could get.

'Look, you'll have to excuse me, but I have a meeting. I've got a pile of information about planning and control, quality management and human resource management for you to study. I'll see you tomorrow I hope.'

Planning and control and logistics – the 'game plan'

Laker had prepared an abstract of facts relating to demand management and logistics (see Exhibit 9.5). Some, but not all, of the information was new to Ashworth, especially that on new product development and shelf life.

The 'game plan' for manufacturing planning and control was based on Joseph Orlickey's (1975) 'plumbing diagram' (see Fig. 9.3). Orlickey originally developed this method of viewing planning and control in the context of manufacturing resource planning (MRP II) methodology. However, it had been widely developed as a paradigm for control in organisations where MRP II was not possible. The purpose of the game plan is to ensure that through regular communication, measurement and control, business plan objectives were met on a daily basis. The methodology could be described as a system of 'objectives down – plans up'.

There are basically three areas in the game plan. First, top management (aggregate planning level). This covers all top-level business planning from sales and operation planning to financial objectives and budgets.

The second level is a logical disaggregation of the top level. However, at this level, planning and control are driven by the master product scheduling (MPS) process, which is expressed in actual products and planning volumes of each product for a specified time horizon. Master scheduling at Snacks Ltd had no more than a two-week horizon and the MPS was reviewed twice a week.

It is a prerequisite that the MPS be achievable in detail. It cannot be a 'wish list from management' or the legitimacy of the whole system would disintegrate. It must be realistic in terms of material and capacity availability. The MPS is the 'bridge' between supply/demand and business objectives. It is also the 'software' which drives and determines material requirements and capacity at a detailed level.

Exhibit 9.5 Notes on demand management and operations logistics

1 *Average product mix*
60% own brand (Snacks Ltd)
40% private brand (Tesco, Sainsbury, etc.)

2 *Delivery performance to first promise to customer*
Better than 96% on time, target is 99%
Delivery performance is measured every day

3 *Lead times*
Total provisioning and manufacturing lead time = 2 days to 2 weeks
Packaging film for existing product = 1 week
Metallised film for existing product = 4 weeks

4 *New product development and lead times*
Company introduces approximately 8 new products each year, only 25% are successful over a 6- to 12-month period.

5 *Product development lead times for private brands*
No problem with raw materials (e.g. maize or pellets),
nearly ex-stock. Large delays are for private brand wrappers
(film or metallised bags). Design is completely under the control of the customers.
The lead time for wrapper design varies from 2 to 6 months for new products.
Development of new product including QA screening = 6 weeks approximately.
Customer acceptance takes, on average, 8 weeks.
Once wrappers are designed the lead times are as in 3 above.

6 *Requested delivery lead times from customers*
Anything from 3 days to 3 weeks.
Usually 3 days for own brand
Up to 3 weeks for private label (Sainsbury, etc.).

7 *Demand management*
See our game plan based on Joe Orlickey's 'plumbing diagram'. However, the following variables are important.

(a) *Production rate*
20,000 cases per day
120,000 cases per working week
i.e. 6 million packets of snacks per week (approx.)

Exhibit 9.5 cont.

(b) *Lot sizing*

'Lot for lot' as a general rule as 80–90% of production is based on firm orders not forecasts. Only 10–20% of production is based on forecasts (i.e. stock) and nearly 100% of this output is for Snacks Ltd brands. Forecasts are quite effectively 'consumed' by orders where we make for stock, despite questionable forecasting.

(c) There is very little seasonality in demand.

However, core products sales drop during school holidays by 30%. Private brand demand surges by 40% approximately before Christmas.

(d) Aggregate production planning horizon is 3 months (under continuous review).

Master scheduling horizon is 1 to 2 weeks (reviewed twice weekly).

8 *Shelf life allowed*

This varies from customer to customer but the range is 16 to 20 weeks from manufacture. Dependent on the customer the product must be no older than 4 to 6 weeks from manufacture if it is to be accepted, e.g. Tescos insist on no more than 4 weeks from manufacture.

The general rule is the larger the customer the shorter the shelf life.

9 *Finished stock in warehouse*

Average 2 weeks of demand

Range 1 to 3 weeks of demand

Target average 1.5 weeks

10 *Caveat on finished stock*

Accuracy of finished goods inventory is only approximately 85%. There is evidence of a significant level of 'shrinkage'. We have no procedures, yet, for 'cycle counting' to improve inventory record accuracy.

11 *Forecasting*

An 'indication' of what is required is forecast but no comprehensive forecasts are given. Applies to both own brand and private brand. Some forecast variance is measured but there is little time and therefore little attempt to measure in detail. This is due to the fact that most of our business is made to order and our lot-sizing policy is 'lot for lot' by order.

12 *Distribution and warehousing*

These operations have been subcontracted to third parties for two major reasons:

1 To reduce our cost base

2 Our core competence is not in transport and distribution but in developing, marketing/merchandising and manufacturing packet snack foods.

Other prerequisites for master scheduling are that:

- foundation data, such as bills of material (BOMs), inventory, routings and capacity data, are at least 95 per cent accurate
- no 'informal' systems are used by anyone in the business.

Ashworth was disturbed by Laker's admission that finished stock accuracy was only 85 per cent. Apparently the company did not carry out 'cycle counting' but had quarterly stock checks for the purposes of producing interim P & L account and balance sheet. Informal systems still operated in the business, but were being stamped out vigorously. One first line manager had been fired for

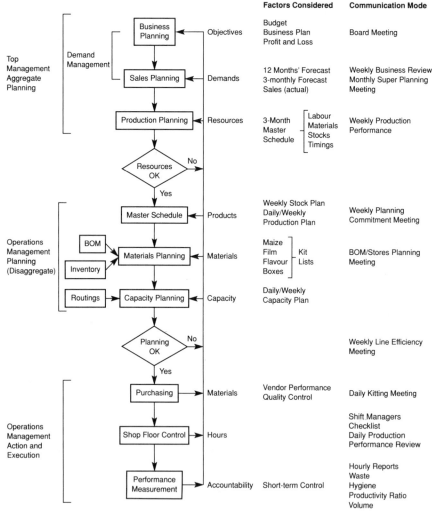

Fig. 9.3 Overview of manufacturing planning and control system and game plan for Snacks and Nibbles Ltd

persistently working to schedules kept in his desk drawer.

The bottom level in the system is that of execution and detailed monitoring of performance. The latter, at Snacks Ltd, was termed short-term control (STC). The indicators were basic but were measured and published on company notice boards, including one in the restaurant, on the hour every hour. The performance indicators used were waste, hygiene, productivity ratio and volume. These were defined in detail and all employees understood their significance.

To implement this type of game plan requires much more than a paradigm. It is essential that at every stage, from business plan downwards, objectives are achievable. Nothing should be overstated for the satisfaction of senior or middle management ego. This does not mean that the business should not attempt to improve continuously both its objective and performance.

Laker's only criticism of the manufacturing game plan was that a vital stage was missing right at the top: the business strategy. It had been argued that this was implicit in the business plan because it was based on expected business activity in terms of market forecasts of volumes and product. Laker's argument was succinct and he drew several analogies, i.e. just as you cannot divorce the production planning stage from business planning, a business plan cannot be created *ad hoc,* it requires a 'top management game plan' to drive it. He was obviously convinced that the company did not have one.

Quality

The approach to quality in development and manufacturing comprehensively covered everything from product development to the aesthetics of the product and its taste. An outline of the product quality parameters is shown in Exhibit 9.6.

Process control in the plant was gradually being taken out of the hands of quality control inspectors and transferred to operators (after appropriate training). Auditing quality control procedures was still the responsibility of quality assurance. 'Quality' was regarded by the company as a 'major requirement for continued success'. Quality assurance had, apparently, started from a low baseline after the buy-out, but abiding by the principles of quality control and consistency was beginning to improve performance (at least in manufacturing).

The need to improve quality arose from the need to reposition the company's products. Snacks Ltd was moving towards more expensive branded products (up to 40p per packet, some even more expensive) and increasing its private label accounts. Before and immediately after the buy-out most production had been concentrated on the 'cheap and cheerful' market (5–10p packets), where product quality was not considered of great importance. If the product was approximately the correct shape and tasted about right then it was OK. With the general repositioning of the company's products the need to improve both product and process control was becoming imperative. Even in the 'economy' market increasing competition was forcing quality to the top of the agenda as

Exhibit 9.6 Summary of specification/development process by product development and QC at Snacks and Nibbles Ltd

---

Bill of Materials (BOM) Specification

What the product is made of
e.g. maize, water, pellets.
Flavour to be used.

Routing Specification

How is the product to be manufactured - which process group?

Testing Procedure and Criteria

Tests for raw materials, WIP and finished product.
Outer packaging material – case size – appearance, printing.

Film or Metallised Film for Packaging

Label information – statutory regulations and legal information,
e.g. Trade Descriptions Act.
Procurement procedures, vendor analysis and selection.

Raw Materials

Ingredient specification – QC procedures at goods inwards.
Procurement procedures and vendor analysis and selection.

Work in Progress (WIP)

SPC (Statistical Process Control) procedures:
Extruded weight and moisture content;
After-drying weight and moisture content;
Flavour control;
Packaging weight control;
Aesthetics, e.g. extruded shape control.

Safety Analysis

Checklists to ensure that:
Ingredients are safe;
Processes are safe for employees.

---

an order-winning criterion, as was the need to secure repeat purchases in a market which was becoming more discriminatory.

Quality, however, did not embrace just product and process control. The company was adopting a quality strategy which covered the whole of marketing logistics from perception of need by the customer to the fulfilment of that need. This required quality policies for customer service, sales and merchandising, customer accounts, customer liaison in product development and delivery and distribution performance. Overall a broad image of quality issues was being addressed by the company. However, there was a caveat to all this and it was most diplomatically expressed by Stephanie Kenworthy when Ashworth met her.

'The management style at Snacks is the subject of much discussion within the operations team, that is, the team who actually run the factory as opposed to the senior management team who are divorced from the factory itself, because (a) they are in a separate office block, and (b) they concentrate on what they perceive to be the real issues. Therefore if management style is the way the workforce is influenced by its leaders to attain desired goals, in particular quality goals, a problem of some significance is sure to arise. The people who should be leading and influencing every aspect of the business in order to manage and steer it through a traumatic period of change are not participating in the factory management as distinct from the business management.

'This has led to a curious state of affairs. First, the company's senior management, including Mike Hoylake, do not get involved with plant goal-setting, motivation, 'walking the job' problem-solving, etc. Instead they adopt what can only be described as a 'fly by wire' approach, concentrating only on the production figures and reacting to them as they feel appropriate. This reaction comes in two forms: they say nothing if performance is perceived to be acceptable or attack everyone if it falls below some arbitrary expectation.

'However, a second strange practice has arisen (I doubt if it's unique to this company): on the one hand, operations management are continually attempting to second-guess what is about to happen to specific business management issues, whilst, on the other, they attempt to create a stable environment within the factory, e.g. setting their own goals and attempting to manage current changes as effectively as possible. This task is made all the more difficult because operations are blindfolded – they do not know what changes are going to occur or when. The result is that day-to-day running of the plant is either difficult to control or out of control. The problem is definitely one of senior management reaction. They are continuously obsessed with what happened last week rather than what is happening now or what may happen next week. This ensures that control is still 'bottom up' and that includes quality control.

'It is generally agreed that this management style is a result of the situation in which Snacks finds itself. The buy-out was heavily financed by investment from the City and this, coupled with an aim to float the company within the next three to five years, has meant that short-term gains are seen as superordinate and the monthly bottom line is regarded as the only test of performance.'

She also echoed something which Laker had referred to earlier: 'Despite the management environment, operations have made a significant contribution to improving the quality of the product and the service to customers through QA and improved manufacturing planning and control. However, these improvements at the sharp end aren't matched by equivalent improvements at the administrative end of the business. In production we are attempting to ensure that all operators pay clear attention to the processes they are operating and to control them in a way that prevents problems occurring, rather than trying to sort problems out after they have happened. This latter type of problem-solving only creates waste and delays in production.'

PEOPLE
HRM basics

The plant operated a three-shift production system, i.e. 6 a.m. to 2 p.m., 2 p.m. to 10 p.m. and 10 p.m. to 6 a.m., Monday to Friday. On Saturday there were only two shifts (excluding the Friday night shift): 6 a.m. to 2 p.m. and 2 p.m. to 10 p.m.

Headcount and cost breakdown

The production-related headcount was as follows:

- directs   182
- indirect warehouse   was 9; prior to subcontracting
- production control   3
- purchasing   2
- maintenance   12
- quality assurance   10

The percentage cost breakdown in production was approximately:

- materials   60 per cent
- labour   10 per cent
- energy   less than 1 per cent
- overhead   the remainder

The cost breakdown was similar to most engineering organisations.

Lost time

The company did not have any strikes but sickness and absenteeism were running at 11 per cent (8 per cent lowest). There were a number of reason for this. In summer the official holidays in the company are not synchronised with local holidays, nevertheless workers always find good reasons for having as much as a week off to compensate for this anomaly.

Laker saw absenteeism as a symptom of a deeper malaise. He had designed a questionnaire to identify the level of morale within the factory in the context of rapid change in the organisation. The response rate (approximately 40 per cent) was quite good for research associated with organisational behaviour. The major themes which emerged from this questionnaire were as follows:

- the workforce would like more control over how the work is presented to them
- feedback is required to see how well the team is performing

- working as a shift or in small teams would be desirable
- communication from management concerning the profitability of the plant could be improved
- training needs to be designed to be specific to the needs of the individual
- the shop-floor workers actually care about their contribution to the performance of the team and would like to be personally thanked when they have performed well.

Laker had considered the responses and had taken the view that changes were needed in organisation, communication, feedback and training in particular. Most of the action he decided to take had no adverse cost effect (some reduced cost). At worst no improvement would take place, and at best he would end up with a more highly motivated, flexible and productive workforce.

He first addressed the organisation structure in manufacturing. It had consisted of a hierarchy with specific responsibilities for each layer, as is shown in Fig. 9.4. The structure and its supporting system allowed little flexibility between the machine operators. Each machine operator reported to a supervisor, who would control his or her activities. The machine operator's role was more that of machine-minder, having very little control over other activities on the shift.

Two of the main themes which had emerged from the research were the need to be in more control and the desire to work in teams. The organisational structure was modified, as shown in Fig. 9.5, to produce the desired change and meet these needs. The supervisor level was removed and replaced by a senior team leader who operated a packing machine along with other team leaders.

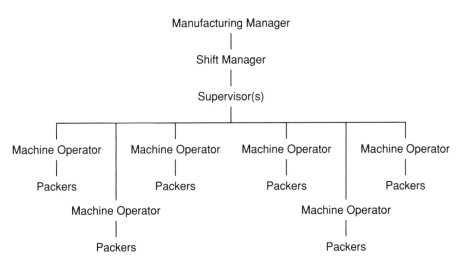

Fig. 9.4 Snacks and Nibbles: Original organisational structure in manufacturing (regimental)

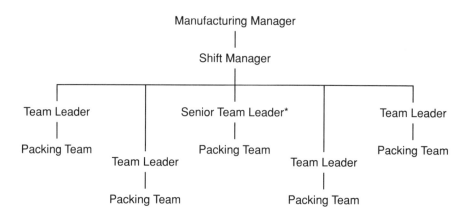

* Also an operator

Fig. 9.5 Snacks and Nibbles: New organisational structure in manufacturing

The structure operated such that a senior team leader would determine the level of team leaders required for each day's production, with any excess joining the packing teams. It was then the senior team leader's responsibility to follow the production plan, fully utilising the labour available. This role was previously carried out by the supervisor, who would inform the machine operators what to make and then walk away and let them continue, returning periodically to comment on the progress being made.

Communication

Once the new organisation structure was in place, improved communication channels were introduced. These involved an initial programme where the senior team leaders, or team leader, were informed of their new role and responsibility. Part of that role was to brief their own teams that they were performing against standards set by Laker. The senior team leaders ran these sessions once every two weeks with senior members of management asked to attend as and when required. To ensure the first three or four sessions were successful a certain degree of input was required by the shift manager. Simple problems were discussed and actioned immediately to give the team the feeling, at least, that they would influence the factory.

The team leader sessions also required a more formal communication seminar. These seminars take place every month. Key performance indicators are presented to the teams (turnover/employee, profit/employee, etc.) by a senior member of the management. It is not the purpose of the meeting to produce action to correct any adverse situation – the information is aggregate and historical – but to give the teams information for discussion. If there are any successes in the previous month's figures, they are usually highlighted to reinforce the team structure and its contribution to the company. Even during a poor month positive feedback concludes the session.

Feedback

The type of communication described above had the effect of improving overall awareness and ensured a forum for discussion. However, it did not influence the factory on an hourly basis, so Laker defined a few hourly performance criteria (referred to as short-term control or STC) and explained them in detail to the team leaders. The STC had served its purpose well and helped focus each shift on its key performance indicators. The purpose was to direct the factory towards more global or aggregate targets which are discussed at team briefing sessions.

Training

The whole emphasis of training at shop-floor level had been to increase flexibility and to extend operator competence across more than one process. It should be noted that the induction and training period for a new employee was approximately four weeks and the period required to become fully competent approximately six months.

Training was now being given in the context of the new organisation structure. The new role and responsibility of the team leader had to be fully understood before implementation. Training was undertaken across all three shifts to ensure the new role could operate effectively. The team leaders were now responsible for their own team of packers and the subsequent output from that team. This increased responsibility gave the team the freedom to ascertain how they would tackle each day's production and in what order.

Once the role was established, training was given to each team leader on specific aspects of the work. External training courses were devised with equipment suppliers to ensure that new equipment was effectively utilised and maintained. It was expected that team leaders would return to Snacks and pass their new knowledge to other team members.

Team leader training remained important, however. Laker wanted the specific involvement of all team members. He had introduced on-line quality control to the packing teams, who now had the specific responsibility for package coding, ensuring average weight, integrity of bag seals and product quality. The teams had welcomed the opportunity to control their own quality in a formal way. It had the added benefit that the Quality Control Department could concentrate upon more important quality aspects within the business such as vendor rating and auditing.

There had been some dramatic improvements in performance during the twelve months since the new organisation and teams had been introduced which appeared fully to justify the changes, shown in Exhibit 9.7.

Exhibit 9.7 Situational changes at Snacks Ltd over 12 months to June 1992

Labour, Productivity and Quality Résumé

1   Productivity increase of 42 per cent.

2   Reduction in shop-floor waste from 11 to 2.3 per cent .
Objective during the next 12 months: 1 per cent.

3   Volume maintained with a significant reduction in workforce.
(Reduction of 50 in workforce.)

4   Plan attainment increased from 64 to 90 per cent.
Objective in next 6 months: 95 per cent at least.

5   Customer service levels increased from 80 to 96 per cent.
Objective during next 6 months: 99 per cent.

6   Absenteeism reduced from 11 to 7 per cent.
Objective over next 12 months: 4–5 per cent.

MARKETING AND SALES

Two days after his arrival at the company Ashworth had arranged a meeting with the Marketing Director, Frank Fischer.

'The trouble with this business,' Fischer intoned mournfully, 'is that every man and his dog wants a slice of the action in the economy sector.'

Ashworth made an obvious observation: 'The big players do seem to be accumulating market share in the economy sector, don't they?'

'They do, but the major brands' market share hasn't changed all that much over five years from 1987 to 1991. In 1987 the brand share of KP, Smiths, Golden Wonder and Walkers was about 78 per cent, with KP the market leader. In 1991 their market share was approximately 77.5 per cent. Not much of a movement except that KP has increased its share at the expense of all the others. Look, here's the trend.' (See Table 9.6.)

Table 9.6 Extruded snacks: brand market shares by value (%)

	1987	1988	1989	1990	1991
KP	32.7	36.0	37.0	37.5	39.0
Smiths	29.5	29.5	29.0	28.0	27.0
Golden Wonder	11.0	9.0	8.0	8.5	8.5
Walkers	5.3	3.9	3.5	3.0	3.0
Private label	8.3	7.8	8.0	8.5	9.0
Other brands	13.2	13.8	14.5	14.5	13.5

Source: Trade Estimates/Euromonitor

Fischer continued: 'And United Biscuits will increase its market share again in 1993 when it has acquired Derwent Valley Foods and the Phileas Fogg brand. But we're not in direct competition with Derwent Valley – yet!'

'Then who do you compete with and how do you intend to compete in the future?'

'That's both a trick question and a double-barrelled one. Let me break it down into a marketing analysis: (a) the effects of competition; (b) market segmentation; and (c) developments in retail distribution.'

The effects of competition

'Snacks Ltd has been in the extruded snacks business for approximately twenty years now and during that period there have been major changes in ownership and control in the industry, but by and large we, believe it or not, have benefited from the growing dominance of top brands such as Walkers, KP, Golden Wonder, etc. They have definitely forced smaller organisations to improve their quality and they have demonstrated to retailers that the market has growth potential. This has not harmed us; on the contrary, we have been quite successful market followers, particularly over the past two years since the buy-out. There is also terrific potential with extruded snacks for product innovation. The same potential doesn't exist to the same extent with crisps and nuts where product shape and variety are limited by the raw materials.'

'Has the recession had any effect on growth?'

'Not a lot. There was a 6 per cent growth in the market from 1990 to 1991. It did have a depressing effect on the premium sector of the market, but the economy sector where we predominate was, and still is, quite resilient. It's funny, and I've not figured it out yet, but the premium sector for crisps increased its share to more than 18 per cent in 1991. The word "premium" in the crisps market means all crisps retailing at more than 20p for a 25-gram packet. It's also interesting to note that although crisp sales in the standard price bracket (below 20p a packet) increased by £14 million, the standard sector share of the market dropped from 84 to 82 per cent. Which brings me to my next point: market segmentation in the extruded snack market.'

Market segmentation

'There are three broad targets in the extruded snacks sector: the family segment, with about 55 per cent; the child segment, about 36 per cent; and the adult segment, accounting for the remaining 9 per cent, but growing at the expense of the child segment. These are then further segmented by price and product shape and flavour.'

'Aren't most of your products targeted at the children's market?'

'Yes they are, it's been our forte for a number of years – especially what you define as "cheap and cheerful" [see Table 9.2].'

'I would have thought that it was a price-sensitive end of the market.'

'It is and it isn't – you must remember that Mummy or Daddy pays for the snacks. Nevertheless we did have to reconsider our pricing policy during 1991. You see our major competitors (that includes KP) and ourselves needed more margin at the "cheap and cheerful" end. We increased our 5p and 10p snacks to 6p and 12p respectively.'

'And what was the market reaction?'

'Adverse. We had significant volume shortfalls after the increase, but although these prices represented a 20 per cent increase, we don't believe that price sensitivity is the whole answer because KP lost only a small share of the "cheap and cheerful" end and is continuing with the 6p brands. We think that a single-coin transaction is more important than price for young purchasers. We'll need to lobby the government for the introduction of 6p and 12p coins. It's amazing how discriminating children are.'

'But why is KP able to continue with 6p brands if a single-coin purchase is a prerequisite?'

'There are a number of reasons: (a) KP offered better value for the 6p than we did; (b) our 6p and 12p products are sold at school tuck-shops and the like, where KP doesn't compete significantly; and (c) KP promoted the repriced product better than we did. The upshot was that we had to relaunch 5p and 10p products this year at a large merchandising and sales effort expense.'

'This might sound obvious,' Ashworth said, 'but aren't you caught in a price trap with these economy products?'

'Yes we are, and currently it's a top priority of mine to get out of it.'

Ashworth intervened again. 'I think that I've diverted you from your definition of the market in terms of product shape, taste, etc.'

'Not really. Product shape/taste and fuller analysis of price points is a natural continuation. Our child-targeted products fall into two categories: animal and monster snacks, which are 5p and 10p economy, and standard shapes such as Puff Balls, which sell at 15p but are also available in 20p and 25p packs.

'Family-targeted products are usually priced at 20p or over and include Puff Balls and Whirls. The equivalent from KP are Hula Hoops.

'The adult market is becoming very complex and a lot of innovative new products are being introduced to maintain interest. We have ethnic snacks such as Mexican Sticks and Chinese Crackers. We also capitalise on current health fads by offering "added fibre" products such as 50g Cheese Fibres and low-fat products. The premium price Dip Snacks which incorporate extruded snacks and a sauce dip are almost exclusively for adults.'

At this point, Fischer produced some information he had prepared: a product contribution analysis (see Table 9.5) and the list of equivalent competitor brands and price points shown in Table 9.7. Although he had already seen the contribution analysis, Ashworth made some mental calculations. 'Is this a sample of production in this financial year?'

Table 9.7 Retail prices of selected extruded snacks

Brand	Size/Weight	Price (pence)	Market Sector
Redmill Krunchie Puffs	No weight on packet	5	Child
Redmill Yankee Stars	– " –	5	Child
Snacks Ltd Cheesy Whirls	– " –	5	Child
Snacks Ltd Monster Teeth	– " –	5	Child
Burtons Potato Puffs	– " –	10	Family/Child
Redmill Animals	– " –	10	Child
Snacks Ltd Monster Snack	– " –	10	Child
Snacks Ltd Salt & Vinegar Whirls	– " –	10	Family/Child
Londis Thunder Cats	– " –	10	Child
Burtons Fish'n'Chips		15	Family
Bensons Chinese Crackers		17	Family – Ethnic
Golden Wonder Wotsits		20	Family
Sooner Snacks Wonder Wheat Crunchies	35 gm	20	Adult/ Health-conscious
Golden Wonder Nik Naks	35 gm	20	Family
Sooner Snacks Crunchy Fries	30 gm	20	Family
KP Hula Hoops		20	Family
KP Frisps		21	Adult/Health-conscious
KP Mexican Chips		26	Adult – Ethnic
KP Capers		27	Adult
Bensons Onion Rings	50 gm	32	Family/Adult
Londis Prawn Cocktail	50 gm	32	Family/Adult
Redmill Prawn Cracker	50 gm	32	Family/Adult
Snacks Ltd Chilli Mexican Sticks	50 gm	35	Family – Ethnic

Prices may be slightly lower in major grocers and slightly higher in CTNs.

'Yes.'

'I understand your concern about the economy end of the market. The 5p and 10p range account for about 70 per cent of volume but only 50 per cent of contribution.'

'Yes, it's a major cause for concern at board level. We don't wish to abandon this sector – it's been our bread and butter for a number of years – but we have to reposition them. If we have to, we'll follow KP. We have to get larger margins if we hope to satisfy the City.'

'But how do you intend to reposition the economy products?'

'Well . . .' Fischer paused to consider, 'we can change the product; the way we brand it; the way we package it; promote it; but more importantly the retail channels we select. In short we have to make these products less price-sensitive; be perceived as good value for money even with a two-coin transaction.'

'But I thought a two-coin transaction was a dead end. Why don't you switch your emphasis to higher-priced bands and avoid competing with KP?'

Fischer appeared irritated. 'We *can't* avoid competing with KP and Smiths and Golden Wonder. Just let me describe the retail channels. Everyone outside the industry is under the impression that the large grocery multiples are the major channels. There are various sizes of grocery outlets, not all are as big as the multiples such as Sainsbury. Multiples, it has to be admitted, are the largest retail channel, accounting for as much as 60 per cent of sales of snack foods. But this proportion has remained fairly constant for at least seven years; it's even fallen slightly.'

'Has any generic channel increased its share then?'

'Oh, yes – which brings us to the third element in our analysis: retail developments.'

Developments in retail distribution

'Confectioners, tobacconists and newsagents (the so-called CTNs) have increased share from about 15 to 20 per cent during the last five/six years.'

'Aren't these the corner shops? I thought they were a dying breed.'

'Far from it – the multiples have forced them to differentiate. There will always be CTNs, in fact a whole new breed is emerging in the shape of large, franchised petrol service stations that not only sell petrol, but have mini-super-markets selling everything from spanners to pot plants and confectionery – but more importantly, snack foods. Have you seen Esso, Shell and BP promotions on TV? The least important promotional aspect in their copy is fuel. They're promoting the non-fuel-retailing side of their business.'

'I can see the advantages this particular sector offers. They have lots of out-lets nationwide, and I suspect they have nearly as much buying power as the larger grocers.'

'They do indeed, but what is of particular interest to me is the impulsive nature of purchasers of snack foods and a CTN and, more specifically, a service station provides an excellent channel for an impulse sale.' Fischer was warming to this subject. 'Just think of the combination: husband, wife and 2.4 children on a day out in the country or at the seaside. Driver needs petrol and the family need a comfort break. Then: "Mum, I'm hungry"; parents convince them-selves they're famished. Possible result: economy snacks for children, premium snacks for parents.'

'An interesting scenario, the implication being that you can sell a wide price range of product based on impulse buying patterns.'

'That's what's emerging and it provides a big advantage over the grocers. CTNs tend to have less price-sensitive customers, whereas the grocery chains have buyers with shopping lists, purchases are more planned, and the custom-ers are more sensitive to price – they expect a bargain.'

'What other outlets are there? I can only think of licensed premises.'

'Pubs and off-licences account for about 10 per cent of all snack food sales but only 6 per cent of extruded snacks. Licensed premises cater for the adult snacks market, particularly in crisps and nuts. These are most often sold as an accompaniment to alcoholic beverages and this leads to the major problem:

licensed premises stock only standard products. They aren't interested in product development. Anyway, there are far more interesting alternatives available to us outside CTNs and grocers.'

'What are they?'

'Well, we supply school tuck-shops all over the country, mainly with our 5p and 10p brands. The main problem with these is their price sensitivity. We also supply caterers, but they only account for about 3 per cent of retail sales of snacks, and of course we fill vending machines at railway stations, universities, schools, etc.'

'That must take a lot of sales effort?'

'It does. We have thirty self-employed sales agents paid only by results.'

'And do they provide the business with market feedback – market research?'

'Whatever information we receive from them is entirely anecdotal and never collated. However, in the cheap and cheerful child market we do have a good idea of what sells the product. Between four and seven, the stronger the flavour the better; between nine and twelve, shapes are the buying influence. I have to admit that in terms of market research we are also big company followers. In fact I would say we are almost, but not quite, order takers and not market makers and we have to change that.'

'How do you intend to go about that?'

'I want this company to be on site – in the multiples and CTNs – with the right product when the bell rings.'

The marketing/sales plan

'But you will still need a marketing strategy or plan to achieve this broad objective,' said Ashworth. 'What market segments are the most profitable to target, for instance?'

'We need a sales plan not a marketing strategy. I want this company to be in a position to target a different market every month if necessary. But more specifically, these are my basic objectives:

- I want Snacks to spread its risks over a wider market
- that means less emphasis on the economy sector and a concerted move towards the multiples and large CTNs
- this will ultimately lead to a wider product range, but ideally we could convert our own-brand products to private brands
- in addition to this, I would like to see a development of our premium brands
- more use of metallised packaging rather than polyethylene film: I admit it's more expensive but it doubles shelf life and that benefits the multiples, CTNs and us – we can increase stock and provide better service levels
- I want more successful brand launches; our success rate in this area is abysmal
- finally, I issued a short-term plan when we relaunched the 5p snack range. Its major objectives are to: get the main 5p brands stocked and featured;

double existing sales in CTNs; regain any lost outlets; remove KP 6p packets from the market nationally; and counter Golden Wonder in Scotland, the North West and Ireland.

These objectives will assist sales in more 10p products.'

Ashworth had to intervene: 'There are just two queries. First, it's a bit of a tall order to expect KP sales to collapse in the manner you have described. Secondly, won't this current emphasis on the economy range deflect you from your longer-term objectives for the multiples and premium market?'

'That's the conventional wisdom: KP isn't bullet-proof and we are offering a price advantage in a price-sensitive market; besides, sales agents become highly motivated when they are given almost impossible objectives to achieve. Your second question is easily answered: we have a large interest in the economy sector at present and we must consolidate that position to finance the business for a concerted move into the multiples and premium brands.'

'What do you see as the major advantages of trading with Sainsbury and the like?'

'First of all, fewer accounts, fewer bad debts and less administration. Second, fewer salesmen, therefore less cost. Third, multiples have more resources for research – we could even use them as test markets for our own brands.'

'Don't most of the multiples insist on their own private brands? Isn't there a possibility that you will lose your own brand identity?'

'Not entirely; we would be able to sell our own brands in about 20 per cent of the multiples and all of the CTNs. Anyway a certain degree of anonymity is not undesirable in this business especially if you're a small player like us. It reduces the risk of attention from the big boys such as United Biscuits.'

At this point Fischer called the meeting to a close. Ashworth left the Marketing Director's office slightly confused. Most of what Fischer had said did not quite add up. He decided that on the next occasion he would press home far more searching questions to pin him down on the business's marketing strategy. 'Perhaps,' he was thinking aloud, 'I ought to call it the sales/marketing plan.'

FINANCIAL DIRECTION, CONTROL AND PHILOSOPHY

After the meeting with Fischer, Ashworth arranged an early appointment with Gillian Snowden, the Financial Director. After discussing her career up to joining Snacks, and the condition of the company at the time of the buy-out, Ashworth remarked: 'I guess that the first year of trading was difficult.'

'Yes it was; we had some sleepless nights, but we stuck to our business plan with one or two modifications.'

'What was the basis of the business plan?'

'To rectify fundamentals such as reducing unnecessary cost and improving cash flow. The place was overmanned and inefficient. We also had to develop new brands and abandon the ones which weren't performing. Our financial target was to increase gross margin to above 50 per cent and pre-tax margin to 15 per cent in the first year. It was ambitious, and we almost achieved those figures. Unfortunately, rising interest rates were responsible for missing pre-tax objectives.'

'They haven't helped to improve last year's result have they?'

'Absolutely! But that provides us with lots of incentive to become more cost effective. Current rates are probably too high, but they're part of our environment. Unfortunately there are too many businesses in this country with a tendency to attribute poor performance to their environments – it's a form of "buck-passing" in my opinion. It used to be credible to blame deteriorating results on the competition (foreigners in particular), the economic climate or some government legislation. Fortunately most of these excuses are becoming "paper thin" because many UK companies do more than survive in adversity. From my experience the winners are those who concentrate on improving internally with effective marketing; better quality products and service; improved control inside the business; better trained workforce and so on. Actually most of the areas addressed by your questionnaire.' (See Exhibit 9.9.)

'I'm pleased you read it, but how would you describe business performance in the first two years and, more generally, how do you intend to improve in the longer term?'

'The business is beginning to fulfil its profit potential. We have continued to improve on the cost side. For example, distribution and warehousing are now variable costs, not a fixed overhead. We subcontracted these functions, not because they're unimportant, but because we aren't distribution and warehousing specialists. The investments we made in new plant, equipment and refurbishments have also paid off in terms of higher productivity, morale and image. However, we have wasted too much money on dud brand launches.'

'Laker and Fischer tell me that only 25 per cent of new brands are successful.'

'I would put the figure nearer 20 per cent, but that's academic. KP does far better than that. Incidentally, have you heard about the débâcle over the retail pricing of core product?'

Ashworth nodded.

'Well, that's an excellent example of launching dud brands. We lost a lot of turnover – in the region of £160,000 – and profit of course. Then there was the cost of relaunching 5p and 10p brands. We made the original decision on a purely computational basis at board level. It was argued that if KP could re-price successfully so could we and it appeared to be a painless route to improved margins. *I* should have known better – we aren't very good at making sophisticated decisions yet.'

'Sophisticated? In what way?'

'It's best explained anecdotally: in the early days we were very busy correcting fundamental, almost day-to-day, problems. For example, it once took more than one month after delivery to invoice almost 25 per cent of our customers.'

'I'll bet that caused a cash problem.'

'It did; we could report a monthly profit and yet our overdraft was rising. But the point is that the problem was fundamental and could be addressed and rectified very quickly by improving systems. Even improvements to budget development and control, with a longer gestation to implement, was a system improvement.' (See Exhibit 9.8 – Summary of July 1992 budget.)

'You see,' she continued, 'all these problems were important, but nonetheless relative minutiae. However, they absorbed 80 per cent of our time and when we had to make sophisticated – strategic – decisions we treated them like a system problem. We were obviously out of practice . . . and that brings me to your question of improving in the longer term.'

'Yes. How do you intend to go about it?'

'Well – though I hate metaphors – we have to learn how to take our eyes off the ball and start looking for the goalposts, i.e. decide on the best direction to take the company rather than being totally absorbed by the monthly accounts. To achieve this there are two fundamental prerequisites: first, we have to maintain external, City, confidence in the company. This, we believe, is now forthcoming. The board's intention is to float the company in three years and reduce gearing to around 25 per cent – currently it's 150 per cent. Secondly, we need to have more self-confidence in our own decisions. That requires higher-quality information from better systems.'

'What kind of systems improvement do you envisage as necessary?'

'There are too many "islands" of information in the business. They consist of unintegrated databases and informal systems throughout all the business functions – finance, sales/marketing, manufacturing, etc. Look: this is the level of information and logistics integration I would like to see at Snacks Ltd.'

She handed Ashworth a sheet of A4 paper (see Fig. 9.6), which he studied for a moment. The logic on the flow chart was almost identical to the diagram he had obtained from Laker (Fig. 9.3).

'What do you think of it then?'

Ashworth gave a studied answer. 'Well, there's nothing novel about it at all. However, its very simplicity disguises a tremendous amount of management change for the business and a potential culture shock for many of the people at Snacks.'

'You're absolutely right; it does represent a sea change in the business. The trauma can be diminished if we manage the change carefully. However, I must make my own position clear. The days are gone when the financial function of a business could adopt a passive role. That attitude represents an abandonment of responsibility in my book, because the ultimate objectives of a commercial

Exhibit 9.8 Snacks and Nibbles Ltd: Summary of cost centre analysis overhead

	July 1992 Actual	July 1992 Budget	Unrevised Budget 92/93
Admin/Fin Overhead			
Admin Payroll	26106	22900	274800
Admin Overhead	29694	23750	251489
Total Overhead	55800	46650	526289
Total Includes:			
Admin Bad Debt	5038	1850	21000
System Development & Training	520	740	8880
System Charges	3809	4000	46020
Sales Overhead			
Sales Payroll	18627	19000	228000
Sales Overhead	59648	71010	852120
Total Overhead	78275	90010	1080120
Total Includes:			
Sales Agents Commission	28875	30900	370800
Sales Promotion	680	3250	40650
Sales Demonstration	975	2600	33800
Sales Advertising	4125	16500	107250
Artwork & Promotional Info	8000	1000	12000
Royalty Payments	1824	2500	29325
Product Development & QC Overhead			
Payroll	11776	11800	153400
Overhead	10545	3400	74800
Total Overhead	22321	15200	228800
Overhead Includes:			
New Product Development Costs	5600	600	55000
Training Costs	510	900	11700
Factory Overhead			
Payroll (Indirect)	48449	45300	611550
Overhead	100491	94700	928450
Total Overhead	148940	140000	1540000
Overhead Includes:			
Power Costs	20580	21210	233310
Engineering Payroll	23400	18000	235000
Management Payroll	25049	27300	386550
Equipment Maintenance	40194	58250	596400

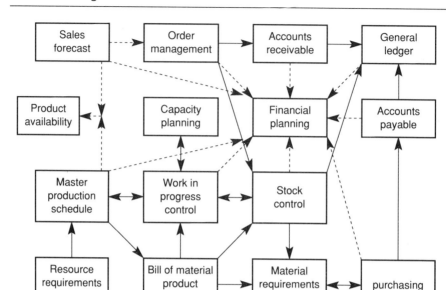

———— formal linkages

------ semi-formal linkages

Fig. 9.6 Snacks and Nibbles Ltd: Outline of proposed integration of management information systems and logistics

organisation are all economic ones; therefore every decision that's made must be directed at achieving them. Let me give you an example. I'm an advocate of more investment in both new products and hardware, but not before we can confidently finance it out of earnings. But more importantly, not before we've determined the best way to compete. At present that is not at all clear to the board. We still have far too many distractions and we're handicapped with low-quality information.'

'You obviously regard information as a strategic asset.'

'It has to be. It's more important than the materials we buy.'

The conversation lasted for a further half hour and during that time Gillian also related her philosophy towards business ethics. Her attitudes were very close to those of Milton Friedman, i.e. that business is most socially responsible and ethical when it attends strictly to its economic mission. She reinforced her argument as follows:

'We have a social and ethical responsibility to every stakeholder in the "value chain" of our business; suppliers, customers, shareholders and employees. Unfortunately most organisations forget the supply side of the enterprise when they talk of being "market driven" and regard the demand side – the customer – as the only important variable. At Snacks we also believe that "The customer is King", but in addition, we believe that one of the basic rules of society (and business) is to pay bills promptly. In this respect we have chosen to be more ethical (I prefer to call it more businesslike) with our suppliers by reducing our creditor days to payment. This policy "drives" a number of internal and beneficial forces:

- it guarantees the need for effective credit control for our customers;
- it has improved our credit screening procedures for potential new accounts;
- it forces us to use working capital more effectively by, for example, increasing stock turnover, which is only achieved by a combination of improved forecasting and continually reducing lead times; and
- just as important, it contributes towards the solvency of our suppliers and improves their trust in us. In return we ask for higher quality, more flexibility and improved delivery performance from them.

'In business, ethics is not an issue which can be discussed in a ideological vacuum. It has to be related to business performance; they are not mutually exclusive as I've tried to demonstrate.'

The meeting had been invaluable to John, but he came away with the distinct impression that Gillian Snowden's systems approach could create tension amongst some of the managing shareholders.

THE SESSION

Ashworth had been at the receiving end of a variety of opinions from the Snacks management concerning its best competitive posture in the future and its current performance in existing markets. The views expressed weren't totally disparate but had been the source of a little confusion for him. He decided to approach Hobart. 'James, I need a clearer picture from your senior and middle management team of the degree of common perception they have regarding the criteria, I call them order-winning criteria, which they believe will give the company competitive advantage within the industry. I also wish to discover how they believe the company is performing against the same criteria. Look, here's the basic format and criteria. I want them to rank both order-winning criteria (OWC) and performance (P).' He showed Hobart the ranking form (see Fig. 9.7).

Hobart considered the criteria and the ranking scheme to be applied. 'It's fairly broad, but comprehensive, and these criteria do touch on most areas of the business. I suppose this will provide us with a rough and ready gap analysis of the business.'

Ashworth went on to explain the procedure he wished to adopt. 'On this first occasion I would like each manager present to rank OWC and performance individually, without any collaboration. I know it appears a little subjective but I want them to rank the importance of each OWC from 1 to 10, i.e. 1 is unimportant, 10 is essential and provides significant advantage. However, it

(OWC) Order-Winning Criteria (Rank) 1 2		Unimportant 1 2		Marginally Important 3 4		Quite Important 5 6		Very Important 7 8		Essential 9 10			
(P) Performance Against Criteria (Rank)		Unacceptable 1 2		Marginal 3 4		Good 5 6		Very Good 7 8		Excellent 9 10		'Q' Qualifying Criteria	
Criteria		OWC	P	OWC	P	OWC	P	OWC	P	OWC	P	Q	P
Price													
Quality													
Product Range													
Product Volumes													
Customisation to Buyer Requirements													
Speed of Delivery													
Reliability of Delivery													
Availability (Geographically)													
Product (Leadership)													
Product (Aesthetics)													
Speed of Introduction of New Products													
Customer Liaison (New Products Schedules)													
Sales/Marketing Team													
Brand Name of Products													
Company Nationality													
Others													
Comments													

Note: 'OWC' and Performance ranking to be considered separately for the following broad market segments:
1   Economy Child Market;
2   Mid range Family Market;
3   Premium Adult Market.

Fig. 9.7 Order-winning criteria and performance

is essential that they identify "qualifying criteria", i.e. those criteria which are a prerequisite if you are to compete seriously at all.'

'I see you have accounted for market segmentation, and it's important because, as an example, price is almost a "qualifying criterion" in the economy market, but there is a degree of price insensitivity in premium markets. There's also the complication of our customer base. That provides another variable for segmentation.'

'I agree with you that the segmentation issue is more complex than I've proposed here, but I don't want the exercise to become overcomplicated at this session. I thought that the basic model of segmentation: child; family; adult markets could be roughly correlated with price segmentation, i.e. economy/child; mid-range/family; premium/adult.'

'What about current performance?'

'The same procedure applies to that. Each manager must rank the current performance of business against the same criteria. A rank of 1 is equivalent to lousy and 10 is excellent. It contains the same subjectivity, but most of your people will have some idea of performance. They can produce additional criteria if they think they are important.'

'What happens if there is no broad consensus?'

'You would have a problem on your hands, but I would be surprised if there was unanimity on every criterion. However, we do have an opportunity to measure the degree of agreement overall. But I do hope you will utilise this exercise beyond that.'

Assembled in the boardroom the following evening were Hobart, the five managers Ashworth had met on his first day and one of Fischer's account managers. Ashworth explained the purpose of the exercise.

'What purpose will all this serve John?' It was Fischer.

'I was about to answer that one. I've had assignments in a wide variety of organisations and uncovered an even wider variety of opinions and perceptions as to what constitutes success, even at board level.'

'Opinions and perceptions.' It was Fischer again. 'We operate in the world of reality. We don't perceive important facts of economic life – we know them and measure them!'

Hobart intervened: 'You can correct me if I'm wrong, Frank, but my understanding is this: there are so many variables which can create success – or failure – in the industry that it's almost certain there will be conflicting views as to which ones are the key result for success. Just for one moment cast a critical eye over the history of this industry. Look at the major structural changes which have taken place; not over twenty years but even during the last five. The criteria we are being asked to consider are dynamic. Their relative importance will change over time depending on dozens of environmental influences – economic climate, new brands, changing public taste, the competitive environment; and that includes competition between our customers. Let me cite one hypothetical scenario: how do you think we should respond if a major account requested us to reduce retail price on a packet of core product by 1p or even 2p?'

'We might have to grin and bear it. It would have an immediate effect on our gross margin. We would have to evaluate the benefits of retaining the business against the cost of lost margin or the cost of losing the account if we refused to reduce recommended retail price. If we wanted to keep the account and maintain margins there would have to be some rapid cost-cutting, but it is hypothetical.'

'It's not that hypothetical – look what Joe Public, not one account, did to our sales when we raised the price of core product. Besides, you're assisting my argument: we've considered only one variable, price, and already you can see it's a minefield. If you think price is an important criterion for success you should also consider our cost performance inside the business.'

'I take your point, but wouldn't it be useful for us to rank the importance to the company of each of these broad market segments? Also, we could possibly use these criteria as a basis for the measurement of customer satisfaction.'

Ashworth chipped in: 'You could certainly rank your markets, it would usefully extend the scope of this exercise. Your second suggestion falls into the category of market research and corporate responsibility.'

Hobart now closed the debate. 'Rank the markets by all means Frank, it's an exercise which is overdue, but remember to assess our current capability and future requirements in new markets whilst you're in the process. Now let's get on with it!'

The outcome of the session (see Fig. 9.8) made interesting reading for all of them.

Summarisation of comments by J Ashworth:

'Price performance related to cost base and competitors.'	*MD and Financial Director*
'Product volumes related to current capability.'	*Manufacturing Director and Financial Director*
'Brand name related to known brand awareness.'	*MD and Marketing Director*
'Customisation as a criterion is really only applicable to private label.'	*Marketing Director, MD, Manufacturing Director*
'Speed of introduction of new products has been evaluated in terms of competitor share of new brand and success rate of our own brand's launches.'	*MD, Marketing Director, Manufacturing Director*

Ranking scores

	Criteria	Economy/Child Market			Mid range/Family Market			Premium/Adult Market		
		Average Rank	Range Min. Max. Ranks	No. of 'Q's	Average Rank	Range Min. Max Ranks	No. of 'Q's	Average Rank	Range Min. Max. Ranks	No. of 'Q's
1	Price	6.8	5 Min 8 Max	3	8	6 Min 10 Max	1	8	6 Min 10 Max	
2	Quality	5.2	3 Min 6 Max	1	9	8 Min 10 Max	2	9	8 Min 10 Max	
3	Product Range	5.9	1 Min 9 Max	–	7	3 Min 9 Max		6.3	2 Min 10 Max	
4	Product Volumes	6	4 Min 8 Max	1	5	3 Min 9 Max		5.4	4 Min 8 Max	
5	Customisation to Buyer Reqirements	3.9	2 Min 6 Max	–	6	4 Min 10 Max		4.7	2 Min 9 Max	
6	Speed of Delivery	6.4	5 Min 10 Max	–	8.1	5 Min 9 Max	–	7.3	5 Min 9 Max	
7	Reliability of Delivery	7	5 Min 9 Max	1	7.8	5 Min 10 Max	1	8.5	7 Min 10 Max	1
8	Availability (Geographically)	6	3 Min 9 Max		6.3	3 Min 9 Max		6.9	3 Min 9 Max	
9	Product (Leadership)	6.4	5 Min 9 Max		7	6 Min 9 Max		8.7	6 Min 10 Max	
10	Product (Aesthetics)	5.6	2 Min 10 Max		6.9	4 Min 9 Max		8.3	7 Min 10 Max	
11	Speed of Introduction – New Products	6.9	3 Min 9 Max		7.3	3 Min 8 Max		7	3 Min 9 Max	2
12	Customer Liaison New Products/Schedules	4.4	3 Min 7 Max		5.4	3 Min 8 Max		5.3	2 Min 9 Max	
13	Sales/Marketing Team	7.1	4 Min 10 Max		6.3	4 Min 9 Max		5.3	3 Min 9 Max	
14	Brand Name of Products	7	5 Min 9 Max		9.3	7 Min 10 Max		9.1	8 Min 10 Max	
15	Company Nationality	3.9	2 Min 7 Max		3.7	3 Min 7 Max		4.4	3 Min 7 Max	
Others										
16	Brand Promotion	6.7	5 Min 8 Max		8.7	7 Min 10 Max		8.3	8 Min 9 Max	
17	Research and Development – New Products	6	4 Min 8 Max		7.8	6 Min 9 Max		8.7	8 Min 10 Max	1
18	Availability (Ex. Stock)	7	–	1	8	°	1	9	–	1
19	Market Research	7	6 Min 8 Max	1	8.2	7 Min 9 Max	–	8.5	7 Min 9 Max	1

Number of Respondents for other Criteria:
Brand Promotion – 3; Research and Development – 4; Availability (Ex.Stock) – 2; March Research – 5.

Fig. 9.8 Order-winning criteria and qualifying criteria

Fig. 9.8 cont.
Performance against criteria ranking scores

	Criteria	Economy/Child Market		Mid range/Family Market		Premium/Adult Market	
		Average Rank	Range Min/Max Ranks	Average Rank	Range Min/Max Ranks	Average Rank	Range Min/Max Ranks
1	Price	3.6	2 Min 7 Max	5.7	4 Min 7 Max	6.9	5 Min 9 Max
2	Quality	5.3	3 Min 8 Max	6	4 Min 9 Max	4.7	3 Min 6 Max
3	Product Range	6.1	4 Min 8 Max	7.4	6 Min 9 Max	7.3	5 Min 10 Max
4	Product Volumes	5		3.7	2 Min 6 Max	4.4	2 Min 6 Max
5	Customisation by Buyer Requirements	5.4	4 Min 8 Max	3	1 Min 5 Max	3.7	2 Min 5 Max
6	Speed of Delivery	6.3	4 Min 9 Max	7.3	5 Min 10 Max	7.7	6 Min 10 Max
7	Reliability of Delivery	6.1	4 Min 9 Max	7.7	4 Min 10 Max	7.4	5 Min 9 Max
8	Availability (Geographically)	8	6 Min 9 Max	5.9	4 Min 8 Max	6.6	5 Min 8 Max
9	Product (Leadership)	5.1	3 Min 7 Max	5	3 Min 7 Max	6	4 Min 9 Max
10	Product (Aesthetics)	3.9	2 Min 6 Max	6	4 Min 9 Max	6	4 Min 8 Max
11	Speed of Introduction – New Products	5.3	4 Min 7 Max	3.3	2 Min 5 Max	4.9	3 Min 7 Max
12	Customer Liaison – New Products/Schedules	4	4 Min 7 Max	3.3	2 Min 6 Max	3.1	1 Min 7 Max
13	Sales/Marketing Team	7.1	5 Min 10 Max	6.1	4 Min 10 Max	6.7	4 Min 10 Max
14	Brand Name of Products	6.4	5 Min 9 Max	7	5 Min 9 Max	5.9	4 Min 9 Max
15	Company Nationality	NOT RANKED BY RESPONDENTS					
Others							
16	Brand Promotion	5.3	4 Min 6 Max	5	4 Min 6 Max	5.7	5 Min 7 Max
17	Research and Development	6.8	5 Min 7 Max	6.8	6 Min 8 Max	6.3	5 Min 8 Max
18	Availability (Ex.Stock)	6.5	4 Min 9 Max	6.5	5 Min 8 Max	6	4 Min 8 Max
19	Market Research	5.8	5 Min 7 Max	5	4 Min 7 Max	4.4	3 Min 6 Max

Ranking of Markets

Four individuals ranked markets in terms of future importance. But not all used the same basis for segmentation.

Managing Director	Markets	All economy/ Own label	All Mid range/ Own label	Private label/ all prices
	Rank	6	8	9
Marketing Director	Markets	CTN/Child	CTN/Family	Multiple/Family
	Rank	7	9	9
Financial Director	Markets	Own label/ Economy	Private label/ Mid range	Own label/ Premium
	Rank	6	7	8
Manufacturing Director	Markets	Economy/Family	Mid range/Family	Premium/Adult
	Rank	6	7	8

A comment frequently made was that each variable of segmentation should be ranked separately, e.g.:

a price points   b age   c distribution   d product type
e geographic region   etc.

ASHWORTH'S SUMMING UP

A little more than two weeks had passed since Ashworth had met James Hobart in Swans. The time had flown and, to date, he pondered; this assignment had been one of the most pleasant, yet demanding, he had undertaken for a long time.

Hobart had provided him with a temporary office and a PC and had ensured that everyone in the company was aware of his task. Despite the very hectic nature of the business, he had met all the senior management at Snacks Ltd several times. They had all answered his questionnaire completely and provided significant quantities of additional information. None of them had been forced to cancel a meeting with him – it was apparent that they had all created space in their diaries.

Ashworth had not confined his interviews to the official and middle management of the company. He had met a wide variety of personnel, both in the manufacturing area and the administration office. He had taken lunch several times in the pleasant surroundings of the new works restaurant talking to supervisors, clerical and direct manufacturing employees. These informal meetings were not only concerned with the exchange of pleasantries. David Laker had facilitated these meetings, but left after making introductions so as not to constrain conversation.

Shop-floor personnel aired typical grievances about working conditions, salaries and job security, yet even these matters did not dominate the conversation.

Ashworth was impressed at the breadth and depth of understanding in areas relating to product knowledge, company marketing policy and the competition. 'After all,' one wrapping operator said, 'who doesn't shop at a supermarket nowadays? Our competitors are on display even when their products are disguised as supermarket brands.' They were also very proud of the achievements in the plant over the past twelve months. Everyone took great interest in the quality and productivity data which was displayed at several points in the plant including the restaurant.

From the top to the bottom of the organisation Ashworth was treated, and beginning to feel, like one of the team. He had even acquired a new nickname – 'Ashen'.

He felt, and probably looked, ashen as he surveyed the information before him. He had a 'mountain' of in-depth information from all the major areas of the business, including his own notes and perceptions which he abstracted following the numerous conversations he had had with directors and employees. He now had the task of making sense of it all in the report he had to publish for James Hobart and his colleagues. He decided that he should avoid any lingering contemplation of the data and the associated temptation of 'analysing it to death'. The major issues, as he saw them, had to be addressed immediately while they were relatively fresh and coherent in his mind. He framed a series of questions relating to both the business and its environment. 'Lets have a go,' he announced to himself as he put fingers to keyboard.

Ashworth's questions

1. Is the current marketing strategy consistent with the manufacturing capability and infrastructure?

2. What key marketing and manufacturing capabilities are required to compete effectively?

3. How can a company with relatively small 'mass' compete with market leaders?

4. Which 'generic' strategies are the most suitable for this type of business? What are the most viable strategic alternatives and how can they be made operational?

5. How does a company which is financially highly geared reconcile the short-term demands and time horizons of bankers and the City with the longer-term 'span of action' necessary for strategic planning and are these demands reconcilable?

6. Is it possible for Snacks Ltd to manage fairly radical change over a relatively short time period whilst simultaneously fulfilling its economic objectives?

7. How effective are the mechanisms which connect broad business objectives and short-term plan execution?

8. What important trade-off decisions are required in the detailed policy making areas of manufacturing in order to ensure the company is capable of achieving its manufacturing task?

9. In business and operations terms how best can the company compete: on quality; on productivity; on new products (brands)/processes etc?

Exhibit 9.9 Extract from John Ashworth's business questionnaire

The purpose of this business questionnaire is to familiarise myself with your industry and business environment.

All the information you provide will be treated confidentially.

Industry Profile

- What is the size of the UK market?
- Are export markets important to the industry?
- If so, what is the current size of the export market?
- What is your market share?
- How is the market segmented?
- How many segments do you serve?
- What proportion of sales do you spend on market research?
- What is your approximate share in the markets you serve?
- Is the industry market growing or contracting and at what approximate rate (disregard fluctuations due to business or economic cycles)?
- Are your markets 'seasonal' in terms of demand?
- Are there forecasts for market growth/decline?
- Who are the industry leaders and what is their approximate market share?
- Who are your major competitors?
- Do you export?
- If so, what proportion of your turnover is exported?
- What is average industry ROCE?
- What is your ROCE?
- What is your turnover?

Exhibit 9.9 cont.

- What are your margins? $\dfrac{\text{Profit before tax}}{\text{Sales}}$

- What are average industry margins?

- What are the main barriers to entry for new competition?
    - e.g. brand identity
        - capital requirement
        - access to distribution
        - access to essential inputs
        - economies of scale
        - other

- For existing competitors what are the 'rivalry determinants'?
    - e.g. industry growth
        - fixed costs/value added
        - product differences
        - brand identity
        - economies of scale
        - other

- Buyers – who are your largest customers as a percentage of your turn-over?

- Geographically – what are the major concentrations of your sales?

- Buyer power and buyer leverage – what are the main variables?
    - e.g. buyer concentration v. firms concentration
        - buyer volume
        - buyer information
        - ability to integrate backwards
        - substitute products
        - price/total purchases
        - product differences
        - brand identity
        - buyer profits
        - decision-maker incentives

- What proportion of your turnover is buyer's own brand?

- How long has your company been in business?

- Could you provide us with a brief company history?

Exhibit 9.9 cont.

Order-Winning and Qualifying Criteria

NB: **Order-Winning Criteria** are those which give you competitive edge and identify you as a preferred supplier.

Qualifying Criteria are those which you must have in order to compete at all or reasonably effectively.

Please rank the criteria from 1 to 10, where 1 is unimportant, 10 essential as an order-winning criterion. Please identify the qualifying criteria.

Price
Quality
Product range
Product volumes
Customisation to individual buyer requirements
Speed of delivery
Reliability of delivery
Availability
Product (leadership)
Product (aesthetics)
Speed of introduction of new products
Customer liaison (new products schedules, etc.)
The sales/marketing team and its personalities
The brand name of your products
The nationality of your company
Others

Manufacturing Audit

Orders

- What is the frequency of order receipt?

- What is the average size of order (value, quantity, etc.) and what is the distribution?

- How does demand vary?
    Seasonally
    Random business
    Other (e.g. business cycle)

- What proportion of (works) orders are initiated on the basis of sales forecasts rather than firm orders?

- Do you measure the accuracy of forecasts in order to improve the process of forecasting?

Exhibit 9.9 cont.

- What is the average lead time from receipt of order to delivery and receipt by customer?

- What is the distribution (or range) of requested lead times?

- Do your major customers provide you with forecasts of their future requirements (short term to medium term)?

Manufacturing Structure

- How would you describe your type of production organisation – batch or line production?

- How are your facilities laid out: by process (functional) or by product (e.g. group technology)?

- What is the span of process (the degree of vertical integration)?

- How many manufacturing processes do you have?

- For the total operations what proportion of items are:
    made to stock
    made to order
    brought in
    (by proportion would be acceptable)?

- What are your ex-works cost breakdown (average and key products) purchase items?
    e.g. direct materials (disaggregate)
        energy
        labour
        overhead

- What is the headcount (proportionally and absolutely) of manufacturing-related labour?
    direct operations
    plant indirects (breakdown by function)
    management/supervision
    production/inventory control
    production/industrial engineers
    purchasing

Manufacturing Operations

- What are the key manufacturing processes?
    By virtue of unique technology
    By virtue of high capacity utilisation

- What is the economic life v. the actual age of key manufacturing facilities?

Exhibit 9.9 cont.

- Is advanced manufacturing technology and/or advanced in-process control an important feature of your process technology?

- Do you have critical bottleneck processes?

- At what stage in manufacturing logistics?

- For key processes, what are:
  set-up times?
  process times (average; range or distribution)?
  capacity utilisation?
  percentage availability?
  defect rates?
  types of control (manual, automatic or combination)?

- What proportion of processes have alternatives and at what cost/penalty?

- What dependence or operator skills do you have for key processes?
  Do you have a skills 'matrix'?
  How many operators are capable of operating the key processes?
  What training period is required for new operators?

- What other specialist technical skills are required (e.g. supervisory, plant maintenance, tool maintenance, etc.)?

- What is the age profile of your equipment?

- What major improvement to manufacturing could be made with 'state of the art' equipment?

- What quantifiable benefits would such equipment provide?
  e.g.   profit-related
         reductions of WIP
         increased throughput of saleable product
         etc.

Manufacturing Performance

- How many 'live' works orders do you have at any one time?

- What is the throughput efficiency (approximately) of orders (i.e. total work content v. total time in plant)?

Exhibit 9.9 cont.

- What is your delivery performance to due date?

- What is the batch size distribution in the plant?

- How are batch sizes determined?
    - e.g. lot for lot (against orders or forecasts)
      - EOQ
      - rule of thumb
      - some other method

For Key Processes

- What is the distribution of WIP (days or hours) in front of the process?

- What is the average availability of the process?

- What is the capacity utilisation?

- What is the average time taken to recover from a breakdown?

- What is the frequency of breakdown?

- Do you have preventive maintenance procedures?

- What percentage of hours are lost per year (in labour terms):
  - Through strikes?
  - Because of sickness?
  - Absenteeism?
  - Others?

Major Components of Lead Time

What is the lead time from receipt of order to commencment of production? (SOP and Admin lead time)

Manufacturing lead time?

Packaging?

Delivery/distribution lead time?

For new products.

- What are the major constraints and variables which delay product intro-duction?
  - Development?
  - Customer liaison?
  - Marketing uncertainty?
  - Vendors of key materials?
  - Others, e.g. quality?

BIBLIOGRAPHY

Christopher, M. (1986) *The Strategy of Distribution Management*, London: Heinemann.

Goldratt, E. and Cox, J. (1984) *The Goal*, Connecticutt: North River Press.

Kanter, R. M. (1983, reprinted 1990) *The Change Masters: Corporate Entrepreneurs at Work*, London: Unwin Hyman.

Kaplan, R. S. (ed.), (1990) *Measures for Manufacturing Excellence*, Harvard Business School.

Lockyer, K. G. (1974) *Factory and Production Management*, 3rd edn, London: Pitman Publishing.

Orlickey, J. A. (1975) *Material Requirements Planning*, NY: McGraw-Hill.

Peters, T. J. and Waterman, R. H. (1982) *In Search of Excellence*, NY: Harper & Row.

Porter, M. E. (1985) *Competitive Advantage: Creating and Maintaining Superior Performance*, NY: The Free Press.

Skinner, W. (1978) *Manufacturing in the Corporate Strategy*, NY: John Wiley & Son.

Vollman, Berry & Whybark (1992) *Manufacturing, Planning and Control Systems*, 3rd edn, Boston: Irwin.

Voss, C. (ed.) (1993) *Made in Britain: The True State of Britain's Manufacturing Industry*, London: IBM/LBS.

CHAPTER 10

Case Study: Braun AG – the KF 40 coffee machine

Karen Freeze

'If we're going to do it, we've got to quit stalling,' exclaimed Albrecht Jestädt, head of development for a new coffee-maker at Braun AG. 'I've said all I can about polypropylene, and I'm convinced we can go with it,' he added, taking another sip of his beer.

At the end of a day in February 1983, Jestädt and his colleagues were discussing Braun's newest design: an elegant, cylindrical coffee-maker, called the KF 40 destined for the mid- and upper end of the mass market. In order to meet management's cost targets, however, they would have to use a much less expensive plastic material than Braun had traditionally used. Whether the material, polypropylene, would destroy Braun's reputation for quality was a matter of intense debate throughout the company. Unlike the very expensive polycarbonate, Braun's traditional material, polypropylene could not be moulded into large, complicated parts (like the KF 40's 'tank') without suffering so-called 'sink' marks on surfaces that were supposed to be flawlessly even. The designers had come up with a solution that involved a major departure from the smooth, winter-white surfaces characteristic of all Braun household products (see Fig. 10.1).

'The decision is obvious,' claimed Gilbert Greaves, business director for household products. 'We need this product *now*, and we have to stop being quite so picky.'

'I think we should be picky,' said Hartwig Kahlcke, the industrial designer on the project. 'But we feel that the rippled design for the tank actually enhances the surface appearance, without compromise.'

'Maybe,' said Hartmut Stroth, recently appointed director of corporate communications. 'But it's no trivial matter. It's true that if we lose a year, we might not get in the market at all. Yet *nothing* is worth losing our reputation for superior quality. Not even the mass market.' Stroth, who had served for over a decade in various communications positions at Braun, was very sensitive to the

This case was prepared by Dr. Karen Freeze, Director of Research of the Design Management Institute, for the purposes of class discussion rather than to illustrate either effective or ineffective handling of an administrative situation.

Fig. 10.1 KF 40

importance of Braun's 'visual equity' and the need for maintaining it: 'Not only do we have to think hard about how this corrugated surface design would fit into the Braun "look", but also about what that look represents. The idea of using design to mask sink marks bothers me in principle, and it may not work in practice, especially if the stuff doesn't hold up. I'm anything but risk-averse in this business, but I need to be convinced.'

'What about the chairman?' asked Kahlcke. 'I know he liked the design, and I know he wants the product. What does he think about the material at this point?'

'You tell me,' answered Lorne Waxlax, chairman of the board and Braun's CEO. He would have to make the ultimate decision and had just dropped in, as was his custom, to get the latest thinking on the KF 40.

HISTORY AND CULTURE

Braun AG (Aktiengesellschaft – joint stock company) began as a family-owned radio and small appliance business founded in 1921 by Max Braun. In the 1940s Braun developed a novelty, the electric razor, which he introduced in 1950. After Braun's death in 1951, his sons, Artur and Erwin, took over the business. Three years later they asked their friend Fritz Eichler, an artist then working in the theatre, to help them find a new approach to their struggling business. Post-war Germany was rapidly recovering, resulting in greater spending for consumer goods, and the Brauns wanted to profit from that trend.

Designing a new company

By enlisting Eichler, history would show, the Braun brothers changed the direction of their company and built not just a successful business, but also a cultural symbol, a distinctive style. That development took more than Eichler's efforts alone, however. In 1955, looking for an architect to help build a new office building, the company hired Dieter Rams, just two years out of architecture school. The twenty-three-year-old Rams was more broadly experienced than most young graduates, having spent three years as an apprentice in carpentry along the way.

Rams became Eichler's protégé, and together they built a small, intense design department at the company's headquarters. Believing that they could single-handedly change the taste of their fellow citizens, Eichler, Rams and colleagues set out to design and build a new kind of product. Eichler believed that such products would find a response in people whom he visualised as

> likeable, intelligent, and natural, with a feeling for authenticity and quality. People, in other words, whose homes are not stage sets for unfulfilled pipe dreams, but simple, practical, and comfortable. And that is exactly how our products should be and look. Products made not for show windows, loud and obtrusive eye-catchers, but, rather, products that one can live with for a long, long time.

Erwin Braun, and then Rams, frequently articulated the company's vision with another metaphor: 'Products should be like the proverbial English butler: unobtrusively in the background, but there when you need him.'

Eicher and Rams believed that their design philosophy should permeate the company, providing a recognisable identity not only in its products, but in every aspect of its relations with customers (see Exhibit 10.1).

By 1983 the Braun design group had come far toward succeeding in their mission. One of their first products, a heavy-duty kitchen mixer (1957), was still in production and still selling well. Their innovative stereo with the plastic see-through lid (1956) had set a world standard, as they turned completely away from bulky furniture cabinets and fake wood in favour of clean, compact plastics. Most famous was their shaver, familiar to men all over the world. Many Braun products had won design awards; thirty-six of them, including Braun's first coffee-maker, had won a permanent place in New York's Museum of Modern Art. (A testimony to the appeal of Braun products was the emergence of a Braun Collectors Club, whose members collected Braun products and published a newsletter.)

The company's mission was carried out not only in its products, but in its people as well. The company's principles had permeated its corporate consciousness and were second nature even at lower levels in the organisation. Almost any employee could tell a visitor that Braun's values were embodied in its products, which had to have three characteristics:

Exhibit 10.1 The principles of Braun's corporate identity

- Braun regards the consumer as a *partner* in its business, not as an *object* of its strategy that is open to manipulation.

- Braun believes that consumer desires relate to genuine needs, and employs its expertise, inventiveness, know-how, etc. to satisfy these needs.

- Braun seeks to satisfy these needs in an optimal way, perhaps even better than the consumer expects.

- However, Braun refuses to persuade people to buy its products on the basis of presentation which meets – or pretends to meet – entirely different needs (which are not amenable to rational consideration) for prestige, ego-support, ostentatious consumption, cosmetic effectiveness, etc.

- Braun refuses to exploit human weaknesses to improve its results, and rejects any means of 'hidden persuasion'.

- Braun also rejects all methods involving purely superficial attraction: in place of this, it has demonstrated that firm concentration on product design which is as good and functional as possible – including external aspects – is also experienced as aesthetically satisfying.

(1) first-class design;
(2) superior quality; and
(3) functions or features ahead of the competition.

'We'll never bring out just a me-too product' echoed in every department.

The Gillette connection

In 1967 the Braun brothers sold the company to an American consumer products giant, Gillette. The Gillette Company, well known for its mass-produced, mass-marketed products like razors, blades, and toiletries, hardly seemed the company to become the parent of an élite-class German firm. But Gillette was no stranger to Europe, having marketed its goods on the continent and in Britain since the turn of the twentieth century. It now saw the Braun acquisition as an opportunity to cover the dry end of the shaving business, as well as to extend its influence upward.

Braun, for its part, had by 1967 grown to over 5,700 employees and operated in 144 countries, but it was too small to compete with the multinationals. Its management saw Gillette as a source of funding to enable them to do so. Shortly afterwards, Braun moved its headquarters from Frankfurt to Kronberg, a few kilometres away.

For the first several years, Gillette left Braun's product strategy intact while infusing some of its management expertise into the organisation. Very few people knew that this German company *par excellence* had an American owner. Braun expanded its operations in other countries and began to extend its target markets beyond the opinion leaders it had originally cultivated.

Braun's Spanish operations were a case in point. Unprofitable since its beginnings, the Spanish plant was taken over in 1971 by Lorne Waxlax, a Gillette manager since 1958. Waxlax largely refocused the operation, emphasising product development, sophisticated manufacturing, market research and television advertising. The Spanish plant manufactured Braun's first successful mass-produced kitchen appliance, the hand blender, and served as the training ground for Braun's mass-produced appliance motors.

By the mid-1970s Braun's business consisted of home appliances (about two-thirds of its revenues), with shavers accounting for over one-half of that. Consumer electronics (cameras and hi-fis) constituted the other third. Because of growing Japanese competition in Europe, however, the company found its position in consumer electronics weakening. Three-quarters of its business was still in Germany.

A new strategy: to rob a bank

In 1980 Gillette replaced Braun's current chairman with Lorne Waxlax. After his five-year stint in Spain, Waxlax had managed Braun's non-Central European export business for three years, and then headed business management for two. Waxlax had long wanted to encourage Braun to get rid of cameras and hi-fi and to focus more effectively on its core technologies in the personal care and appliance businesses. As chairman, Waxlax could finally proceed with this strategy.

While narrowing Braun's product line, Waxlax also recommended extending Braun's horizons to a larger piece of the consumer market. He paraphrased the legendary bank robber Willy Sutton: 'You don't rob a gas station; you rob a bank, because that's where the money is.' Waxlax saw 'banks' in six segments of the consumer appliance business: coffee-makers, irons, toasters, hair-dryers, shavers and food preparation products. They were big, and they were constant; the market for coffee-makers in Europe alone was over 9 million units per year. Even a small percentage share would make a good business, but Waxlax was 'always going for a big share'.

This new strategy was eagerly embraced by business management, and also embarked on with enthusiasm by Braun's designers. Contrary to what many people may have assumed, given the company's reputation for high-class design, the designers were no snobs. Rams made very clear his philosophy: good design should be for everyone.

Implementing the strategy

On a hot August day in 1981, when half of Germany was on holiday and the other half getting ready to leave, Waxlax wrote two memoranda to Gilbert Greaves, business director for household products, asking him to check into the possibilities for Braun in coffee-makers and irons.

It was a well-timed request. (See financial details in Table 10.1.) Having sold off an unprofitable camera business and consolidated hi-fis by 1981, Braun could now invest in new core projects and strengthen its premier position in shavers. The company was now down from over 9,000 to around 7,700 employees, two-thirds of them in Germany. Waxlax and his top managers wished to focus on Braun's core products and expertise, its reputation for excellence in design, and the opportunities within grasp at the upper end of the mass market. Balancing these three dimensions of the company – technology, design and business management – while maintaining the integrity of its corporate mission was management's key challenge.

Table 10.1 Braun group financial information

	Millions of dollars		
	1980	1981	1982
Net sales	496.1	451.4	403.4
Profit from operations	23.6	22.8	33.3
Identifiable assets	384.3	325.2	301.5
Capital expenditures	21.5	23.6	20.4
Depreciation	17.3	18.9	16.6

THE BUSINESS ENVIRONMENT
Products and markets

By 1983 Braun was well established in several product families. Electric shavers were its biggest and most widely marketed product line, accounting for half the company's revenues. In many countries Braun held first place in market share; wherever it was present, it was among the top three. The household division, whose image was represented by its classic kitchen machine, produced coffee-makers, stick mixers, press juicers, food processors, food choppers, and irons as well. In the personal care area, hair-dryers and curling irons were the most successful, having established market leadership in Europe.

Braun's exports were continuing to grow: in 1982 they accounted for 75 per cent of its turnover.

Competition: coffee

Braun's major competitors in the middle-to-high-end coffee machine segment were two German companies, Krups and Rowenta. Braun's market research defined this segment in terms of price points: DM 70 retail or above. In

Germany and France, two of the biggest markets for coffee-makers, half the units were sold in that range. The market researchers were confident that the features of the KF 40 and its cousins, to be offered across the entire spectrum from DM 72 to DM 136, would be competitive in Europe, where the greater part of the market (about 70 per cent of 9 million units annually) was for replacements. An open question was how soon Krups and Rowenta would copy Braun's design, as was their custom.

The US market was considerably less certain. And yet Waxlax felt it was crucial if Braun was to maintain a volume that would permit a tolerable return on investment. 'You don't go for the small appliance business because of the margins. You have to have high volumes.' Americans had been introduced to filter coffee systems through Mr Coffee, a low-end product. Would they be willing to pay for Braun quality? With the currency exchange rate at DM 2.40 to $1, it was reasonable to expect imports to the US to grow. The market for filter coffee machines was already running at about 11 million units, and penetration was still low. Braun's distribution system in the US was practically nonexistent, however, and Waxlax wondered if it could be sufficiently developed in time.

CORPORATE STRUCTURE AND OPERATIONS

Braun AG in 1983 was a relatively efficient organisation, unemcumbered by layers of bureaucracy. Helped logistically by the central location of all of its functions near Frankfurt, it enjoyed relatively open and effective communication among its various disciplines and departments. Its success spawned an *esprit de corps* that made teamwork natural. 'We got to a lot of birthday parties in order to help keep it that way,' the chairman said.

The company was divided into three main functions: business management, technical operations and group sales. These, as well as smaller functions (including strategic planning, financial, public relations, and personnel and design), all reported to the chairman, who was the company's chief executive officer (see Fig. 10.2).

Business management

Business management, established in 1976, was a co-ordinating body that was essentially identical with strategic marketing. As it looked in 1983, the marketing function was relatively new at Braun. Until Gillette came along, Braun had assumed that if you made a good product, it would sell. And it generally did. But in 1975 marketing became more important, as the domestic and international marketing people came together under a single group. A director for each product group reported to the head of business management, as did the director of communications, which included packaging.

Business management often had conflicts with design because, said the mar-

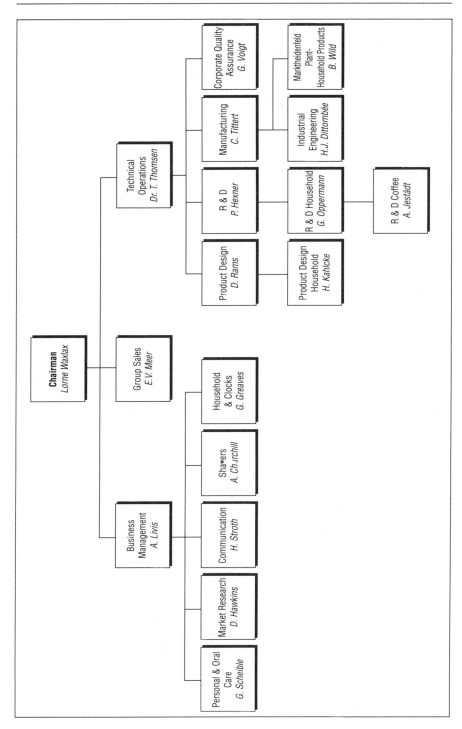

Fig. 10.2 Braun corporate structure

keters, the latter insisted on certain principles that were not always viable in the marketplace. 'The problem with designers,' Greaves sighed, 'is that they think they design for eternity. Rams will hand me a 1965 design and expect me to go for it today.' Sometimes the conflicts were trivial. For example, 'one time we argued with Kahlcke over the baseplate of the mixer. Because of his obsession with details, he wanted it changed. I told him that was ridiculous, since no one would ever see it,' recounted Greaves. 'The cord storage was not in the base, so there was no reason whatsoever to turn the mixer over. But Kahlcke got his way!'

Market research

The market research department reported directly to the director of business management as well. 'We feel that market research needs to be independent of marketing so it won't be so easy to corrupt it,' explained Waxlax. Market researchers often originated product ideas, or discovered segments where they believed Braun should be and then presented their ideas to management. They were often given the task of scoping out potential fields for Braun, such as coffee-makers and irons. This might involve a look at statistical information, or it might involve customer interviews as well, perhaps showing competitors' products alongside a new Braun design. Sometimes working with quality assurance, market research filmed people actually using an appliance – ironing, drying their hair, etc. – to understand more accurately just how better design might make these activities more efficient. Industrial design, for its part, believed that market research was pointless, 'because people cannot know what they will want in the future'.

Testing of Braun products already in the market was part of market research as well. Working with colleagues from quality assurance, the market researchers were responsible for testing products directly in the hands of users. For example, they conducted so-called 'placement tests' using products from the pre-production ('0') series, usually in about 200 locations. Throughout the life of a product, they continued to provide data that led to improvements.

Communications

The communications department helped guard the Braun image – i.e. its corporate identity – and transmit its values. Its director, Hartmut Stroth, had come to Braun in 1976 and soon was working closely with Fritz Eichler and Rams, who had established the communications function in the mid-1950s as a complement to product design. Because Eichler viewed design as Braun's greatest asset, he began early to analyse and articulate its significance. When Stroth became director of communications in 1982, he continued to work with Eichler, who remained on the board of directors after his retirement as head of design.

Technical operations

Because its mission was to bring innovation and quality to consumers, Braun invested heavily in technology. All key technically related disciplines were based at company headquarters in Kronberg, under Dr Thomas H. Thomsen, recently appointed director of technical operations. Thomsen had come to Braun in 1982 from Gillette, where he had been head of engineering in both London and Boston. He had also been plant manager for Gillette in Berlin. His academic background included mechanical engineering and materials science in Darmstadt, and three years' post-doctoral work in metallurgy at the Massachusetts Institute of Technology.

Thomsen found it valuable to have R&D, engineering, quality assurance, materials management, industrial design and manufacturing under one command: 'When these disciplines are together, you pick up problems early,' he explained. Moreover, at Braun people tended to move around among various departments.

R&D

The R&D department employed some 220 people and enjoyed an annual budget of DM 27 million. Braun Spain also supported a considerable R&D effort. Most of the R&D people were directly responsible for product development, but some served in the applied research group, established in 1981 to attract first-rate scientists and engineers. 'This group,' explained Waxlax, 'concentrates on things that take longer to develop, like cutting systems, ceramics, innovative motors – things that interest and attract the best scientists. Once they've been here a while, they see how much fun it is to work on products, and so they move to product development. Then we go out and get some new people for applied research.' The idea behind the group was to ensure that Braun would always be the technical leader, the innovator, in its field.

R&D was headed by Dr Peter Hexner, an American ex-army colonel who had recently come from Gillette, having headed its advanced technology department for ten years. He brought frankness, energy, tenaciousness, and a PhD in physics from MIT to Braun. Hexner also saw his job as balancing the demands of design. 'We have the classic conflicts,' he asserted. 'Design wants an elegant shaver a centimetre thick,' Hexner continued with hyperbole, 'and I have to knock reality into their heads: you can't fit a motor into a case a centimetre thick!'

The new R&D manager for household products (including coffee-makers) was Gunter Oppermann, a twenty-year Braun engineer who had recently come from the hi-fi group.

Engineering

Engineering was the company's link between R&D and manufacturing. Its 200 engineers worked with R&D, plant engineers, industrial designers and others on the product development team to ensure that the product could be optimally produced. Engineering's responsibilities included translating R&D's ideas into manufacturable products, planning investments in tools, moulds and all other equipment needed for manufacturing, and calculating production costs and determining if and how they could be reached.

The company's machine tool making department, a part of manufacturing engineering, was also located at headquarters. Twelve tool designers and three others worked for Friedhelm Bau, a long-time Braun employee. The shop was capable of making tools, moulds, presses, etc., for both metal and plastic. It was limited in capacity to 80 per cent of the company's needs. 'If we had more staff, however, they'd have nothing to do in slow times.'

For the rest, the department went to outside suppliers – especially for outsized tools that they were not equipped to make. These tools – including many for the injection-moulding machines – were a critical component of all products. Large moulds, for example, took nine to twelve months to build, six of them actual construction. 'If you make a mistake,' explained Bau, 'you can't just fix it.'

Manufacturing

Manufacturing at Braun was characterised by state-of-the-at technology and a high degree of vertical integration. The small plant at company headquarters in Kronberg, for example, produced key components for all Braun products, especially those with proprietary significance or a high degree of precision. The company's larger plants were located in Walldürn and Marktheidenfeld, West Germany, where over three-quarters of its manufacturing operations took place. The rest took place in Barcelona, Spain, and in Carlow, Ireland. Very small plants were located in Mexico City, Buenos Aires, and Saõ Paulo. The coffee machine was to be produced at Marktheidenfeld.

Built in 1961, Marktheidenfeld had expanded over the years to 32,000 square metres and 870 employees. It manufactured about 16,000 units per day, including clocks, hair-dryers, and kitchen appliances. The latter were low-volume products, however; the KF 35 coffee-maker, for example, was produced at around 700 per day. The plant had not been set up for high-volume products, however, and would need considerable investment in machinery and the building of new assembly lines to handle the KF 40. Because of the high cost of German labour, the question of further offshore manufacturing and outside suppliers was frequently raised, especially by the marketing department.

Bernard Wild, plant director at Marktheidenfeld (and formerly head of central engineering), was opposed to both on principle: 'Whenever you go outside, even to suppliers for parts you can't do yourself, you give up know-how. Even in explaining what you want, or helping a supplier make what you need, you are giving away know-how and creating competition. This industry is very competitive, and when the profits are to be made where the know-how is, it's better to keep it inside.' Waxlax concurred: 'It's usually more expensive to go outside.'

That meant, of course, that Braun had to figure out how to compete in spite of high labour costs, which were concentrated in assembly. One solution was automated assembly, well under way in Braun plants. Automation was applied in other ways as well; for example, the plant at Marktheidenfeld had recently completed a fully automated 2,000-square-metre warehouse with capacity for 6,650 pallets operated by only two employees.

More challenging, however, was to use the company's design and engineering talents to design a product so that it required minimal assembly. 'Anyone can make a cheap product with many parts and hire cheap labour offshore to screw them on. But not everyone can reduce as many parts as possible to one,' said Wild. 'We can prove that advanced industrial nations don't have to forfeit manufacturing just because their labour costs are high. Our resources are in our brains and imaginations – our know-how.'

Quality assurance

The quality department's status was determined by Braun's third product requirement: that all its products be better than those of all the competition. During the initial stages of product development, when a concept was being explored, the quality people worked with business management to analyse the competitors' products. Together they scrutinised their features – e.g. ease of use, cleaning, service – as well as details of construction and principal functions. 'We take them apart and analyse them down to the last screw,' explained Werner Utsch, a quality engineer who was responsible for the coffee-maker project. 'We then make a profile of the competition and decide what Braun would have to have in order to succeed.'

Another important consideration was an independent consumer protection testing programme, the *Stiftung Warentest*, much like *Consumer Reports* in the US. 'The criteria for testing are announced in advance, so you know, as a company, what standards you have to meet. We at Braun have to exceed those standards,' explained Utsch. It was crucial that any consumer product pass this test, because failures were well publicised, and could mean death in the German marketplace. Braun's general approach was to try to duplicate these tests on prototypes and new products. Its goal was to obtain the top *'sehr gut'* rating, not easily achieved.

The quality department ran an experimental kitchen for the household line, which was fully equipped to test products under user conditions. 'Sometimes we even get to eat the results.' Less satisfying, but perhaps more important, were such tedious tests as those for switches. 'We test things like the strength needed to switch on the appliance. It should be neither too stiff nor too easy to turn on,' Utsch continued.

Testing of the final product never ended. 'When the 0-series is under way, we finally have enough samples to run destructive tests. Like 'crash tests' to find out what happens when a product drops off an 80-centimetre table. It has to survive the fall with only very slight cosmetic damage or it isn't a Braun product.' Tests are also run to simulate jiggling and jostling in cars and suitcases, etc.

Quality and design were perhaps the closest of any two disciplines in the company, and each respected the suggestions of the other. 'We don't let them get by with, for example, a sharp edge anywhere, because that's a safety problem. They don't mind.'

Industrial design

Braun's design department, headed by Dieter Rams since 1961, was relatively small. It employed only sixteen people altogether, including seven designers and seven model-builders, plus an assistant and a secretary. Rams felt that good communication among them was related to the size of the group, and therefore did not intend to add to his staff. 'Besides, we don't have the space.' Turnover was rare – all had been in the company over ten years. 'The designers are really a family,' noted chairman Waxlax. 'They don't quarrel in front of outsiders.' Most had been winners of the Braun Prize, a design award offered by Braun to design students since 1968.

By 1983 Rams's international stature often resulted in his being equated with Braun design almost exclusively. Appearances to the contrary, he found this star status awkward: 'I constantly have to stress that I don't do everything: I'm simply the motor that drives the department. I try to give other people the credit they deserve.'

Industrial design had recently acquired a dual-reporting status. Until late 1982 Rams had reported only to the chairman. But because of time limitations, Waxlax assigned ID to technical operations, where most problems could be solved. The direct line to the chairman remained, but was used only for the most important issues and impasses.

Rams did not take his relationship to the chairman for granted. 'I've had a good understanding with every chairman I've worked with,' he said, 'but often designers aren't so lucky. We often educate business management people to the point where they begin to understand design and are supportive to us, but then they leave.'

BRAUN DESIGN: WHAT FUNCTIONALISM REALLY IS

Braun's design philosophy, which began to emerge in 1955, was articulated with consistency and authority by Dieter Rams. Rams measured his own and his department's work by standards that he frequently articulated in writing and lectures. In his view, the term 'design' had been unconscionably misused and therefore widely misunderstood. Remembering an advertisement in New

York about 'the best-designed cookies', he nearly exploded with disdain: 'Technological design is something other than cookies!!' Good design, he said:

- is honest, and does not use tricks and strategems to make a product seem more innovative or valuable than it really is
- is unobtrusive and neutral, allowing people room to express their individual personalities
- is as little design as possible, omitting everything that is unimportant in order to emphasise what is important, simplifying at every turn
- does not play on human weakness, greed, vanity, status-consciousness, etc.
- is timeless and lasting, unfettered by fashion and its transience, and thus helps conserve our natural resources.

(See Exhibit 10.2 for Rams's ten commandments of good design.)

Design's mandate

In an industry setting, Rams said, good design must be supported by top management. Moreover, it requires teamwork – constant interaction among disciplines. Finally, good design requires that designers be given certain responsibilities and authority; otherwise they can arrive, at most, at 'superficial product cosmetics'.

According to Rams, designers needed four things. First, they had to be responsible for configuring all elements of the product that will have an influence on the product's final appearance. Second, designers needed the authority to determine the dimensions of a product – e.g. the positioning and ergonomic design of its operating functions; third, they must be the ones to decide on surface structures, colours, product labelling, and imprinting; fourth, they needed to co-operate with the engineers on construction problems – e.g. manufacturability – whenever the form of a product directly depends on the construction.

That Rams practised what he preached was evident in many stories told about his activities at Braun. Once, for example, he noticed how the conventional angle of the handle to the hair-dryer fan caused strain on one's wrist. This observation led to a Braun first: the angled handle on the hair-dryer, subsequently an industry standard. Nor did he hesitate to make a point vividly: When looking at the placement of the controls on a model of a food processor made by one of his staff, he got down on his knees to demonstrate that – regardless of the extra cost involved – the controls should be on top, where they could easily be seen and operated by the user – not at the bottom of the appliance.

Rams had recently accepted a teaching position at the Academy of Fine Arts in Hamburg, where he spent four days a month teaching industrial design. The challenge of articulating his ideas to students forced him to clarify his thinking and led to a stream of papers and speeches.

Exhibit 10.2 Ten principles of good design

1. Good design is innovative.

2. Good design enhances the usefulness of a product.

3. Good design is aesthetic.

4. Good design displays the logical structure of a product; its form follows its function.

5. Good design is unobtrusive.

6. Good design is honest.

7. Good design is enduring.

8. Good design is consistent right down to details.

9. Good design is ecologically conscious.

10. Good design is minimal design.

Braun has an uncompromising commitment towards the pursuit of excellence in performance-orientated design. Every product designed and manufactured by Braun must adhere to these commandments of good design. So, too, should every consumer demand such quality in the selection of a product – be it furniture, clothing, an automobile or a home appliance.

Dieter Rams
Braun's Chief Designer

Rams's critics considered him too austere, too 'functionalist', by which they meant that he took too seriously the edict that 'form follows function'. Nevertheless, his work was an effective counterweight to the popular assumption that designers merely dreamed up the external form of a product. Moreover, Rams adamantly stood by his own definition of 'functional': that the purpose of good design is to fulfil the *primary function* of a product, including its need to be appealing to the user so that it would be a welcome object in his or her environment.

Organisation and facilities: designed for designing

Each designer at Braun was responsible for a certain product line – e.g. shavers or household products – but they traditionally offered ideas in other areas as well. 'They need to have a product specialty,' explained Rams, 'so they can work with their counterparts from other disciplines efficiently.'

Nestled on the ground floor of the main administration building, the design department offered a bright and roomy working space for its people, each of whom had a large workstation. An inside room with shelves to the ceiling stored old models, more or less grouped according to product line. This was a storehouse of ideas, a record of the visualisation process. Here were the low-density blue foam models, high-density white foam models, and more sophisticated models made of wood or Plexiglass, painted to look real. The history of shaving or food processing could be seen here; as indeed, could the imaginings of designers as they thought 'coffee' over the years.

Adjacent to the designers' workplace was the model shop, which consisted of four rooms devoted to model-building. In one large room, seven model builders, equipped with sophisticated machinery, made the time-consuming, precisely detailed models for both development and market test purposes. Next door the designers too could explore concepts and verify ideas by making their own foam models. One small room was reserved for spray painting.

Designers at work: visualisation through models

Design entered product development most often at the 'idea' stage, long before a formal project was undertaken. A designer might have an idea, for example, for the next generation of a product. After exploring the idea and verifying its potential through working with foam models, he could have a 'real' model made even before working extensively with R&D or any other department. Or an engineer or R&D or marketing person might develop an idea individually or together and then come to design when he or she needed to embody it in a model. Any discipline might suggest certain features or modifications of a product.

Regardless of the idea's origin, the designers always hurried to visualise it – to translate the idea into a visual medium – in a rough sketch and then, very quickly, in a three-dimensional, low-density foam model. 'We never do renderings,' any Braun designer would say, 'because you can't fully communicate your idea that way. The three-dimensional model is a fuller experience – you can see more and therefore think better.' As the project proceeded, the models became increasingly more detailed and lifelike.

Braun designers at first used their models internally, with colleagues from other disciplines, to help develop the initial concept. Then they often became the focus of the monthly product development meetings held with the chairman. At a later stage they were used by market researchers to test customer reactions.

Designer as team member

Given the fact that all key disciplines at Braun were located in the same building or, at most, in buildings next door (engineering and manufacturing), much communication about development took place informally, and no one really kept track of where ideas came from and when they first got together with a colleague from another department. That design, because of its reputation, often received disproportionate credit for a product occasionally irked some engineers and scientists, whose contributions were less visible. Well aware of this problem, the company's chairman accepted the responsibility of keeping the rivalry healthy.

Industrial design's relationship to other departments varied. Within the 'triangle of power' (design – technology – marketing), design felt most akin to technology. The designers kept up with new developments in such fields as materials science, for example. 'We understand technology, so when we have an idea, it is not unrealistic technically. We don't come up with totally impossible ideas,' explained Rams.

The same went for manufacturing. The group knew what it meant to design a product for manufacturability; if they were having difficulties, all they had to do was go down the hall and across the parking lot to the engineering building. Such interaction among all disciplines was daily fare at Braun.

Marketing was something else. Rams: 'I don't mind if technology has greater influence than design; we understand each other and can work things out. But when marketing gets power, it can be bad.' For example, sometimes marketing got its way with regard to colour. 'Why should we pay attention to colour fads? Just because red cars are popular one year, why should we have a red hairdryer? It's not integral to the design.'

The design department was also responsible for product graphics – whatever was printed directly upon the product itself. Design wanted such graphics to be subtle, to aid the user intuitively. Marketing sometimes wanted them to be more obvious, especially when the Braun logo was involved.

PRODUCT DEVELOPMENT

Product development had been relatively informal until 1980, when three people, representing R&D, business management and manufacturing engineering, came together to develop procedures that would make the process more operational and efficient. The result was a product development manual that was formally introduced in 1981. It covered the responsibilities of key persons in a team (called an MTS team, for marketing–technology–strategy), definitions of elements in project development (e.g. different kinds of models), product specification guide, stages ('categories') and sign-off points in the process, etc. (see Exhibit 10.3).

The product programme manager was responsible for maintaining these procedures. His function was largely administrative and co-ordinative; he was not always a heavyweight team member. He chaired team meetings, and represented the team *vis-à-vis* management, reporting directly to the head of technical operations or business management. (See Exhibit 10.4 for the product programme manager's formal responsibilities.)

Exhibit 10.3 Contents of product development handbook

	Chapter
Project Procedures for New Products	1
Introduction	1.1
Goals	1.2
Assumptions	1.3
Tasks, Competence, Responsibilities	2
Project team	2.1
Project manager	2.2
Project team representatives	2.3
Project Development Procedure	3
Assumptions/principles	3.1
Implementation	3.2
Definition of terms	3.3
Exceptions	3.4
Project Profile	4
Explanations	4.1
Forms for project profile	4.2
Project Reporting	5
Project book	5.1
Reporting to the chairman	5.2
Summary	6
Product development flow chart	6.1

The team itself did not have a formal leader. Various people took over as the stage in the product development process dictated. Stronger personalities could be influential; Jestädt, for example, first as product programme manager, then as R&D manager for coffee, had quickly emerged as the leader of the coffee machine project.

Monthly reports to the chairman were very important. For purposes of record-keeping, they all had a standard format, divided into four sections: Description, Status, Further Steps and Problems (or Risks). These monthly reviews were seen as a good way to motivate people to keep moving toward the project goal. On the other hand, Waxlax did not like to use them as a threat: 'The trick is to know whether the deadline is truly viable or not. It's easy for marketing to insist on a deadline – they don't have to do the work. I believe the

Exhibit 10.4 Formal responsibilities of the project manager and project team members

---

The Project Team

Tasks
- Collective development of the project goals and procedures (the Project Profile) on the basis of the product concept determined by the MTS team as well as the product profile.
- The assignment of functional-specific tasks to the relevant team member.
- The independent solving of problems in order to reach the goals articulated by the project profile.
- The development of alternatives when deviations from the project profile are necessary and the formulation of written proposals for changes for approval of the MTS team.

Authority
- Shortening of the planned course of product development when possible through changes in the project profile.

Responsibility
- The responsibility of the project team consists of the responsibility of the individual team members and the project manager.

The Project Manager

Tasks
- Overall co-ordination of the project from planning to production start-up and control over fulfilment of project goals.
- Requisition of representatives from functional departments and the establishment of a project team.
- Calling and running of project meetings; preparation of meeting reports.
- Maintenance of the Project Book.
- Written records of project assignments.
- Planning and implementation of phase reviews at the end of each development category and whenever needed.
- Reports to product line manager.

Authority
- The right to direct information from team members and their superiors in the respective departments.
- The right to make necessary changes in the project profile and to submit written proposals for changes for approval by the MTS team.

Responsibility
- For co-ordination of
    - individual assignments in all functions.
    - project procedures.

Exhibit 10.4 cont.

- information flow (including among team members).
- supervision of costs, deadlines, and performance in accordance with the project profile.
- For the content of the project profile and project reports.
- For ensuring that any changes in the product objectives set by the MTS team are made only in exceptional circumstances and only with the approval of the MTS team.

The Team Members

Tasks
- Handling of tasks in his functional area.
- Ensure readiness, in co-operation with the product line supervisor, for his department's contribution to the project.
- Timely reports to the project manager about the completion of his department's tasks or deviation therefrom, in accordance with the project profile.
- Communicate information from his product line superior and other colleagues in his department.
- Nominate further representatives from his department (in agreeement with the product line supervisor).

Authority
- Each team member can request that the project manager call a team meeting.
- Each team member has operating room, within the project profile, for solving problems.

Responsibility
- The team members of individual departments bear responsibility for the technical performance of their part of the work.
- The team members are responsible for ensuring the flow of information from their departments that pertains to the project.

Source: From *Handbuch Projektablauf von neuen Produkten*, section 2

engineers know better than I how fast the team can go, and for that reason I don't want to force it unduly.'

Waxlax saw the meetings as an efficient way to keep up to date on all that was going on and to keep on top of problems and conflicts as they came up. His style as a conflict mediator was not necessarily to minimise it. He viewed conflict as positive for the company: 'It's often the guy who is against something who forces it to become better.' He also viewed the monthly review meetings in a constructive light: 'It is a chance for me to encourage people,' he added.

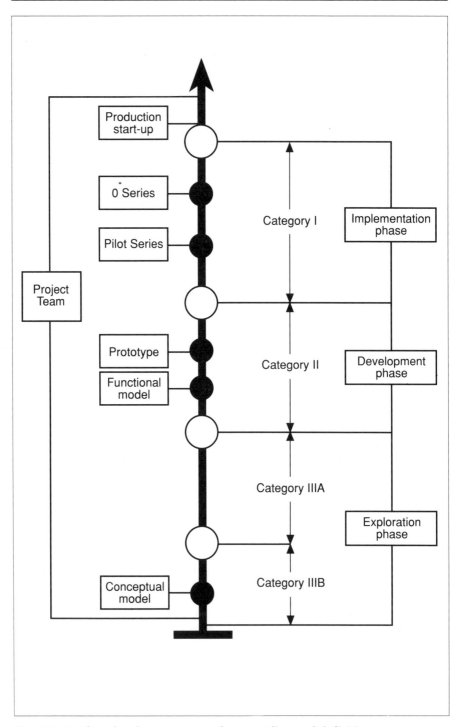

Fig. 10.3 Product development procedures: outline and definitions

The point at which a project became formal and began to adhere to the *Projektablauf* (project procedures) varied. When, for example, a project had proceeded informally rather far in its development before entering the formal product development process, the formality of the earlier stages might be skipped over. It might remain simply to formalise the project and delineate the product specifications. In its early stages, a project like the KF 40 might have provided monthly reports to the chairman for some time before becoming a formal project. (See Fig. 10.3 for the Braun product development process line.)

In addition to the core team, people from other groups and disciplines became involved as the project proceeded. 'There might be forty people at a product development meeting at its high point,' Waxlax pointed out.

THE KF 40 PROJECT

Braun had entered the coffee-maker business in 1972 with the KF 20 (shown in Fig. 10.4), a novel cylindrical design that won many design awards and was enthroned in the Museum of Modern Art in New York. Available in strong red and yellow, it had entered the consciousness of upper-income coffee drinkers in both Europe and the US. It was, however, a very expensive machine, and expensive to produce, retailing at about DM 120.

A few years later, the company introduced the KF 35 (see Fig. 10.5), a sleeker version of the then popular 'L-shape' epitomised by Mr Coffee. It cost about 40 per cent less than the KF 20 to produce, retailing at about DM 90. The design

Fig. 10.4 KF 20

department was not fully satisfied with it: 'I always thought it looked like a chemical lab sitting on the table,' declared Rams, disdainfully. The unit enjoyed only average sales, about 150,000 units annually.

Gilbert Greaves, an English linguist turned businessman, had worked for Gillette for several years and had come to Braun as marketing manager for household products in 1979. Upon receiving Walxax's coffee machine memo in August 1981, he set to work with his people and in two months came up with a rough description of a product Braun could sell:

> *It should have a shortened filter, slimmer jug [than the competition]; it should come in different colours, the water tank should be opaque, the tubes should be completely covered up, the filter should be tight and compact, the thermal jug should be more elegant, lighter, handier, taller, slimmer, and presentable on the coffee table.*

That idea, which marketing articulated in October 1981, evolved into a 'product profile' that Greaves circulated to key people on 2 December 1981. (See Exhibit 10.5 for a summary of Greaves's memo.)

What the KF 35 successor has to be

In his memo Greaves discussed, as Waxlax had asked, the issue of the cost/volume relationship, and presented the direct costs and price points in connection with assumed volumes. He also analysed the market segments where Braun could realistically compete. He determined that (a) a range of models – at least two – would be necessary; (b) this range was defined so that it could be

Fig. 10.5 KF 35

Exhibit 10.5 Excerpts from memorandum 'Product profile – coffee machine range' from Gilbert Greaves to G. Voigt

2 December 1981

Background

A key element in determining the viability of a filter-coffee-machine entry is the investment/volume required. The problem is that volume depends on the range offered. [But a wide range] necessitates different tools for housings, water tanks, etc., thus increasing the investment cost for entry.

A further element determining the range is price segmentation. In Germany 52 per cent of the unit volume is sold under DM 59; [this would require] a direct cost we cannot realistically expect from Braun.

Conclusions:

1. A range of models will be needed.

2. A range has been defined which can be constructed on a 'building block' system to minimise tooling investments.

3. This range will enable Braun to compete in medium to high price segments only . . . retail sale prices above DM 70. We will have to compete on feature, not on price.

This document, [based on a market survey], will serve as an input to R&D to evaluate costs, feasibility, and timing based on the [following] volume estimates.

Range:

The Braun range will be differentiated from competition by the following characteristics:

1. The premium model in the range will have a thermal flask. Into this thermal flask the coffee can be filtered direct. Coffee can be held off the hot-plate in the flask at 80 degrees Celsius for 45 minutes. This prevents evaporation and aroma loss.

2. All models in the Braun range will be compatible with a special 'Coffee ground dispenser'. This stores 500g of ground coffee in an airtight hopper and has a metering system allowing the ground coffee to be dispensed by cups into the coffee machine filter.

3. All models in the Braun range will have a laterally pivoting filter allowing the filter to be swung out of the machine and underneath the hopper so that the consumer does not need to handle the coffee grounds at any time. The filter can be lifted out to dispense with the paper filter and coffee grounds.

Exhibit 10.5 cont.

The range will consist of the following models:	1	2	3	4	5	6	7	
Standard Features								
Cup à 125 cc	8	8	8	12	12	12	12	
Anti Drip	●	●	●	●	●	●	●	
Pivoting Filter	●	●	●	●	●	●	●	
Translucent Tank	●	●	●	●	●	●	●	
Pilot Switch	●	●	●	●	●	●	●	
Warming Plate	●	●	●	●	●	●	●	
Cord Compartment	●	●	●	●	●	●	●	
Optional Features								
Glass Jug	●	●	●	●	●	●		
Thermal Jug							●	
Coffee Dispenser			●			●	●	
Calcification Indicator			●			●	●	
Detachable Tank		●	●		●	●	●	
Fixed Tank	●			●				
Target Direct Cost	22	23	29	24	25	31	36	
Target Price Point DM	74	78	99	82	85	105	122	
Target Price Point £	18.5	19.5	24.75	20.5	21.25	26.25	30.5	
Annual Volume Assumptions (000)								**Total**
Year 1	150	50	60	50	50	40	100	500
Year 2	225	75	90	75	75	60	150	750
Year 3	300	100	120	100	100	80	200	1000

constructed on a 'building block system' to 'minimise tooling investments'; and (c) the range would enable Braun to compete in medium to high price segments, at retail prices about DM 70. This would mean that Braun had to compete with key players – Krups, Rowenta, Siemens and AEG – on feature, not price. To be profitable, it would have to cost fully one-third less in direct costs than the KF 35, or 60 per cent less than the KF 20.

This document was sent to R&D for feasibility analyses. R&D's first reaction to the target costs was 'Nonsense! you can't make a coffee-maker for DM 23 in this company!' (Direct costs at Braun included *only* labour and materials.) Nor did engineering take the idea well: 'To be honest,' industrial engineer Hans-Jürgen Dittombée confessed, 'we thought the cost targets were impossible. We are responsible for technical planning and didn't see how we could get there.'

Exploration: from impossible to maybe

One of the people working with Greaves on the project was a young, energetic product programme manager, Albrecht Jestädt, a mechanical engineer with experience in production and engineering. Upon hearing R&D's and engineering's reactions, Jestädt refused to take 'no' for an answer, and set about looking for alternatives. If Braun can't manufacture it, at least we can sell an OEM product that we design, he reasoned. Over the next year, he explored options in and outside Germany and managed to find a manufacturer in Switzerland who could meet the cost requirements.

A shared vision

Meanwhile Jestädt and the designer for household products, Hartwig Kahlcke, teamed up and began to develop the product. Kahlcke, a quiet contrast to the ebullient Jestädt, had come to the design department ten years earlier, and had worked on the KF 35. Kahlcke had worked extensively with the Spanish group because they did so many household products. He and Jestädt worked well together: 'We share a vision,' Jestädt declared, 'and we're both willing to do what we have to to realise it.' That vision had as its starting point the KF 20 and its still novel cylindrical design. How could they use the cylinder within the cost parameters? They had to use less material and only one heating element to start with. 'Our first design was really terrific – the water tank completely surrounded the filter. But then we realised that we had to think modularly, so manufacturing costs would be minimised, and so we had to drop it,' Jestädt recalled.

Jestädt and Kahlcke knew that the cylindrical form not only was appealing, but it used less material than the 'chemical lab', the KF 35. Going back and

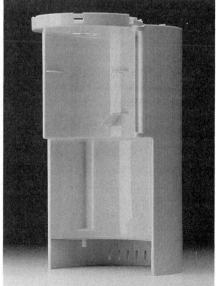

Fig. 10.6 The initial KF 40 concept   Fig. 10.7 The KF 40 'tank'

forth they came up with five or six blue foam models before settling on what they believed was the optimal configuration: a cylinder within a cylinder, operating on the same principle as the KF 35 but much more compact. The main novelty: it would be operated from the front, and thus it would take less space and look even slimmer on the kitchen worktop. (See Fig. 10.6 for initial concept.)

A single heating element

At the same time, other disciplines continued working on the project. R&D, after exclaiming 'impossible' at the very idea, took up the challenge and looked at how to get the cost out of the heating element and many other dimensions of the machine. The cost target presupposed a single heating element for both heating the water and keeping the coffee hot, rather than the two needed for the KF 20. Within those parameters, they still needed to explore their options carefully. They finally decided that they could go for aluminium rather than copper in the heating element, which would be cheaper, but it would mean different dimensions for the various parts because of differences in conductivity. Keeping the coffee temperature at 82°C was considered an absolute must by the designers and marketing alike, even though they knew it was, essentially, an insoluble problem because of the length of time that coffee might be held.

How to attach a handle invisibly

Kahlcke and Rams wanted to glue the handle on the pot, and asked engineering to explore adhesives. The design reasons were both aesthetic and functional: the conventional method of attaching the handle to the coffee jug was the metal band, which both interrupted the line of the jug and collected dirt. In the course of working on the adhesives, it had become clear that manufacturing engineering would have to design an automated glueing process, in order to keep the costs down. The good news by spring 1983 was that the new design and manufacturing process was expected to cost less than the conventional metal-band method. R&D still had not found the ideal adhesive, however, one that would hold for years under heat, impact and moisture.

Stop that drip!

R&D had other challenges as well. Marketing had found that an anti-drip device would be very attractive for customers, but as usual, Braun wanted to go at least one step beyond the competition. The idea was to prevent drips either from the filter (when one pulls out the coffee-pot) or from the water tube (when one swings the filter out). It was supposed to be a relatively easy assignment but, as Oppermann pointed out, 'simple is most difficult', and that was what the project was about. The drip-stop was a case in point. 'It has to be dual-action (stopping the flow when you pull out the pot *or* the filter), and we have to go around some outside patents. We thought about toilet flushers as a model and started from there. We don't want the device to stick, and yet it must be sturdy.'

When a coffee-maker makes coffee

Quality assurance was working on several aspects of the new machine, including its end product. 'We found that we didn't really know anything about coffee,' Utsch said with chagrin, 'so we had to analyse and test some more, and that has led us to work with the coffee producers.' The tests revealed valuable information: 'We have found that our competition doesn't know much about coffee either.' The next step would be blind taste tests, for which they needed a functional model.

What does the market tell us?

The market researchers continued gathering data as well. In October 1982 they tested the thermal jug concept and determined that it would be an essential selling feature. The next month they tested filter systems; the swivel filter won hands down. At this time, contrary to results a year earlier, the market wanted a detachable, transparent water tank. It was 'significantly preferred over a non-transparent one' and 'should be included . . . if the price is not prohibitive to the customer'. (See Exhibit 10.6 for market test results.)

Jestädt and Kahlcke had, however, already developed a modular design that could not accommodate a transparent tank.

To design means to think

Operating from the principle that 'no parts = no assembly costs', Jestädt and Kahlcke were striving to collapse the number of parts into as few as possible. This was where Ram's motto, 'To design means to think (*Designarbeit ist Denkarbeit*)', converged with Bernard Wild's view of Braun's know-how. Working with machine tool experts, headed by Bau, Jestädt and Kahlcke had designed a configuration that incorporated many large and small parts that in the past would have been screwed together. The water tank was now part of the appliance housing, and the whole large piece, known simply as the 'tank', was now central to their product concept, for it accounted for a good chunk of the savings in assembly costs (see Fig. 10.7). It was, however, the largest, most complicated part ever attempted in polypropylene injection moulding at Braun, and as such would be risky. (See Exhibit 10.7 for note on injection moulding.)

The manufacturing challenge

Manufacturing and toolmaking engineers were involved from the beginning of the project. Bernard Wild, plant manager at Marktheidenfelt, had prepared an analysis of plant requirements in order to achieve the projected volumes for the new coffee-maker. As soon as polypropylene was proposed, Bau and his group at Kronberg started working with plastic suppliers and toolmakers in Berlin, who had experience with designing large tools for polypropylene. Bau was convinced that the large tank could be moulded on the three 330-ton

Exhibit 10.6 Report on coffee-maker tests: 10 January 1983

Title	Date of Report		Comments
	Month	Year	
Coffee machine group discussions	10	1981	Desired improvements of the Braun coffee machine with thermal jug: Shortened filter, slimmer jug, should come in different colours, the water tank should be opaque, the tubes should be completely covered up, the filter should be tight and compact, the thermal jug should be more elegant, lighter, handier, taller, slimmer and presentable on the coffee table.
Thermos jug concept	10	1982	The concept of a thermos jug with aroma test protective lid is preferred by the majority of respondents over a conventional glass jug with removable hot-plate. There's a theoretical potential for a detachable heating or heat protection device.
Coffee filter system	11	1982	The best filter system for our new coffee acceptance test machine would be a swivel filter and the best water tank would be a transparent one.
Coffee machine features	12	1982	BMR would recommend the following concept test features to be considered for the new coffee machine range: built-in decalcifier, jug with heat and aroma preservation, swivel filter system, transparent detachable water tank, capacity 10–12 cups.

Source: Company documents

Exhibit 10.7 Note on injection moulding

Injection-moulding technology permits the high-speed moulding of thin, often complex parts out of metal or plastic. It involves (a) melting the material to a liquid state; (b) injecting the liquid under pressure into a metal mould; (c) waiting a number of seconds until the liquid cools and solidifies; (d) opening the mould; (e) withdrawing the part; (f) closing the mould again. To be precise and consistent, the process needs computer controls and robotised handling.

The easiest form to mould in this way is the cone, because it comes out from the mould easily. As soon as there are straight sides and protruding features, the design problem is vastly more complicated. Industrial designers, engineers, and tool designers work together to develop a design that can be produced effectively. For example, the mould needs to open at some point, and a flash line, preferably a very thin one, will show. The designers need to determine where the line's effects are minimal, and design the mould accordingly.

In the case of plastic injecting moulding, the material is not held in liquid form. Rather, it is fed to the machine in small beads, like small white beans, which are melted instantly under pressure at the nozzle. This way the temperature can be controlled and there is less waste.

An important point in the design of a mould is the cooling rates of the plastic. This rate is determined by the properties of the plastic itself and by the shape of the part – its thickness at any given point and the distance of that point from the nozzle through which the liquid is injected. Because the part cannot be removed until all of it has solidified, these problems must be taken into consideration when designing the part. Moreover, the injection temperature of the plastic and the temperature of the cooling water have to be kept constant via computer controls.

A mould may be very complicated, with more than one axis. Then the order in which the parts of the mould are opened and removed has to be carefully thought through. The 'tank' part of the Braun coffee machine incorporated parts that would conventionally have been cast in at least five separate components and then screwed or snapped together. To save labour costs, the company invested in knowledge and tooling up front. This enabled them to keep production in high-wage Germany.

Some plastics are easier to cast than others. Those with low density, like polypropylene, are less stable, and this needs to be compensated for in the design of large parts. A large wall, for example, needs to be thicker or have a supporting shape built into the design. Because of the design implications of the variations in plastics, the same mould cannot be used for multiple kinds of plastic.

Exhibit 10.7 cont.

> The quality of the moulded part is determined not only by the design of the mould, but also by the interior surface finish of the mould. The quality of the metal, usually a special alloy steel, and the finishing technology used (e.g. erosion, grinding, polishing) determine how well a mould can meet its tolerances and how long it will last.

moulding machines available at Marktheidenfelt. One machine could make 1,500 mouldings per day. With estimated volumes at 500,000 the first year, increasing to 2 million units in the fourth year, the plant needed to be prepared to manufacture 10,000 units a day, given the 220 days per year that the plant operated. They were assuming a one-minute cycle time for the 'tank' part, but could not be certain of it. They could start with two moulds (for 10- and 12-cup units), plus one for the thermal carafe, but if the product took off, they would need more machines. Each machine cost about DM 500,000. The estimated cost for each mould was DM 250,000, and they would eventually need five of them, according to Hans-Jürgen Dittombée, manager of industrial engineering: two each for the 10-cup and 12-cup versions and one mould for the thermal carafe. The cost was not only in Deutschmarks, but also in time. The lead time for tooling was around nine months for the large moulds. Because the moulds were not interchangeable for various types of plastics, the choice of plastic was crucial to engineering's planning.

Polypropylene: a question of Braun-ness

Braun had pioneered the use of plastics as early as the 1950s, when it abjured the use of fake wood and overstuffed designs for its products. Its designers, engineers and toolmakers were experienced in making both clear and opaque parts from several different kinds of plastic. For the outer housing of its appliances, the company had traditionally used polycarbonate, a dense, stable material that could be fashioned into precision parts with smooth surfaces. Polycarbonate was, however, too expensive for the new coffee machine's requirements.

For that reason, Jestädt had begun working with ABS, which sold for about half polycarbonate's going rate (see Table 10.2 for information on plastics). Even that, as it turned out, would probably be too expensive. The alternative, polypropylene, was the material of choice for low-end producers, and had never before been considered by Braun, except for interior parts that could benefit from its lower density and other features. The amount of polypropylene needed for each unit was estimated at 700–950 grams. The problem with polypropylene for use in injection moulding was its instability during the cooling process. Having a lower specific weight than the denser plastics, it tended to shrink unevenly and fall off, or 'sink', at edges and meeting points. The resultant 'sink

Table 10.2 Properties of plastics

	Polycarbonate	ABS	Polypropylene
Cost DM/kg (1983)	8.5	3.95	2.8
Specific weight	1.2	1.05	0.9
Melting temperature	220°C	200°C	165–170°C
Softening temperature	160°C	140°C	120°C
Colour-fastness	yes	no	yes
Shrinkage	0.5–0.7%	0.3–0.9%	0.3–2.5% (1–2.5% unfilled)

marks' marred the surface and looked 'cheap'. Nor did polypropylene become as rigid as the more expensive materials, thus posing additional design challenges. Large parts were therefore especially vulnerable to a flimsy feel and had to be designed with the need to control that problem. It might mean thicker walls or a shape in the mould that would buttress the form from within.

When polypropylene was first suggested, many colleagues familiar with its problems immediately objected: it will not be a *Braun* product if we use this cheap stuff, they warned. Despite such adamant objections, Jestädt and Kahlcke began working with chemical suppliers and toolmakers to explore ways of improving the quality of polypropylene parts. In autumn 1982 they achieved a breakthrough: why not let necessity be the mother of design in this case? If we can't get a perfectly smooth surface, let's minimise the effect of the sink marks by treating the surface in some way. This inspiration led to the idea for a corrugated surface that would both mask flaws and actually enhance the design as well.

No! said the purists, for whom Braun design was synonymous with absolutely smooth, winter-white surfaces. 'It's a compromise,' said Utsch, 'and I don't like compromises.' Utsch, head of quality assurance for the project, kept pointing to polypropylene's tendency to scratch: 'It's just too soft. Even a fingernail can scratch it. And if you wipe it with the same sponge you wiped the worktop with, you can scratch it with food particles or coffee grounds.' Even the head of design, Rams himself, was sceptical at first, but quickly came to support the solution. 'It is the obvious way to go, given the project requirements.'

Polypropylene did have some advantages other than its price, Oppermann pointed out: 'It doesn't absorb water, so it won't stain easily. And, as far as we can tell, it won't get brittle as fast as polycarbonate, so it won't chip easily.'

Jestädt, ever confident, insisted on exploring further. Willing to take risks, R&D director Hexner supported R&D's involvement in trying to make polypropylene work. Like everyone else, he knew that if it didn't work, it would be extremely costly. 'They are talking about a *huge* and very complicated tool for the tank. If it doesn't work, we'll have to throw it away and be another year behind.' But Hexner didn't see any choice: 'We've been given the job of making this thing at a ridiculous cost. My people say that it's possible only with polypropylene, and I agree.' To Hexner the 'purists' were entirely unrealistic. 'If a Braun product *has* to have a smooth surface, then you have two choices: go with flaws, or forget it. And that is ridiculous!'

Hexner's boss, Dr Thomsen, did not think it ridiculous to consider further choices. Neither did Waxlax. 'We could make a business with, say, ABS. But it would be a different business,' Thomsen contended. Waxlax was worried about the US market implications: 'We'd either have to drop the US market, and that means low volumes, or restrict it to the higher-priced department store segment.'

Jestädt and Kahlcke, meanwhile, were not insensitive to the design concerns. The ridges of the corrugated surface would have to be absolutely smooth, with no peaks or valleys, so that they would not catch any dirt. That job was turned over to the toolmakers. By the end of 1982 Bau's department was confident that the job could be done using the 330-ton moulding machines at Marktheidenfeld. An outside consultant had suggested that the tools should be larger (500 tons) for a part the size of the tank, but that would mean an additional investment of DM 2 million for five new machines.

The OEM threat

In December 1982 Jestädt had presented his plan for a Swiss company to manufacture the new design. At the same meeting, someone brought in a cheap, DM-29 coffee-maker from a supermarket and challenged those present: 'If these guys can sell a coffee-maker for DM 29, you can surely make one for DM 23.' As the discussion proceeded, the group realised that the new design was so special that it would be dangerous to let it out to a subcontractor; they would have to keep it inside in order to ensure a competitive lead.

At that point it was decided to build a trial tool to test the material, and Waxlax approved DM 140,000 for the test and the tool. The point was, according to a project report for 12 December, simply to 'clarify if polypropylene is suitable for the appliance housing material'. That was the point, according to engineer Dittombée. 'I am confident that we can master polypropylene *technically*,' he said, 'but the discussion is about whether *Braun* can – or should – use it.'

After this meeting Jestädt reported to R&D that they would have to complete this project, like it or not. They said to him, 'OK, then *you* do it!' Greaves facilitated the change in responsibility by getting Jestädt promptly moved to the R&D department. At Braun, such pragmatic flexibility was common. For the next two months Jestädt continued to fill the role of product programme manager as well.

Exhibit 10.8 Project report, coffee-maker KF 40: 26 January 1983

Product Description:

KF 40:   10-cup version with swinging filter, anti-drip, and cord storage
DC target: FY 1982/83: DM 23.50

KF 45:   same as KF 40, but with switch for brewing 3–4 cups
DC target: FY 1982/83: DM 24.30

Status:
Blueprints for the construction of a functional model have been prepared, and it is currently being built.

Further steps:

• Prepare drawings for parts and tools	by 28 January 1983
• Requisition parts and tools; produce the A.R.	by 18 March 1983
• Have the A.R. approved	by 29 April 1983
• Finish the functional model	by 25 March 1983
• Test the functional model by QC	by 16 May 1983
• Build the design model	by 30 March 1983
• Complete drawings for tool orders	by 16 May 1983
• Go or no-go decision	by 17 May 1983
If go, then Category I release	
• Planned start-up of production	April 1984

Risks:
The above schedule does not include the production of prototypes. Only if the tests of the functional model reveal no major problems will it be possible to meet the planned deadlines.

Project: Coffee Makers KF 40 and KF 45   Signed: A. Jestädt, Project Mgr.
Project Number: 542   Date: 26 January 1983   Version:1

A material decision

Over the next four months the coffee-maker project became more intense. At the report to management at the end of January 1983, drawings for the functional model were presented, and a schedule established (see Exhibits 10.8 and 10.9). The new 10-cup coffee-maker now had a name: the KF 40. A second model, the KF 45, would have a 3–4 cup switch, costing one DM more. According to this schedule, the functional model would be ready by the end of March, with final tool drawings complete on 16 May. The formal go/no-go decision would be made on 17 May, followed by a 'category I' sign-off, which released the drawings so that tools could be ordered. Production ramp-up was estimated to begin in April 1984, to reach 3,000 units per day within three months.

All this assumed that the KF 40 could be made with polypropylene and that all the other problems, such as the drip-stop, could be solved in time. By

Exhibit 10.9 Project report, coffee-maker KF 40: 22 February 1983

Product Description:

KF 40:   10-cup version with swivel filter, anti-drip, and cord storage
DC target: FY 1982/83: DM 23.50

KF 45:   same as KF 40, but with additional switch for brewing 3–4 cups
DC target: FY 1982/83: DM 24.30

Status:
- Requisition drawings are prepared
- Tools and parts are being requisitioned
- Design model is being built

Further steps:
- Construct the functional model   by 25 March 1983
- Requisition parts and tools and make the A.R.   by 18 March 1983
- Test of functional model by quality control   by 16 May 1983
- Complete the design model   by 30 March 1983
- Make the drawings for the tool orders   by 16 May 1983
- Go or no-go decision   by 17 May 1983
  If go, then Category I release
- Planned start-up   April 1984

Risks:
The above schedule does not include the production of prototypes. Only if the tests of the functional model reveal no major problems will it be possible to meet the current deadlines.

Project: Coffee Makers KF 40 and KF 45   Signed: A. Jestädt, Project Mgr.
Project Number: 542   Date: 22 February 1983   Version: 2

producing this schedule, business management had already cast its vote of confidence. Waxlax knew that Greaves tended to be conservative in his forecasts, and therefore one didn't have to worry about unrealistic figures in his analyses. Neither engineering nor design wanted to be pushed, however, and that Waxlax respected. The decision was a strategic one: a big risk – but one with a big payoff if they succeeded. The risk was not so much financial, though DM 1 million in moulds and two years in development costs would not be insignificant. Should they walk away from the project or rethink their positioning with a more expensive plastic? That option could reduce the risks, but required a new strategy. Waxlax intended to take his time in listening to all points of view.

INDEX

The index refers to the Preface and Chapters 1 to 10 (excluding the end-of-chapter bibliographies). Numbers are filed as though spelled out, e.g. '3M' is filed as though 'Three . . .'.

Entries are filed in word-by-word alphabetical order, in which spaces between words are taken into account; 'market surveys' therefore files before 'marketing'.